Eighteenth Century
German Criticism

The German Library: Volume 11
Volkmar Sander, General Editor

EIGHTEENTH CENTURY GERMAN CRITICISM

Edited by Timothy J. Chamberlain

CONTINUUM • NEW YORK

1992
The Continuum Publishing Company
370 Lexington Avenue, New York, NY 10017

The German Library
is published in cooperation with Deutsches Haus,
New York University.
This volume has been supported by a grant from
Robert Bosch Jubiläumsstiftung.

Printed in the United States of America

Library of Congress Cataloging-in-Publication Data

Eighteenth century German criticism / edited by Timothy J. Chamberlain.
    p.   cm. — (German library ; v. 11)
    ISBN 0-8264-0700-5. — ISBN 0-8264-0701-3 (pbk.)
    1. German literature—18th century—History and criticism.
2. Literature—History and criticism.   3. Criticism—Germany—
—History—18th century—Sources.   I. Chamberlain, Timothy James.
II. Title: 18th century German criticism.   III. Series.
PT78.E36   1992
830.9'006—dc20   91-16431
                                                           CIP

Acknowledgments will be found on page 284,
which constitutes an extension of the copyright page.

Contents

Introduction

In Germany as in France and England, the eighteenth century is an age of criticism. As in literary production, at the beginning of the century German criticism lagged behind, but by 1800 a rich and diverse debate had helped raise the quality of German literature to a level Goethe defends with rather excessive modesty in his last essay in this volume, with work that had begun to exert an influence outside Germany, and that retains more than historical interest. Far more is of importance than can be included in a volume of this scope, and some of the most significant contributions are included elsewhere in The German Library Series. Volume 79, *German Essays on Art History,* edited by Gert Schiff, may be consulted for Winckelmann's highly influential essay "On the Imitation of the Painting and Sculpture of the Greeks," and for the young Goethe's rhapsody on Gothic architecture, "On German Architecture." Important works on the theater may be found in volume 83, *Essays on German Theater,* edited by Margaret Herzfeld-Sander, especially excerpts from Lessing's *Hamburg Dramaturgy* and Lenz's *Notes on the Theater.* Volume 13, *Selected Works of Immanuel Kant,* edited by Ernst Behler, contains the first part of *The Critique of Judgment,* particularly important for the criticism of the Romantics, and of Schiller, whose major critical works appear in volume 17, edited by Walter Hinderer. Finally, volume 21, *German Romantic Criticism,* edited by A. Leslie Willson offers important texts from the critics of the next generation, beginning in the 1790s. In addition, volume 10, *Eighteenth Century German Writings,* edited by Ellis Shookman, provides a selection of literary works from the period corresponding to this volume.

While the absence of a number of important texts in this volume may be regretted, it allows significant gains in breadth. Herder is represented here somewhat more adequately than usual (though he really deserves a volume of his own), and a number of critics can be made available in English for the first time. Klopstock's theory of sacred and sublime poetry, Wieland's cosmopolitan vision of literature, Blanckenburg's notable *Essay on the Novel*, and Bürger's arguments for popular literature are among the gains. The overall effect, I hope, is to diminish the traditional emphasis on Weimar Classicism and Romanticism as the telos of all eighteenth-century criticism. While not wanting to deny the aspects of history and development, the state of criticism in eighteenth-century Germany would be better described in terms of diversity, debate, and pluralism, and this volume takes some steps toward reflecting that state of affairs.[1]

Indeed, debate raged. Sometimes friendly and informal, as in the exchange between Lessing, Nicolai, and Mendelssohn; sometimes respectful, as in Herder's response to Lessing; sometimes scornful and insulting, as in the later retorts to Gottsched, Hamann's satire against rationalists like Johann David Michaelis and Voltaire, or Goethe's review of Sulzer; sometimes condescending and crushing, as in Schiller's review of Bürger. Even criticism not composed in direct response to actual opposed views often employed the form of such a response, such as the fictional letters of Herder on folk poetry, of Lenz on Werther, or of Wieland. The critics involved shared a keen sense of themselves as participants in a debate about which they cared passionately, and the energy of their disputes is still palpable today.

An introduction of this scope cannot hope to provide a detailed history or analysis of this debate.[2] All that can be offered is a brief survey of some of the most significant areas of discussion. Beyond that, the texts may speak for themselves, and readers wishing further information may be referred to the bibliographical suggestions in the notes to this introduction, and in the biographical sketches that accompany each critic's work.

German Literature—French and English Models

Although in the course of the century, demand focused increasingly on the need for an original national German literature, much of the debate long assumed the necessity of taking some other literature as a model. For Gottsched, the undoubted superiority of the French meant that the Germans could best achieve a literature of their own by following the French example. In his *Critical Poetics* (1730), he therefore closely followed French classical models, and the teachings of Nicolas Boileau, which led in particular to an insistence on probability, a suppression of the imagination, and rigid formal laws such as the doctrine of the three unities of the theater. While later critics, starting already with the Swiss theorists Bodmer and Breitinger around 1740, criticized this rigidity, and began a turn to English models, Gottsched's influence should not be underestimated, particularly since it was combined with his substantially helpful reform of the German language,[3] and coincided with the ascendancy of French culture at German courts. Frederick the Great of Prussia preferred speaking French to German, and proved more likely to support French writers and philosophers such as Voltaire, La Mettrie and Helvétius than Germans. In 1780, Frederick's own survey of German literature—in French, of course[4]—still deplored the barbarism of German literature, including among other recent works Goethe's play *Götz von Berlichingen* (1773), which had taken a decisive step towards establishing a national German literature, and which Wieland and Lenz discuss in this volume.

While Frederick the Great was an extreme case, the nobility in general modeled itself on the French, and the turn to English literature as an alternative[5] reflects not simply a need for new inspirations, nor even the recognition of essential similarities between the German and English languages and peoples—though both undoubtedly play a significant part—but also a quest on the part of the rising middle class, which was growing in numbers, wealth, and literacy, for a vehicle more suited to its own aspirations. England, as the ancient enemy of the French, and the country with the greatest measure of democracy and the strongest middle class, proved the best alternative.

The change in orientation shows clearly in the attitude toward Shakespeare. While Gottsched had poured scorn on the Englishman's dramas for their failure to abide by the rules, Lessing and Wieland admired him, and Herder, Goethe, and Lenz adulated him as the great northern modern genius. Along with Shakespeare, other English writers became popular and influential: Milton inspired Klopstock, and Edward Young, Oliver Goldsmith, and Laurence Sterne enjoyed great success. The vogue of Richardson, strong from the 1740s to the 1770s, was supplemented by Fielding, whose *History of Tom Jones* was rightly adjudged by Blanckenburg to set new standards for the novel. English and Scottish critics such as Shaftesbury, Edward Young, Hugh Blair, and Thomas Blackwell became influential.

Yet although German literature clearly benefited greatly from English examples, it would be too simple to speak of a rejection of the French in favor of the English. The importance of new French criticism is particularly striking. Dubos helped Nicolai and Mendelssohn overcome Gottsched's didacticism;[6] Lessing acknowledged his debt to Diderot,[7] and the importance of Rousseau for his concept of pity has been demonstrated.[8] Rousseau's influence can also be seen in the work of Herder, Goethe and Lenz, and in the midst of the "Sturm und Drang," Mercier's essay on the theater appeared in a translation by Heinrich Leopold Wagner.

Standing above the fray, Wieland impresses the modern reader by his balance and tolerance, which far from being a sign of weakness or equivocation, as has sometimes been charged, rests on a strong cosmopolitan vision of literature within the cultural context of Europe, rather than the single nation. What Wieland failed to appreciate was simply the necessary instrumental role of the polemics against the French and the demonstrative embrace of the English, in establishing a German literature that by the end of the century had essentially freed itself from the imitation of foreign models.

On Ancient Poetry

For Gottsched, the accomplishments of the French were made possible by the adherence to Greek models, which, being founded on the rational analysis of the beauty of unchanging nature, enjoyed an unrivaled, eternally valid position. While Gottsched's neoclassicism became suspect later in the century because of his reliance on the French, Greek antiquity attained even greater force from Winckelmann's interpretation of Greek artists and his advocacy of their imitation in his essay "On the Imitation of the Painting and Sculpture of the Greeks" (1755).[9] Bypassing the French and Romans, Winckelmann's essay gained attraction by its return to the sources, which accorded with a general feeling of distress at the belatedness and artificiality of modern culture. His discovery in the Greeks—startlingly enough, in the Laocoön group—of "noble simplicity and tranquil grandeur" appealed to a generation inspired by Rousseau, and his advocacy of simple, linear form became an ideal of all art for the renewed classicism of Goethe and Schiller. Moreover, Winckelmann inspired others, notably Goethe and Moritz, to visit Italy themselves (Greece being still inaccessible) in quest of traces of antiquity. Meanwhile, Homer remained the preeminent poetic genius of all time, and the irrelevance of Sophocles for modern dramatists felt by Goethe and Lenz was not meant to call into question his status as a tragic poet.

Yet several challenges arose to the exemplary status of Greek culture, including its literature.

Firstly, Herder's historical understanding of the origins and character of Greek culture, developed from Winckelmann's notions about the influence of climate and society on culture, implied the equal validity in their own circumstances of cultures arising in different periods and parts of the world. Indeed, the only cultures that lack validity are those made inauthentic and derivative by importing their culture from foreign regions and times. For all its beauty, therefore, Greek art is not eternally valid for all nations, and neither can nor should be replicated. The Germans can still learn from it, to be sure, but they may have more to learn from cultures closer to their own in climate (e.g., that of the ancient Celts), and in time (e.g., Elizabethan England). Yet even here, Herder is less concerned with lessons the Germans may be able to learn than to take delight in the individuality of each culture, as reflected in his passion for folk songs from England, Spain, Greenland, the Baltic states, and North and South America.

Herder's fundamental challenge brought with it a new privileging of the authentic products of indigenous culture, which could be taken as models, not so much in form, as in the manner and exemplary individuality of their production. Herder shared with many contemporaries an enthusiasm for Ossian, believing as most did that the prose versions put out by James Macpherson in the 1760s were indeed, as claimed, translations of originals collected in the Scottish highlands, and going back to the legendary third-century Celtic hero and bard.[10] Still more important was folk poetry, as the authentic expression of the people, untainted by foreign models. Herder followed his own theoretical work with a collection of folk songs drawn from many nations (1778–79). The most famous anthology of German folk songs, Arnim and Brentano's *The Boy's Magic Horn* (1806–8) is unthinkable without Herder.

More influential even than folk poetry was Shakespeare, whose impact finds ecstatic expression in Goethe's rhapsody "On Shake-speare's Day" (1771), and achieves its full theoretical justification in Herder's essay "Shakespeare" (1773). Yet here, too, Herder hints that even Shakespeare is receding rapidly from our view. Everywhere Herder sees movement, dynamism, a world in flux. Indeed, a large part of the attraction of Shakespeare rests in the feeling of a dynamic, fluid world his plays convey, and in the bringing of history onto the stage as a process and force.

A second challenge, also present in Herder and Goethe, concerns the nature of society, and is developed most fully by Blanckenburg. Whereas the Greeks participated fully as citizens in the affairs of their state, modern Europeans have no say in political matters. Blanckenburg does not lament this fact, and indeed argues that it may be the basis of the potential superiority of modern literature, since its liberation from events that concern the citizen enables it to concentrate on a philosophical cultivation of man. Lacking a public role, that is, literature turns inward, to ideas, feelings, and character.[11] Blanckenburg thus stands at the beginning of the reflection of inwardness as a quality of German culture, later alternately regretted and embraced.[12] For Blanckenburg, one major consequence is the loss of relevance of Greek culture, and in particular the supersedence of the epic poem by the novel.

A final challenge to Greek literature is the appeal by Klopstock and Hamann to a still older and more inspired source, namely the poetry of the Bible. While this specific model bore little fruit, it did serve to undermine the authority inherent in the supposed temporal primacy of the Greeks, and by drawing explicit attention to the spiritual inferiority of Greek pagans compared with modern Christians, further diminished Greek claims, and helped to prepare the ground for a literature emphasizing inwardness. At the same time, the failure of this model to inspire greater poetry or later criticism provides an early indication of the waning of Christianity in intellectual and cultural life.

Criticism and Related Disciplines

Literary criticism and theory in the eighteenth century are inextricably entwined with other fields of inquiry, in particular with the theory of the visual arts, semiotics, psychology, philosophy, and theology.

Lessing's *Laocoön* and Herder's *Critical Forests* explore the distinction between the arts of literature and painting. Goethe's "Simple Imitation of Nature, Manner, Style" and Moritz's essay "On the Concept of That Which Is Perfect in Itself," on the other hand, focus on the visual arts to elaborate ideas applicable in all the arts, in accordance with the newly developing classicism. The preoccupation with the visual arts goes back in the first instance to Winckelmann, and continues with the Romantics.

Lessing concerns himself in his *Laocoön* with the ancient injunction to the poet to emulate the painter, given classic expression in Horace's formula *ut pictura poesis*. Impressed by Winckelmann's work, he is nonetheless dismayed at Winckelmann's claim that the sculptor of the Laocoön group surpasses Virgil, and seeks in the first instance to explain why there must be a distinction between the portrayal of Laocoön by the sculptor and that by the poet.[13] Lessing finds, firstly, that for the ancients, beauty was the supreme law in the visual arts, so that the distortions arising from physical pain such as that suffered by Laocoön could not be represented in a sculpture, and had to be toned down. Secondly, since it is restricted to the representation of a single moment, a sculpture cannot choose a transitory moment such as the climax of agony, since this would then be prolonged eternally. Rather, a moment should be chosen that enables the imagination to extrapolate, since a climax beyond which the imagination cannot proceed is less effective. The poet, on the other hand, is limited neither to the depiction of beauty, since he can also show the more significant inner perfections of a character, nor to a single moment. Hence, there is nothing to prevent him from having a character scream in agony, as Virgil has Laocoön scream.

While these restrictions on the visual arts strike the modern reader as unduly narrow, Lessing's more fundamental distinction between the arts, based on semiotics, retains greater interest. Here (in chapter 16), he argues from the difference between the coexistence in space of the signs used by painting and the consecutiveness in time of the signs used by poetry, to conclude that painting should primarily depict bodies, while poetry should concentrate on actions. Although the examples he adduces in support of this view of poetry are taken from Homer, one can clearly detect Lessing the dramatist behind this argument, which in effect condemns the descriptive poetry popular in the earlier eighteenth century. Even taking the arbitrary nature of linguistic signs into account (chapter 17), the vivid impressions produced by these signs in poetry remain consecutive, and therefore cannot be employed to describe a whole body without the writer ceasing to be a poet.

These distinctions are explored further by Herder in his response to Lessing in the *Critical Forests*. Given his emphasis on flux and change, already evident in his view of the ancient world and of Shakespeare, it is hardly surprising that Herder rejects the notion that visual art should eschew the transitory, since that is not only a metaphysical impossibility, but also would rob art of its most expressive qualities. But the restriction of visual art to a single moment may indeed explain its need for beauty, which Herder argues gives the imagination of the viewer the greatest scope.

In dealing with Lessing's semiotic arguments, Herder pays considerably greater attention than his precursor to the arbitrariness of the signs employed by poetry. The entire force of poetry, he claims, lies in the meaning invested in linguistic signs by arbitrary means. Precisely this arbitrariness, he insists, by enlisting the imagination and the memory, overcomes the "natural" consecutiveness of linguistic signs, giving them an immediacy and vividness poetry can share with painting. The evidence of Homer fails to convince Herder for two reasons. Firstly, Homer's style is progressive not because poetry is unable to depict bodies, but rather because the essence of his poem is to convey an energetic effect. Secondly, Homer's progressive style is *his* epic style, and cannot provide any absolute standards for poetry as a whole. Indeed, even other epic poets may adopt a quite different approach.

Clearly, a major factor in Herder's response to Lessing is his wariness towards prescriptive rules of the kind that Lessing, in this sense at least still well within the framework of neoclassicism, insists on. Herder's individualism allows for the greatest variety, both in poetry and in painting (though he is less concerned with the latter). His arguments in this "Grove" do not represent his whole truth, and that Herder himself overstated the case here becomes clear when one takes into account the essay on Ossian and folk poetry, where he shows a keen awareness of the musical qualities of poetry—of alliteration, assonance, and other aspects of rhythm. Nonetheless, his insistence on the meaning of words as the key to the force, or power, of poetry, and his corresponding emphasis on effect (*Wirkung*) remain central to his theory of signs and of verbal art.

The focus on the visual in Moritz's short essay emerges from his use of visual metaphors for the consideration of beauty. The contrast between the beautiful and the useful becomes most vivid with reference to the visual world, where the distinction between the craftsman and the artist seems particularly necessary and fruitful. Further, given the appropriation by the Enlightenment of literature as the most rational form of art, visual art can exemplify more closely than literature the freedom from utility that Moritz demands. However, the original title of his work indicates his intention that the "concept of that which is perfect in itself" should become a unifying principle in all the arts. Moritz's insistence on purposefulness without purpose anticipates Kant's *Critique of Judgment* (1790), and clearly prepares the way for Schiller's aesthetics.[14]

While Moritz's essay displays a proximity to Kant, other philosophers provided a context for critics earlier in the century. Gottsched's insistence on the employment of sound reason, his rather prosaic understanding of this faculty, belief in the beautiful harmony of nature, and finally uncompromising advocacy of probability place him firmly within the camp of the Enlightenment philosophy of Leibniz and Wolff. The enduring influence of this philosophy can be observed in the 1770s, when Blanckenburg makes the cogency of cause and effect the crucial criterion for a good novel, and sees this realized in the work of Fielding and Wieland. Even Lenz's insistence on the effect of literature, for example in his speech on *Götz von Berlichingen,* may be seen within this tradition.[15]

If Gottsched and to some extent Blanckenburg emphasize the clear cognition of Wolff, attained to by the "higher" powers of the soul, i.e., reason, the midcentury sees the development of aesthetics by Alexander Baumgarten as a theory of the confused and obscure cognition of the senses, analogous to and perhaps not inferior to clear rational cognition.[16] Whatever its limitations, sensuous cognition shares with divine cognition the spontaneous, unmediated grasp of the whole, a quality granted increasing importance in the course of the century. It was to this sensuous cognition that aesthetics appealed, and aesthetic pleasure could lead to its refining and perfecting. Mendelssohn, Lessing, and Herder build on this theory, the former two in particular making it a central point in their debate on the tragedy. Mendelssohn's reluctance to allow sensuous cognition a practical ethical role (here he remains a follower of Wolff) leads him to grant aesthetic experience a certain independence, and indeed he later formulated the idea of a faculty of approval (*Billigungsvermögen*) which anticipates Kant's "judgment" (*Ur-*

teilskraft). Lessing, on the other hand, argues that the "lower" powers of the soul have a vital influence on our will, and finds in pity an inseparable aesthetic pleasure and moral effect.

Literary theory also reacts against philosophy. Lenz, for example, while accepting aspects of the philosophy of Leibniz and Wolff, and of the precritical Kant, energetically rejects the claims of the French materialists La Mettrie and Helvétius, whose mechanism seems to him to deny individual freedom.

The most uncompromising rejection of Enlightenment philosophy comes from Hamann, who ironically appropriates for himself the mantle of Socrates.[17] But whereas the Enlightenment saw in Socrates the forerunner of critical reason, Hamann reinterpreted him by taking seriously both his confessions of ignorance, as exposures of the inadequacy of human thought, and his claim to be inspired by a divine inner voice (*daimon*). The whole drift of Hamann's work is to accuse his contemporaries of a sinful and foolish pride in human reason, and to reassert the claims of faith, inspiration, and intuition, and it was this that aroused the enthusiasm of Herder, Goethe, and other younger contemporaries. This did not, however, lead them to heed his admonition at the end of the *Aesthetica in nuce* to "fear God and give glory to Him," and in his call to a renewal of poetry by a return to piety Hamann remained without serious followers.

Epic, Dramatic, and Lyric Poetry

In the classical poetics still adhered to by Gottsched, the major genres were the epic poem and tragedy. In the course of the century, tragedy retained its importance, though its exact nature was debated, while the epic poem lost much of its significance. To be sure, Lessing, Mendelssohn, Herder, and Blanckenburg continue to pay their respects to Homer, but the relevance and validity of the epic poem in the modern world seem increasingly questionable. In his correspondence with Mendelssohn, Lessing ventures the restriction that the epic merely holds up the greatness of physical courage, and Mendelssohn has no qualms about agreeing with him. But if this is so, then it has little to offer a society that is more interested in cultivating the social virtues in the way outlined by Lessing.

It is Blanckenburg who reckons most fully with the epic, concluding that in fact, because the epic is a public work for a society in which all citizens have an interest in public affairs, it has little relevance in the modern world. More suited to these changed circumstances, in Blanckenburg's view, is the novel, which is able to show the development of character, and hence, by being more inward, is more philosophical. Thus Blanckenburg justifies his challenging claim that the novel can be for the modern world what the epic was for the ancient—a claim more controversial at the time than now. Novels, though increasingly the reading matter of choice for the broader literate public, still had a bad reputation as frivolous, formless entertainment, and it was not until the Romantics a generation later that this view was overcome.

Tragedy meanwhile retained its dignity and force, but only by being repeatedly redefined. In his *Treatise on Tragedy*, which he summarizes for Lessing in the letter that opens the *Correspondence on Tragedy*, Nicolai, drawing on Dubos and on discussions with Mendelssohn, broke with the didactic claim of neoclassicism that tragedy should serve to improve manners, and instead advanced the thesis that it should move the audience to vehement emotions. The pleasure given by this effect should be the dramatist's aim, a conclusion with which Mendelssohn concurs. His defense of admiration in his correspondence with Lessing—which prepares the way for Schiller's emphasis on the sublime[18]—rests on the dramatic, not the moral effect of this emotion. Lessing was uneasy with the proposed disjunction of dramatic and moral effect, still believing that tragedy should improve the audience, but agreeing that the stimulation of emotions was a powerful means to this end effect. Lessing's particular contribution is to emphasize the stimulation of pity, in accordance with the maxim, "the most compassionate man is the best man." Hence, tragedy no longer, as for Gottsched, serves the purpose of warning against specific faults, but solely of developing the virtue of pity, a position Lessing substantially retains in his *Hamburg Dramaturgy*.

For Herder and the young Goethe, the classical genres are of little relevance: the modern theater, Herder argues in his essay on Shakespeare, cannot be what the ancient was, because drama is a product of historical, social, and religious conditions and traditions. To attain the same effect—fear and pity—Shakespeare therefore had to employ utterly different means; formal rules have only local validity. While Herder still writes of tragedy, Goethe, who like his teacher

Herder was particularly impressed by Shakespeare's representation of history, called his epoch-making *Götz von Berlichingen* (1773) simply a *Schauspiel* or "play."

One of the most idiosyncratic views of the theater is presented by Lenz, who in his *Notes on the Theater* argued for a reversal of Aristotelian categories: for him, tragedy revolves around a character, while comedy has to do with events. Though praising Goethe's *Götz von Berlichingen* for its inspiring central character—thus aligning it with his understanding of tragedy—Lenz himself wrote plays that, in accordance with his theory, he termed comedies. Not surprisingly, this concept was much misunderstood, and Lenz felt compelled to attempt an explanation of his usage of the term in his review of *The New Menoza*. While tragedy may be a higher genre, even in Lenz's view, in practical terms he argues that the German audience as it currently exists is not yet ripe for tragedy, so that comedy in his sense is necessary.

In the course of the century, lyric poetry enjoyed a major reevaluation that brought it to its modern position as the purest and most essentially poetic of all forms of literature. Klopstock played a crucial role in this development by advocating a sublime poetry that would undertake to move the soul in all its powers. In terms of the three conventional aims of rhetorically based poetics, the framework within which he clearly operates, Klopstock placed a new emphasis on *movere,* in contrast to the Enlightenment preference for *prodesse* and *delectare,* poetry that instructs and delights.[19] Although the essay included here originally accompanied his epic poem, *The Messiah,* the essential ideas are equally relevant to his odes, and proved more influential for lyric poetry.

A second great impetus was Herder's focus on folk poetry, which made of ballads and shorter lyrics the most authentic and original poetic products. Nonetheless, while he agreed with Klopstock and Lessing in devaluing didactic and descriptive poetry, he remained wary of narrow prescriptions, and accords poetry the greatest range both in his early *Critical Forests* and in his late *Letters for the Advancement of Humanity*.

Bürger, enthusiastically following Herder's advocacy of folk poetry, allows lyric poetry a much narrower range, polemicizing against not just didactic and philosophical poetry, but all poetry too abstruse to be accessible to the feeling and imagination, the "outer" and "inner" senses of the majority. This called forth a stern and uncompromising response from Schiller, just in the process of developing his classical aesthetics. For Schiller, Bürger's popular poetry brings with it the risk of an impoverishment of literature, by reducing it to the lowest common denominator, or appealing to mass opinion. Where Bürger had defined taste in thoroughly popular terms as the composite voice of the people, a democratically defined norm, and had distinguished between taste and beauty in a provocative manner, Schiller insists on ideal standards of taste to which the true poet should endeavor to raise his readers. Only in this way, Schiller argues, will poetry fulfill its function.

The Purpose of Poetry

Throughout the eighteenth century, the purpose of literature remains a fundamental issue for criticism. For Gottsched, to delight and—especially—instruct is purpose enough. Obedience to the laws of poetry should guarantee delight, while the appropriate choice of subjects will serve to instruct. To give a specific example, tragedy should have the twofold task of showing the audience the consequences of certain flaws in behavior, which are therefore to be avoided, and of preparing the audience to face vicissitudes with courage, as for example Gottsched's own Cato does.

As discussed in the context of the relation of criticism and philosophy, Mendelssohn and Nicolai provide important arguments for overcoming Gottsched's narrow didacticism by allowing the aesthetic pleasure afforded by literature a more significant role, irrespective of moral intent. Lessing reaffirms the mission of the theater to improve the manners of the public, but understands the means and specific ends quite differently. Firstly, he rejects the aim of preparing the audience to face vicissitudes, on aesthetic grounds, since a Stoic makes a poor hero for a play. Secondly, he discounts the effectiveness of warning the audience against specific faults. Thirdly, he argues that tragedy should arouse in the audience only one emotion, namely pity, and that the exercise of this pity, as the supreme social virtue, is the ultimate purpose of tragedy. Fourthly, just as tragedy should exercise the faculty of pity, so comedy should exercise the faculty of perceiving ridiculous behavior. Rather than warning against specific faults, that is, such as avarice or hypochondria, it should have a more general effect on our mental powers. Thus while Lessing perpetuates the Enlightenment tradition that literature should have an improving effect on the public, he stands against the earlier Enlightenment in emphasizing the development of faculties within the individual psyche, rather than specific virtues.

The two other critics of this generation represented here express quite divergent views. Wieland—closer to Mendelssohn—sees the true calling of literature in the ennobling of human nature, a process in which the contemplation of beauty clearly plays no small role. Klopstock stresses the potential of poetry for inspiring the human soul and raising it to greater heights. Though secular poetry may also stir the heart with sublime images, he has in mind religious themes in particular as the most lofty and noble subjects of all. Whereas Lessing's vision of literature plants it firmly in a social context, and Wieland's looks to broad cultural progress, for Klopstock the individual's relation to the absolute becomes a sufficient end in itself.

For critics of the following generation, these latter two positions point the way. Herder's eclectic tastes are reflected in his rather diverse view of the purpose of poetry: in his early writings, the effect on the individual's feeling of life seems most important, whereas in his later work the notion of cultural progress toward the full realization of humanity for all mankind becomes his final word. Goethe's reflections on the purpose of literature are relatively sparse and peripheral to his major concerns. For him, literature has an intrinsic interest that makes the issue of broader relevance secondary, and indeed he rejects such applications of literature in his review of Sulzer's work. His essay on Shakespeare follows the line begun by Klopstock, showing clearly that literature can be a personal inspiration, serving to promote a more intense and energetic feeling of life. In the later essays by Goethe in this volume, art is apparently an end in itself, though the ideas of his collaborator Schiller need to be taken into account here.

Lenz's inconsistency reveals the contradictions of his age. On the one hand, he insists on effectiveness as the major criterion in judging art. This effectiveness may apparently rest in the inspiring encounter with a great character, in the stimulation of the audience to thought, or in the exploration of aspects of the human heart of which we would otherwise be unaware. Indeed, in his letters on *Werther,* this latter point seems the most crucial, so that literature in effect becomes a means to self-knowledge. On the other hand, there are moments when literature seems to exist in its own right, to have the independent existence Lenz's rejection of mechanism may imply. *Werther,* for example, may be the display of Werther's sufferings, just as the *Iliad* displays Achilles' wrath. To demand moral teachings from the poet is barking up the wrong tree.

This relative distance from moral instruction becomes a dominant theme in the writing of the period. Though Blanckenburg insists that the poet should instruct and entertain, what he has in mind is clearly not that which earlier critics envisaged, but rather instruction in human nature, showing how human beings become what they are. At most, this has the general effect on the reader of enlightening him or her in the correct philosophy, in developing that is the general disposition to understand life. While Blanckenburg retains the notion of perfect characters, his confession as to the attraction of the character of Tom Jones reveals the general tenor of his work more accurately.

Moritz takes an essential step towards arguing the autonomy of art from extrinsic ends, seeing the purpose of art precisely in its appearance of purposefulness without actual purpose. We take a selfless pleasure in beauty, enjoying the contemplation of a perfection that has no practical relevance to us. However, precisely because our pleasure is selfless, art ennobles the one who contemplates it, allowing the overcoming of selfish, limited concerns in a quasimystical manner. Clearly, Moritz's pietistic upbringing influences his aesthetic principles.

Schiller, finally, argues from a similar conception of aesthetic autonomy and purposefulness without purpose (though derived from Kant rather than Moritz) to present literature with a lofty and inspired goal: the reintegration of human wholeness in a life characterized by fragmentation and alienation. The experience of harmony, beauty, and idealization can free us from necessity and limitation, and thus ennoble us by restoring our full humanity. Schiller's review of Bürger's poems already finds him working with these ideas, most fully elaborated in the *Letters on the Aesthetic Education of Man* (1795).

The Audience

From Gottsched to Lessing, critics agree that literature addresses an increasingly cultured and educated middle class, and conceive of their own work as a constitutive contribution to this process. In the course of the century, the potential audience expands as literacy increases, a process that accelerates in the last third of the century.[20]

Hence, the question as to whether the writer should continue to address a relatively cultivated elite, or should appeal to a broader audience becomes urgent. For Bürger, there is no question: the poet should accommodate himself to public demand; writers who complain that the public shows insufficient interest in their work have only themselves to blame, since they are clearly writing in an inaccessible and uninteresting manner. Lenz and Blanckenburg regard the matter somewhat differently. The broad reading public is a fact, and the writer has a responsibility to keep this audience in mind, and to write accordingly. However, this means not just writing in a way that will appeal to the general public, but also writing in such a way as to raise that public to a more cultivated level. Schiller also envisages this as an ideal goal, but in practice seems resigned to the fact that the poet must write for an elite. In this he follows, though in a secularized mode, Klopstock's explicit appeal to the spiritual elite.

A Note on the Texts

For reasons of space, most of the texts included are excerpts, a procedure all the more justifiable given their (often deliberate) fragmentariness. I have indicated editions where the full texts may be found in German. Throughout this volume, editor's notes are enclosed in [brackets] to distinguish them from author's notes. With the exception of the most obvious, names not explained in notes may be found in the biographical notes at the end of the volume.

T. J. C.

Notes

1. For some indications of this diversity, see Richard Critchfield and Wulf Koepke, introduction in *Eighteenth-Century Authors and Their Aesthetic Theories: Literature and the Other Arts,* ed. Critchfield and Koepke (Columbia, South Carolina: Camden House, 1988), pp. 1–10.

2. For general accounts, see Klaus L. Berghahn, "From Classicist to Classical Literary Criticism, 1730–1806," trans. John R. Blazek, in *A History of German Literary Criticism, 1730–1980,* ed. Peter Uwe Hohendahl (Lincoln, Nebraska; London: University of Nebraska Press, 1988), pp. 13–98; René Wellek, *A History of Modern Criticism: 1750–1950,* vol. 1, *The Later Eighteenth Century* (New Haven: Yale University Press, 1955); Bruno Markwardt, *Geschichte der deutschen Poetik,* second edition, 5 vols. (Berlin: de Gruyter, 1956–67). For information about the

social and political background, it is still worth consulting W. H. Bruford, *Germany in the Eighteenth Century: The Social Background of the Literary Revival* (Cambridge: Cambridge University Press, 1935). For the philosophical context, see Ernst Cassirer, *The Philosophy of the Enlightenment,* trans. Fritz C. A. Koelln and James P. Pettegrove (Princeton: Princeton University Press, 1951).

3. See Eric A. Blackall, *The Emergence of German as a Literary Language, 1700–1775,* second edition (Ithaca; London: Cornell University Press, 1978), especially chapters 4 and 5.

4. *De la Littérature allemande,* available in a bilingual French-German edition, edited by Christoph Gutknecht and Peter Kerner (Hamburg: Buske, 1969).

5. Although requiring correction in some areas, the best overview is provided by Lawrence Marsden Price, *The Reception of English Literature in Germany* (Berkeley: University of California Press, 1932).

6. See Jochen Schulte-Sasse, "Der Stellenwert des Briefwechsels in der Geschichte der deutschen Ästhetik," in his edition of Gotthold Ephraim Lessing, Moses Mendelssohn, Friedrich Nicolai, *Briefwechsel über das Trauerspiel* (Munich: Winkler, 1972), pp. 189, 198.

7. See Richard Critchfield, "Lessing, Diderot, and the Theatre," in *Eighteenth-Century German Authors and Their Aesthetic Theories,* ed. Critchfield and Koepke, pp. 11–28.

8. See Hans-Jürgen Schings, *Der mitleidigste Mensch ist der beste Mensch: Poetik des Mitleids von Lessing bis Büchner* (Munich: Beck, 1980).

9. E. M. Butler's study of the impact of Winckelmann's Greece, *The Tyranny of Greece over Germany* (Cambridge: Cambridge University Press, 1935), remains provocative; the title indicates her perspective.

10. For a survey of the Ossian controversy, see J. S. Smart, *James Macpherson: An Episode in Literature* (London: Nutt, 1905).

11. This inwardness of course is not without political implications; see Jürgen Habermas, *The Structural Transformation of the Public Sphere: An Inquiry into a Category of Bourgeois Society,* trans. Thomas Burger, with the assistance of Frederick Lawrence (Cambridge, Massachusetts: MIT Press, 1989), chapter 2, especially pp. 51–56.

12. In *The German Tradition of Self-Cultivation: "Bildung" from Humboldt to Thomas Mann* (Cambridge: Cambridge University Press, 1975), W. H. Bruford, for example, addresses the question, "Was there perhaps some inherent defect from the beginning in what Mill calls 'the culture of the inward man' in Germany?" (p. ix).

13. For an outstanding discussion of *Laocoön,* see David E. Wellbery, *Lessing's "Laocoon": Semiotics and Aesthetics in the Age of Reason* (Cambridge: Cambridge University Press, 1984).

14. For a brief discussion of this essay, see Mark Boulby, *Karl Philipp Moritz: At the Fringe of Genius* (Toronto: University of Toronto Press, 1979), pp. 151–52; on the further development of these ideas in the essay *On the Imitation of the Beautiful in the Plastic Arts* (1788), pp. 171–83.

15. For another connection between Lenz and Leibniz, see Allan Blunden, "J. M. R. Lenz and Leibniz: A Point of View," *Sprachkunst* 9 (1978): 3–18.

16. See Schulte-Sasse, "Der Stellenwert des Briefwechsels," especially pp. 168–79; also Wellbery, *Lessing's "Laocoon,"* chapters 1 and 2.

17. For a useful discussion, see James C. O'Flaherty, *Hamann's "Socratic Memorabilia": A Translation and Commentary* (Baltimore: Johns Hopkins Press, 1967), especially pp. 1–47.

18. See Schings, *Der mitleidigste Mensch ist der beste Mensch,* pp. 36, 46–47.

19. For a study of Klopstock within the rhetorical tradition, see Hans-Henrik Krummacher, "Friedrich Gottlieb Klopstock," in *Deutsche Dichter des 18. Jahrhunderts,* ed. Benno v. Wiese (Berlin: E. Schmidt, 1977), pp. 190–209; also Kevin

Hilliard, *Philosophy, Letters, and the Fine Arts in Klopstock's Thought* (London: University of London Institute of Germanic Studies, 1987).

20. On the development of the reading public, see Rolf Engelsing, *Analphabetentum und Lektüre: Zur Sozialgeschichte des Lesens in Deutschland* (Stuttgart: Metzler, 1973), pp. 53–89.

Eighteenth Century
German Criticism

Johann Christoph Gottsched

Johann Christoph Gottsched (1700–1766), an adherent of the Wolffian school of early Enlightenment philosophy, and professor of logic and metaphysics at Leipzig University, promoted linguistic reform to create a single educated German language, and literary reform to establish a national German literature on the model of French neoclassicism. To his major theoretical work, the *Critical Poetics* (1730), were added practical efforts to reform the theater, aided by the leading actress Friederike Neuber and her company, and by the translations and original writings of his wife, Luise Adelgunde Gottsched (1713–62). Gottsched attempted to assemble a repertoire of modern German plays, and himself wrote a model tragedy, *The Dying Cato* (1732). He also produced works on the German language, rhetoric, and philosophy, and pioneered the moral weekly in Germany, following the example of the English *Spectator*. Though later attacked and even ridiculed by the Swiss critics Bodmer and Breitinger, and by Lessing, his writings initiated the serious literary debate of the eighteenth century, and the attempt to develop a national literature.

Critical Poetics

Part 1. Chapter 3. On the Good Taste of the Poet.

§15. If it is asked, further, how good taste may be promoted among adults, then I answer, by no other means than by the employment of sound reason. One should consider nothing beautiful or ugly because one has heard it so called, or because all one's acquaintances consider it so, but rather, one should investigate it in and of itself, to see whether it is really so. One must consult one's own five senses, which will soon learn to uncover all deceptions—to distinguish false beauty from true, veneer from real marble, tinsel from genuine gold. By this means, in ancient times Greece invented the rules of most of the liberal arts, thus making good taste immutable there for a number of centuries. Painting, architecture, sculpture, music, poetry, and rhetoric were invented there and brought almost to perfection. That is because the Greeks were the most rational people in the world. Everyone there engaged in philosophy; everyone judged freely and thought independently. Thus they discovered by and by the true beauties of nature. They took care to notice where agreement and order gave rise to perfection; and where on the other hand the confusion of repulsive things aroused a displeasing condition. The most profound among them derived from the precise observation of successfully realized masterpieces the rules in which all their beauty had its origin. And as therefore these rules were not mere mental phantoms but were drawn up from actual examples that were deemed beautiful according to the judgment of the best minds, it has always been seen that the rules and examples of the Greeks, in all liberal arts, have been the best guidance to good taste.

§16. What I have said here of the Greeks can also be said with appropriate modifications of the Romans. The distinction is this: that the latter had the Greeks to thank for their good taste, and as they received it late, so also they retained it only for a short time. But after the barbarian peoples had filled the whole Western world with a corrupted taste, so once again the Greeks were the only ones who restored good taste in Italy. Thence it has gradually spread to Germany, France, Holland, and England, yet has barely been able anywhere completely to gain the upper hand. So the surest means to preserve good taste is to keep to the rules which have come down to us from the ancient critics and masters. . . .

§19. Finally it has also been asked whether a writer has not cause to adapt himself to the taste of his times, his place or his court, rather than to the rules of art? The opinion is voiced, that is, that the first rules of the liberal arts were drawn up only in accordance with the taste of the Athenian people, in that the critics there appealed to those masterpieces that had received general applause, and based their theories on these. Now why should we, it is said, direct our head according to Athenian willfulness? What need have we to see with foreign eyes, taste with foreign tongues, and think according to a foreign pattern? Why should we today not have the right to consider beautiful that which pleases us ourselves, but rather be obliged to prefer that which the ancient Greeks found pleasing two thousand years ago?

§20. The objection appears important, for it flatters our vanity. It would be unanswerable if it were mere willfulness which declared a thing beautiful. If, further, the Athenians had no other advantages over us, and we were their equals in every respect, then we could oppose them with justice. However, in both instances matters are quite different. The beauty of an artwork rests not on vain presumption, but rather has its firm and necessary basis in the nature of things. God has created everything according to number, measure, and weight. Natural things are beautiful in themselves, and so if art also wants to produce something beautiful, it must imitate the pattern of nature. Exact proportion, order, and the right measurement of all parts of which a thing consists are the source of all beauty. The imitation of perfect nature can therefore give an artwork the perfection whereby it becomes pleasing and appealing to the understanding; and deviation from its pattern will always give rise to something formless and tasteless.

Part 2. Chapter 10. On Tragedies.

§5. Among the Greeks, then, even in Aristotle's judgment, tragedy was brought to perfection. In this condition it was in it could very well be called a *Trauerspiel*,[1] because it had the intention of awakening sadness, fear, pity, and admiration among the audience, by means of the misfortunes of great men and women. For this reason, Aristotle describes it as an imitation of an action by which a noble person brings on himself hard and unanticipated misfortunes.[2] The poet therefore wants to teach truths by means of the stories, and prepare the audience for their own sorrows by showing them such vicissitudes suffered by the great ones of this world. For example, *Oedipus,* one of the most famous tragedies of Sophocles, represents the lamentable end to which this Theban king came on account of his appalling deeds; although he stumbled into them almost without it being his fault. And that is just what Aristotle wants when he says the heroes of a tragedy must be neither really bad, nor really good:[3] not really bad, because otherwise one would feel no pity for their misfortune, but would rejoice at it; but also not really good, because otherwise one could easily accuse Providence of injustice, if it had punished innocent people so severely. . . .

§15. The entire fable has only one main intention, that is, one moral thesis: therefore it must also have a single principal action, on account of which everything else occurs. . . . In general, English plays transgress against this rule.

§16. Unity of time is the second thing that is indispensable in tragedy. The story of a heroic poem can last many months, as shown above; the reason is that it is only read. But the story of a play, which is really performed by living people in a few hours, can only last one circuit of the sun, as Aristotle puts it,[4] i.e., one day. For what sort of probability would there be in wanting to present the hero in the first scene in the cradle, somewhat further along as a lad, then as a youth, a man, an old man, and finally even in the coffin. In *Don Quixote*, Cervantes has made fun of foolish plays of this kind by Spanish poets.[5] If the English have not been quite so bad, it is certainly not much better. Shakespeare's *Julius Caesar* begins before the murder of Caesar, and lasts until after the Battle of Philippi, where Brutus and Cassius fell. Or how can it be probable to see night fall several times on stage, while yet oneself remaining seated always in the same place, without eating, drinking, or sleeping? The best stories are therefore those that would not require more time to happen in reality than they do in performance, i.e., about three or four hours, and this is the way the stories of most Greek tragedies are. At most, they require six, eight, or in the extreme case twelve hours for their whole course, and a poet must go no further if he does not want to act contrary to probability. . . .

§18. The third property of tragedy is unity of place. The audience remains seated in one place; consequently, the persons in the play must also remain all in one place, which the audience can view without moving. So in *Oedipus*, for example, the scene is the forecourt of the royal Theban palace, where Oedipus lives. Everything that transpires in the whole tragedy takes place before this palace: nothing that is actually seen occurs in the rooms, but rather outside on the square before the palace, before the eyes of the whole people. These days, when our princes do all their business in their chambers, it is therefore more difficult to make such stories probable. For this reason poets generally take old histories for their plays, or else they represent to us a great audience room in which many people can appear. Indeed, they occasionally also make use of a curtain, which they let fall and raise again, when they need two rooms for the story.[6] It is therefore obvious how ridiculous it is when, according to Cervantes' account, Spanish tragedies show the hero in the first scene in Europe, in the second in Africa, in the third in Asia, and finally even in America. . . .[7] It is therefore not permitted in a tragedy written according to the rules to change the scene. Where one is, one must stay; and so one must not be in a forest in the first act, in a city in the second, at war in the third, and in the fourth in a garden, or at sea. These are nothing but faults against probability: but a story that is not probable is worthless, for probability is its prime quality.

Translated by Timothy J. Chamberlain

Notes

This translation is based on the third edition of Gottsched's *Versuch einer Critischen Dichtkunst* (1742). This edition is reproduced in Johann Christoph Gottsched, *Ausgewählte Werke*, vol. 6, ed. Joachim Birke and Brigitte Birke (Berlin; New York: Walter de Gruyter, 1973).

1. [Literally, "play of mourning or sorrow."]
2. [*Poetics,* chapter 13.]
3. [*Poetics,* chapter 13.]
4. [See *Poetics,* chapter 5.]
5. [*Don Quixote,* part 1, chapter 48.]
6. [Gottsched employs this device in *Der sterbende Cato.*]
7. [*Don Quixote,* part 1, chapter 48. Only one such play is mentioned, and it has only three acts, set in Europe, Asia, and Africa; the speaker speculates that a fourth act would doubtless have taken place in America.]

Gotthold Ephraim Lessing, Friedrich Nicolai, Moses Mendelssohn

Gotthold Ephraim Lessing (1729–81) first studied theology at Leipzig, but soon abandoned his studies to move to Berlin, where he was among the first Germans to support himself by writing. The production of his early years includes comedies and fables, together with criticism and translation; his first major success was the domestic tragedy *Miss Sara Sampson* (1755). In 1759, together with his friends Nicolai and Mendelssohn, he launched the *Letters Concerning the Newest Literature,* which rapidly became the leading critical journal in Germany. In the famous Seventeenth Letter (The German Library, volume 83), he made a devastating attack on Gottsched. As secretary to a Prussian general in Breslau between 1760 and 1765, he devoted himself to antiquarian studies, the major result being *Laocoön* (1766). From 1767 to 1770, he was in Hamburg as advisor to the theater and house critic, producing the *Hamburg Dramaturgy* (1767–69; selections in The German Library, volume 83). His three most mature and durable dramas are the comedy *Minna von Barnhelm* (1767), the tragedy *Emilia Galotti* (1772), and the dramatic poem *Nathan the Wise* (1779), written during Lessing's years as ducal librarian in Wolfenbüttel (1770–81).

The major modern edition of Lessing's works is *Werke,* ed. Herbert G. Göpfert (Munich: Hanser, 1970–79). A useful introduction in English is F. Andrew Brown's *Gotthold Ephraim Lessing* (New York: Twayne, 1971). A good selection of Lessing's works appears in The German Library, volume 12.

Friedrich Nicolai (1733–1811), a bookseller and publisher by profession, was a leading figure in the Berlin Enlightenment. Among his major critical enterprises were the *Letters Concerning the Newest Literature* (1759–65) and the *Allgemeine deutsche Bibliothek* (General German Library) (1765–92). His novel *Life and Opinions of Master Sebaldus Nothanker* (1773), influenced by Sterne, took a satirical stand against superstition, intolerance, and religious excesses, drawing the praise of Wieland, Bürger, and others, though provoking Hamann's ire. His satire against the Storm and Stress in *The Joys of Young Werther* (1775) and *A Fine Little Yearbook* (1777–78) involved him in further controversies, although the latter work, while mocking what Nicolai perceived as irrational excesses, actually contains the first serious collection of German folk songs. A further work of importance was the monumental *Description of a Journey through Germany and Switzerland in the Year 1783* (1783–96). Nicolai's unfair posthumous reputation as an intolerant, narrow-minded dogmatist resulted from Goethe's and Schiller's campaign against him in the *Xenien* (1796), and assaults by Fichte and the Romantics in the following years.

Moses Mendelssohn (1729–86) came to Berlin from Dessau in 1743 to pursue his studies of the Talmud, but his interests soon broadened to Enlightenment philosophy. His friendship with Lessing and Nicolai stimulated his interest in literature, and he collaborated with them in the *Letters Concerning the Newest Literature*. He also produced pioneering work in psychology, notably *On the Sentiments* (1755), while his most famous work, *Phaedon; or, the Immortality of the Soul* (1767) earned him the title of the "German Socrates" and almost universal respect. Denied membership in the Royal Academy by Frederick the Great, presumably because he was a Jew, Mendelssohn earned his living as a clerk and then manager in the silk business. His later life was troubled by celebrated disputes with the Swiss physiognomist Johann Kaspar Lavater, who challenged him publicly to refute Christianity or convert to it, and with Friedrich Heinrich Jacobi, whose claim that Lessing had become a Spinozist before his death Mendelssohn challenged. Throughout his life, Mendelssohn remained a pillar of the Jewish community in Berlin, translating the Psalms and the Five Books of the Torah (Pentateuch) into German, and working for improved political and social conditions for German Jews. In *Jerusalem* (1783), he attempted to demonstrate the compatibility of his political liberalism and religious orthodoxy. For a thorough study in English, see Alexander Altmann, *Moses Mendelssohn: A Biographical Study* (Alabama: University of Alabama Press, 1973).

Correspondence on Tragedy

Nicolai to Lessing   Berlin, August 31, 1756

. . . I await your thoughts on the domestic tragedy eagerly.[1] I only wish you could have looked through my *Treatise on Tragedy*, which is already in press, before it was printed.[2] Moses (who I am sure, however, is too indulgent) may have applauded it, but I myself am not satisfied. Even though I spent a quarter of a year on it, I still didn't have time to think through certain things sufficiently, and for that reason I completely omitted the theory of the domestic tragedy, because it seemed to me important enough to deserve a treatise of its own. Nothing would have been more welcome to me on this subject than your comments.

In the meantime let me give you a notion of my theses. Firstly you must know that because the treatise is written in the main for those who want to submit tragedies for the competition,[3] I have assumed as given all the general theses on which everyone agrees; for I was nauseated at the prospect of repeating once more all the theses that have already been repeated a hundred times. I only intended to consider the theory of tragedy from a new angle, and therefore aimed to include nothing in the treatise but what is in a certain degree novel. Above all I have attempted to refute Aristotle's thesis, so often repeated, that it is the purpose of tragedy to purge the passions or to shape public manners. It is, if not false, at least not generally true, and is to blame that many German tragedies are so bad. I therefore place the purpose of tragedy in the arousing of the passions and say: the best tragedy is that which arouses the passions most powerfully, not that which is suited to purging the passions. I attempt to make this end the unifying principle behind all the qualities of tragedy. The most important matter is and remains the action, because this contributes the most to the arousal of the passions. The essential qualities of the action are grandeur, continuity, simplicity. The tragic grandeur of an action doesn't consist in its being accomplished by great or noble characters, but in its being suited to arousing vehement passions. The continuity of an action consists in its never being interrupted by another action; and the simplicity in its not being so entangled by incidental actions that an effort is needed to perceive its design. If it has the last two qualities, it has at the same time the quality critics have already long since enjoined under the name of unity. The unity of the action is absolutely necessary; without it certainly parts can be beautiful, but never the whole. The unities of time and place do not need to be so strictly observed, and it is best not to fix time and place all too precisely. Tragedies may be classified according to the passions they are intended to arouse into: (1) tragedies that attempt to arouse fear and pity. These I call affecting tragedies, and they include all domestic tragedies, also all those in which domestic interest dominates, such as *Merope*,[4] *Medea*,[5] etc. (2) Tragedies such as *Brutus*[6] and *Cato*,[7] which employ fear and pity to arouse admiration, I call heroic. (3) Tragedies in which the arousal of fear and pity is accompanied by admiration are mixed tragedies, such as *The Earl of Essex*,[8] etc. (4) Tragedies that are supposed to arouse admiration without the help of fear and pity are not practicable, because the hero arouses the greatest admiration in misfortune, but then he also arouses pity. *Canute*[9] might be a failed example of this genre. From the qualities of the action I derive the manner of the plot. The exposition must be natural. The continuation of the action contains the means to its end or resolution. As soon as we begin to be in doubt as to what ends the means serve, the plot is thickened; as soon as we begin to suspect these ends, the resolution begins; as soon as the ends are fully certain, the resolution is also consummate, no matter where the change of fortune may occur. The poet in general imitates nature, but only insofar as it is sensuous; thus the tragic poet imitates nature, but only insofar as it arouses passions. Therefore if the poet can represent an object in two different ways, of which the one is more natural, but the other arouses more passion, the latter is superior. For example, using confidants is natural, but cold; therefore, assuming all other things remain the same, one should rather make a monologue, which admittedly isn't so natural, but can be more passionate. Again, the tragic quality in characters lies in that they arouse violent passions, not that they improve manners. The tragic characters are a virtuous man who becomes unhappy through a mistake he commits, and a villain who also becomes unhappy, but who to a certain extent gains our sympathy by a false ethical system (a thesis of Moses'). Thus Canute is an example of a good king, but for precisely that reason not a tragic hero, because he doesn't commit a mistake. Ulfo, on the other hand, irrespective of his godlessness, gains our sympathies through his false system of honor to such a degree that in a certain way he appears heroic to us; precisely for that reason he is tragic.[10] The flaw in a character is nothing evil but rather an action or inclination that, precisely in that it turns out unfortunately for the hero, becomes a fault; thus for example in Sophocles' *Oedipus,* Oedipus's flaw is not the murder of Laius, which is outside the action, but the curiosity from which the resolution proceeds. In just the same way, Schlegel could have made Canute's kindness itself the flaw; this would have made his tragedy look completely different. That is, the kindness of Canute in giving Ulfo an army to command after their reconciliation, would need to have the consequence (the seeds of which are already there) that Ulfo murdered Canute, and even in death Canute forgave Ulfo, etc. Concerning expression, it is assumed as given that the poet thinks nobly; but he must also express himself nobly, sensuously, and beautifully. Flaws in expression are demonstrated with little effort using the example of Gottsched's translation of *Alzire.*[11] These are roughly my thoughts. I have expounded them in a somewhat muddled manner, just as the treatise itself is none too orderly. . . .

Lessing to Nicolai   November 1756

. . . Sincere thanks for the brief excerpt from your *Treatise on Tragedy.* It pleased me very much in many ways, among others because it gives me the opportunity to contradict. Do give due consideration to everything I will say in response; for it may well be that I haven't given it all sufficient thought. . . .

It is possible that we owe many a wretched but well-meant play to the principle: *Tragedy should be improving.* It is possible, I say, because this comment of yours sounds a little too ingenious for me to be inclined to consider it true right away. But this I recognize as true, that no principle can help to produce better tragedies, if one has become truly familiar with it, than this: *Tragedy should arouse passions.*

If one supposes for a moment that the first principle is just as true as the second, one can still cite adequate reasons why in practice the former must have more bad consequences, and the latter more good consequences. It is not because it is a *false* principle that the former has bad consequences, but rather because it is more remote than the latter, because it merely cites the end goal, whereas the latter cites the means. If I have the means, I have the end, but not vice versa. You must therefore have stronger reasons for departing from Aristotle here, and I wish you had cast some light on them for me; for now you can attribute it to that omission that you have to read my thoughts on how I believe the ancient philosopher's theory should be understood, and how I imagine that the tragedy can exercise an improving influence by engendering passions.

The crucial point will be what kind of passions tragedy arouses. In its characters it can allow all passions to hold sway that are compatible with the dignity of the subject matter. But are all these passions also aroused in the audience at the same time? Does a member of the audience become joyful? enamored? angry? vengeful? I'm not asking whether the poet brings him to the point of approving these passions in the character in the play, but rather whether he brings him to the point of *feeling* these passions himself, and not just feeling that someone else is feeling them?

In short, I find that the only passion that tragedy arouses in the audience is pity. You will say, "Doesn't it also awaken fear? Doesn't it also awaken admiration?" As I understand them, fear and admiration are not passions. What are they then? If in your presentation you have hit on what fear is, *eris mihi magnus Apollo,*[12] and if you have hit on what admiration is, *Phyllida solus habeto.*[13]

Sit yourselves here on your judges' seats, gentlemen, Nicolai and Moses. Let me say what I understand by the two terms.

Fear in *tragedy* is nothing more than being suddenly surprised by pity, whether I know the object of my pity or not. For example, the priest finally blurts it out: "You, Oedipus, are the murderer of Laius!" I am frightened, for suddenly I see the righteous Oedipus unhappy; my pity is suddenly aroused. Another example: a ghost appears; I am frightened: the thought that it would not appear if its appearance were not to cause misfortune to one character or another, the obscure imagining of this misfortune, even though I don't yet know whom it will strike, surprise my pity, and this surprised pity is called fear.[14] Correct me if I am wrong.

Now to admiration! Admiration! *Oh in tragedy,* to express myself a little like an oracle, it is pity that has become superfluous. The hero is unhappy, but he is so above his misfortune, he is even so proud of it, that in my thoughts too it begins to lose its fearful aspect, so that I envy him more than I feel sorry for him.

The rungs therefore are these: fear, pity, admiration. But the ladder is called pity, and fear and admiration are nothing but the first and last steps, the beginning and end of pity. For example, I suddenly hear that now Cato is as good as in Caesar's hands. *Fear!* After this I become acquainted with the former's estimable character, and then also with his misfortune. *Fear is resolved into pity.* But now I hear him say: "The world which serves Caesar is no longer worthy of me." *Admiration imposes limits on pity.* The poet needs fear to announce pity, and admiration as it were as a resting point for pity. The path to pity becomes too long for the audience if the initial fear doesn't gain his attention at once, and pity gets worn out if it cannot take respite in admiration. If it is therefore true that the whole art of the tragic poet aims to succeed in arousing and prolonging pity alone, then I now say the purpose of tragedy is this: it should expand *our capacity for feeling pity*. It should not merely teach us to feel pity for this or that unfortunate character, but rather it should make us feel in general that the unfortunate man must at all times move us and win our sympathies, in whatever form he appears. And now I appeal to a thesis Moses may perhaps demonstrate to you for the present if you want to spite your own feelings by doubting it.[15] *The most compassionate man is the best man,* the most inclined to all social virtues, to all types of magnanimity. He who makes us feel pity therefore makes us better and more virtuous, and the tragedy that does the former also does the latter, or—it does the former so that it can do the latter. Apologize to Aristotle, or refute me.

I proceed in the same way with comedy. It should help us to acquire the skill of easily perceiving all types of ridiculousness. Anyone who possesses this skill will attempt to avoid all types of ridiculous behavior, and precisely thereby become the best-mannered and most ethical man. And thus the usefulness of comedy is also rescued.

The use of both, of tragedy as well as comedy, is inseparable from pleasure; for a good half of pity and laughter is pleasure, and it is a great advantage for the dramatic poet that he can be neither useful nor pleasant without being the other.

I am so satisfied at present with these whims of mine that if I were to write a poetics of the drama I would preface it with extensive treatises on pity and laughter. I would even compare the two, I would show that weeping arises from a mixture of sadness and joy, just as much as laughter from a mixture of pleasure and displeasure; I would indicate how laughter can be transformed into weeping by allowing on the one hand pleasure to grow into joy and on the other displeasure into sadness; I would—you wouldn't believe all the things I'd do.

I will just add a few examples of how easily and correctly not just the most important rule known, but also a host of new rules proceeds from my principle, rules without which writers normally make do with mere intuition.

Tragedy should awaken just as much pity as ever it can; consequently all the characters one allows to become unhappy must have good qualities, consequently the best character must also be the most unhappy, and merit and misfortune remain in constant proportion to one another. That is, the poet must introduce no villain devoid of all goodness. The hero or the best person mustn't, like a god, survey his virtues quietly and untroubled. A flaw of Canute, to the observation of which you have arrived by another route. But do notice that I'm not talking here about the conclusion, for I leave it up to the poet as he sees fit whether he prefers to crown virtue by a happy conclusion, or to make it still more interesting to us by an unhappy ending. I only demand that the characters who engage my sympathies the most should be the unhappiest *for the duration of the play*. But the conclusion doesn't belong to this duration.

Fear, I have said, is surprised pity; let me add a word here. Surprised and *undeveloped* pity; consequently, why the surprise if pity remains undeveloped? A tragedy full of fear, without pity, is lightning without thunder. There should be as many cracks of thunder as lightning flashes, if the flash isn't to become so indifferent to us that we gape at it with childish pleasure. Admiration, as I have expressed myself, is pity become superfluous. But as pity is the principal achievement, so it must consequently become superfluous as seldom as possible; the poet mustn't expose his hero too much, nor too persistently to mere admiration, and I find Cato as a Stoic a poor tragic hero. The admired hero is the subject of the epic; the *pitied* that of the tragedy. Can you recall a single passage in Homer, Virgil, Tasso or Klopstock where the hero awakens pity? Or a single ancient tragedy where the hero is more admired than pitied? From these remarks you can also now infer what I think of your classification of tragedies. Begging your pardon, but it falls away completely. . . .

Lessing to Mendelssohn   November 13, 1756

. . . Please think over, test, improve what I have written to Nicolai. If you fulfill my request, it will be just as if I myself had once again thought over, tested, and improved it. Your better thoughts are nothing more than my second thoughts. So as soon as you, for example, find my concept of weeping false, I will immediately discard it too, and consider it nothing more than a violent extension of my concept of laughter. At present I still think it is true, for I reason as follows: all sorrow accompanied by tears is sorrow over something good that has been lost; no other pain, no other unpleasant feeling is accompanied by tears. Now if something good has been lost, not only the idea of loss but also the idea of the good thing is present, and both are inseparably bound together, the pleasant idea and the unpleasant idea. What if this association were always the case where weeping occurs? In the case of tears of pity it's obvious. In the case of tears of joy it also holds true: for then one only weeps for joy when one has previously been miserable and now suddenly sees oneself made happy; but never when one has previously not been miserable. Only so-called tears of remorse create a problem for me, but I am very much afraid the memory of the pleasure of the sin one only now begins to recognize as criminal plays a good part in it; unless tears of remorse are nothing other than a kind of tears of joy, as one simultaneously feels one's wretchedness in having trod the path of vice, and one's bliss in again stepping out on the path of virtue.

I only ask you in addition to pay attention to the admirable harmony, which, in accordance with my explanation of weeping, I believe I see here between the corresponding changes of the body and the soul. One can laugh so that tears come to one's eyes; physical weeping is as it were the highest degree of physical laughter. And what more is needed in the soul in the case of laughter, if it is to turn to weeping, than that the pleasure and displeasure from whose mixture laughter arises, both grow to the highest degree, and remain mixed in just the same way? For example, the head of a child in a great ceremonial wig is a ridiculous object; and the great statesman who has grown childish an object worthy of tears. . . .

Mendelssohn to Lessing   Berlin, November 23, 1756

. . . In truth, your last letter to Nicolai contains so many remarkable points that I must request a space of time to give mature consideration to all your thoughts before I can answer them. If boredom in Leipzig has inspired in you these excellent thoughts, I am almost tempted to wish boredom on you more frequently. Meanwhile, for now I request a few clarifications on your thoughts about admiration. If you are off the mark in this subject, I promise myself I can tear down your whole system.

If we notice good qualities in a person, which surpass the opinion we have had of him or of human nature in its entirety, we fall into a pleasant emotion we call admiration. Now since all admiration has its basis in uncommonly good qualities, this emotion must already in and of itself occasion pleasure in the heart of the spectator, without regard for the pity the admired person can do without. Indeed, the wish must even arise in the spectator to emulate the admired hero if possible; for the desire to emulate is inseparable from the intuitive cognition of a good quality, and I am sure I do not need to cite to you the evidence of experience to show that this desire has frequently had the most excellent effect.

I admit that admiration frequently tones down the pity we had previously proffered suffering virtue, or, if you will, completely suspends it for a space. But it doesn't always do this, and when it does, this is merely a chance effect, which cannot possibly exhaust its whole worth, because it has this effect in common with the utter death of the hero. The dead Zaïre[16] demands our pity just as little as the dying Gusmann,[17] and yet it is something more than subdued pity that occasions our enthusiasm at the excellent behavior of the latter, and, if I am not mistaken, gives rise in every human breast to the wish to be capable of an equally sublime attitude. When Mithridates,[18] though finding himself in the most constricting circumstances, is still hatching a plan to attack Rome and explains it to his sons so excellently that we even perceive the possibility of its being carried out, he indisputably arouses admiration. But has Mithridates' unfortunate fate in the war against the Romans ever moved us to pity? Wouldn't it be an unforgivable error on the part of the poet if he wanted to subdue a pity, which as it were has followed its course offstage and has barely the remotest influence on the plot? So beg forgiveness of admiration, this mother of virtue, for having thought so unfavorably of her worth. It is not merely a resting point of pity, only there so as to make room again for new pity to arise. No! The sensuous feeling of pity gives way to a higher feeling and its gentle shimmer vanishes when the radiance of admiration penetrates our heart. Let the admirers of the ancients think up ways to excuse the fact that the greatest poets of Greece never brought admirable characters onto the stage. As far as I am acquainted with their tragedies, I can't remember a single trait of one character who might deserve our admiration from the point of view of his morality. Their sculptors have made better use of this dignified emotion. They have almost always allowed a certain heroism to accompany the passions, thereby raising their characters somewhat above nature, and connoisseurs admit that their statues are almost inimitable in this respect.[19]

Let me break off my tiresome chatter here. I can't reveal to you my thoughts about fear and weeping before I have spoken with Nicolai about them. It always seems to me as if every illusion of fear, even without the help of pity, must be pleasant. Let an example of this be the painted serpent cited by Aristotle,[20] or rather the appearance of a ghost on the stage you yourself cite. The manner in which you attempt to reduce this fear to pity is all too ingenious for it to be natural. We shall expand further on all this once we have organized our thoughts about the effect of theatrical illusion, and its conflict with clear cognition. . . .

Lessing to Mendelssohn   Leipzig, November 28, 1756

. . . What you say about admiration suits me very well. In my letter to our friend I didn't intend just to explain this emotion in general, but also to indicate what effect it produces in tragedy—an effect you yourself do not entirely deny.

We begin to feel admiration, you say, when we notice in a person good qualities that surpass our previous opinion of him or of human nature in its entirety. In this explanation I find two separate things that deserve two separate names, which they really do have in our language. When I notice in a person good qualities that surpass my opinion of *him,* then what that's called is not, I *admire* him, but rather, I am *amazed* at him. . . .

So, when a villain or any other person shows a good quality I hadn't suspected in him, it is not admiration but amazement that arises, and this, far from being something pleasing, deserves rather to be called a flaw in the poet, because there must be no more to a character than one thinks one finds in it at the beginning. If the miser suddenly becomes generous, the boaster modest, one is *amazed,* but one can't admire the character.

Now if this distinction isn't false hairsplitting, then admiration will only occur where we discover qualities so radiant that we would not have believed them of human nature in its entirety. I think the following points will help make it possible to perceive this more precisely.

What sort of shining qualities is it that we admire? Are they distinct qualities, or are they only the highest degrees of good qualities? Are they the highest degrees of all good qualities, or only of a few of them?

The word "admiration" is used so often by the greatest admirer, the rabble, that I hardly dare decide anything on the basis of linguistic usage. Its—i.e., the rabble's—capacities are so meager, its virtues so limited, that it only has to discover capacities and virtues in a moderate degree if it is to admire. Whatever is above its narrow sphere it believes is above the sphere of human nature in its entirety.

So let us only investigate those cases where better people, people of feeling and insight, admire. Investigate your own heart, dearest friend! Do you admire the benevolence of Augustus,[21] the chastity of Hippolytus,[22] the childlike love of Chimène?[23] Do these and other such qualities go beyond the notion you have of human nature? Or doesn't the very emulation they awaken in you show on the contrary that they are still within that notion?

So, what qualities *do* you admire? You admire a Cato, an Essex—in a word, nothing but examples of unshakable firmness, uncompromising steadfastness, of courage that cannot be frightened, of heroic contempt for danger and death; and the better your heart, the more delicate your feeling, the more you admire all these examples. You have too correct a notion of human nature for you not to consider all insensitive heroes beautiful monsters, more than human, but not good people at all. So you admire them with justice; but precisely for the reason that you admire them, you will not emulate them. At least it has never occurred to me to become the equal of a Cato or an Essex in stubbornness, however much I may admire them on account of this stubbornness, which I would absolutely despise and condemn if it didn't seem to be a stubbornness of virtue.

So I will not ask forgiveness of admiration, but rather I demand that you should beg the pardon of virtue for making it a daughter of admiration. It is true virtue is very often a daughter of emulation, and emulation is a natural consequence of the intuitive cognition of a good quality. But must it be an admirable quality? Far from it. It must be a good quality of which I consider people in general, and therefore also myself, capable. And far from excluding these qualities from tragedy, my opinion, on the contrary, is that no tragedy can exist at all without them, because without them one can arouse no pity. I only want to exclude those great qualities that we can comprehend under the general name of heroism, because each of them is connected with insensitivity, and insensitivity in the object of my pity weakens my pity.

Let us here take lessons from the ancients. What better teachers can we choose, other than nature? In order to arouse pity all the more certainly, Oedipus and Alcestis[24] were stripped of all heroism. The former laments like a woman, and the latter wails even more than a woman usually would; the authors wanted to make them too sensitive, rather than insensitive; they preferred to have them pour out too many laments, to shed too many tears, than none at all.

You say, it doesn't detract from the value of admiration that it weakens or even suspends pity, because it has this in common with the death of the hero. Here excessive acumen leads you astray. Among a thousand people there will be only one sage who doesn't consider death the greatest evil, and being dead a perpetuation of this evil! Pity therefore still doesn't end when death comes; but even if it did, this circumstance would be nothing more than the reason for the rule that the play must also end with the death of the hero. But can the play conclude with admiration? But if I said that the tragic poet, far from allowing admiration to be his main object, must on the contrary make it merely a resting point for pity, then what I meant to say by that was that he should give his hero only sufficient steadfastness to ensure that he doesn't succumb to his misfortune in an undignified manner. He must make him sensitive of his misfortune; he must let him feel it strongly; for otherwise we couldn't feel it. And he must only occasionally let him exert himself in a way that for a few moments seems to reveal a soul able to stand up to fate; but the next moment, this great soul must again become the prey of its feelings of pain.

I think what you say about Racine's Mithridates supports me rather than you. The noble scene where he reveals to his sons the plan to march on Rome is precisely the reason why we can feel no pity for him for his unfortunate fate in the war against the Romans. I see him already marching triumphantly into Rome, and this makes me forget all his unfortunate battles. And what does that make this scene in Racine other than a beautiful filler? You admire Mithridates, this admiration is a pleasant emotion; in a Charles XII[25] it can awaken emulation, but does that make it untrue that it is more suited to a heroic poem than to a tragedy?

But let me stop chattering, and at last take into account that I'm writing to one sparing with words. Let me not have said what I have said until now against admiration, whether it is good or bad; let all that you say about it be true. Nonetheless, it must be banished from tragedy.

For—But let me first preface this with a clarification taken from the origin of tragedy. The ancient tragedies are taken from Homer, as regards their content, and the very genre of these poems arose from the singing of his epics. Homer, and following him the rhapsodists, selected certain episodes from them that they used to sing on ceremonious occasions, or perhaps from door to door to earn their bread. They must have soon found out by experience which episodes the people preferred most to hear. One only hears heroic deeds once with particular pleasure; their novelty is what moves us most. But tragic events move us as often as they are heard. These, therefore, in preference to other events in Homer, were selected, and at first sung as narratives, as they stand in Homer, until the idea was hit upon to divide them up into dialogue, so that what we now call tragedy arose from this process. Now couldn't the ancients just as well have made a dialogic whole out of the heroic deeds? To be sure, and certainly they would have done so if they hadn't considered admiration a less apt teacher of the people than pity.

And that is a point you yourself can prove best. Admiration, as it is generally understood, according to which it is nothing but the peculiar pleasure at a rare perfection, improves by means of emulation, and emulation presupposes a clear cognition of the perfection I want to emulate. How many possess this cognition? And where this is lacking, doesn't admiration remain unfruitful? Pity on the other hand improves directly; improves without us having to contribute something to the process; improves the man of understanding as well as the dunce. . . .

Mendelssohn to Lessing [Berlin, first half of December, 1756]

. . . I'm sending you your letter with this one, because I intend to refute it piece by piece, but I beg you to return it to me. It shall serve to restore my modesty; for it proves what a small opponent I must be that you believe it possible to defend yourself against me with such poor weapons! To business!

I think the current political events[26] have led you to confuse *admiration* and *amazement*. An unsuspected event whose reason I cannot get to the bottom of occasions in me *amazement*. Thus I am amazed at thunder, electricity, the actions of a person that do not seem to be grounded in his moral character, and finally you, if *you* want to make me believe in so faulty a distinction. On the other hand I admire a person in whom I notice a good quality of which I didn't believe him capable, but which nonetheless is grounded in his moral character. . . .

. . . In general, every action that cannot be reconciled with the known character of the person acting occasions in us amazement, and in dramatic plays is a fault of the poet, except when the *amazement* is ultimately resolved into *admiration*, i.e., when as the play develops we learn circumstances that make the action really probable. I consider the most excellent kind of plot one in which the actions of an otherwise virtuous person appear to be in conflict with his character, but are finally all found to flow from a single source. Clarissa's family must stand there as if struck by lightning when their amazement at the inconsistent behavior of their little Claire is suddenly resolved into *admiration* of her victorious innocence.[27]

I return to my definition of admiration. When a preeminently virtuous person (Cato) acts in a way that surpasses as it were human nature, or when an ambiguous character acts in such a way as to give us a better opinion of his convictions, then *admiration* arises. Now I will investigate my own heart. "Do I admire the benevolence of Augustus?" Yes! And so do Cinna and the Roman populace, because they haven't believed the imperious emperor capable of any such gentleness. "The chastity of Hippolytus?" No! "The childlike love of Chimène?" Yes! Inasmuch as I wouldn't have believed any woman capable of such heroic power over her passion.—Thus far my heart can still be more or less reconciled with my understanding. However, I also admire a Cato, an Essex, etc., on account of their uncommon heroic virtues, and yet it has never occurred to me to emulate them in this. How can this be, since after all a quality I admire must of necessity appear worthy of imitation? This is the problem you have found, but not resolved. I will endeavor to do it for you.

All our judgments are based either on clear rational deductions or on obscure perceptions,[28] which in matters concerning truth are generally termed *insight*, but in matters relating to beauty *taste*. Rational deductions are based on symbolic cognition, on the workings of the higher powers of the soul, obscure perceptions on the other hand on intuitive cognition, on the workings of the lower powers of the soul. You are aware that taste or insight (common sense) can frequently conflict with symbolic cognition, indeed, that the former frequently have greater influence on our will than the latter. (Some quite new thoughts on the conflict of the lower and higher powers of the soul have occurred to me, which I will submit to your judgment in the near future.) The morality of the theater does not belong before the judgment seat of symbolic cognition. If the poet, *through his perfectly sensuous discourse,*[29] can convince our intuitive cognition of the worth and worthlessness of his characters, then he has our applause. We gladly suppress the clear rational deductions that oppose our illusions; just as we transpose ourselves by means of illusion into another climate, other circumstances, and among other people, in order to feel the power of the imitation as emphatically as possible. (I can't go into this any further before Nicolai has time to develop with me the thoughts on theatrical illusion we promised you.) So off with your clear conviction of the vanity of stubborn heroism! It can disturb neither the admiration nor the immediate resolution to emulate, if the poet has managed to take possession of the lower powers of our soul. But it can prevent this immediate wish from ever growing into reality, because when the illusion is ended, reason grasps the wheel again. On the other hand, in the case of a person who doesn't have a sufficient store of clear cognition to counterbalance the illusion, the wish to emulate will persist, and even give rise to deeds. Let Charles XII be an example, and also that Englishman who killed himself after seeing *Cato* performed, since subsequently the following epigram was found on him: "What Cato does and Addison approves cannot be wrong."—Now a large number of phenomena are explained as it were of themselves. Can you really still ask me now whether I believe that admiration can impel us to emulation more effectively than the simple contemplation of good qualities? Can you still doubt now that the intuitive cognition of perfection becomes more sensuous by means of admiration, because it surprises us unexpectedly or because we encounter the apparent perfection in such a degree that it triumphs over nature and fate, as it were, and shows us the undismayed hero where we expected a sighing human being bent under his burden?—"So admiration can also commend to us as worthy of imitation actions we recognize rationally as unvirtuous?" I hear you ask.—Certainly! And this is one of the reasons that moved Nicolai to assert that the ultimate purpose of tragedy is actually not to improve manners.

Yet you mustn't think that your pity enjoys an advantage over my admiration in this respect. Pity, too, can bring us to unvirtuous attitudes if it is not governed by reason, by the cold symbolic reason that must be wholly banished from the theater if pleasure is intended.

I'll go with you into the school of the ancient poets, but when we leave them, come with me into the school of the ancient sculptors. I haven't seen their works of art, but Winckelmann, who I am confident has excellent taste, says (in his excellent treatise on the imitation of the works of the Greeks) that their sculptors never let their gods and heroes be carried away by unbridled passion. One always finds in them *nature at rest* (as he calls it), and the passions accompanied by a certain tranquility of mood by which the painful sensation of pity is covered as it were by a veneer of admiration and reverence. He cites for example Laocoön, sketched poetically by Virgil, and carved in marble by a Greek artist. The former expresses the pain excellently, the latter on the other hand allows him to conquer the pain to a certain extent, and surpasses the poet in the measure that the mere feeling of pity is to be considered inferior to pity intermingled with admiration and reverence. . . .

But why haven't you answered my objection? How, in the scene by Racine, can an admiration please us that is supposed to subdue a pity we haven't felt at all? You say, Racine wrote the scene as a filler? All right! But yet it is beautiful, therefore admiration is beautiful even where it has no pity to still.

I like your final proof, taken from the origin of tragedy, to some extent. But I doubt whether you will find admirable characters such as Cato, Grandison, Brutus, etc., in Homer. At that time their heroic merits, which aroused admiration, consisted in fighting. At the end of the game, Achilles is nothing but a brave slugger, and Agamemnon has no merit beyond being a king of kings. In Homer's times, the Greeks seem to have thought of their kings roughly as the French currently think of theirs. Ulysses is a cunning general, and Calchas a mediocre priest who can't arouse nearly as much admiration as your Theophanes.[30] (I forgot your Theophanes. He arouses the freethinker's admiration, even though he knows that his good qualities don't surpass human nature in its entirety.) I don't mean to put Homer down at all by this comment, and believe on the contrary that as a whole none of the poets who have succeeded him has equaled him, but as far as great characters who arouse admiration are concerned, it seems to me that many have surpassed him.

I have one additional small comment. You assert that the poet must necessarily make his hero feel the misfortune if we are to be moved, and term admiration in this context once again *the resting point of pity*. The latter designation requires no further refutation. The former point, on the other hand, I concede, but for a quite different reason. The poet must convince our senses that his hero knows the danger his imperturbability enables him to transcend. The imitation does not become sufficiently sensuous by a mere narration of the difficult circumstances in which his hero finds himself. But if we are already concerned for the hero in advance, if the poet has possessed the skill to convince our senses in some other way that the hero foresees his misfortune, and that all those present fear for him, because they see the greatest danger before their eyes— then he can let him appear completely triumphant over threatening fate. In the story of Grandison, the hero is challenged by the worthless Hargrave.[31] All Grandison's near and dear are almost beside themselves for pain, and tremble for his precious life. But how astonished one is when Grandison himself appears with his customary cheerfulness, and regards the greatest vexation he could have encountered with more than indifference! He feels nothing, but Byron, Charlotte, etc., feel all the more, and the reader is seized by a joyful admiration that surely leaves behind the warmest wish to emulate him.

So much in refutation of your concepts of admiration! . . . .

Lessing to Mendelssohn   Leipzig, December 18, 1756.

Dearest friend!

You're right, in my letter to you I chatted rather carelessly. Feel free to save it, but for my humiliation rather than yours. Let it remain a permanent demonstration for you of what absurd stuff I can write when I *let my thoughts mature as I write,* as I saw fit to express myself. Let me now test whether they have become more mature from your objections and animadversions. I wipe the whole slate clean, as if I had not yet stated anything at all on the subject of admiration. Back to square one!

In the first letter to Nicolai I had written on this subject: *in tragedy, admiration must be nothing but the resting point of pity.* Did you understand me properly? Nicolai made his second genre of tragedies those intended to arouse admiration with the help of fear and pity. In this genre therefore admiration becomes the main object, that is, the misfortune which befalls the hero is supposed not just to move us, but also to give the hero the opportunity to exhibit his extraordinary perfections, the intuitive cognition of which is supposed to awaken in us the pleasant emotion you term *admiration*.

Now such a tragedy, I say, would be a heroic poem in dialogue form, not a tragedy. As I put it in my letter to Nicolai, the *admired* hero is the subject matter of the heroic poem. Now since, after all, you will surely credit me with considering a heroic poem (a poem full of admiration) a beautiful poem, I can't see how you can accuse me of wanting to rob admiration of all its beauty and pleasantness. It is a pleasant emotion, fine; but can this earn it the foremost place in a tragedy? Tragedy, says Aristotle (chapter 14), should not afford us every kind of pleasure without distinction, but only the pleasure peculiarly appropriate to it.

Why should we confuse the different species of poetry needlessly, and let their borders overlap? Just as admiration is the main object in the heroic poem, and all other emotions, particularly pity are subordinated to it, so let pity be the main object in tragedy, and let every other emotion, particularly admiration, merely be subordinate to it, that is, let it serve no purpose but to help arouse pity. The heroic poet makes his hero unfortunate, in order to bring his perfections to light. The writer of tragedies brings his hero's perfections to light in order to make his misfortune all the more painful to us.

Great pity cannot exist unless the object of pity has great perfections, and great perfections, expressed sensuously, cannot fail to produce admiration. But in tragedy, these great perfections should never occur without great misfortunes, should always be precisely connected with these misfortunes, and should therefore awaken not admiration alone, but admiration and pain, that is, pity. And that is what I mean. Admiration, then, doesn't occur in tragedy as an emotion in itself, but merely as one-half of pity. And in this regard I was also right to explain it not as an emotion in itself, but only in its relation to pity.

And in this relation, I still say, *it should be the resting point of pity*, namely in cases where it is supposed to have an effect *in its own right*. But since you insist on the example of *Mithridates* for a second time, I have to believe you understood my words to mean by this resting point that admiration should help to still pity. But that's not what I mean by it at all, quite the contrary. Just listen!

We cannot persist in a strong emotion for long; so we can't endure a strong feeling of pity for long, either; it weakens itself. Even mediocre poets have noticed this, and saved strong feelings of pity to the end. But I hate French tragedies, which don't squeeze any tears out of me before the end of the fifth act. The true poet distributes pity throughout his whole tragedy; he finds opportunities everywhere for passages in which he shows the perfections and misfortunes of his hero connected in a moving fashion, in which, that is, he awakens tears. But because the whole play cannot be an unbroken sequence of such passages, he intermingles them with passages that deal solely with his hero's perfections, and in these passages admiration occurs in its own right. But what are these passages other than resting points, as it were, where the audience is supposed to recover so as to be able to feel pity anew? The previous feeling of pity isn't supposed to be stilled by this, that never entered my mind, and would run directly contrary to my system.

But as these passages—I shall call them *empty scenes* (although they don't always have to be whole scenes), because admiration, or the depiction of the hero's extraordinary perfections is the only technique to make the *empty scenes,* where the action stands still, tolerable—as these *empty scenes,* as I say, should be nothing but a preparation for future feelings of pity, they must not deal with any perfections of the kind that destroy pity. I will give an example, but you must forgive me its ridiculous side. Let's assume I said to someone, "Today is the day when Titus is to convey his old father in a wheelbarrow all the way down along a rope stretched from the highest tip of the tower right across the river." Now if I wanted to awaken pity for Titus on account of this dangerous action, what do I have to do? I would have to elaborate the good qualities of Titus and his father, and make them both people who, being so worthy, deserve all the less to have to expose themselves to such a danger. But pity's path to my listener's heart is immediately cut off, isn't it, as soon as I say to him, "Titus is a tightrope artist who has already attempted this feat more than once." And yet I have done nothing more than acquainted the audience with one of Titus's perfections. True, but it was a perfection that infinitely diminished the danger, and therefore deprived pity of its sustenance. The tightrope artist is now admired, but not pitied.

But what does a poet make of his hero but a tightrope artist, if, when he wants to have him die, that is, when he wants to move us most by his misfortunes, he makes him prattle quantities of the finest boasts about his contempt for death, and his indifference to life? In exactly the proportion in which, on the one hand, admiration increases, pity diminishes on the other hand. For this reason I consider Corneille's *Polyeucte* flawed; even if it will never cease to please on account of quite different beauties. Polyeucte strives to become a martyr, he yearns for death and martyrdom, he regards them as the first step into an abundantly blissful life. I admire the pious enthusiast, but I would have to fear angering his spirit in the bosom of eternal happiness if I wanted to feel pity for him.

Enough of this. You can understand me adequately to refute me, if I deserve it. But as the pen is running on, let me now explain my thoughts on the difference between the effects of admiration and the effects of pity. From admiration springs the resolution to emulate; but, as you say yourself, this resolution is only *momentary*. If it is to become reality, either the subsequent clear cognition must make it so, or the emotion of admiration must persist so strongly that the resolution becomes the deed before reason can grasp the wheel again. That is what you mean, isn't it?—Now I say: in the first instance, the effect is to be ascribed not to admiration, but to clear cognition; and for the second instance to occur, requires nothing less than a *dreamer*. For dreamers are surely nothing but people in whom the lower powers of the soul triumph over the higher? That doesn't matter, you may say, there are plenty of these dreamers in the world, and it's a good thing if even dreamers do virtuous deeds. All right, then it must be one of the poet's prime duties to awaken admiration only for really virtuous actions. For if he were permitted to give the gloss of admiration to unvirtuous actions too, then Plato would be right in wanting them banned from his Republic. So Nicolai shouldn't have argued that because wine not infrequently gives rise to bloody quarrels, the claim that it gladdens the human heart is false; or because poetry often commends bad actions as worthy of admiration, its end purpose cannot be to improve manners.

I go still further, and ask you to consider whether the virtuous deed a person does out of mere emulation, without clear cognition, is really a virtuous deed, and can be credited to him as such? Further, I insist that admiration of a beautiful action can only impel one to emulate precisely that same action, in precisely the same circumstances, and not all beautiful actions; it improves us, if it does improve us, only by means of specific instances, and therefore also only in specific cases. One admires Gusmann, for example, who forgives his murderer.[32] Can this admiration, without the assistance of clear cognition, impel me to forgive all my opponents? Or does it only impel me to forgive that mortal enemy whom I have made for myself by my own misdeeds? I think only the latter.

How infinitely better and more certain are the effects of my pity! Tragedy should only *exercise* the general faculty of pity, and not induce us to feel pity in this case or that. Even assuming that the poet makes me feel pity for an unworthy object, namely by showing me bogus perfections, by which he misleads my *insight* in order to win my heart, this doesn't matter, as long as my pity is aroused, and accustoms itself, as it were, to being aroused more and more easily. I allow myself to be moved to pity in a tragedy in order to gain proficiency in pity; does that occur with admiration? Can one say, "I want to feel admiration in the tragedy, in order to gain proficiency in admiration"? I believe the man who has the greatest proficiency in admiration is a fop; just as the person who has the greatest proficiency in pity is undoubtedly the best person.

But haven't I perhaps returned to my old tricks? Am I not declaring admiration absolutely useless by what I have said so far, even though I concede it the heroic poem in its entirety as its arena? It might almost appear so; so I shall at least dare to confide to you an idea that admittedly sounds rather strange, but because it rescues no lesser personages than Homer and myself, is perhaps not unworthy of your investigation.

There are certain physical abilities, certain degrees of physical strengths, which we do not have power over at will, even though they really are present in the body. A madman, for example, is incomparably stronger than he was when his reason was sound; also fear, anger, despair, and other emotions too awaken in us a greater degree of strength that doesn't stand at our command until we have fallen into this emotion or that.

My second preliminary remark is this. All physical skills are learned with the aid of admiration; at least the *fine points* of all physical skills. Take a jumper. He can show his pupils the actual mechanism of only a very few jumps; often he can say no more than, "Just watch, just watch how I do it!" That is, just admire me properly and then attempt it, it will go of its own accord. And the more perfectly the master models the jump, and the more he excites the admiration of his pupil by this perfection, the easier the latter will find it to imitate him.

Out with my idea, then! What if Homer deliberately described only physical perfections as worthy of admiration? He can easily have been just as good a philosopher as I. He can easily have believed, like me, that though admiration can make our bodies brave and skillful, it cannot make our souls virtuous. Achilles, you say, is in Homer nothing but a brave slugger; maybe. But nonetheless he is an admirable slugger, who can give rise in another to the resolution to emulate. And as often as this other person finds himself in circumstances similar to those of Achilles, the example of this hero will occur to him again, the admiration he felt will be renewed, and this admiration will make him stronger and more skillful than he would have been without it. But let's assume Homer had made Achilles an admirable model of magnanimity. Now as often as a person with a fiery imagination saw himself in similar circumstances to his, he could certainly also remember the admiration he felt, and in consequence of this admiration act with equal magnanimity; but would that make him magnanimous? Magnanimity has to be a constant quality of the soul, and not merely issue forth from it by fits and starts.

I'm convinced that my words often detract from my meaning, that I not infrequently express myself too vaguely or too carelessly. So, dearest friend, try to put yourself by your own reflection into the spirit of my system. And perhaps you'll find it much better than I can imagine it to be.

Compared with me, you will always be *sparing with words,* after all, for I have formed the firm intention of scribbling this second sheet full, too. To start with I wanted to make of the following a separate letter to Nicolai, but I don't want to deliberately heap up his debts. Do read chapter 13 of Aristotle's *Poetics.* There the philosopher says: the hero of a tragedy must be an intermediate character; he must be neither all too immoral, nor all too virtuous; if he were all too immoral, and earned his misfortune by his crimes, then we couldn't feel pity for him; but if he were all too virtuous, and yet became unhappy, then pity would be transformed into horror and disgust.

I'd like to know how Nicolai can reconcile this rule with the admirable qualities of his hero. But that's not what I want to write about now.

Here I myself am against Aristotle, who seems to me to have laid down a false explanation of pity as his foundation.[33] And if I am less far off the truth, I have only *your* better concept of pity to thank for it. Is it true that the misfortune of an all too virtuous person awakens horror and disgust? If it is true, then horror and disgust must be the highest degree of pity, which they nonetheless are not. Pity, which grows in precisely the proportion in which perfection and misfortune increase, ceases to be pleasant to me and becomes more unpleasant, the greater on the one hand the perfection, and on the other the misfortune is.

At the same time it is nonetheless also true that there must be a certain ἁμαρτια, a certain flaw in the hero, by which he has brought his misfortune on himself. But why this ἁμαρτια, as Aristotle calls it? Could it be, because without it he would be perfect, and the misfortune of a perfect person awakens disgust? Surely not. I think I have found the only correct cause. It is this: because without the flaw, which brings the misfortune upon him, his character and his misfortune would constitute no *whole,* because the one would not be grounded in the other, and we would think about each of these two things separately. An example will make my meaning clearer. Let Canute be a model of the most perfect goodness. If he is to arouse pity, then I must bring a great misfortune upon him through the flaw that he doesn't let his goodness be governed by cleverness, and heaps dangerous blessings on Ulfo, whom he should only forgive; Ulfo must imprison and murder him. Pity in the highest degree! But let's assume I didn't have Canute perish as a result of his abused goodness; I had him suddenly struck down by lightning, or crushed by the collapse of his palace. Horror and disgust without pity! Why? Because there is not the least connection between his goodness and the thunder, or the collapsing palace, between his perfection and his misfortune. They are two different things, which cannot produce a single communal effect such as pity, but rather each of which has its own effect.—Another example! Think of the old cousin in the *London Merchant;*[34] when Barnwell stabs him, the audience is horrified, without feeling pity, because the good character of the old man contains absolutely nothing that could serve as a reason for this misfortune. But as soon as one then hears him pray to God for his murderer and cousin, the horror is transformed into a truly delightful pity, and quite naturally so, because this magnanimous deed flows from his misfortune and has its basis in the same. . . .

P.S. To make sure this letter has all the qualities of an intolerable letter, let me even provide it with a P.S.

Twice already you have called on the authority of the Greek sculptors, who, you believe, understood their art better than the Greek poets. Read the conclusion of chapter 15 of Aristotle's *Poetics* and then tell me whether the rule of the embellishment of the passions was unknown to them.

The hero is unfortunate in the epic, and is also unfortunate in the tragedy. But the way in which he is unfortunate in the one must never be the same as in the other. I can't remember finding the difference between these two kinds of misfortune properly defined anywhere. The misfortune of the hero in the epic mustn't be a consequence of his character, because otherwise, according to my above remark, it would arouse pity. Rather, it must be a misfortune of fate and chance, in which his good or bad qualities play no part. "Fato profugus," as Virgil says of his Aeneas.[35] With tragedy the opposite holds, and a heroic poem can never be made of Oedipus, for example, and anyone wanting to make one of this story would in the end have made nothing more than a tragedy in books. For it would be wretched if these two genres of poetry were to have no more essential distinction than the use of unbroken dialogue and dialogue interrupted by the narrative of the poet, or the division into acts and books.

When you work out a finished version of your thoughts on illusion with Nicolai, don't forget that the whole theory of illusion actually has nothing to do with the dramatic poet, and the performance of his play is the work of an art other than poetry. Tragedy must retain its full power even without performance and actors, and in order to express this to the reader it has no more need of illusion than any other story. Consult Aristotle once again on this account, towards the end of chapter 6 and the beginning of chapter 14.

Now I've completely finished. Farewell!

Mendelssohn (and Nicolai) to Lessing   [Berlin, January 1757]

. . . I must tell you immediately at the outset that in most matters I am of just the same opinion as you. "Why not in all?" you ask. Patience! I shall examine your thoughts one by one. Right at the beginning you allot quite different jurisdictions to the two tragic passions, admiration and pity, and want the former to dominate in the field of the heroic poem, but the latter on the stage. In this context you ask, "Why should we confuse the different species of poems needlessly, and let their borders overlap?" Here you have taken as your defense a prejudice I have so often heard you yourself contest. What is the basis of this imagined drawing of borders? With regard to the works of nature it has been established in the past century that they are not divided by their mistress into any particular, separate classes. Why shouldn't we let art become an imitator of nature in this, too? If linguistic usage, the authority of the ancients, the division of the arts into their separate species, and a thousand other prejudices have given the name *tragedy* only to those dramatic pieces that arouse primarily pity, then those who teach language can keep to this prescription. But reason speaks otherwise; it counts every great and dignified event among the objects of tragedy, *as long as it is capable of a higher degree of imitation by means of lively representation.* . . . So don't exclude a single passion from the theater. As long as the imitated passion can convince us intuitively of the excellence of the imitation, it deserves to be performed on the stage. Even hatred and disgust can please on the stage, in spite of Aristotle and all his adherents, because it is enough if the imitated passion can convince us that the imitation resembles the original. . . .

However, let us draw a little closer together. I concede that pity can more easily create an intuitive illusion for us than admiration. I mean, it is easier to persuade us that the imitation resembles the original by imitating pity than to achieve this by means of admiration. But you must admit to me, too, that art reveals itself in all its radiance when it dares to imitate the most subtle features of nature and to represent a great soul in its brightest light, when it copies the image of a hero who rises courageously under the burden of his afflictions, lifts his head to the clouds, and undismayed hears around his feet the thunder roar, which, taken by aesthetic illusion, we have watched gathering around him with the greatest anxiety. The path is difficult, very difficult, and only great minds can hope to tread it with success! I admit it; but when has my Lessing been bothered about paths on which mediocre minds are to proceed? . . .

Just don't make excuses for your expression, "Admiration is the resting point of pity." Certainly the elaboration of the perfections that adorn the hero, or rather the making known of his character, can not infrequently fill out a minor scene and provide a resting point of pity. But this is not *admiration,* but rather esteem, a lower degree of admiration, which entertains us for a while, just as we often introduce moving passages in comedy, in order to give us a break from laughter. But where admiration is supposed to be the chief emotion, in a Cato, a Brutus, a Grandison, and—why don't I say it?—a Theophanes, it must perform something more than such subaltern service. In general it is the fate of all theatrical passions that they are almost completely unrecognizable when they appear accompanying other passions. Love, for example, is a raging and horrifying passion where, as in Hippolytus, it dominates the stage;

but how childish and ridiculous it is in a thousand French plays, where it only fills out a few minor scenes. I don't want to excuse Polyeucte, but when you compare him with the fellow who's to tumble down from the tower, I think the acrobat has lost the *tertium comparationis*. The hero must value moral goodness incomparably higher than physical goodness. If pain, fetters, slavery, and death conflict with a duty, he must not hesitate to hasten towards all these evils in order to preserve his innocence unblemished. This inner victory, which his divine soul wins over the body, delights us and sets us into an emotion no sensuous pleasure approaches in pleasing quality. The mere admiration of physical skills you still allow your wheelbarrow pusher is without emotion, without that inner feeling and gut warmth (if I may so express myself) with which we admire for example the magnanimity of an Orestes and Pylades. (In passing I remind you that these are perhaps the only characters of the ancients who arouse true admiration.) I say nothing of a certain situation in a Chinese tragedy you yourself always used to admire.[36] At the command of the tyrant, an old man is miserably thrashed by his friend, by precisely the friend for whose sake he doesn't want to reveal a certain secret. He looks back almost angrily at the man who is performing on his back what the tyrant commands. Now he will open his mouth and with a single word free himself from the terrible pains. But no! He sees his friend, remembers his duty, and the cruel power that forces his friend to become his executioner. His anger is transformed into melancholy, he sighs and remains faithful to his duty. Here is magnanimity, here is steadfastness, here is the inner struggle and the most splendid victory which mortals ever won! . . .

If Nicolai claims poetry can contribute nothing to the improvement of manners,[37] then he is obviously wrong. . . . But if he claims the improvement of manners cannot be the chief purpose of tragedy, because the imitation can still be perfect even if the underlying morality doesn't fully accord with reason—then I believe the most eager advocates of poetry have to concur with him. The æsthetic illusion really is capable of silencing for a while the higher powers of the soul, as I make quite clear in my "Thoughts on Illusion."[38] But that even the capacity to pity . . . doesn't always have a good effect, is made clear by my thoughts on moral sensitivity, which without the help of the power of judgment only makes our feeling more tender and drives us to chase after both true and apparent goods with greater desire. Your thoughts on the physical skills and the admiration they arouse please me uncommonly, and you put me to shame when you complain about the inability to express your thoughts correctly. What can I reply to this without paying you a compliment in return?

Just don't elevate the admiration of physical skills at the expense of the soul! You are dead wrong if you believe that magnanimity in specific individual cases merely arouses the wish to behave magnanimously in similar cases. From my *Thoughts on Controlling the Inclinations* you will see how beneficial it is to virtue when general abstract concepts are reduced to individual cases. This reduction can occur through experience, through examples, or also through fiction. Our symbolic cognition is in each case transformed into an intuitive cognition, the power of the motivations is animated, and their sum becomes greater than the sum of sensuous pleasure that opposes them. . . .

Lessing to Mendelssohn   Leipzig, February 2, 1757

. . . We are after all surely in agreement, dearest friend, that all passions are either vehement desires or vehement aversions? Also, that with every vehement desire or aversion we are conscious of our existence in a greater degree, and that this consciousness cannot be other than pleasant? Consequently, all passions, even the most unpleasant of all, are pleasant as passions. But I don't have to tell you of all people that the pleasure connected with the stronger definition of our powers can be so infinitely outweighed by the displeasure we feel at the objects with respect to which our powers are so defined that we are no longer conscious of it at all.

Everything I deduce from this will gain the greatest clarity when applied to Aristotle's example of the painted serpent.[39] *If we suddenly glimpse a painted serpent, the more violently frightened we are by it, the better it pleases us.*

This I explain thus: I am frightened by the serpent depicted so well because I take it for a real serpent. Let the degree of this fright as an unpleasant passion, or rather the degree of displeasure I feel at this frightening object, be ten; then I can call the degree of pleasure connected with the feeling of the passion one, or ten if the degree of displeasure were to grow to one hundred. So while I feel ten, I cannot feel one, that is, as long as I take the snake for a real one, I cannot feel any pleasure at it. But now I suddenly become aware that it isn't a real serpent, that it's merely a picture. What happens? The displeasure over the frightening object (ten) falls away, and nothing remains but the pleasure which is connected with the passion as a mere stronger definition of our powers; one remains, and this is what I now feel, and I can feel this in the degree of eight or ten, if the degree of displeasure was eighty or one hundred instead of ten.

Now to what end do we use illusion here? Let me test my explanation on a contrary example too, in order to demonstrate its correctness all the more indubitably.—There in the distance I become aware of the most beautiful, adorable woman, who seems to wave to me with her hand in a mysterious way. I begin to feel an emotion, longing, love, admiration, whatever you like to call it. So here the pleasure at the object (ten) is joined with the pleasant feeling of the emotion (one), and the effect of both is eleven. Now I set out toward it. Heavens! It's nothing but a painting, or a statue! Now, according to your explanation, dearest friend, the pleasure should be all the greater, because the emotion has intuitively persuaded me of the perfection of the imitation. But that runs counter to all experience; rather, I become annoyed; and why do I become annoyed? The pleasure at the perfect object falls away, and only the pleasant feeling of the emotion remains. I come to your second consequence: "(b) Hence in imitation all unpleasant emotions please us. The musician can make us angry, etc." To this I reply: the imitation of unpleasant emotions pleases us because they awaken similar emotions in us directed toward no specific object. The musician saddens me, and I find this sadness pleasant because I feel this sadness merely as an emotion, and every emotion is pleasant. For if you suppose the case that during this musical sadness I really think of something sad, then the pleasantness certainly ceases.

An example from the physical world! It is well known that if one gives two strings an identical tension, and makes one of them sound by touching it, the other also sounds without being touched. Let us give the strings feelings; we can assume that they may find every *vibration,* but not every *touch* pleasant; rather, only the particular touch that brings forth in them a certain vibration is pleasant. The first string, therefore, which vibrates through touch, may experience pain, whereas the second, although its vibration resembles the first, experiences pleasure, because it was not touched, at least not so directly. So it is also in tragedy. The character onstage comes to feel an unpleasant emotion, and I do too. But why do I find this emotion pleasant? Because I am not the character on stage himself, who experiences the direct effect of the unpleasant idea—because I feel the emotion only as an emotion, without associating a specific unpleasant object with it.

Secondary emotions of this kind, however, which arise in me when I perceive such emotions in others, hardly merit the name of emotions, which is why I said already in one of my first letters that tragedy actually arouses no emotion in us but *pity*. For the characters in the play don't feel this emotion, and we don't feel it merely because they feel it, but rather it arises originally in us from the effect of the objects on us; it isn't a *secondary*, communicated emotion. . . .

Lessing to Nicolai   Leipzig, April 2, 1757

. . . *Fear* and *pity*.[40] Can't you tell me why both Dacier and Curtius take terror and fear for words of identical meaning? Why they translate Aristotle's φοβος, which the Greek uses *consistently*, now with the one word, now with the other? After all, surely they are two different things, fear and terror? And what if this whole terror, which so much nonsense has been spouted about, in accordance with the wrongly understood Aristotelian concepts, were based on nothing but this inconsistent translation? Please read chapters 2 and 8 of the second book of Aristotle's *Rhetoric*—for I must tell you, by the way, that I can't imagine that anyone who has not read this second book and the whole of Aristotle's *Nichomachean Ethics* can understand this sage's *Poetics*. Aristotle explains the word φοβος, which Curtius most often translates as *Schrecken* [terror], but Dacier alternately *terreur* and *crainte,* by the displeasure at an impending evil, and says, all those things awaken fear in us, which awaken pity when we see them affecting others, and all those things awaken pity that, if we ourselves face them, must awaken fear.[41] In consequence of this, fear, in Aristotle's opinion, cannot be a direct effect of tragedy, but rather it must be nothing more than a *reflected idea.* Aristotle would merely have said, "Tragedy should purge our passions by means of pity," if he hadn't also wanted immediately to indicate the way by which this purging by means of pity becomes possible; and on this account, he added *fear,* which he considered this means. The first part of his opinion has a certain validity; but the latter is false. Pity purges our passions, but not by means of fear, an idea to which Aristotle was brought by his false concept of pity. You can discuss this further with Moses; for on this point we are in agreement, as far as I know. Now, throughout Aristotle's *Poetics,* keep this explanation of *fear* in mind wherever you find *terror* (for it has to be called fear everywhere, and not terror), and then tell me what you think of Aristotle's theory. . . .

Translated by Timothy J. Chamberlain

Notes

Not intended originally for publication, the correspondence was first published in 1794, and received the title *Briefwechsel über das Trauerspiel* in 1910. A useful modern edition exists, with the same title, edited by Jochen Schulte-Sasse (Munich: Winkler, 1972).

1. [Lessing had announced his intention to write on this subject.]
2. [Nicolai's treatise appeared in his journal *Bibliothek der schönen Wissenschaften und der freien Künste* in 1757.]
3. [The *Bibliothek* had announced a competition for the best original tragedy.]
4. [By Voltaire, or by Maffei.]
5. [By Euripides or Corneille; the subject matter rather than the actual version is what matters.]
6. [By Voltaire.]
7. [By Addison or Gottsched; again, the subject matter is what Nicolai means.]
8. [By Thomas Corneille (1625–1709), or by John Banks (c. 1650–1706).]
9. [By J. E. Schlegel.]
10. [Ulfo is Canute's antagonist in Schlegel's tragedy.]
11. [By Voltaire.]
12. [Virgil, *Eclogues* 3.104: "You shall be for me the great Apollo."]
13. [Virgil, *Eclogues* 3.107: "You alone shall have Phyllis."]
14. [Mendelssohn had given this definition of tragic fear in his *Letters on the Sentiments* (1755).]
15. [Mendelssohn had written on this in his *Letters on the Sentiments.*]
16. [In Voltaire's play of the same name.]
17. [In Voltaire's play *Alzire.*]
18. [In Racine's play by the same name.]
19. [Lessing takes up the difference between literature and sculpture in *Laocoön.*]
20. [Mendelssohn apparently has in mind the beginning of chapter 4 of the *Poetics,* though Aristotle does not specifically mention a serpent; this idea may have come from Boileau's *L'art poétique,* canto 3.]
21. [In Corneille's *Cinna.*]
22. [In Racine's *Phaedra.*]
23. [In Corneille's *Le Cid.*]
24. [In the play of the same name by Euripides.]
25. [Of Sweden (1682–1718). His fate as a ruler of great but doomed ambitions was famous.]
26. [The correspondence took place in the early part of the Seven Years' War (1756–63).]
27. [The reference is to Richardson's novel *Clarissa.*]

28. [This discussion is based on the theory of cognition developed by Leibniz and Wolff; see Jochen Schulte-Sasse's analysis in his edition of *Briefwechsel über das Trauerspiel,* especially pp. 168–89.]

29. [Mendelssohn is citing Baumgarten's well-known definition of a poem in his *Meditationes philosophicae de nonnullis ad poema pertinentibus* (Meditations on certain questions concerning poetry) (1735): "oratio sensitiva animi perfecta."]

30. [In Lessing's comedy *Der Freigeist* (The freethinker), 1749.]

31. [The reference is to Richardson's novel *Sir Charles Grandison.*]

32. [In Voltaire's *Alzire.*]

33. [Lessing later reconsidered this criticism; see *Hamburg Dramaturgy,* nos. 75ff. (German Library, vol. 83).]

34. [By George Lillo. The first bourgeois tragedy on the German stage. Barnwell actually stabs his uncle, not his cousin.]

35. [*Aeneid* 1.2: "compelled by fate to flight."]

36. [*Zhao-shi gu-er,* which Lessing knew in a French translation.]

37. "If"—but take note, my dear Lessing, that I don't claim this. [Nicolai's note.]

38. [Part of Mendelssohn's *Von der Herrschaft über die Neigungen* (On controlling the inclinations), which Mendelssohn sent Lessing with this letter, and to which he refers a number of times.]

39. [In the following, Lessing is responding to Mendelssohn's "Thoughts on Illusion," especially paragraph 14: "The best means to persuade ourselves intuitively of the value of imitation is when unpleasant passions are aroused in us by means of illusion.

"(a) If we suddenly catch sight of a painted serpent, the more we were scared by it the better it pleases us. Aristotle believes we were delighted because we were freed from the danger we thought we were in. But how unnatural this explanation is! I believe rather that the brief scare convinces us intuitively that the painting is a successful copy of the original.

"(b) Hence all unpleasant emotions please us when aroused by imitation. The musician can make us angry, sorrowful, despairing, etc., and we are thankful to him for the unpleasant passions he has aroused in us. But it is clear that in these cases the subsequent judgment, that these emotions are only aroused by imitation, must follow immediately on the emotion itself, because otherwise the unpleasant feeling that arises from the emotion would be greater than the pleasant feeling that is an effect of the imitation.

"(c) For these reasons the limits of the well-known law may be defined: the fine arts are an imitation of nature, but not nature itself."]

40. [Cf. *Hamburg Dramaturgy,* nos. 75ff. (German Library, vol. 83).]

41. [Aristotle, *Rhetoric* 2.8.]

Gotthold Ephraim Lessing

Laocoön: An Essay on the Limits of Painting and Poetry

Preface

The first person to compare painting with poetry was a man of fine feeling who observed that both arts produced a similar effect upon him. Both, he felt, represent absent things as being present and appearance as reality. Both create an illusion, and in both cases the illusion is pleasing.

A second observer, in attempting to get at the nature of this pleasure, discovered that both proceed from the same source. Beauty, a concept we first derive from physical objects, has general rules applicable to a number of things: to actions and thoughts as well as to forms.

A third, who examined the value and distribution of these general rules, observed that some of them are more predominant in painting, others in poetry. Thus, in the one case poetry can help to explain and illustrate painting, and in the other painting can do the same for poetry.

The first was the amateur, the second the philosopher, and the third the critic.

The first two could not easily misuse their feelings or their conclusions. With the critic, however, the case was different. The principal value of his observations depends on their correct application to the individual case. And since for every one really discerning critic there have always been fifty clever ones, it would have been a miracle if this application had always been made with the caution necessary to maintain a proper balance between the two arts.

If Apelles and Protogenes, in their lost writings on painting, confirmed and explained its laws by applying already established rules of poetry, we may be certain that they did so with the same moderation and accuracy with which the principles and lessons of painting are applied to eloquence and poetry in the works of Aristotle, Cicero, Horace, and Quintilian. It is the prerogative of the ancients never to have done too much or too little in anything.

But in many respects we moderns have considered ourselves far superior when we transformed their pleasant little lanes into highways, even though shorter and safer highways themselves become mere footpaths as they lead through wildernesses.

The brilliant antithesis of the Greek Voltaire[1] that painting is mute poetry and poetry a speaking painting was doubtless not to be found in any textbook. It was a sudden fancy—among others that Simonides had—and the truth it contains is so evident that one feels compelled to overlook the indefinite and untrue statements that accompany it.

The ancients, however, did not overlook them. In restricting Simonides' statement to the effect achieved by the two arts, they nevertheless did not forget to stress that, despite the complete similarity of effect, the two arts differed both in the objects imitated as well as in the manner of imitation (ὕλῃ καὶ τρόποις μιμήσεως).

Still, many recent critics have drawn the most ill-digested conclusions imaginable from this correspondence between painting and poetry, just as though no such difference existed. In some instances they force poetry into the narrower limits of painting; in others they allow painting to fill the whole wide sphere of poetry. Whatever one is entitled to must be permitted to the other also; whatever pleases or displeases in one must necessarily please or displease in the other. And so, full of this idea, they pronounce the shallowest judgments with the greatest self-assurance and, in criticizing the work of a poet and a painter on the same subject, they regard the differences of treatment observed in them as errors, which they blame on one or the other, depending on whether they happen to prefer painting or poetry.

Indeed, this spurious criticism has to some degree misled even the masters of the arts. In poetry it has engendered a mania for description and in painting a mania for allegory, by attempting to make the former a speaking picture, without actually knowing what it could and ought to paint, and the latter a silent poem, without having considered to what degree it is able to express general ideas without denying its true function and degenerating into a purely arbitrary means of expression.

To counteract this false taste and these unfounded judgments is the principal aim of the following chapters. They were written as chance dictated and more in keeping with my reading than through any systematic development of general principles. Hence they are to be regarded more as unordered notes for a book than as a book itself.

Yet I flatter myself that even in this form they will not be treated wholly with contempt. We Germans suffer from no lack of systematic books. We know better than any other nation in the world how to deduce anything we want in the most beautiful order from a few postulated definitions.

Baumgarten acknowledged that he owed the greater part of the examples in his *Aesthetics* to Gesner's dictionary. Although my reasoning may not be so compelling as Baumgarten's, my examples will at least smack more of the source.

Since I started, as it were, with the Laocoön and return to it a number of times, I wished to give it a share in the title too. Other short digressions on various points of ancient art history contribute less to my intent and are included only because I can never hope to find a more suitable place for them.

I should like to remark, finally, that by "painting" I mean the visual arts in general; further, I do not promise that, under the name of poetry, I shall not devote some consideration also to those other arts in which the method of presentation is progressive in time.

Chapter 1

The general and distinguishing characteristics of the Greek masterpieces of painting and sculpture are, according to Herr Winckelmann, noble simplicity and quiet grandeur, both in posture and in expression. "As the depths of the sea always remain calm," he says, "however much the surface may be agitated, so does the expression in the figures of the Greeks reveal a great and composed soul in the midst of passions."

> Such a soul is depicted in Laocoön's face—and not only in his face—under the most violent suffering. The pain is revealed in

every muscle and sinew of his body, and one can almost feel it oneself in the painful contraction of the abdomen without looking at the face or other parts of the body at all. However, this pain expresses itself without any sign of rage either in his face or in his posture. He does not raise his voice in a terrible scream, which Virgil describes his Laocoön as doing;[2] the way in which his mouth is open does not permit it. Rather he emits the anxious and subdued sigh described by Sadoleto. The pain of body and the nobility of soul are distributed and weighed out, as it were, over the entire figure with equal intensity. Laocoön suffers, but he suffers like the Philoctetes of Sophocles;[3] his anguish pierces our very soul, but at the same time we wish that we were able to endure our suffering as well as this great man does.

Expressing so noble a soul goes far beyond the formation of a beautiful body. This artist must have felt within himself that strength of spirit which he imparted to his marble. In Greece artists and philosophers were united in one person, and there was more than one Metrodorus. Philosophy extended its hand to art and breathed into its figures more than common souls.[4]

The remark on which the foregoing comments are based, namely that the pain in Laocoön's face is not expressed with the same intensity that its violence would lead us to expect, is perfectly correct. It is also indisputable that this very point shows truly the wisdom of the artist. Only the ill-informed observer would judge that the artist had fallen short of nature and had not attained the true pathos of suffering.

But as to the reasons on which Herr Winckelmann bases this wisdom, and the universality of the rule he derives from it, I venture to be of a different opinion.

I must confess that the disparaging reference to Virgil was the first cause of my doubts, and the second was the comparison with Philoctetes. I shall proceed from this point and record my thoughts as they developed in me.

"Laocoön suffers like the Philoctetes of Sophocles." But how does Philoctetes suffer? It is strange that his suffering should have left such different impressions. The laments, the cries, the wild curses with which his anguish filled the camp and interrupted all the sacrifices and sacred rites resounded no less terribly through the desert island, and it was this that brought about his banishment there. What sounds of despondency, of sorrow and despair in the poet's presentation ring through the theater! It has been found that the third act of his work is much shorter than the others. From this, the critics claim,[5] we may conclude that the ancients were little concerned with having acts of equal length. I agree with this, but I should prefer to rely on some other example than this for support. The cries of anguish, the moaning, the disjointed ἆ ἆ, φεῦ, ἀπαταῖ, ὤμοι μοι the whole lines of παπᾶ, παπᾶ of which this act consists and which must be spoken with prolonged stresses and with pauses quite different from those of connected speech, have in actual performance doubtless made this act just about as long as the others. It seems much shorter on paper to the reader than it probably did to a theater audience.

A cry is the natural expression of physical pain. Homer's wounded warriors not infrequently fall to the ground with a cry. Venus shrieks aloud at a mere scratch,[6] not because she must be made to represent the tender goddess of sensuality, but because suffering nature must have her due. Even iron Mars screams so horribly on feeling the lance of Diomedes that it sounds like the shouting of ten thousand raging warriors and fills both armies with terror.[7]

High as Homer raises his heroes above human nature in other respects, he still has them remain faithful to it in their sensitiveness to pain and injury and in the expression of this feeling by cries, tears, or invectives. In their deeds they are beings of a higher order, in their feelings true men.

I know that we more refined Europeans of a wiser, later age know better how to govern our mouths and our eyes. Courtesy and propriety force us to restrain our cries and tears. The aggressive bravery of the rough, early ages has become in our time a passive courage of endurance. Yet even our ancestors were greater in the latter than the former. But our ancestors were barbarians. To master all pain, to face death's stroke with unflinching eye, to die laughing under the adder's bite, to weep neither at the loss of one's dearest friend nor at one's own sins: these are the traits of old Nordic heroism.[8] Palnatoko decreed that his Jomsburghers were not to fear anything nor even so much as mention the word "fear."

Not so the Greek! He felt and feared, and he expressed his pain and grief. He was not ashamed of any human weakness, but it must not prevent him from attaining honor nor from fulfilling his duty. The Greek acted from principles whereas the barbarian acted out of his natural ferocity and callousness. In the Greek, heroism was like the spark hidden in the flint, which sleeps quietly as long as no external force awakens it, and robs it of its clarity or its coldness. In the barbarian, heroism was a bright, consuming, and ever-raging flame that devoured, or at least blackened, every other fine quality in him. When Homer makes the Trojans march to battle with wild cries, while the Greeks go in resolute silence, the commentators rightly observe that the poet thereby intends to depict the former as barbarians and the latter as civilized peoples. I am surprised that they did not notice a similar contrast of character in another passage.[9] Here the opposing armies have agreed to a truce and are busy burning their dead, which does not take place without the shedding of hot tears on both sides (δάκρυα θερμὰ χέοντες).[10] But Priam forbids his Trojans to weep (οὐδ᾽ εἴα κλαίειν Πρίαμος μέγας).[11] He does this, Madame Dacier says, because he is afraid they may grow too softhearted and take up the battle on the following day with less courage. True! But why, may I ask, should only Priam fear this? Why does Agamemnon not issue the same command to the Greeks? The poet's meaning goes deeper: he wants to tell us that only the civilized Greek can weep and yet be brave at the same time, while the uncivilized Trojan, to be brave, must first stifle all human feeling. Νεμεσσῶμαί γε μὲν οὐδὲν κλαίειν is the remark that Homer has the sensible son of wise Nestor make on another occasion.[12]

It is worthy of note that among the few tragedies that have come down to us from antiquity there are two in which physical pain is not the least part of the misfortune that befalls the suffering heroes, Philoctetes and the dying Hercules.[13] And Sophocles lets even the latter wail and moan, weep and cry out. Thanks to our well-mannered neighbors,[14] those masters of propriety, a wailing Philoctetes or a bawling Hercules today would be the most ridiculous and unbearable figure on stage. One of their most recent poets has, to be sure, ventured on a Philoctetes,[15] but did he dare to show his audience the *true* Philoctetes?

There is even a Laocoön among the lost plays of Sophocles. If only fate had saved this one for us! From the slight references of some of the ancient grammarians we cannot determine how the poet treated his subject. But of this much I am certain: he did not portray Laocoön as more stoical than Philoctetes and Hercules. Stoicism is not dramatic, and our sympathy is in direct proportion to the suffering of the object of our interest. If we see him bearing his misery with nobility of soul, he will, to be sure, excite our admiration; but admiration is only a cold sentiment whose barren wonderment excludes not only every warmer passion but every other clear conception as well.

I come now to my conclusion: if, according to the ancient Greeks, crying aloud when in physical pain is compatible with nobility of soul, then the desire to express such nobility could not have prevented the artist from representing the scream in his marble. There must be another reason why he differs on this point from his rival the poet, who expresses this scream with deliberate intention.

Chapter 2

Whether it be fact or fiction that Love inspired the first artistic effort in the fine arts,[16] this much is certain: she never tired of guiding the hands of the old masters. Painting, as practiced today, comprises all representations of three-dimensional bodies on a plane. The wise Greek, however, confined it to far narrower limits by restricting it to the imitation of beautiful bodies only. The Greek artist represented only the beautiful, and ordinary beauty, the beauty of a lower order, was only his accidental subject, his exercise, his relaxation. The perfection of the object itself in his work had to give delight, and he was too great to demand of his audience that they be satisfied with the barren pleasure that comes from looking at a perfect resemblance, or from consideration of his skill as a craftsman. Nothing in his art was dearer to him or seemed nobler than its ultimate purpose.

"Who would want to paint you when no one even wants to look at you?" an old epigrammatist[17] asks of an exceedingly deformed man. Many an artist of our time would say, "Be as ugly as possible, I will paint you nevertheless. Even though no one likes to look at you, they will still be glad to look at my picture, not because it portrays you but because it is a proof of my art, which knows how to present such a monster so faithfully."

To be sure, the propensity to this wanton boasting of mere skills, not ennobled by the intrinsic worth of their subjects, is too natural for even the Greeks not to have had their Pauson and their Pyreicus. They had them, but they treated them with stern justice. Pauson, whose subjects did not even have the beauty of ordinary nature and whose low taste made him enjoy best the portrayal of what is faulty and ugly in the human form,[18] lived in the most abject poverty.[19] And Pyreicus, who painted barbershops, filthy workshops, asses, and kitchen herbs with all the zeal of a Dutch artist—as if such things in nature had so much charm or were so rare!—acquired the name of Rhyparographer,[20] or the painter of filth. Indeed, the debauched rich paid their weight in gold for his paintings, as if to offset their intrinsic worthlessness by putting a fictitious value upon them.

The authorities themselves did not deem it beneath their dignity to force the artist to remain in his proper sphere. It is well known that the law of the Thebans commanded idealization in art and threatened digression toward ugliness with punishment. This was no law against bunglers, which has been generally supposed, even by Junius himself.[21] It condemned the Greek Ghezzis,[22] that unworthy artistic device through which a likeness is obtained by exaggerating the ugly parts of the original—in a word, the caricature.

The law of the Olympic judges[23] sprang from the same idea of the beautiful. Every victor in the Olympic games received a statue, but only the three-time winner had a portrait-statue erected in his honor.[24] This was to prevent the increase of mediocre portraits among works of art, for a portrait, although admitting idealization, is dominated by likeness. It is the ideal of one particular man and not of man in general.

We laugh when we hear that among the ancients even the arts were subject to the civil code. But we are not always right when we do so. Unquestionably, laws must not exercise any constraint on the sciences, for the ultimate goal of knowledge is truth. Truth is a necessity to the soul, and it is tyranny to impose the slightest constraint on the satisfaction of this essential need. But the ultimate goal of the arts is pleasure, and this pleasure is not indispensable. Hence it may be for the lawmaker to determine what kind of pleasure and how much of each kind he will permit.

The plastic arts in particular—aside from the inevitable influence they exert on the character of a nation—have an effect that demands close supervision by the law. If beautiful men created beautiful statues, these statues in turn affected the men, and thus the state owed thanks also to beautiful statues for beautiful men. (With us the highly susceptible imagination of mothers seems to express itself only in producing monsters.)

From this point of view I believe I can find some truth in some of the ancient tales that are generally rejected as outright lies. The mothers of Aristomenes, Aristodamas,[25] Alexander the Great, Scipio, Augustus, and Galerius all dreamed during pregnancy that they had relations with a serpent. The serpent was a symbol of divinity,[26] and the beautiful statues and paintings depicting Bacchus, Apollo, Mercury, or Hercules were seldom without one. Those honest mothers had feasted their eyes on the god during the day, and their confused dreams recalled the image of the reptile. Thus I save the dream and abandon the interpretation born of the pride of their sons and the impudence of the flatterer. For there must be some reason why the adulterous fantasy was always a serpent.

But I am digressing. I wanted simply to establish that among the ancients beauty was the supreme law of the visual arts. Once this has been established, it necessarily follows that whatever else these arts may include must give way completely if not compatible with beauty, and, if compatible, must at least be subordinate to it.

Let us consider expression. There are passions and degrees of passion that are expressed by the most hideous contortions of the face and that throw the whole body into such unnatural positions as to lose all the beautiful contours of its natural state. The ancient artists either refrained from depicting such emotions or reduced them to a degree where it is possible to show them with a certain measure of beauty.

Rage and despair did not degrade any of their works. I venture to say that they never depicted a Fury.[27] Wrath was reduced to seriousness. In poetry it was the wrathful Jupiter who hurled the thunderbolt; in art it was only the stern Jupiter.

Anguish was softened into sadness. Where this softening was impossible, where anguish would have been disparaging as well as distorting—what did Timanthes do? We know the answer from his painting of the sacrifice of Iphigenia: he imparted to each bystander the particular degree of sadness appropriate to him but concealed the face of the father, which should have shown the most intense suffering. Many clever things have been said about this. One critic,[28] for instance, says that he had so exhausted himself in depicting the sorrowful faces of the bystanders that he despaired of his ability to give a still more sorrowful one to the father. Another says that by so doing he admitted that the anguish of a father in such circumstances is beyond expressing.[29] For my part, I see no incapacity on the part of either the artist or his art. The intensity of the emotions intensifies the corresponding expression in the features of the face; the highest degree will cause the most extreme expression, and nothing is easier in art than to express this. But Timanthes knew the limits the Graces had set for his art. He knew that the anguish appropriate to Agamemnon as the father would have to be expressed through distortions, which are always ugly. He went as far as he could in combining beauty and dignity with the expression of anguish. He would have preferred to pass over the ugly or to soften it, but since his composition did not permit him to do either, there was nothing left him but to veil it. What he might not paint he left to conjecture. In short, this concealment is a sacrifice that the artist has made to beauty; it is an example, not of how one pushes expression beyond the limits of art, but how one should subject it to the first law of art, the law of beauty.

If we apply this now to the Laocoön, the principle I am seeking becomes apparent. The master strove to attain the highest beauty possible under the given condition of physical pain. The demands of beauty could not be reconciled with the pain in all its disfiguring violence, so it had to be reduced. The scream had to be softened to a sigh, not because screaming betrays an ignoble soul, but because it distorts the features in a disgusting manner. Simply imagine Laocoön's mouth forced wide open, and then judge! Imagine him screaming, and then look! From a form that inspired pity because it possessed beauty and pain at the same time, it has now become an ugly, repulsive figure from which we gladly turn away. For the sight of pain provokes distress; however, the distress should be transformed, through beauty, into the tender feeling of pity.

The wide-open mouth, aside from the fact that the rest of the face is thereby twisted and distorted in an unnatural and loathsome manner, becomes in painting a mere spot and in sculpture a cavity, with most repulsive effect. Montfaucon showed little taste when he pronounced an old bearded head with gaping mouth to be Jupiter uttering oracles.[30] Must a god shout when he reveals the future? Would a pleasing outline of the mouth cast suspicion on his words? Nor do I believe Valerius when he says that Ajax was represented as screaming in the above-mentioned picture of Timanthes.[31] Far inferior painters, in a period when art was already in decay, did not allow even the most savage barbarians to open their mouths wide enough to scream though they were seized with terror and fear of death beneath the victor's sword.[32]

It is certain that this softening of extreme physical pain to a less-intense degree is observable in a number of ancient artworks. The suffering Hercules in the poisoned garment, by an unknown master, was not the Hercules of Sophocles, who screamed so horribly that the rocks of Locris and the headlands of Euboea resounded. He was sullen rather than wild.[33] The Philoctetes of Pythagoras Leontinus seemed to communicate his pain to the spectator, and yet the effect of this pain would have been destroyed by any feature even slightly suggestive of horror. One might ask how I know that this master made a statue of Philoctetes. From a passage in Pliny, which is so obviously interpolated or mutilated that it should not have had to wait for me to emend it.[34]

Chapter 3

As I have already said, art has been given a far wider scope in modern times. It is claimed that representation in the arts covers all of visible nature, of which the beautiful is but a small part. Truth and expression are art's first law, and as nature herself is ever ready to sacrifice beauty for the sake of higher aims, so must the artist subordinate it to his general purpose and pursue it no farther than truth and expression permit. It is enough that truth and expression transform the ugliest aspects of nature into artistic beauty.

But even if we were willing to leave these ideas for the moment unchallenged as to their value, we would still have to consider, quite independently of these ideas, why the artist must nevertheless set certain restraints upon expression and never present an action at its climax.

The single moment of time to which art must confine itself by virtue of its material limitations will lead us, I believe, to such considerations.

If the artist can never make use of more than a single moment in ever-changing nature, and if the painter in particular can use this moment only with reference to a single vantage point, while the works of both painter and sculptor are created not merely to be given a glance but to be contemplated—contemplated repeatedly and at length—then it is evident that this single moment and the point from which it is viewed cannot be chosen with too great a regard for its effect. But only that which gives free rein to the imagination is effective. The more we see, the more we must be able to imagine. And the more we add in our imaginations, the more we must think we see. In the full course of an emotion, no point is less suitable for this than its climax. There is nothing beyond this, and to present the utmost to the eye is to bind the wings of fancy and compel it, since it cannot soar above the impression made on the senses, to concern itself with weaker images, shunning the visible fullness already represented as a limit beyond which it cannot go.

Thus, if Laocoön sighs, the imagination can hear him cry out; but if he cries out, it can neither go one step higher nor one step lower than this representation without seeing him in a more tolerable and hence less interesting condition. One either hears him merely moaning or else sees him dead.

Furthermore, this single moment, if it is to receive immutable permanence from art, must express nothing transitory. According to our notions, there are phenomena, which we conceive as being essentially sudden in their beginning and end and which can be what they are only for a brief moment. However, the prolongation of such phenomena in art, whether agreeable or otherwise, gives them such an unnatural appearance that they make a weaker impression the more often we look at them, until they finally fill us with disgust or horror. La Mettrie, who had himself portrayed in painting and engraving as a second Democritus, seems to be laughing only the first few times we look at him. Look at him more often and the philosopher turns into a fop. His laugh becomes a grin. The same holds true for screaming. The violent pain that extorts the scream either soon subsides or else destroys the sufferer. When a man of firmness and endurance cries out he does not do so unceasingly, and it is only the seeming perpetuity of such cries when represented in art that turns them into effeminate helplessness or childish petulance. This, at least, the artist of the Laocoön had to avoid, even if screaming had not been detrimental to beauty, and if his art had been allowed to express suffering without beauty.

Among the ancient painters Timomachus seems to have been the one most fond of subjects that display extreme passion. His raving Ajax and his infanticide Medea were famous paintings, but from the descriptions we have of them it is clear that he thoroughly understood and was able to combine two things: that point or moment the beholder not so much sees as adds in his imagination, and that appearance that does not seem so transitory as to become displeasing through its perpetuation in art. Timomachus did not represent Medea at the moment when she was actually murdering her children, but a few moments before, when a mother's love was still struggling with her vengefulness. We can foresee the outcome of this struggle; we tremble in anticipation of seeing Medea as simply cruel, and our imagination takes us far beyond what the painter could have shown us in this terrible moment. But for this very reason we are not offended at Medea's perpetual indecision, as it is represented in art, but wish it could have remained that way in reality. We wish that the duel of passions had never been decided, or at least had continued long enough for time and reflection to overcome rage and secure the victory for maternal feelings. This wisdom on the part of Timomachus has earned him lavish and frequent praise and raised him far above another, unknown painter who was foolish enough to depict Medea at the height of her rage, thus endowing her brief instant of madness with a permanence that is an affront to all nature. The poet, who reproaches him for this, says quite sensibly, in addressing the picture itself: "Art thou then constantly thirsting for the blood of thy young? Is there ever a new Jason, a new Creusa there to incense you endlessly?—A curse on you, even in the painting!" he adds angrily.[35]

We are able to form some judgment of Timomachus's raging Ajax from the account given by Philostratus.[36] Ajax did not appear raging among the herds, binding and slaughtering cattle and rams, mistaking them for men. He was depicted sitting there exhausted after these deeds of insane heroism, and contemplating suicide. That is really the raging Ajax, not because he is raging at this moment, but because we see that he has been raging and because we can recognize the enormity of his madness most vividly from the desperate shame he himself now feels at his actions. We see the tempest in the wrecks and corpses it has cast ashore.

Chapter 4

I review the reasons given why the master of the Laocoön was obliged to exercise moderation in expressing physical pain and find that all of them have been derived from the special nature of the visual arts, their limitations, and their requirements. Hence any one of those causes could scarcely be applied to poetry.

Without investigating here the extent to which the poet is able to depict physical beauty, we may accept this much as unquestionable: since the whole infinite realm of perfection lies open to his description, this external form, beneath which perfection becomes beauty, can at best be only one of the least significant means by which he is able to awaken our interest in his characters. Often he ignores it entirely, being convinced that once his hero has won our favor his other qualities will either occupy us to such a point that we do not think of his physical form or, if we do think of it, we will be so captivated that we give him of our own accord if not a beautiful form, at least an ordinary one.

Least of all will he have to consider the sense of sight in any single trait that is not expressly intended to appeal to it. When Virgil's Laocoön screams, does it occur to anyone that a wide-open mouth is necessary in order to scream, and that this wide-open mouth makes the face ugly? Enough that "clamores horrendos ad sidera tollit"[37] has a powerful appeal to the ear, no matter what its effect on the eye! He who demands a beautiful picture here has failed to understand the poet.

Moreover, there is nothing to compel the poet to compress his picture into a single moment. He may, if he so chooses, take up each action at its origin and pursue it through all possible variations to its end. Each variation that would cost the artist a separate work costs the poet but a single pen stroke; and if the result of this pen stroke, viewed by itself, should offend the hearer's imagination, it was either anticipated by what has preceded or is so softened and compensated by what follows that it loses its individual impression and in combination achieves the best effect in the world. Thus, if it were really improper for a man to cry out in the violence of pain, what prejudice can this slight and transitory impropriety create in us against a man whose other virtues have already inclined us in his favor?

Virgil's Laocoön cries out, but this screaming Laocoön is the same man whom we already know and love as a prudent patriot and loving father. We do not relate his cries to his character, but solely to his unbearable suffering. It is this alone we hear in them, and it was only by this means that the poet could convey it clearly to our senses.

Who, then, would still censure him? Who would not have to confess, rather, that while the artist was right in not permitting Laocoön to cry out, the poet has done equally well in having him do so? . . .

Chapter 16

But I shall attempt now to derive the matter from its first principles.

I reason thus: if it is true that in its imitations painting uses completely different means or signs than does poetry, namely figures and colors in space rather than articulated sounds in time, and if these signs must indisputably bear a suitable relation to the thing signified, then signs existing in space can express only objects whose wholes or parts coexist, while signs that follow one another can express only objects whose wholes or parts are consecutive.

Objects or parts of objects that exist in space are called bodies. Accordingly, bodies with their visible properties are the true subjects of painting.

Objects or parts of objects that follow one another are called actions. Accordingly, actions are the true subjects of poetry.

However, bodies do not exist in space only, but also in time. They persist in time, and in each moment of their duration they may assume a different appearance or stand in a different combination. Each of these momentary appearances and combinations is the result of a preceding one and can be the cause of a subsequent one, which means that it can be, as it were, the center of an action. Consequently, painting too can imitate actions, but only by suggestion through bodies.

On the other hand, actions cannot exist independently, but must be joined to certain beings or things. Insofar as these beings or things are bodies, or are treated as such, poetry also depicts bodies, but only by suggestion through actions.

Painting can use only a single moment of an action in its coexisting compositions and must therefore choose the one that is most suggestive and from which the preceding and succeeding actions are most easily comprehensible.

Similarly, poetry in its progressive imitations can use only one single property of a body. It must therefore choose that one that awakens the most vivid image of the body, looked at from the point of view under which poetry can best use it. From this comes the rule concerning the harmony of descriptive adjectives and economy in description of physical objects.

I should put little faith in this dry chain of reasoning did I not find it completely confirmed by the procedure of Homer, or rather if it had not been just this procedure that led me to my conclusions. Only on these principles can the grand style of the Greek be defined and explained, and only thus can the proper position be assigned to the opposite style of so many modern poets, who attempt to rival the painter at a point where they must necessarily be surpassed by him.

I find that Homer represents nothing but progressive actions. He depicts bodies and single objects only when they contribute toward these actions, and then only by a single trait. No wonder, then, that where Homer paints, the artist finds little or nothing to do himself; and no wonder that his harvest can be found only where the story assembles a number of beautiful bodies in beautiful positions and in a setting favorable to art, however sparingly the poet himself may paint these bodies, these positions, and this setting. If we go through the whole series of paintings as Caylus proposes them, one by one, we find that each is a proof of this remark.

At this point I shall leave the count, who wants to make the artist's palette the touchstone of the poet,[38] in order to analyze the style of Homer more closely.

Homer, I say, generally gives only one single characteristic to each object. To him a ship is a black ship, or a hollow ship, or a fast ship, or at most a well-manned black ship. He goes no further than this in describing a ship. But the departure, the sailing away, the putting in to shore are the things he combines in a detailed picture—one the artist would have to break up into five or six individual pictures if he wanted to put the whole of it on canvas.

Even when Homer is forced by peculiar circumstances to fix our attention longer on a single object, he still does not create a picture the artist could imitate with his brush. On the contrary! By means of countless artistic devices he places this single object in a series of stages, in each of which it has a different appearance. In the last stage the artist must wait for the poet in order to show us complete what we have seen the poet making. For example, if Homer wants to show us Juno's chariot, he shows Hebe putting it together piece by piece before our eyes. We see the wheels and axle, the seat, the pole, the traces, and the straps, not as these parts are when fitted together, but as they are actually being assembled by Hebe. It is only to the wheels that Homer devotes more than a single epithet; he shows us the eight bronze spokes, the golden rims, the bronze tires, the silver hubs, one by one. We might almost say that since there was more than one wheel, exactly as much additional time had to be devoted to them in the description as would have been required to fasten them on separately in reality.

Ἥβη δ' ἀμφ' ὀχέεσσι θοῶς βάλε καμπύλα κύκλα,
χάλκεα ὀκτάκνημα, σιδηρέῳ ἄξονι ἀμφίς.
τῶν ἤτοι χρυσέη ἴτυς ἄφθιτος, αὐτὰρ ὕπερθεν
χάλκε' ἐπίσσωτρα προσαρηρότα, θαῦμα ἰδέσθαι·
πλῆμναι δ' ἀργύρου εἰσὶ περίδρομοι ἀμφοτέρωθεν.
δίφρος δὲ χρυσέοισι καὶ ἀργυρέοισιν ἱμᾶσιν

ἐντέταται, δοιαὶ δὲ περίδρομοι ἄντυγές εἰσιν.
τοῦ δ᾽ ἐξ ἀργύρεος ῥυμὸς πέλεν· αὐτὰρ ἐπ᾽ ἄκρῳ
δῆσε χρύσειον καλὸν ζυγόν, ἐν δὲ λέπαδνα
κάλ᾽ ἔβαλε, χρύσει᾽·³⁹

And when Homer wants to show us how Agamemnon was dressed, he has the king put on his garments, one by one, before our eyes: the soft chiton, the great cloak, the beautiful sandals, the sword. Now he is ready and takes up his scepter. We see the garments while the poet is describing the act of dressing; another poet would have described the garments themselves down to the smallest fringe, and we should have seen nothing of the action itself.

μαλακὸν δ᾽ ἔνδυνε χιτῶνα,
καλὸν νηγάτεον, περὶ δὲ μέγα βάλλετο φᾶρος·
ποσσὶ δ᾽ ὑπὸ λιπαροῖσιν ἐδήσατο καλὰ πέδιλα,
ἀμφὶ δ᾽ ἄρ ὤμοισιν βάλετο ξίφος ἀργυρόηλον.
εἵλετο δὲ σκῆπτρον πατρώϊον, ἄφθιτον αἰεί·⁴⁰

Here the scepter is called merely paternal and imperishable, just as a similar one is elsewhere described[41] merely as the golden-studded scepter, χρυσείοις ἥλοισι πεπάρμενον. But what does Homer do when we require a more complete and accurate picture of this important scepter? Does he describe the wood and the carved knob in addition to the golden studs? Of course he would do so if the description were intended for a handbook of heraldic art, so that at some later time an exact duplicate of it could be made. And I am quite certain that many a modern poet would have given us just such a heraldic description, in the naive belief that he himself had painted a picture because the painter can follow his description with the brush. But what does Homer care how far he outstrips the painter? Instead of an illustration he gives us the story of the scepter. First it is being made by Vulcan; next it glitters in the hands of Jupiter; now it is a symbol of the dignity of Mercury; now it is the martial wand of the warlike Pelops; now it is the shepherd's staff of the peaceful Atreus, etc.

σκῆπτρον ἔχων· τὸ μὲν Ἥφαιστος κάμε τεύχων·
Ἥφαιστος μὲν δῶκε Διὶ Κρονίωνι ἄνακτι,
αὐτὰρ ἄρα Ζεὺς δῶκε διακτόρῳ Ἀργεϊφόντῃ·
Ἑρμείας δὲ ἄναξ δῶκεν Πέλοπι πληξίππῳ,

αὐτὰρ ὁ αὖτε Πέλοψ δῶκ' Ἀτρέϊ, ποιμένι λαῶν·
Ἀτρεὺς δὲ θνῄσκων ἔλιπεν πολύαρνι Θυέστῃ,
αὐτὰρ ὁ αὖτε Θυέστ' Ἀγαμέμνονι λεῖπε φορῆναι,
πολλῇσιν νήσοισοι καὶ Ἄργεϊ παντὶ ἀνάσσειν·[42]

And so finally I know this scepter better than if a painter were to place it before my eyes or a second Vulcan in my very hands. I should not be surprised if I found that one of the ancient commentators on Homer had praised this passage as being the most perfect allegory of the origin, development, strengthening, and ultimate hereditary succession of royal power among men. I should smile, to be sure, if I were to read that the forger of the scepter, Vulcan, as the personification of fire, of that which is most important to man's preservation, represented the alleviation of all those general wants that induced the first men to submit to a single ruler. Or if I were to read that the first king, a son of Time (Ζεὺς Κρονίων), was a venerable patriarch who was willing to share with or even relinquish his power entirely to an eloquent and able man, a Mercury (Διακτόρῳ Ἀργειφόντῃ). Or that the clever orator, at a time when the young nation was threatened by foreign enemies, handed over his authority to the bravest warrior (Πέλοπι πληξίππῳ). And that the brave warrior, after he had subdued the enemy and secured the realm, could manipulate this power into his son's hands; who in turn, and as a peace-loving regent and benevolent shepherd of his people (ποιμὴν λαῶν), brought them prosperity and superabundance, and at whose death the way was paved for the richest of his relatives (πολύαρνι Θυέστῃ) to appropriate by means of gifts and bribes, and afterwards to secure for his family as if it were a property he had purchased, that which only confidence had bestowed before and merit had considered a burden rather than an honor. I should smile at all this, but it would strengthen my regard for the poet to whom so much can be attributed. But this is not my present concern, and I am regarding the history of the scepter merely as an artistic device, by means of which the poet causes us to linger over a single object without entering into a tiring description of its parts.

Again, when Achilles swears by his scepter to avenge the contemptuous way in which Agamemnon treated him, Homer gives us the history of this scepter. We see it verdant on the hills; the iron divides it from the trunk, deprives it of its leaves and bark and renders it suitable to serve the judges of the people as a symbol of their godlike dignity.

ναὶ μὰ τόδε σκῆπτρον, τὸ μὲν οὔποτε φύλλα καὶ ὅζους
φύσει, ἐπειδὴ πρῶτα τομὴν ἐν ὄρεσσι λέλοιπεν,
οὐδ' ἀναθηλήσει· περὶ γάρ ῥά ἑ χαλκὸς ἔλεψε
φύλλα τε καὶ φλοιόν· νῦν αὐτέ μιν υἷες Ἀχαιῶν
ἐν παλάμῃς φορέουσι δικασπόλοι, οἵτε θέμιστας
πρὸς Διὸς εἰρύαται.[43]

Homer was not so much concerned with describing two staffs of differing shape and material as to give us a clear image of the difference in power the two staffs symbolized. The one the work of Vulcan; the other, cut from the mountainside by some unknown hand. The one an ancient possession of a noble house; the other destined to fit the hand of any who might chance to grasp it. The one wielded by a monarch over many islands and over all of Argos; the other held by one from the midst of the Greeks, to whom, with others, the guardianship of the laws had been entrusted. This was the real difference between Agamemnon and Achilles; a difference Achilles himself, in spite of all his blind rage, could not help but acknowledge.

But it is not only where Homer combines such further aims with his descriptions that he disperses the image of his object over a kind of history of it; he does this also where his sole object is to show us the picture, in order that its parts that we find side by side in nature may follow one another in his description just as naturally, and keep pace, as it were, with the progress of the narrative. For example, he wishes to show us the bow of Pandarus: a bow of horn, of such and such a length, well polished and tipped on both ends with gold. What does he do? Does he drily enumerate all these things, one after the other? Far from it! That would be to show us such a bow and to describe how it was to be made, but not to paint it. He begins with the wild goat hunt, from whose horns the bow was made. Pandarus had lain in wait for the goat in the rocks and had killed it. The horns were of an extraordinary size, and for that reason he ordered them to be made into a bow. The work on the bow begins, the artisan joins the horns together, polishes them and tips them with metal. And so, as I have said, we see in the poet's work the origin and formation of that which in the picture we can only behold as completed and formed.

τόξον ἐύξοον ἰξάλου αἰγὸς
ἀγρίου, ὅν ῥά ποτ' αὐτὸς ὑπὸ στέρνοιο τυχήσας
πέτρης ἐκβαίνοντα, δεδεγμένος ἐν προδοκῇσιν,

βεβλήκει πρὸς στῆθος· ὁ δ' ὕπτιος ἔμπεσε πέτρῃ.
τοῦ κέρα ἐκ κεφαλῆς ἐκκαιδεκάδωρα πεφύκει·
καὶ τὰ μὲν ἀσκήσας κεραοξόος ἤραρε τέκτων,
πᾶν δ' εὖ λειήνας, χρυσέην ἐπέθηκε κορώνην.[44]

If I were to set down all the examples of this sort, I should never finish the task. They will occur in great number to everyone who is familiar with his Homer.

Chapter 17

But the objection will be raised that the symbols of poetry are not only successive but are also arbitrary; and, as arbitrary symbols, they are of course able to represent bodies as they exist in space. Examples of this might be taken from Homer himself. We need only to recall his shield of Achilles to have the most decisive instance of how discursively and yet at the same time poetically a single object may be described by presenting its coexistent parts.

I shall reply to this twofold objection. I call it twofold because a correct deduction must hold good even without examples; and, conversely, an example from Homer is of importance to me even when I am unable to justify it by means of deduction.

It is true that since the symbols of speech are arbitrary, the parts of a body may, through speech, be made to follow one another just as readily as they exist side by side in nature. But this is a peculiarity of speech and its signs in general and not as they serve the aims of poetry. The poet does not want merely to be intelligible, nor is he content—as is the prose writer—with simply presenting his image clearly and concisely. He wants rather to make the ideas he awakens in us so vivid that at that moment we believe that we feel the real impressions the objects of these ideas would produce on us. In this moment of illusion we should cease to be conscious of the means the poet uses for this purpose, that is, his words. This was the substance of the definition of a poetical painting given above. But the poet is always supposed to paint, and we shall now see how far bodies with their coexistent parts adapt themselves to this painting.

How do we arrive at a clear conception of an object in space? We first look at its parts singly, then the combination of parts, and finally the totality. Our senses perform these various operations with such astonishing rapidity that they seem to us to be but one single operation, and this rapidity is absolutely necessary if we are to receive an impression of the whole, which is nothing more than the result of the conceptions of the parts and of their combination. Now let us assume that the poet takes us from one part of the object to the other in the best possible order; let us assume that he knows how to make the combination of these parts ever so clear to us; how much time would he use in doing this? That which the eye takes in at a single glance he counts out to us with perceptible slowness, and it often happens that when we arrive at the end of his description we have already forgotten the first features. And yet we are supposed to form a notion of the whole from these features. To the eye, parts once seen remain continually present; it can run over them again and again. For the ear, however, the parts once heard are lost unless they remain in the memory. And even if they do remain there, what trouble and effort it costs to renew all their impressions in the same order and with the same vividness; to review them in the mind all at once with only moderate rapidity, to arrive at an approximate idea of the whole!

Let us test this on an example, which may be called a masterpiece of its kind:

> Dort ragt das hohe Haupt vom edeln Enziane
> Weit übern niedern Chor der Pöbelkräuter hin,
> Ein ganzes Blumenvolk dient unter seiner Fahne,
> Sein blauer Bruder selbst bückt sich und ehret ihn.
> Der Blumen helles Gold, in Strahlen umgebogen,
> Thürmt sich am Stengel auf, und krönt sein grau Gewand,
> Der Blätter glattes Weiss, mit tiefem Grün durchzogen,
> Strahlt von dem bunten Blitz von feuchtem Diamant.
> Gerechtestes Gesetz! dass Kraft sich Zier vermähle
> In einem schönen Leib wohnt eine schönre Seele.
>
> Hier kriecht ein niedrig Kraut, gleich einem grauen Nebel,
> Dem die Natur sein Blatt im Kreuze hingelegt;
> Die holde Blume zeigt die zwei vergöldten Schnäbel,
> Die ein von Amethyst gebildter Vogel trägt.
> Dort wirft ein glänzend Blatt, in Finger ausgekerbet,
> Auf einen hellen Bach den grünen Wiederschein;
> Der Blumen zarten Schnee, den matten Purpur färbet
> Schliesst ein gestreifter Stern in weisse Strahlen ein.
> Smaragd und Rosen blühn auch auf zertretner Heide,
> Und Felsen decken sich mit einem Purpurkleide.[45]

These are herbs and flowers the learned poet paints with great art and fidelity to nature. Paints, I say, but without producing a trace of illusion. I do not mean to say that anyone who has never seen these herbs and flowers can form practically no notion at all of them from his painting. It may be that all poetic painting demands a previous knowledge of its subject. Nor will I deny that the poet might awaken a more vivid idea of some of its details in one who has the advantage of such knowledge. I ask him only: what about the conception of the whole? If this is to be more vivid, too, then no single part must be given prominence, but all parts must seem equally illuminated. Our imagination must be able to survey them all with the same rapidity in order to construct from them in one moment what can be seen in one moment in nature. Is that the case here? And if it is not, how can it have been said that "the most faithful drawing by a painter would appear weak and dull in comparison with this poetic description"?[46] It remains infinitely inferior to what lines and color can express on canvas, and the critic who praised it in this exaggerated manner must have looked at it from a completely false point of view. He must have paid greater regard to the foreign ornaments the poet has interwoven with it, to its elevation above vegetable life, to the development of those inner perfections that external beauty serves merely as a shell, than to this beauty itself and the degree of vividness and fidelity of the picture the painter and the poet respectively can give us. For all that, it is only the last that is of importance here, and whoever would say that the mere lines—

> Der Blumen helles Gold in Strahlen umgebogen,
> Thürmt sich am Stengel auf, und krönt sein grau Gewand,
> Der Blätter glattes Weiss, mit tiefem Grün durchzogen,
> Strahlt von dem bunten Blitz von feuchtem Diamant

—that these lines, in regard to the impression they make can compete with the imitation of a Huysum, must either never have questioned his feelings or else have wanted deliberately to belie them. It may be very nice to recite them, holding the flower in one's hand; but by themselves they say little or nothing. In every word I hear the poet at work, but I am a long way from seeing the object itself.

Once more, then: I do not deny to language altogether the power of depicting the corporeal whole according to its parts. It can do so because its signs, although consecutive, are still arbitrary. But I do deny it to language as the medium of poetry, because the illusion, which is the principal object of poetry, is wanting in such verbal description of bodies. And this illusion, I say, must be wanting because the coexistent nature of a body comes into conflict with the consecutive nature of language, and although dissolving the former into the latter makes the division of the whole into its parts easier for us, the final reassembling of the parts into a whole is made extremely difficult and often even impossible.

In every case, therefore, where illusion is not the object and where the writer appeals only to the understanding of the reader and aims only at conveying distinct and, insofar as this is possible, complete ideas, these descriptions of bodies, excluded from poetry, are quite in place; and not only the prose writer, but also the didactic poet (for where he becomes didactic he ceases to be a poet) can use them to great advantage. For instance, in his *Georgics* Virgil describes a cow good for breeding in this way:

> Optima torvae
> Forma bovis, cui turpe caput, cui plurima cervix,
> Et crurum tenus a mento palearia pendent.
> Tum longo nullus lateri modus: omnia magna:
> Pes etiam, et camuris hirtae sub cornibus aures.
> Nec mihi displiceat maculis insignis et albo,
> Aut iuga detractans interdumque aspera cornu,
> Et faciem tauro proprior: quaeque ardua tota,
> Et gradiens ima verrit vestigia cauda.[47]

Or a beautiful colt:

> Illi ardua cervix
> Argutumque caput, brevis alvus, obesaque terga;
> Luxuriatque toris animosum pectus, etc.[48]

Is it not obvious here that the poet was much more concerned with the description of the parts than with the whole? He wants to enumerate for us the characteristics of a beautiful colt, or a useful cow, in order to put us in a position to judge the worth of this or that specimen if we should encounter one or more of them. But whether or not all these characteristics can be put together readily into one vivid picture is a matter of utter indifference to him.

With the exception of this use, the detailed depictions of physical

objects (without the above-mentioned Homeric device for transforming what is coexistent in them into what is really consecutive)
have always been recognized by the best critics as being pieces of
pedantic trifling, to which little or no genius can be attributed.
When the poetaster, says Horace, can do nothing more, he begins to
paint a grove, an altar, a brook meandering through pleasant mead-
ows, a rushing stream, a rainbow:

> Lucus et ara Dianae,
> Et properantis aquae per amoenos ambitus agros,
> Aut flumen Rhenum, aut pluvius describitur arcus.[49]

The mature Pope[50] looked back on the descriptive attempts of the
poetic works of his youth with great contempt. He demanded expressly that whoever would bear the name of poet with dignity must
renounce the mania for description as early as possible, and he
called a purely descriptive poem a banquet of nothing but sauces.[51]
In regard to von Kleist I am able to assure you that he prided himself
very little on his "Spring." Had he lived longer, he would have given
it a completely different form. He considered giving it a plan and
searched for a means of having the host of images, which he seemed
to have drawn at random from the infinite realm of rejuvenated
nature, arise and follow one another in some natural order before
his eyes. At the same time he would have done what Marmontel, no
doubt prompted by his *Eclogues,* advised several German poets to
do. He would have converted a series of images scantily interwoven
with feelings into a succession of feelings sparingly interlaced with
images.[52]

Chapter 18

And yet should Homer himself have lapsed into this lifeless description of material objects? I do hope that there are but few passages
one can find to support this; and I feel certain that these few
passages are of such a nature as to confirm the rule to which they
seem to be the exception.

It remains true that succession of time is the province of the poet
just as space is that of the painter.

It is an intrusion of the painter into the domain of the poet, which
good taste can never sanction, when the painter combines in one

and the same picture two points necessarily separate in time, as does Fra Mazzuoli when he introduces the rape of the Sabine women[53] and the reconciliation effected by them between their husbands and relations, or as Titian does when he presents the entire history of the prodigal son, his dissolute life, his misery, and his repentance.

It is an intrusion of the poet into the domain of the painter and a squandering of much imagination to no purpose when, in order to give the reader an idea of the whole, the poet enumerates one by one several parts or things I must necessarily survey at one glance in nature if they are to give the effect of a whole.

But as two equitable and friendly neighbors do not permit the one to take unbecoming liberties in the heart of the other's domain, yet on their extreme frontiers practice a mutual forbearance by which both sides make peaceful compensation for those slight aggressions that, in haste and from force of circumstance, the one finds himself compelled to make on the other's privilege: so also with painting and poetry.

To support this I will not cite the fact that in great historical paintings the single moment is always somewhat extended, and that perhaps there is not a single work comprising a wealth of figures in which each one of them is in exactly that motion and position it should be in at the moment of the main action; some are represented in the attitude of a somewhat earlier, others in that of a somewhat later moment. This is a liberty the master must justify by certain refinements in the arrangement—in the way he uses his figures and places them closer to or more distant from the main action—which permits them to take a more or less momentary part in what is going on. I shall merely make use of a remark made by Mengs concerning Raphael's drapery. "In his paintings," he says, "there is a reason for every fold, whether it be because of its own weight or because of the movement of the limbs. Sometimes we can tell from them how they were before, and Raphael even tried to attach significance to this. We can see from the folds whether an arm or a leg was in a backward or forward position prior to its movement; whether the limb had moved or is moving from contraction to extension, or whether it had been extended and is now contracted."[54] It is indisputable that in this case the artist is combining two different moments into one. For since that part of the drapery that lies on the foot immediately follows it in its forward motion—unless the drapery be of very stiff material and hence entirely unsuitable for painting—there is no moment in which the garment can form any other fold whatsoever except what the actual position of the limb requires. However, if it is permitted to form a different fold, then the drapery is represented at the moment preceding and the limb at the following. Nevertheless, who would be so particular with the artist who finds it advantageous to show us these two moments at the same time? Who would not praise him rather for having had the understanding and the courage to commit such a minor error for the sake of obtaining greater perfection of expression?

The poet deserves the same forbearance. His progressive imitation actually allows him to allude to only one side, only one characteristic of his material objects at one time. But when the happy structure of his language permits him to do this in a single word, why should he not be allowed to add a second word now and then? And why not even a third, if it is worth the trouble? Or even a fourth? I have already said that for Homer a ship is only a black ship, or a hollow ship, or a swift ship, or at the most a well-manned black ship. This is to be understood of his style in general. Here and there we find a passage in which he adds a third descriptive epithet: Καμπύλα κύκλα, χάλκεα, ὀκτάκνημα,[55] round, bronze, eight-spoked wheels. And also a fourth: ἀσπίδα πάντοσ᾽ εἴσην, καλὴν, χαλκείην, ἐξήλατον,[56] a uniformly smooth, beautiful, embossed bronze shield. Who would censure him for this? Who would not rather thank him for this little extravagance when he feels what a good effect it can have in some few suitable passages?

But I shall not allow the particular justification of either poet or painter to be based on the above-mentioned analogy of the two friendly neighbors. A mere analogy neither proves nor justifies anything. The following consideration must be their real justification: just as in the painter's art two different moments border so closely on one another that we can, without hesitation, accept them as one, so in the poet's work do the several features representing the various parts and properties in space follow one another in such a rapid succession that we believe we hear them all at once.

It is in this, I say, that the excellence of Homer's language aids him unusually well. It not only allows him the greatest possible freedom in the accumulation and combination of epithets, but it finds such a happy arrangement for these accumulated adjectives that the awkward suspension of their noun disappears. Modern languages are lacking entirely in one or more of these advantages. For example, the French must paraphrase the καμπυλα κυκλα, φάλκεα, ὀκτάκνημα with "the round wheels, which were of bronze and had eight spokes." They give the meaning but destroy the picture. Yet the picture is everything here and the meaning nothing; and without the former the latter turns the liveliest of poets into a tiresome bore, a fate that has often befallen our good Homer under the pen of the conscientious Madame Dacier. The German language, on the other hand, can usually translate Homer's epithets with equally short equivalent adjectives, although it is unable to imitate the advantageous arrangement of Greek. We can say, to be sure, *die runden, ehernen, achtspeichigten* [the round, brazen, eight-spoked], but *Räder* [wheels] drags behind. Who does not feel that three different predicates, before we learn the subject, can produce only an indistinct and confused picture? The Greek combines the subject and the first predicate, and leaves the others to follow. He says, "round wheels, brazen, eight-spoked." And so we know immediately what he is speaking of. In conformity with the natural order of thought, we first become acquainted with the thing itself and then with its accidents. Our [German] language does not enjoy this advantage. Or should I say, it does enjoy it but can seldom make use of it without ambiguity? Both amount to the same thing. For if we place the adjectives after the subject, they must stand *in statu absoluto,* i.e., in uninflected form. Hence, we must say *runde Räder, ehern und achtspeichigt* [round wheels, brazen and eight-spoked]. However, in this *statu* the German adjectives are identical with the German adverbs, and if we take them as such with the next verb that is predicated of the subject, they not infrequently produce a completely false, and in any case a very uncertain meaning.

But I am lingering over trifles, and it may appear as if I were going to forget the shield, the shield of Achilles, that is—the famous picture that more than anything else caused Homer to be considered by the ancients a master of painting.[57] A shield, it will be said, is a single material object the poet cannot present by describing its coexistent parts. And yet Homer, in more than a hundred splendid verses, has described this shield, its material, its form, all the figures that filled its enormous surface, so exactly and in such detail that it was not difficult for modern artists to produce a drawing of it exact in every part.

My answer to this particular objection is that I have already answered it. Homer does not paint the shield as finished and complete, but as a shield that is being made. Thus, here too he has made use of that admirable artistic device: transforming what is coexistent in his subject into what is consecutive, and thereby making the living picture of an action out of the tedious painting of an object. We do not see the shield, but the divine master as he is making it. He steps up to the anvil with hammer and tongs, and after he has forged the plates out of the rough, the pictures he destines for the shield's ornamentatior rise before our eyes out of the bronze, one after the other, beneath the finer blows of his hammer. We do not lose sight of him until all is finished. Now the shield is complete, and we marvel at the work. But it is the believing wonder of the eyewitness who has seen it forged.

Translated by Edward Allan McCormick

Notes

Original title: *Laokoon: oder über die Grenzen der Malerei und Poesie* (1766).

1. [Lessing is referring to Simonides of Ceos (died 469 B.C.), whose famous saying that painting is mute poetry and poetry a speaking picture is found in Plutarch's *De Gloria Atheniensium* 346f.: τὴν μὲν ζωγραφίαν ποίησιν οιωπῶσαν προσαγορεύει, τὴν δὲ ποίησιν ζωγραφαν λαλοῦσαν. Just why Lessing calls Simonides "the Greek Voltaire" is uncertain, for there is little in the Greek writer's works to remind one of Voltaire. One commentator has suggested that Lessing is attempting to discredit Simonides by such a comparison, "for Voltaire was then notorious for shiftiness and frivolity" (W. G. Howard, *Lessing's Laokoon* [New York, 1910], p. 341). It seems more probable, however, that Lessing was struck by the fact that both were men of great intellectual power and versatility and both long enjoyed favor at court, Simonides at the court of Hiero of Syracuse, and Voltaire at the court of Frederick of Prussia.]

2. [Virgil, *Aeneid* 1.222.]

3. ["Philoctetes, the leader of seven ships of archers against Troy (*Iliad* 2.716), is bitten by a snake on the island of Chrysa, near Lemnos, and, by the advice of Odysseus, left behind at Lemnos because the stench of his wound and his cries are intolerable. He is, however, in possession of the bows and arrows of Heracles, without which, as has been foretold, Troy cannot be captured. Accordingly, Odysseus undertakes to bring Philoctetes to Troy. But since Odysseus knows that he cannot by fair means prevail upon Philoctetes to come, he induces Neoptolemus, son of Achilles, to try a subterfuge. The play of Sophocles opens with Odysseus and Neoptolemus at Lemnos, looking for Philoctetes. Neoptolemus is fated to take Troy, but only with the bow and arrows of Heracles, and with the help of Philoctetes. Although a noble-minded youth, he allows himself to be persuaded by Odysseus, on the ground that the end justifies the means. Odysseus withdrawing, Neoptolemus represents to Philoctetes that he has deserted the Greek host before Troy, because the arms of his father have been taken from him and given to Odysseus. He thus wins the confidence of Philoctetes, and the sufferer beseeches Neoptolemus to take him home in his ship. The youth promises to do this; but he is so deeply touched by the misery Philoctetes endures when his wound festers and a paroxysm comes over him, that, although the bow is now in his hands and Philoctetes is completely in his power, he cannot proceed with the intended stratagem. Thereupon Odysseus steps forth; but he can accomplish nothing with Philoctetes. Not until Heracles speaks as a god from the heavens, and

declares it to be the will of fate that Philoctetes shall aid in the destruction of Troy, does he consent to accompany Neoptolemus and Odysseus thither" (Howard, *Lessing's Laokoon*, pp. 343–44).]

4. *Von der Nachahmung der griechischen Werke in der Malerei und Bildhauerkunst* [On the imitation of Greek works in painting and sculpture], pp. 21, 22.

5. Brumoy, *Théâtre des Grecs* 2:89.

6. *Iliad* 5.343: Ἡ δὲ μέγα ἰάχουσα. ["now the goddess cried loudly." Diomedes wounded Venus very slightly with his spear while the goddess was pursuing Aeneas.]

7. *Iliad* 5.859.

8. Th[omas] Bartholinus, *De causis contemptae a Danis adhuc gentilibus mortis*, chapter 1.

9. *Iliad* 7.421.

10. ["shedding hot tears."]

11. ["but mighty Priam forbade them to weep."]

12. *Odyssey* 4.195. ["Weeping does not make me indignant." Spoken by Peisistratus, son of Nestor, about the tears we shed for the deceased.]

13. [Lessing is alluding to the hero of one of Sophocles' tragedies, *The Women of Trachis*, who, after being poisoned by a garment given him by his wife Deianeira, burns himself to death on Mount Aetna in Thessaly.]

14. [The French, of whom Lessing once said (*Hamburg Dramaturgy*, no. 80) that they had no genuine tragedies at all.]

15. Chataubrun [Chateaubrun].

16. [Pliny (*Natural Histories* 35.151) tells the story of a Corinthian potter, Dibutades, whose daughter fell in love with a youth who was to depart on a long journey the following day. While sitting beside him on the evening before the journey, she noticed the outline of his face reflected on the wall and quickly traced it in order to keep the memory of her lover fresh. Dibutades filled in the outline with clay and fired it with his clay wares, thus becoming the inventor of the art of bas-relief. It is to this story that Lessing alludes here.]

17. Antiochus (*Antholog[ia Graeca]* 2.4 [11.412]). In his commentary on Pliny (35.36), Hardouin credits this epigram to a certain Piso, but among all the Greek epigrammatists there is no such name to be found.

18. For this reason Aristotle refused to let Pauson's pictures be shown to young people, so that their imagination might be kept as free as possible from all representations of the ugly (*Politics* 8.5, p. 526, ed. Conring). Boden suggests reading Pausanias instead of Pauson in this passage, because the former is known to have painted licentious pictures (*de Umbra poetica*, comment. I, p. xiii). As though one had to learn first from a philosophical lawgiver that such licentious temptations ought to be kept away from young people! Had he taken the trouble to refer to the famous passage in the *Poetics* (chapter 2), he would never have expounded his theory. There are commentators (e.g., Kühn on Aelian, *Variae Historiae* 4.3) who maintain that the distinction Aristotle draws there between Polygnotus, Dionysius, and Pauson actually lies in the fact that Polygnotus painted gods and heroes; Dionysius, people; and Pauson, animals. But all of them painted human figures; and the fact that Pauson once painted a horse is no proof that he was exclusively an animal painter, which Boden takes him to have been. Their rank was determined by the degree of beauty they were able to impart to their human figures, and the reason that Dionysius could paint only people, and was therefore called the anthropographus (man-painter), was because he copied nature too slavishly and could not raise himself to that ideal beneath which it would have been sacrilege to paint gods and heroes.

19. Aristophanes, *Plutus* 602, and *Acharnians* 854.

20. Pliny 35.37, ed. Hard[ouin].

21. *De Pictura vet[erum]* 2.4 §1.
22. [A term given to caricaturists. Count Pier Leone Ghezzi (1674–1755) was a Roman painter and engraver of caricatures who was well-known in Lessing's time.]
23. [The *Hellanodicae* (ἑλλανοδίκαι) were the nine chief judges at the Olympic games. Three were assigned to the track events, three to the pentathlon, and the others to the remaining contests.]
24. Pliny 34.9.
25. [Lessing has confused Aristodamas with Aratus, son of Aristodama. The passage to which Lessing refers is Pausanias 4.14.5. Aratus of Sicyon was a famous statesman and founder of the Achaean League (271–13 B.C.).]
26. It is an error to suppose that the serpent was the symbol only of a healing deity. Justin Martyr (*Apolog.* 2.55, ed. Sylburg) says expressly: παρὰ παντὶ τῶν νομιζομένων παρ' ὑμῖν θεῶν, ὄφις σύμβολον μέγα καὶ μυστήριον ἀναγράφεται [*Apologia Secunda (pro Christianis ad Senatum Romanum)*, chapter 27: "Near every one of the divinities worshiped by you a serpent is painted on as an important symbol and mystery"]; and it would be a simple matter to name a whole series of monuments on which the serpent accompanies deities who had no connection whatever with healing.
27. [The Furies, also called "Eumenides," were the avenging deities in classical mythology. They are represented as the daughters of Earth or of Night, and as winged maidens with serpents twined in their hair and blood dripping from their eyes. It was their duty to punish men, both in life and after death. Later writers usually speak of three Furies: Tisiphone, Alecto, and Megaera.] If we were to go through all the works of art Pliny, Pausanias, and others mention, or search through all the ancient statues, bas-reliefs, and paintings still extant, we should not find a Fury anywhere. I except figures that belong more to the language of symbols than to art, such as are to be found chiefly on coins. Yet Spence, since he was determined to find Furies, would have done better to borrow them from the coins (*Seguini Numis.*, p. 178; *Spanhem. de Praest. Numism. Dissert.*, 13:639; Spanheim, *Les Césars de Julien*, p. 48) than to introduce them ingeniously into a work which they definitely do not exist. He says in his *Polymetis* (*Dial.* 16, p. 272): "Although Furies are quite rare in the works of ancient artists, there is one story in which they have generally introduced them. I am referring to the death of Meleager. In bas-reliefs on this subject they often encourage or urge Althaea to burn the fatal brand on which the life of her only son depended. For even a woman would not have gone so far in her revenge without a little prodding from the devil. In one of these bas-reliefs, published by Bellori (in the *Admirandis*), we see two women, to all appearances Furies, standing beside Althaea at the altar. For who else but Furies would have wanted to attend such a sacrifice? That they do not seem horrible enough for this role is doubtless the fault of the copy. The most remarkable thing about this work, however, is the round disk to be seen near the lower center, which evidently displays the head of a Fury. Perhaps it was the one to whom Althaea, whenever she had resolved on any evil action, addressed her prayers, and especially now on this occasion had every reason to . . . ," etc. One can prove anything by the use of such tricky logic. Who else, asks Spence, would have attended such a ceremony? My answer is, the maidservants of Althaea, who had to light the fire and keep it burning. Ovid says (*Metamorphoses* 8.460, 461): "Protulit hunc (stipitem) genitrix, taedasque in fragmina poni Imperat, et positis inimicos admovet ignes" ["And now the mother bore it away and had sticks of resinous fir (*taedas*) collected in a heap, and into this she sent the power of destroying fire"]. Both figures actually have in their hands such *taedas,* long pieces of resinous fir, which the ancients used for torches, and one of them has just broken one of the pieces, as her attitude shows. And, in my opinion, that is no Fury on the disk near the center of the work. It is a face that has on it an expression of violent pain and is doubtless meant to be the head of Meleager himself. (*Metamorphoses* 8.515):

> Inscius atque absens flamma Meleagros in illa
> Uritur: et caecis torreri viscera sentit
> Ignibus: et magnos superat virtute dolores.

["Unknowing and far off, Meleager is made fiery by the flame, and he feels a mysterious flame burning his insides. But he forcefully restrains the mighty pains."] The artist needed this as a transition, as it were, to the subsequent scene of the same story, which shows Meleager dying. The figures that Spence calls Furies Montfaucon takes to be Parcae (*Antiquité expliquée*, 1:162), with the exception of the head on the disk, which he too calls a Fury. Bellori himself (*Admiranda*, tab. 77) leaves undecided whether or not they are Parcae or Furies—an "or" that is enough to show that they are actually neither the one nor the other. The remainder of Montfaucon's explanation also lacks accuracy. The female figure leaning on her elbows against the bed should have been called Cassandra and not Atalanta, who is sitting in an attitude of mourning with her back to the bed. The artist has shown a great deal of perception in having Atalanta sit apart from the family, since she is only the mistress and not the wife of Meleager, and since her grief at a misfortune she herself inadvertently brought about could only have embittered his relatives.

28. Pliny 35.35 [36]: "Cum moestos pinxisset omnes, praecipue patruum, et tristitiae omnem imaginem consumpsisset, patris ipsius vultum velavit, quem digne non poterat ostendere." [After he had painted them all with melancholy expressions, and especially the uncle, and had exhausted every possible picture of sadness, he concealed the face of the father, being unable to depict it in a worthy manner.]

29. "Summi moeroris acerbitatem arte exprimi non posse confessus est." [He confessed that the bitterness of greatest grief could not be expressed by art.] Valerius Maximus 8.11.

30. *Antiquité expliquée*, 1:50.

31. That is to say, he specifies the degree of sadness actually expressed by Timanthes in this way: "Calchantem tristem, moestum Ulyssem, clamantem Ajacem, lamentantem Menelaum" [Calchas sad, Ulysses deeply troubled, Ajax crying out, Menelaus loudly wailing]. The screaming Ajax must have been an ugly figure, and since neither Cicero [*ad M. Brutum Orator*, sec. 22] nor Quintilian [*Institutio Oratoria* 2.13.12] mention it in their descriptions of this painting, I have all the more reason to believe it to be an addition, by which Valerius thought he could enrich the picture from his own imagination.

32. Bellorii *Admiranda*, tab. 11, 12.

33. Pliny 35.19.

34. "Eundem" (that is to say, Myro), we read in Pliny (34.19), "vicit et Pythagoras Leontinus, qui fecit stadiodromon Astylon, qui Olympiae ostenditur: et Libyn puerum tenentem tabulam, eodem loco, et mala ferentem nudum. Syracusis autem claudicantem: cuius hulceris dolorem sentire etiam spectantes videntur." [And the same one overcame Pythagoras also, who made (a statue of) Astylos, who is shown in Olympia, as well as a Libyan youth holding a tablet. This he did in the same place and also a naked body holding apples. However, in Syracuse (he made) a lame figure, in whom even the beholders appear to feel the pain of the sores.] Let us examine these last words more closely. Is it not obvious that they refer to a person known everywhere because of a painful ulcer? *Cuius hulceris.* And is this *cuius* to refer to the mere *claudicantem*, and the *claudicantem* perhaps to the *puerem*, which is back in the preceding clause? No one has the right to be more celebrated on account of such an ulcer than Philoctetes. Hence I read *Philoctetem* instead of *claudicantem*, or at least maintain that the former of the two words was pushed out of the MS by the latter, and that the correct reading would be *Philoctetem claudicantem.* Sophocles speaks of his στίβον κατ' ἀνάγκην ἔρπειν ["crawling along the

road under constraint"], and he must have had a limp, since he could not step firmly with the affected foot.

35. Philippus (*Anthol[ogia Graeca]* 4.9.10 [16.137]).

> 'Αιεὶ γὰρ διψᾷς βρέφεων φονον. ἡ τις 'Ιήσων
> Δεύτερος, ἤ Γλαύκη τις πάλι σοὶ πρόφασις;
> "Ἐῤῥε καὶ ἐν κηρῶ παιδοκτόνε . . .

[Lessing himself translates this passage from Philippus in the preceding four lines of the text.]

36. *Vita Apoll[onius]* 2.22.

37. [*Aeneid* 1.222: "He lifted up his voice in horrible cries to the heavens."]

38. [Lessing's play on the words *palette* (*der Farb[en]stein*, literally "color-stone") and *touchstone* (*der Probierstein*, literally "testing-stone") is untranslatable, and the irony of the lines is unfortunately much weaker in the English version. The translation of *Farbstein* as "palette" is somewhat free, since the word actually means "pigment cake," or, in Lessing's time, the stone on which the painter prepared his colors.]

39. [Then Hebe in speed set about the chariot the curved wheels
eight-spoked and brazen, with an axle of iron both ways.
Golden is the wheel's felly imperishable, and outside it
is joined, a wonder to look upon, the brazen running-rim,
and the silver naves revolve on either side of the chariot,
whereas the car itself is lashed fast with plaiting of gold
and silver, with double chariot rails that circle about it,
and the pole of the chariot is of silver, to whose extremity
Hebe made fast the golden and splendid yoke, and fastened
the harness, golden and splendid
(Iliad 5.722–31, tr. Lattimore)]

40. [. . . and put on his tunic,
beautiful, fresh woven, and threw the great mantle over it.
Underneath his shining feet he bound the fair sandals
and across his shoulders slung the sword with the nails of silver,
and took up the sceptre of his fathers, immortal forever.
(Iliad 2.43–47, tr. Lattimore)]

41. [*Iliad* 1.246.]

42. [. . . Powerful Agamemnon
stood up holding the scepter Hephaistos had wrought him carefully.
Hephaistos gave it to Zeus the king, the son of Kronos,
and Zeus in turn gave it to the courier Argeïphontes,
and Lord Hermes gave it to Pelops, driver of horses
and Pelops again gave it to Atreus, the shepherd of the people.
Atreus dying left it to Thyestes of the rich flocks,
and Thyestes left it in turn to Agamemnon to carry
and to be lord of many islands and over all Argos.
(Iliad 2.101–8, tr. Lattimore)]

43. [In the name of this scepter, which never again will bear leaf nor
branch, now that it has left behind the cut stump in the mountains,
nor shall it ever blossom again, since the bronze blade stripped
bark and leafage, and now at last the sons of the Achaians
carry it in their hands in state when they administer
the justice of Zeus. And this shall be a great oath before you.
(Iliad 1.234–39, tr. Lattimore)]

44. [Straightway he unwrapped his bow, of the polished horn from
a running wild goat he himself had shot in the chest once,
lying in wait for the goat in a covert as it stepped down
from the rock, and hit it in the chest so it sprawled on the boulders.
The horns that grew from the goat's head were sixteen palms' length.
A bowyer working on the horn then bound them together,
smoothing them to a fair surface, and put on a golden string hook.
(*Iliad* 4.105–11, tr. Lattimore)]

45. [The two strophes Lessing quotes are taken from a well-known poem, "Die Alpen" (The Alps), by Albrecht von Haller:

> There towers the noble gentian's lofty head,
>   Far o'er the common herd of vulgar plants,
> A whole flower people 'neath his flag is led,
>   E'en his blue brother bends and fealty grants.
> In circled rays his flowers of golden sheen
>   Tower on the stem, and crown its vestments gray;
> His glossy leaves of white bestreak'd with green
>   Gleam with the watery diamond's varied ray.
> O law most just! that Might consort with Grace,
>   In body fair a fairer soul has place.
>
> Here, like gray mist, a humble earth-plant steals,
>   Its leaf by Nature like a cross disposed;
> The lovely flower two gilded bills reveals,
>   Borne by a bird of amethyst composed.
> There finger-shaped a glancing leaf endues
>   A crystal stream with its reflection green:
> The flower's soft snow, stain'd with faint purple hues,
>   Clasps a striped star its blanchèd rays within.
> On trodden heath the rose and emerald bloom,
>   And craggy hill a purple robe assume.
>   (*Lessing's Prose Works,* ed. Edward Bell
>   [London, 1890], p. 99)]

46. Breitinger's *Kritische Dichtkunst* [Critical poetics], 2:807.

47. ["The best cow is ugly-shapen; her head coarse, her neck of the largest, with dewlaps hanging down from chin to leg; and to her length of flank there is no limit; large of limb and of foot, and with shaggy ears under inward-curving horns. Nor would I quarrel with one marked with spots of white, or one reluctant to the yoke and sometimes hasty with her horn, and almost like a bull to view, and tall all her length, with a tail that sweeps her footprints below her as she moves" (*Georgics* 3.51–62, tr. Mackail).]

48. [" . . . his are a high crest and fine head, a short belly and fleshy back, and a breast rippling in proud slopes of muscle" (*Georgics* 3.79–80, tr. Mackail).]

49. *Ars Poetica* 16. [Translated in the text above.]

50. [Doubtless *Windsor Forest,* published in 1713, but for the most part written in 1704, is especially referred to here.]

51. Prologue to the *Satires* [lines 340–41, 148–49]:

> That not in Fancy's maze he wander'd long,
> But stoop'd to truth, and moraliz'd his song.
>
> . . . who could take offence,
> While pure Description held the place of Sense?

Warburton's remark on this last passage may be considered as an authentic explanation by the poet himself:

> He uses PURE equivocally, to signify either chaste or empty; and has given in this line what he esteemed the true Character of descriptive Poetry, as it is called. A composition, in his opinion, as absurd as a feast made up of sauces. The use of a pictoresque imagination is to brighten and adorn good sense; so that to employ it only in Description, is like children's delighting in a prism for the sake of its gaudy colours; which when frugally managed, and artfully disposed, might be made to represent and illustrate the noblest objects in nature.

Both poet and commentator seem to have looked at the matter more from its moral than from its artistic side. But so much the better; it appears as worthless from one point of view as from the other.

52. *Poétique Française*, 2:501: "J'écrivois ces réflexions avant que les essais des Allemands dans ce genre (l'Eglogue) fussent connus parmi nous. Ils ont exécuté ce que j'avois conçu; et s'ils parviennent à donner plus au moral et moins au détail des peintures physiques, ils excelleront dans ce genre, plus riche, plus vaste, plus fécond, et infiniment plus natural et plus moral que celui de la galanterie champêtre." [I wrote these reflections before the attempts of the Germans in this genre (eclogue) became known to us. They have put into practice what I already knew and if they should succeed in paying more attention to the moral content and less to the details of description, they would excel in this genre, which is richer, more extensive, more fruitful, and infinitely more natural and moral than that of the gallantry of the pastoral.]

53. [Described in the *Aeneid* 8.635ff.]

54. *Gedanken über die Schönheit und über den Geschmack in der Malerei* [Thoughts on beauty and taste in painting], p. 69.

55. *Iliad* 5.722.

56. *Iliad* 12.294.

57. Dionysius Halicarnassus, *Vita Homeri,* in Thomas Gale, *Opuscula mythologica,* [*ethica et physica,* 1671,], p. 401. [Lessing is not citing Dionysius but is taking his information from Gale.]

Notes by Edward Allan McCormick

Friedrich Gottlieb Klopstock

Friedrich Gottlieb Klopstock (1724–1803) broke new ground in German poetry with his religious epic *The Messiah* (1748–73), inspired by Milton, and his *Odes* (1771), written in emulation of Pindar and pioneering the use of free rhythms in German verse. He thus combined the turn to English models and the return to the Greeks, which together played a decisive role in the development of German literature in the second half of the eighteenth century. Additionally, he fueled the growing patriotic interest in the German past with his trilogy of plays (*Bardiete*) on Arminius, *Hermann's Battle* (1769), *Hermann and the Princes* (1784), and *Hermann's Death* (1789). From 1751 until his death, Klopstock received a pension from the king of Denmark, though from 1770 on he lived mainly in Hamburg. Hailed as a genius by the Storm and Stress, he exercised a powerful influence on Goethe, Schiller, and Hölderlin. His most important contribution to theory, as to poetic practice, is in the sphere of the sublime. The most useful edition is *Ausgewählte Werke,* ed. Karl August Schleiden, 4th edition, 2 vols. (Munich: Hanser, 1981). For a recent study in English, see Kevin Hilliard, *Philosophy, Letters, and the Fine Arts in Klopstock's Thought* (London: University of London Institute of Germanic Studies, 1987).

On Sacred Poetry

. . . Higher poetry is a work of genius, and it should only rarely employ a few traces of wit, for painterly effects.

There are works of wit that are masterpieces, without the heart having contributed anything to them. However, genius without heart would only be half-genius.

The ultimate and highest effects of works of genius are that they move the entire soul. Here we can ascend through several gradations of increasingly strong feeling. This is the arena of the sublime.

Anyone who thinks there is little difference between touching the soul lightly and moving it in its entirety in all its mighty powers does not have a sufficiently dignified opinion of the soul.

It is demanded of one who undertakes to move our soul thus that he strike each of its strings wholly, in its own way. In this process the soul notices every jarring note, even the most subtle. One who has reflected on this properly will often have decided rather not to write at all.

Yet one who succeeds in this undertaking has produced in us feelings neither the highest philosophical conviction nor the other kinds of poetry can induce. With regard to their strength and duration, these impressions bear some resemblance to the example given by a great man.

Higher poetry is quite incapable of seducing us to evil by dazzling images. The moment it wanted to do that it would cease to be what it is. For however petty some people do want to make themselves, they can yet never bring themselves down so far as to allow anything other than what is really noble and sublime to stir all the powers of their soul in this great, universal way.

The ultimate purpose of higher poetry, and at the same time the true mark of its worth, is moral beauty. And it is also this alone that deserves to move our entire soul. The poet we have in mind must raise us above our shortsighted way of thinking and tear us from the stream that carries us along. It must remind us powerfully that we are immortal, and also that we could be much happier even in this life.

The human being led to this height and viewed from this perspective is the proper listener demanded by higher poetry.

It is possible to go far in this field even without revelation. Even Homer is very moral, except for his history of the gods, which he didn't invent. But when revelation becomes our guide, we climb from a hill to a mountain.

Young's *Nights* are perhaps the only work of higher poetry that could merit having no faults at all. If we take from him what he says as a Christian, we are left with Socrates. But how far the Christian is elevated above Socrates!

Perhaps the following additional notes are not superfluous in regard to what I have to say about sacred poetry.

We customarily accord the soul understanding, imagination, and will as its chief powers. Memory doesn't belong among them, though it always works in concert with them. Anyone undertaking works of higher poetry looks at this as follows, in accordance with his final purpose.

For him, imagination is more frequently a painter of the great and terrible beauties of nature than of objects in it that touch us gently. When he is painting the former, he succeeds in the strongest traits when he approaches passion by the ardor of his depiction.

He likes best to set before the understanding those truths that deserve to be known, and that only the righteous man understands completely.

And in the will, or the heart, this many-sided and mightiest power of the soul, he attempts above all to strike those feelings that enlarge it, and teach it to be great and noble.

But his purpose goes further than only to arouse a single power of the soul, while the others slumber, to entertain it gently and entice from it quiet applause. Though this intention has also produced masterpieces! He brings us—and succeeds in this particularly when the actor or reader has understood him—he brings us with rapid force to the point that we cry out, rejoice out loud; pause in meditation, think, fall silent; or become pale, tremble, weep. Criticism should barely engage to search out the causes of these effects, which are so rapid and mighty. They are of such varied nuances, and these have so manifold a relation to one another that it is infinitely difficult to explicate them all correctly. And when they are explicated, even though the reader of meditative taste may enjoy investigating them, the poet knew them already, and knew still more; or, even if he learned something new, he still wouldn't become more of a poet from it. In addition, these subtle explications, which draw the thread through the whole labyrinth, are too vulnerable to the danger of becoming incorrect by their very subtlety. Yet something may be said about them. . . .

When it has attained its full maturity, the sublime moves the entire soul. Which soul does it move most? The one that itself is lofty, that rarely admires, but when it must, also admires more than any petty soul can. The sublime affects mediocre souls only as a certain impact, which they do not feel completely, because they are more shaken by it than they feel it. The powers of our soul are in such harmony with one another, they flow constantly into one another, if

I may put it thus, that, when one of them is affected strongly, the others feel it too, and simultaneously come into play in their own way. The poet shows us an image. He gives it such even proportions and such correctness that it also appeals to the understanding, or he manages to convey to it certain traits that border closely on the feeling of the heart. The unadorned truth, which alone seemed to occupy the understanding, has nonetheless assumed some of the bright aspects of the image beneath his hand, or it shows itself with such dignity and loftiness that it appeals to the noblest desires of the heart to transform the truth into virtue. If it is the heart that the poet seizes, how quickly this inflames us! The whole soul is enlarged, all images of the imagination awake, all thoughts become greater. For although some passions completely interrupt a certain tranquil manner of thinking, the moved heart in general impels our thoughts on to quickness, greatness, and truth. What a new harmony of the soul we then discover in ourselves! With what an unaccustomed élan thoughts and feelings arise in us! What plans! What decisions!

But often a certain mediocrity still attaches to this elevation of ours. We feel that we wanted to raise ourselves still higher. Our soul is still larger. It can encompass still more. We still lacked religion. We were still only in the sphere of truths we devised ourselves. How happy, nonetheless, is the one who knows much, thinks much, and feels much in this sphere. But how happy he who has even just begun to understand and to feel the much higher truths of religion.

Religion in revelation itself is a healthy virile body. Our doctrinal books have made a skeleton of it. Yet they have their great use in their intentions.

The author of the sacred poem imitates religion; as he, in a not very dissimilar sense, should imitate nature. . . .

When I said previously that the poet must imitate religion as he should imitate nature, I didn't mean the style in which revelation is written. I meant the main design of religion: great wondrous events that have occurred, still more wondrous that shall occur! Truths of the same kind! The decorum of religion! The loftiness! The simplicity! The gravity! The sweetness! The beauty—as far as it may be attained by a human imitation. The imitation of the prophets as far as their works are masterpieces of rhetoric with regard to their expression is something else.

The Greeks, the Romans, and the French have a Golden Age in their arts, which is restricted to a short period. (I don't know why we have forgotten to give the English one too. They have had masterpieces for a long time now, and still produce them, at least in the work of Glover.)[1] The Golden Age of the Hebrews is of much longer duration. It begins with Moses or Job. And the manner of writing of the Orientals in general and that of revelation in particular, are two different things.

The higher beings who were outside creation as it is known to our philosophical cognition, have returned into it by means of revelation. But they had also to be given form for our imagination, in accordance with our way of thinking. It is probable that finite spirits that also occupy themselves in particular with the observation of the physical world have bodies. And it is not completely without probability that beings that God also employs so much to promote the bliss of mankind received a body resembling that assumed by the mediator of this bliss. Here the author of the sacred poem is led to a completely new scene of the imagination. Here in particular he can approach most closely his great goal of giving the images such traits that he simultaneously occupies the understanding or sets the feelings of the heart in motion. Here, simplicity and loftiness are the finishing touches required.

And what astonishing truths religion sets before the understanding! How they restore to our soul that loftiness with which it was created! And how diverse they are! Each of their twigs gives the wanderer wearied by petty things shade in which he can rest his fill and breathe his truer life. Be perfect, as God is perfect! says the great founder of our religion.[2] If the poet does not want to utter these truths in vain, he must say them in such a way that they occupy the heart just as much as the understanding.

To stir the heart completely is in general in every kind of oratory the highest task that the master can set himself and the listener can demand of him. To do it by means of religion is a new height which for us, without revelation, was obscured by clouds. Here the poet and the reader learn most surely whether the other is a Christian. Nothing less may that one be who wants to move our whole heart in this sphere, nor he who wants to feel the poet completely here. For will the poet, even with the most fortunate genius, be able to bring forth these movements in us without really feeling the beauty of religion, and without a righteousness of the heart, which does not want to glitter, far less to shine?

The freethinker, and the Christian who only half understands his religion, see only a great arena of ruins where the meditative Christian sees a majestic temple. And how could they see anything else? For not infrequently even details they fail to recognize transform the temple into ruins for them. And yet—if this boldest of all analogies is permitted—they have studied mythology, in order to understand Homer.

Translated by Timothy J. Chamberlain

Notes

Original title: *Von der heiligen Poesie*. First published in 1755 as preface to vol. 1 of *The Messiah*.

1. [Richard Glover (1712–85), known at the time for his epic poem *Leonidas* (1737).]
   2. [Matthew 5:48.]

Johann Georg Hamann

Johann Georg Hamann (1730–88) studied theology in Königsberg and then, after a spell as a tutor, turned to commerce. On a business trip to London in 1757, he experienced a conversion to a mystical form of Christianity, and devoted the remainder of his life to an energetic campaign against the rationalism of the Enlightenment. In deliberately cryptic and rhapsodic writings, notably the *Socratic Memorabilia* (1759) and the *Crusades of the Philologist* (1762), which includes his *Aesthetica in nuce,* he exalted inspiration, instinct, and the emotions, and opposed to neoclassicism the poetry of the Hebrews and folk poetry. An important influence on Herder, he was admired by writers of the Storm and Stress as the "Magus of the North." In later years, he produced a profound challenge to Kant on linguistic grounds in his *Metacritique on the Purism of Reason* (1781), and took issue with Mendelssohn in his *Golgotha und Scheblimini!* (1784). The standard edition is *Sämtliche Werke,* ed. Josef Nadler, 6 vols. (Vienna: Herder, 1949–57). For an account in English, see James C. O'Flaherty, *Johann Georg Hamann* (Boston: Twayne, 1979).

Aesthetica in nuce: A Rhapsody in Cabalistic Prose

Judges 5:30

A prey of divers colors in needlework, meet for the necks of them that take the spoil.

Elihu in the Book of Job, 32:19–22

Behold, my belly is as wine which hath no vent; it is ready to burst like new bottles.

I will speak, that I may be refreshed: I will open my lips and answer.

Let me not, I pray you, accept any man's person, neither let me give flattering titles unto man.

For I know not to give flattering titles; in so doing my maker would soon take me away.[1]

Horace

The uninitiate crowd I ban and spurn!
Come ye, but guard your tongues! A song that's new
    I, priest of the Muses, sing for you
      Fair maids and youths to learn!
Kings o'er their several flocks bear sway. O'er kings
Like sway hath Jove, famed to have overthrown
    The Giants, by his nod alone
      Guiding created things.[2]

Not a lyre! Nor a painter's brush! A winnowing fan for my Muse, to clear the threshing floor of holy literature! Praise to the archangel on the remains of Canaan's tongue![3]—on white asses[4] he is victorious in the contest, but the wise idiot of Greece[5] borrows Euthyphro's[6] proud stallions for the philological dispute.

Poetry is the mother tongue of the human race; even as the garden is older than the plowed field, painting than script; as song is more ancient than declamation; parables older than reasoning;[7] barter than trade. A deep sleep was the repose of our farthest ancestors; and their movement a frenzied dance. Seven days they would sit in the silence of deep thought or wonder;—and would open their mouths to utter winged sentences.

The senses and passions speak and understand nothing but images. The entire store of human knowledge and happiness consists in images. The first outburst of Creation, and the first impression of its recording scribe;—the first manifestation and the first enjoyment of Nature are united in the words: Let there be Light! Here beginneth the feeling for the presence of things.[8]

Finally GOD crowned the revelation of His splendor to the sense with His masterpiece—with man. He created man in divine form—in the image of God created He him. This decision of our prime originator unravels the most complex knots of human nature and its destiny. Blind heathens have recognized the invisibility man has in common with GOD. The veiled figure of the body, the countenance of the head, and the extremities of the arms are the visible schematic form in which we wander the earth; but in truth they are nothing but a finger pointing to the hidden man within us.

Each man is a counterpart of God in miniature.[9] The first nourishment came from the realm of plants; wine—the milk of the ancients; the oldest poetry was called botanical[10] by its learned commentator[11] (to judge from the tales of Jotham and of Joash);[12] and man's first apparel was a rhapsody of fig leaves.

But the LORD GOD made coats of skins and clothed them—our ancestors, whom the knowledge of good and evil had taught shame. If necessity is the mother of invention, and made the arts and conveniences, then we have good cause to wonder with Goguet first how the fashion of clothing ourselves could have arisen in Eastern lands, and second why it should have been in the skins of beasts.[13] Let me risk a conjecture that seems to me at least ingenious. I place the origin of this costume in the universal constancy of animal characters,[14] familiar to Adam from consorting with the ancient poet (known as Abaddon in the language of Canaan, but called Apollyon in the Hellenistic tongue).[15] This moved primal man to hand on to posterity beneath this borrowed skin an intuitive knowledge of past and future events. . . .

Speak, that I may see Thee! This wish was answered by the Creation, which is an utterance to created things through created things, for day speaketh unto day, and night proclaimeth unto night. Its word traverses every clime to the ends of the earth, and its voice can be heard in every dialect. The fault may lie where it will (outside us or within us): all we have left in nature for our use is fragmentary verse and *disjecta membra poetae*.[16] To collect these together is the scholar's modest part; the philosopher's to interpret them; to imitate them,[17] or—bolder still—to adapt them, the poet's.

To speak is to translate—from the tongue of angels into the tongue of men, that is, to translate thoughts into words—things into names—images into signs; which can be poetic or curiological,[18] historic or symbolic or hieroglyphic—and philosophical or characteristic.[19] This kind of translation (I mean, speech) resembles more than aught else the wrong side of a tapestry:

And shows the stuff, but not the workman's skill;[20]
or it can be compared with an eclipse of the sun, which can be
looked at in a vessel of water.[21]

Moses's torch illumines even the intellectual world, which also has
its heaven and its earth. Hence Bacon compares the sciences with
the waters above and below the vault of our vaporous globe.[22] The
former are a glassy sea,[23] like unto crystal with fire; the latter, by
contrast, are clouds from the ocean, no bigger than a man's hand.[24]

But the creation of the setting bears the same relation to the
creation of man as epic to dramatic poetry. The one takes place by
means of the word, the other by means of action. Heart, be like unto
a tranquil sea! Hear this counsel: let us make men in our image,
after our likeness, and let them have dominion!—Behold the deed:
and the LORD GOD formed man of the dust of the ground—
Compare word and deed: worship the mighty speaker with the Psalm-
ist;[25] adore the supposed gardener[26] with her who bore the news
to the disciples; honor the free potter[27] with the Apostle to the
Hellenistic scribes and philosophers of the Talmud![28]

The hieroglyphic Adam is the history of the entire race in the
symbolic wheel:—the character of Eve is the original of Nature's
beauty and of systematic economy, which is not flaunted as a sacred
method, but is formed beneath the earth and lies hidden in the
bowels, in the very reins of things.

Virtuosos of the present aeon, cast by the LORD GOD into a deep
trance of sleep! Ye noble few! Take advantage of this sleep, and make
from this Endymion's rib[29] the newest version of the human soul,
which the bard of midnight songs[30] beheld in his morning
dream[31]—but not from close at hand. The next aeon will awake like
a giant from a drunken sleep to embrace your muse and rejoice and
bear witness: Yea, that is bone of my bone and flesh of my flesh!

If some modern literary Levite[32] were to take passing note of this
rhapsody, I know in advance that he will bless himself like Saint
Peter[33] at the vision of the great sheet knit at the four corners, upon
which he fastened his eyes and saw four-footed beasts of the earth,
and wild beasts, and creeping things, and fowls of the air . . . "Oh
no, thou one possessed, thou Samaritan"—(that is how he will scold
the philologist in his heart)—"for readers of orthodox tastes, low
expressions and unclean vessels[34] are not proper"—*Imposs-
ibilissimum est, communia proprie dicere*[35]—Behold, that is why
an author whose taste is but eight days old, but who is circum-
cised,[36] will foul his swaddling clothes with white gentian[37]—to the

honor of human excrement! The old Phrygian's fabled ugliness[38] was never so dazzling as the aesthetic beauty of Aesop the younger.[39] Today, Horace's typical ode to Aristius[40] is fulfilled, that the poet who sings the praises of sweet-smiling Lalage, whose kiss is still sweeter than her laughter, has made dandies out of Sabine, Apuline, and Mauretanian monsters.[41] True, one can be a man without finding it necessary to become an author. But whoever expects his good friends to think of the writer apart from the man, is more inclined to poetic than to philosophical abstractions.[42] Therefore do not venture into the metaphysics of the fine arts without being initiated into the orgies[43] and Eleusinian mysteries. But the senses belong to Ceres, and to Bacchus the passions, the ancient foster parents of Nature the beautiful:

> Come to us, Bacchus, with the sweet grape cluster hanging
> From thy horns, and, Ceres, wreathe thy temples with the corn ears![44]

If this rhapsody might even be honored by the judgment of a Master in Israel,[45] then let us go to meet him in holy prosopopoeia,[46] which is as welcome in the realm of the dead as it is in the realm of the living[47] (. . . si NUX modo ponor in illis):[48]

Most Worthy and Learned Rabbi!

"The postilion of the Holy Roman Empire, who bears the motto *Relata refero* on the shield of his escutcheon,[49] has made me desirous of the second half of the homilies *da sacra poesi.*[50] I yearn for them, and have waited in vain until this day, even as the mother of the Hazorite captain looked out of her window for her son's chariot and cried through the lattice[51]—so do not think ill of me if I speak to you like the ghost in *Hamlet,* with signs and beckonings, until I have a proper occasion to declare myself in *sermones fideles.*[52] Will you believe without proof that *Orbis pictus,*[53] the book by that renowned fanatic, schoolmaster, and philologist Amos Comenius,[54] and the *Exercitia* of Muzelius[55] are both far too learned for children still pract-ic-ing their spell-ing, and verily, verily, we must become even as little children if we are to receive the spirit of truth that passeth the world's understanding, for it seeth it not, and (even if it were to see it) knoweth it not— —Ascribe the fault to the foolishness of my way of writing, which accords so ill with the original mathematical sin of your oldest writings, and still less with the witty rebirth of your most recent works, if I borrow an example from the spelling book that doubtless may be older than the Bible. Do the elements of the ABC lose their natural meaning, if in their infinite combinations into arbitrary signs they remind us of ideas that dwell, if not in heaven, then in our brains? But if we raise up the whole deserving righteousness of a scribe upon the dead body of the letter, what sayeth the spirit to that? Shall he be but a groom of the chamber to the dead letter, or perhaps a mere esquire to the deadening letter? God forbid! According to your copious insight into physical things,[56] you know better than I can remind you that the wind bloweth where it listeth—regardless of whether one hears it blowing; so one looks to the fickle weathercock to find out where it comes from, or rather, whither it is going."

> O outrageous crime! Shall the precious work be destroyed?
> Rather let the venerable power of the laws be infringed.
> Bacchus and sweet Ceres, come to our aid![57]

The opinions of the philosophers are variant readings of Nature, and the precepts of the theologians variants of the Scriptures The author is the best interpreter of his own words. He may speak through created things and through events—or through blood and fire and vapor of smoke,[58] for these constitute the sacramental language.

The Book of Creation contains examples of general concepts GOD wished to reveal to His creatures through His Creation. The Books of the Covenant contain examples of secret articles GOD wished to reveal to man through man. The unity of the great Author is mirrored even in the dialect of his works—in all of them a tone of immeasurable height and depth! A proof of the most splendid majesty and of total self-divesting! A miracle of such infinite stillness that makes GOD resemble Nothingness, so that in all conscience one would have to deny His existence, or else be a beast.[59] But at the same time a miracle of such infinite power, which fulfills all in all, that we cannot escape the intensity of His affection!

If it is a question of the good taste of the devotions, which are constituted by the philosophical spirit and poetic truth, and if it is a matter of the statecraft[60] of the versification, can we present a more credible witness than the immortal Voltaire, who virtually declares religion to be the cornerstone of epic poetry and whose greatest lament is that his religion[61] is the reverse of mythology?

Bacon represented mythology as a winged boy of Aeolus, the sun at his back, and with clouds for his footstool, fleeting away the time piping on a Grecian flute.[62]

But Voltaire, High Priest in the Temple of Taste, can draw conclusions as tellingly as Caiaphas,[63] and thinks more fruitfully than Herod.[64] For if our theology is not worth as much as mythology, then it is simply impossible for us to match the poetry of the Heathens, let alone excel it[65]—which would be most appropriate to our duty and to our vanity. But if our poetry is worthless, our history will look leaner than Pharaoh's kine; but fairy tales and court gazettes will take the place of our historians. And it is not worth the trouble of thinking of philosophy; all the more systematic calendars instead!—more than spiderwebs in a ruined castle. Every idle fellow who can just about manage dog-Latin or Switzer-German, but whose name is stamped by the whole number M or half the number of the academic beast[66] is a blatant liar, and the benches and the clods sitting on them would have to cry "outrage!" if the former only had ears, and the latter, ironically called listeners, only exercised their ears to listen with—

> Where is Euthyphro's whip, timid jade?
> So that my cart does not get stuck. . . .

Mythology here, mythology there![67] Poetry is an imitation of Nature the beautiful—and the revelations of Nieuwentijdt,[68] Newton, and Buffon will surely be able to replace a tasteless mythology? Indeed they should, and they would too, if they could. So why does it not happen?—Because it is impossible, say your poets.

Nature works through the senses and the passions. But whoso maims these instruments, how can he feel? Are crippled sinews fit for movement?

Your lying, murderous philosophy has cleared Nature out of the way, and why do you demand that we should imitate her?—So that you can renew the pleasure by murdering the young students of Nature too.

Verily, you delicate critics of art, go on asking what is truth, and make for the door, because you cannot wait for an answer to this question. Your hands are always washed, whether you are about to eat bread, or whether you have just pronounced a death sentence. Do you not also ask: what means did you employ to clear Nature out of the way? Bacon accuses you of flaying her with your abstractions. If Bacon is a witness to the truth, well then, stone him—and cast clods of earth or snowballs at his shade— — —

If one single truth, like the sun, prevaileth, it is day. But if you behold instead of this One truth, as many as the sands of the seashore; and here close by, a little light[69] that excels in brightness[70] a whole host of suns; that is a night beloved of poets and thieves. The poet[71] at the beginning of days is the same as the thief[72] at the end of days.

All the colors of the most beautiful world grow pale if once you extinguish that light, the firstborn of Creation. If the belly is your god, then even the hairs on your head are under his guardianship. Every created thing becomes alternately your sacrifice and your idol. Cast down against its will, but hoping still, it groans beneath your yoke, or at your vanity; it does its best to escape your tyranny, and longs even in the most passionate embrace for that freedom with which the beasts paid Adam homage, when GOD brought them unto man to see what he would call them; for whatsoever man would call them, that was the name thereof.

This analogy of man to the Creator endows all creatures with their imprint and their stamp, on which faithfulness and faith in all Nature depends. The more vividly this idea of the image of the invisible GOD[73] dwells in our heart, the more able we are to perceive his loving-kindness in his creatures; and to taste, and see it and grasp it with our hands. Every impression of Nature in man is not only a memorial, but also a warrant of fundamental truth: who is the LORD. Every countereffect of man in GOD's created world is charter and seal that we partake of the divine nature,[74] and that we are his offspring.[75]

Oh for a muse like a refiner's fire, and like a fuller's soap![76]— — She will dare to purify the natural use of the senses from the unnatural use of abstractions,[77] which distorts our concepts of things, even as it suppresses the name of the Creator and blasphemes against Him. I speak with you, O ye Greeks, for you deem yourselves wiser than the chamberlains with the gnostic key; go on and try to read the *Iliad* if you have first, with your abstractions, sifted out the two vowels alpha and omega, and then give me your opinion of the poet's sense and sound!

Sing,—G-ddess, the wr-th -f Peleus's s-n- chilles[78]

Behold, the scribes of worldly wisdom, great and small, have over-whelmed the text of Nature, like the Great Flood. Were not all its beauties and riches bound to turn into water? But you perform far greater miracles than ever delighted the gods,[79] with oak trees[80] and pillars of salt, with petrifactions, alchemical transformations and fables, to convince the human race. You make Nature blind, that she might be your guide! Or rather, you have with your Epicureanism[81] put out the light of your own eyes, that you might be taken for prophets who spin your inspirations and expositions out of your own heads. Oh, you would have dominion over Nature, and you bind your own hands and feet with your Stoicism,[82] that you may warble all the more movingly in your Poetic Miscellanies at the diamond fetters of fate.

If the passions are limbs of dishonor, do they therefore cease to be weapons of virility? Have you a wiser understanding of the letter of reason than that allegorical chamberlain of the Alexandrian Church had of the letter of the Scriptures when he castrated himself in order to reach heaven?[83] The prince of this aeon takes his favorites from among the greatest offenders against themselves; his court fools are the worst enemies of Nature in her beauty; true, she has Corybants and Gauls as her potbellied priests, but *esprits forts* as her true worshipers.[84]

A philosopher such as Saul[85] sets up laws for celibates—passion alone gives hands, feet, and wings to abstractions and hypotheses, and to pictures and signs gives spirit, life, and tongue. Where will you find a swifter syllogism? Where is the rolling thunder of elo-quence begotten? And where its companion, the single-syllabled lightning flash?[86]

Why should I paraphrase *one* word for you with an infinity of them, you readers whose estate, honor, and dignity make you so ignorant? For they can observe for themselves the phenomena of passion everywhere in human society; even as everything, however remote, can touch our hearts in a particular direction; even as each individ-ual feeling extends over the range of all external objects;[87] even as we can make the most general instances our own by applying them to ourselves personally, and expand any private circumstance into the public spectacle of heaven and earth. Each individual truth grows into the foundation of a design more miraculously than the fabled cowhide grew into the extent of a state, and a plan greater than the hemisphere comes together in the focus of perception. In short, the perfection of the design, the strength of the execution—the conception and birth of new ideas and new expressions—the labor and the rest of the wise man, the consolation and the loathing he finds in them, lie hidden from our senses in the fruitful womb of the passions.

"The philologist's public, his world of readers, seems to resemble that lecture hall Plato filled by himself."[88] Antimachus continued confidently, as it is written:

> like the leech that does not drop off the skin until
>   it is sated.[89]

Just as if our learning were a mere remembering, our attention is constantly being drawn to the monuments of the ancients, to shape our minds through memory. But why stop at the fountain of the Greeks, all riddled with holes as it is, and abandon the most living sources of antiquity? Perhaps we do not really know ourselves what it is in the Greeks and Romans that we admire even to idolatry.[90] This is where that accursed lying[91] in our symbolic textbooks comes from, for to this day they are daintily bound in sheep's parchment, but within, verily, within they are whited sepulchres and full of hypo-critical wickedness.[92]

We treat the ancients like a man who gazes on his visible face in a looking glass, but who, having looked upon it, straightway goes and forgets how he was formed. A painter sits for his self-portrait in a wholly different spirit. Narcissus (the bulbous plant of *beaux esprits*) loves his picture more than his life.[93]

Salvation comes from the Jews.[94] I had not yet seen their philosophical writings, but I was certain of finding sounder concepts in them—to your shame, Christians! Yet you feel the sting of that worthy name by which ye are called[95] as little as you feel the honor GOD did himself in taking the vile name of Son of Man.

Nature and Scripture then are the materials of the beautiful spirit that creates and imitates—Bacon compares matter with Penelope. Her importunate suitors are the scribes and philosophers.[96] The tale of the beggar who appeared at the court of Ithaca you know, for has not Homer translated it into Greek, and Pope into English verse?

But how are we to raise the defunct language of Nature from the dead? By making pilgrimages to the fortunate lands of Arabia,[97] and by going on crusades to the East, and by restoring their magic art. To steal it, we must employ old women's cunning, for that is the best sort. Cast your eyes down, ye idle bellies, and read what Bacon has to say about the magic art.[98] Silken feet in dancing shoes will not bear you on such a weary journey, so be ready to accept guidance from this hyperbole.[99]

O Thou who tearest the heavens and camest down from them, before whose arrival the mountains melt as hot water boils on a bright fire, that Thy name shall be proclaimed among its enemies, who nevertheless call themselves by it; and that anointed heathens may learn to tremble before the wonders that Thou doest, which are beyond their understanding. Let new false lights rise in the Orient! Let the pert cleverness of their magi be roused by new stars into bearing their treasures in person to our country. Myrrh, frankincense, and their gold, which mean more to us than their magic art! Let kings be gulled by it, and their philosophical muse rage at children and children's lore;[100] but let not Rachel weep in vain!— —

Why should we swallow death from the pots,[101] to make the garnish palatable for the children of the prophets? And how shall we appease the vexed spirit[102] of the Scripture: "Will I eat the flesh of bulls, or drink the blood of goats?"[103] Neither the dogmatic thoroughness of the orthodox Pharisees nor the poetic extravagance of the freethinking Sadducees will renew the mission of the spirit that inspired GOD's holy men (in season or out of season) to speak and write. That dearly loved disciple of GOD's only-begotten Son, which is in the bosom of the Father, has declared it to us:[104] that the spirit of prophecy liveth in the testimony of the name of the ONE GOD, who alone maketh us blessed and through whom alone we may inherit the promise of this and the next life; the name no one knows except he who receives it, the name that is above all names, that all things that dwell in Heaven and upon the earth and beneath the earth should bow their knee in the name of JESUS; and that all tongues should confess that JESUS CHRIST is the LORD to the glory of GOD the creator, to whom be praise in all eternity, Amen!

Thus the testimony of JESUS is the spirit of prophecy,[105] and the first sign by which He reveals the majesty of His humble figure transforms the holy books of the covenant into fine old wine, which deceives the steward's judgment[106] and strengthens the weak stomach of the critics. "If you read the prophetic books without understanding Christ," says the Punic[107] Father of the Church, "what insipidity and foolishness you will find! If you understand Christ in them, then what you read will not only be to your taste, but will also intoxicate you."[108]—"But to put a curb on the proud and wicked spirits here, Adam must surely have been dead before he would suffer this thing and drink the strong wine. Therefore have a care that you drink no wine while you are still a suckling child; every doctrine has its measure, time, and age."[109]

After GOD had grown weary of speaking to us through Nature and Scripture, through created things and prophets, through reasonings and figures, through poets and seers, and had grown short of breath, He spoke to us at last in the evening of days through His Son—yesterday and today!—until the promise of His coming, no longer as a servant, shall be fulfilled—

> Thou art the King of Glory, O Christ,
> Thou art the everlasting Son of the Father,
> Thou didst not abhor the Virgin's womb.[110]

We would pass a judgment for slander if we were to call our clever sophists fools and idiots when they describe the Lawgiver of the Jews as an ass's head and when they compare the proverbs of their great singers to dove's dung.[111] But the day of the LORD, a Sabbath darker than the midnight in which indomitable armadas are but as a stubble field—the gentlest zephyr, herald of the last Thunderstorm—as poetical as the LORD of Hosts could think and express it—will drown the blasts of even the sturdiest trumpeter— —Abraham's joy shall reach its pinnacle—his cup shall run over, then with his own hand GOD shall wipe away Abraham's last tear, more precious than all the pearls wantonly wasted by the last queen of Egypt;[112] the last tear shed over the last ashes of Sodom and the fate of the last martyr[113] GOD will wipe from the eye of Abraham, from the father of the faithful.

That day of the LORD, which gives the Christian courage to preach the LORD's death, will publish and make known the most stupid village idiots among all the angels for whom the fires of hell are waiting. The devils believe and tremble! But your senses, crazed by the cunning of reason, tremble not. You laugh when Adam the sinner chokes on the apple, and Anacreon the wise man on the grape pip. Do ye not laugh when the geese fill the Capitol with alarm, and the ravens feed the lover of his country, whose spirit was Israel's artillery and cavalry? You congratulate yourselves secretly on your blindness when GOD on the cross is numbered among the criminals, and when some outrage in Geneva or Rome, in the opera or the mosque,[114] reaches its apotheosis or purgation.

> Paint two snakes! Consecrated ground, my lads:
> Not the place for a piss! I take my leave[115]

> (Persius)

The birth of a genius will be celebrated, as usual, to the accompanying martyrdom of innocents—I take the liberty of comparing rhyme and meter to innocent children, for our most recent poetry seems to put them in mortal danger.

If rhyme belongs to the same genus as paronomasia and word-play,[116] then its origins must be almost as old as the nature of language and our sense impressions. The poet who finds the yoke of rhyme too heavy to bear is not therefore justified in denigrating its talents.[117] The failed rhyme might otherwise have given this frivolous pen as much occasion for a satire as Plato may have had to immortalize Aristophanes' hiccups in *The Symposium,* or Scarron his own hiccups in a sonnet.[118]

The free structure that great restorer of lyric song, Klopstock, has allowed himself is, I would guess, an archaism, a happy imitation of the mysterious workings of sacred poetry among the ancient Hebrews. And, as the most thorough critics of our time[119] shrewdly observe, what we apprehend in it is nothing but "an artificial prose whose periods have been broken down into their elements, each one of which can be read as a single line in a particular meter; and the reflections and feelings of the most ancient and holy poets seem of their own accord" (perhaps just as randomly as Epicurus's cosmic atoms) "to have arranged themselves into symmetrical lines that are full of harmony, although they have no (prescribed or mandatory) meter."[120]

Homer's monotonous meter ought to seem at least as paradoxical to us as the free rhythms of our German Pindar.[121] My admiration or ignorance of the causes for the Greek poet's use of the same meter throughout was modified when I made a journey through Courland and Lithuania. In certain parts of these regions, you can hear the Lettish or non-German people at work, singing only a single cadence of a few notes, which greatly resembles a poetic meter.[122] If a poet were to emerge among them, it would be quite natural for him to tailor all his lines to this measure initiated by their voices. To place this small detail in the appropriate light ("perhaps to please the foolish—who wish to burn it with their curling irons"),[123] compare it with several other phenomena, trace their causes, and develop their fruitful consequences would take too much time.

> Surely enough of snow and icy showers
> From the stern north Jove hath in vengeance called,
> Striking with red right hand his sacred towers,
> And Rome appalled—
>
> Ay, the whole earth—lest should return the time
> Of Pyrrha's blank amaze at sights most strange,
> When Proteus drove his finny herd to climb
> The mountain range.   Horace[124]

Gloss

As the oldest reader of this rhapsody in cabalistic prose, I feel obliged by the right of primogeniture to bequeath to my younger brethren who will come after, one more example of a merciful judgment, as follows:

Everything in this aesthetic nutshell tastes of vanity, vanity! The Rhapsodist[125] has read, observed, reflected, sought, and found agreeable words, quoted faithfully, gone round about like a merchant ship, and brought his farfetched cargo home. He has calculated sentence for sentence as arrows are counted on a battlefield;[126] and circumscribed his figures as stakes are measured for a tent. Instead of stakes and arrows he has, with the amateurs and pedants of his time, . . . written obelisks and asterisks.[127]

Let us now hear the sum total of his newest aesthetic, which is the oldest:

Fear GOD, and give glory to Him; for the time of His judgment is come; and worship Him that made heaven, and earth, and the sea, and the fountains of waters![128]

Translated by Joyce P. Crick, with modifications by H. B. Nisbet

Notes

"Aesthetics in a Nutshell;" the title is probably modeled on that of Christoph Otto von Schönaich's (1725–1809) *Die ganze Ästhetik in einer Nuß* (Complete aesthetics in a nutshell), 1754, a satirical work against Klopstock.

1. [This, and the previous quotation from Judges, are given by Hamann in the original Hebrew.]

2. [Hamann quotes Horace in the original Latin (as he does with subsequent Latin authors). The translation is by John Marshall (1908).]

3. [The "Archangel" (Michael) is an allusion to Johann David Michaelis (1717–91), theologian and philologist, whose rationalistic approach to the poetic language of the Old Testament aroused Hamann's strong opposition.]

4. Judges 5:10.

5. [The "wise idiot" is Socrates—and Hamann himself.]

6. See Plato's *Cratylus*:

> HERMOGENES: Indeed, Socrates, you do seem to me to be uttering oracles, exactly like an inspired prophet.
>
> SOCRATES: Yes, Hermogenes, and I am convinced that the inspiration came to me from Euthyphro the Prospaltian [Hamann's text: the son of Pantios]. For I was with him and listening to him for a long time early this morning. So he must have been inspired, and he not only filled my ears but took possession of my soul with his superhuman wisdom. So I think this is our duty: we ought today to make use of this wisdom . . . but tomorrow, if the rest of you agree, we will conjure it away and purify ourselves, when we have found someone, whether priest or sophist, who is skilled in that kind of purifying. . . . But ask me about any others [i.e., other names] you please, "that you may see what" Euthyphro's "horses are." [Plato, *Cratylus*, translated by H. N. Fowler, Loeb Classical Library (London, 1926), 396d-97a and 407d; the quotation at the end is from Homer, *Iliad* 5.221f.]

7. " . . . as hieroglyphs are older than letters, so are parables older than arguments," says Bacon, my Euthyphro.

8. Ephesians 5:13: "For whatsoever doth make manifest is light."

9. Manilius, *Astron.* lib. IV [Marcus Manilius, *Astronomica* 4.895].

10. "For being as a plant which comes from the lust of the earth without a formal seed, poetry has sprung up and spread abroad more than any other kind of learning" (Bacon, *de Augm. Scient.* lib. II cap. 13). See Councillor Johann David Michaelis's observations on Robert Lowth, *de sacra poesi Praelectionibus Academicis Oxonii habitis*, p. 100 (18).

11. [The allusion is again to Michaelis. The latter's work on Lowth, referred to in Hamann's footnote (10), is his annotated edition of Robert Lowth's (1710–87) lectures on Hebrew poetry, *Praelectiones de Sacra Poesi Hebraeorum* (originally published in England in 1753). The quotation from Bacon in the same footnote is from *De augmentis scientiarum*, book 2, chapter 13. Translations of this and subsequent Latin quotations from Bacon's works are from the English versions in vols. 4 and 5 of Francis Bacon, *Works*, edited by James Spedding, Robert Leslie Ellis, and Douglas Denon Heath, 14 vols. (London, 1857–74); the present quotation is from 4:318.]

12. Judges 9; 2 Chronicles 25:18.

13. [The reference is to Antoine Yves Goguet (1716–58), *De l'origine des lois, des arts et des sciences et leur progrès chez les anciens peuples* (1758), 1:114f.

Goguet maintained that the original purpose of clothing cannot have been to protect man from the elements, since it was worn in countries whose climate made such protection unnecessary.]

14. [A satirical reference to Lessing, whose essay *On the Use of Animals in Fables* (1759) argues that the writers of fables employed animals rather than men because of the "universally known constancy of animal characters"; see G. E. Lessing, *Werke*, edited by Herbert G. Göpfert, 8 vols. (Munich, 1970–79), 5:398. Hamann, of course, finds Lessing's rationalistic explanation unacceptable.]

15. [Abaddon . . . Apollyon: see Revelation 9:11.]

16. ["the limbs of the dismembered poet" (Horace, *Satires* 1.4.62).]

17.   You learn to compose verses with a divided name;
    Thus you will become an imitator of the singer Lucilius.
                    Ausonius *Epist.* V [Ausonius, *Epistolae* 16.37–38].

18. For an explanation, consult Wachter's *Naturae et Scripturae Concordia. Commentatio de literis ac numeris primaevis aliisque rebus memorabilibus cum ortu literarum coniunctis.* Lips. et Hafn. 1752, in the first section. [The philologist Johann Georg Wachter (1673–1757), in the work referred to, distinguished three phases in the development of writing (curiological, symbolic, or hieroglyphic, and characteristic) from pictorial representation to abstract signs. Hamann adds the terms *poetic, historic,* and *philosophical* to indicate parallel phases in the development of human thought.]

19. The following passage in Petronius is to be understood as being of this kind of sign. I am obliged to quote it in its context, even if it has to read as a satire on the philologist himself and his contemporaries [Hamann's satirical reference and quotation are aimed at the rationalistic philology of Michaelis (and its prolix expression)]: "Your flatulent and formless flow of words is a modern immigrant from Asia to Athens. Its breath fell upon the mind of ambitious youth like the influence of a baleful planet, and when the old tradition was once broken, eloquence halted and grew dumb. In a word, who after this came to equal the splendor of Thucydides? (He is called the Pindar of historians.) [Hamann's parenthesis] Or of Hyperides? (who bared Phryne's bosom to convince the judges of his good cause) [Hamann's parenthesis] Even poetry did not glow with the color of health, but the whole of art, nourished on one universal diet, lacked the vigor to reach the gray hairs of old age. The decadence in painting was the same, as soon as Egyptian charlatans had found a shortcut to this high calling." [Petronius, *Satyricon,* 2; translated by Michael Heseltine, Loeb Classical Library (London, 1913)]. Compare this with the profound prophecy which Socrates put into the mouth of the Egyptian king Thamus about the inventions of Thoth, such that Phaedrus was moved to cry: "Socrates, you easily make up stories of Egypt or any country you please" [Plato, *Phaedrus* 275b].

20. [See the Earl of Roscommon, *Poems* (London, 1717), p. 9 (on a prose translation of Horace).]

21. The one metaphor comes from the Earl of Roscommon's *Essay on Translated Verse* and Howell's *Letters.* [James Howell (c. 1594–1666), *Familiar Letters* (1645–55).] Both, if I am not mistaken, borrowed the comparison from Saavedra. [That is, Cervantes (Miguel Cervantes de Saavedra).] The other is borrowed from one of the most excellent weekly journals, *The Adventurer.* [No. 49, 24 April 1753.] But there they are used *ad illustrationem* (to adorn the garment), here they are used *ad involucrum* (as a covering for the naked body), as Euthyphro's muse would distinguish.

22. [The reference is to Bacon's distinction between two types of knowledge: divine revelation, and the empirical data of the senses (Bacon, *Works,* 1:520).]

23. [See Revelation 4:6.]

24. [See 1 Kings 18:44.]

25. Psalms 33:9.

26. John 20:15–17.

27. Romans 9:21.

28. [The reference is to St. Paul, as Apostle to the Gentiles and a scholar learned in the Scriptures.]

29. [A combined reference to the creation of woman from Adam's rib (Genesis 2:21–23) and to Endymion, the beautiful youth whom the moon goddess Selene visited while he slept.]

30. [A reference to Edward Young's (1683–1765) poem *Night Thoughts* (1742–44).]

31. See Dr. Young's *Letter to the Author of Grandison on Original Composition*. [A reference to Edward Young's *Conjectures on Original Composition, in a Letter to the Author of Sir Charles Grandison* (1759).]

32. [A reference to Moses Mendelssohn; the "passing Levite" alludes to Luke 10:32 (the parable of the Good Samaritan).]

33. Acts 10:11.

34. [See Mark 7:4 and 8.]

35. [Horace, *Ars poetica* 127 (*Difficile est proprie communia dicere*): "It is difficult to deal adequately with familiar subjects"; or, in Hamann's context, "It is utterly impossible to call vulgar things by their proper name."]

36. [See Genesis 17:12.]

37. [According to Adelung's dictionary "white gentian" was a vulgar expression in German for the white excrement of dogs.]

38. [A reference to the proverbial ugliness of Aesop.]

39. [A reference to Lessing, whose *Fables* were published in 1759.]

40. Lib. I, od. 22. [Horace, *Odes* 1.22; ode on Lalage to Aristius Fuscus.]

41. [The geographical names are taken from Horace's ode (1.22) to Aristius; the target of satire is again Lessing, who wrote frivolous Anacreontic poetry in his early years.]

42. [A reference to Lessing's contention, in the *Letters concerning Recent Literature*, that the private life of an author is irrelevant to his writing (see Lessing, *Werke*, ed. Göpfert, 5:43).]

43. "Orgia nec Pentheum nec Orpheum tolerant." Bacon, *de Augm. Scient.* lib. II, cap. XIII. ["Orgies cannot endure either Pentheus or Orpheus" (that is, both were torn to pieces by frenzied Maenads); see Bacon, *Works*, 4:335.]

44. Tibullus lib. II, eleg. 1. [Tibullus, *Elegies* 2.1.]

45. [Another reference to Michaelis; also to John 3:10.]

46. "L'art de personifier ouvre un champ bien moins borné et plus fertile que l'ancienne Mythologie." [The art of personification opens a field much less restricted and more fertile than ancient mythology.] Fontenelle sur la poésie en général. Tom. VIII.

47. [Personification (prosopopoeia) was employed in ancient rhetoric not only as an everyday figure of speech, but also as a means of introducing deceased personages as spokesmen in dialogues. (Hamann himself is about to address an ironic dialogue to the "Rabbi" Michaelis.)]

48. ["if as a NUT I count as one of them" (Ovid, *Nux* 19); an allusion to the title of Hamann's essay.]

49. [A reference to the weekly newspaper *Ordentliche Wöchentliche Kayserliche Reichs-Postzeitung*, published in the Imperial city of Frankfurt; its motto was *Relata refero* (I report reports).]

50. [Hamann refers to the newspaper announcement of the publication of the second part of Lowth's work on Hebrew poetry (see note 11 above), which appeared in 1761.]

51. [See Judges 5:28.]

52. [*sermones fideles:* true expressions (as distinct from the "cabalistic" style of the present work.] John 3.11. The following passage from Bacon, *de Augm.* lib. IX

may help to guard against the crude and ignorant idea of pronouncing the present imitation of cabalistic style to be good or bad: "In the free way of interpreting Scripture, there occur two excesses. The one presupposes such perfection in Scripture, that all philosophy likewise should be derived from its sources; as if all other philosophy were something profane and heathen. This distemper has principally grown up in the school of Paracelsus and some others; but the beginnings thereof came from the Rabbis and Cabalists. But these men do not gain their object; and instead of giving honor to the Scriptures as they suppose, they rather embase and pollute them . . . and as to seek divinity in philosophy is to seek the living among the dead, so to seek philosophy in divinity is to seek the dead among the living. The other method of interpretation that I set down as an excess, appears at the first glance sober and modest, yet in reality it both dishonors the Scriptures themselves, and is very injurious to the Church. This is, (in a word), when the divinely inspired Scriptures are explained in the same way as human writings. But we ought to remember that there are two things that are known to God the author of the Scriptures, but unknown to man; namely, the secrets of the heart, and the successions of time. And therefore as the dictates of Scripture are written to the hearts of men, and comprehend the vicissitudes of all ages; with an eternal and certain foreknowledge of all heresies, contradictions, and differing and changing estates of the Church, as well in general as of the individual elect, they are not to be interpreted only according to the latitude and obvious sense of the place; or with respect to the occasion whereon the words were uttered; or in precise context with the words before or after; or in contemplation of the principal scope of the passage; but we must consider them to have in themselves, not only totally or collectively, but distributively also in clauses and words, infinite springs and streams of doctrines, to water every part of the Church and the souls of the faithful. For it has been well observed that the answers of our Savior to many of the questions that were propounded to Him do not appear to the point, but as it were impertinent thereto. The reason whereof is twofold; the one, that knowing the thoughts of his questioners not as we men do by their words, but immediately and of himself, he answered their thoughts and not their words; the other, that He did not speak only to the persons then present, but to us also now living, and to men of every age and nation to whom the Gospel was to be preached. And this also holds good in other passages of Scripture." [Bacon, *Works*, 4:116–18.]

53. [*Orbis pictus sensualium* (1657) by the Czech scholar and educationalist Johann Amos Comenius (1592–1671), an illustrated textbook designed to teach children by concrete, visual methods.]

54. See Kortholt's collection of letters by Leibniz, vol. 3, ep. 29.

55. [Friedrich Muzelius (1684–1753), philologist and author of school textbooks.]

56. [A reference to Michaelis's emphasis on geographical and climatic factors in his rationalistic exegesis of the Scriptures.]

57. [Quoted by Hamann in Latin from *Anthologia Latina* 672, lines 4, 20, and 8. The quotation expresses Hamann's unease at the violence done to Scripture by such interpreters as Michaelis.] See the poetic edict of the emperor Octavius Augustus, according to which Virgil's last will *de abolenda Aeneide* [i.e., that the *Aeneid* should be destroyed] is said to have been nullified. One can concede wholeheartedly what Dr. George Benson [George Benson (1699–1762), liberal theologian and author of various paraphrases, with commentaries, of books of the New Testament. (Michaelis had translated some of Benson's work.) Benson rejected the notion of the multiple sense of Scriptural passages, arguing for the unity of sense (that is, every passage has only a single meaning). Antoine Houdart de la Motte (1672–1731) and Samuel Clarke (1675–1729) applied the same thesis to Homer; for further details, see Sven-Aage Jørgensen's notes to his edition of Hamann's *Sokratische Denkwürdigkeiten* and *Aesthetica in nuce* (Stuttgart, 1968), pp. 102–4] has to say about the

unity of sense, though he has scarcely developed his ideas, rather pulled them together with little thought, selection, or smoothness. If he had tried to convey some earthly propositions about the unity of reading, his thoroughness would strike us more strongly. One cannot leaf through the four volumes of this paraphrastic explanation without a sly smile, nor miss the frequent passages where Dr. Benson, the beam of popery in his own eye, inveighs against the mote in the Roman Church's, passages where he imitates our own official theologians when they applaud any blind and overhasty bright idea honoring the creature more than the creator. First I would want to ask Dr. Benson whether unity cannot exist without multiplicity? A lover of Homer is exposed to the same danger of losing his unity of sense by French paraphrasts like de la Motte or thoughtful dogmatists like Samuel Clarke. The literal or grammatical sense, the corporeal or dialectical sense, the Capernaitic [Capernaitic: pertaining to the doctrine of transubstantiation] or historical sense are all profoundly mystical, and they are determined by minor circumstances of such a fleeting, arbitrary, spiritual nature that without ascending to heaven we cannot find the key to their understanding. We must not shrink from any journey across the seas or to the regions of such shadows as have believed, spoken, suffered for a day, for two, for a hundred or a thousand years—oh mysteries!—. The general history of the world can tell us hardly as much about them as can be writ on the narrowest tombstone, or as can be retained by Echo, that nymph of the laconic memory. The thinker who wants to intimate to us the schemes that thoughtful writers in a critical place devise in order to convert their unbelieving brethren must have the keys to heaven and hell. Because Moses placed life in the blood [see Leviticus 17:11], all the baptized rabbis are afraid of the spirit and life of the prophets, which make a sacrifice of the literal understanding, the child of their heart (ἐν παραβολῇ) [as an example] and turn the streams of Eastern wisdom to blood. A dainty stomach will have no use for these stifled thoughts.—*Abstracta initiis occultis; Concreta maturitati conveniunt*, according to Bengel's *Sonnenweiser*. ["The abstract is appropriate to dark beginnings, the concrete to maturity": inaccurate quotation from Johann Albrecht Bengel's (1687–1752) *Gnomon* (= German *Sonnenweiser*) *Novi Testamenti* (1742). Hamann wishes to suggest by this quotation that the true prophetic sense of the Scriptures, denied by the literalist Benson, will come to light in the fullness of time.] (*plane pollex, non index.*) ["Plainly a thumb, not an index finger": pun from Cicero, *Epistles to Atticus* 13.46, as a humorous indication (*index*) of the importance of the preceding quotation.]

58. Acts 2:19.

59. Psalms 73:21, 22.

60. "La seule politique dans un Poème doit être de faire de bons vers," says M. Voltaire in his credo on the epic [Voltaire's *Idée de la Henriade*]. [The only policy in a poem should be to write good lines.]

61. Whatever M. Voltaire understands by religion, *Grammatici certant et adhuc sub Judice lis est* [Horace, *Ars poetica* 78: "Scholars argue, and the case is so far undecided." Hamann now transfers his satire to Voltaire as a leader of the rationalistic Enlightenment]; the philologist has as little to worry about here as his readers. We may look for it in the liberties of the Gallican Church, or in the flowers of sulphur of refined Naturalism, but neither explanation will do any harm to the unity of the sense.

62. "I take mythological fables to be a kind of breath from the traditions of more ancient nations, which fell into the pipes of the Greeks." *De augm. scient.* lib. II, cap. XIII [Bacon, *Works* 4:317].

63. "Qu'un homme ait du jugement ou non, il profite également de vos ouvrages: il ne lui faut que de la MEMOIRE" [Whether or not a man has the power of judgment, he benefits equally from your works: all he needs is MEMORY], is what a writer who utters prophecy has said to M. Voltaire's face. "The rhapsodist should not forget this": Socrates in Plato's *Ion* [*Ion* 539e].

64. Photius (in his *Amphilociis Quaest.* CXX, which Johann Christoph Wolf

has added to his cornucopia of critical and philological whimsies [Johann Christoph Wolf (1683–1739) quotes the passage from Photius (820–91) in his *Curae philologicae et criticae*, vol. 4 (Hamburg, 1735)]) looks for a prophecy in the words of Herod to the Wise Men of the East—"that I may come and worship him also"—and compares them with Caiaphas's statement in John 11:49–52. He observes: "There are perhaps other remarks of this kind, spoken by one of evil intention and murderous heart, which are ultimately prophetic." Photius conceives Herod as a Janus *bifrons* [the Roman god of doorways, with two faces looking in opposite directions], who represented the Gentiles by his race and the Jews by his office. Many malicious and empty utterances (on which both master and servant pride themselves) might appear in a wholly different light if we were to ask ourselves from time to time whether they are speaking of their own accord or whether they should be understood as prophetic.

65. [A reference to the *querelle des anciens et des modernes*.]

66. [Typically oblique reference to the academic degrees of Master (M) and Doctor (D, the Roman numeral for 500, and half of M or 1,000).]

67. Fontenelle sur la Poésie en général. "Quand on saura employer d'une manière nouvelle les images fabuleuses, il est sûr qu'elles feront un grand effet." [When it is understood how to employ fabulous images in a new manner, it is certain they will have a great effect.]

68. [Bernhard Nieuwentijdt (1654–1720), Dutch scientist and physico-theologian; he, Newton, and Buffon are named simply as representatives of modern science, the Enlightenment's faith in which Hamann did not share.]

69. " . . . et notho . . .—. . . lumine . . ." Catull. *Carm. Sec. ad Dian.* ["and with borrowed light," Catullus, *Hymn to Diana* 15f.]

70.   "And yet more bright
Shines out the Julian star, as moon outglows
      Each lesser light"
[Horace, *Odes* 1.12, lines 46–48; translation by John Marshall]

71. 2 Corinthians 4:6.

72. Revelation 16:15.

73. "the image of the invisible God," Colossians 1:15.

74. "partakers of the divine nature," 2 Peter 1:4; "to be conformed to the image of his Son," Romans 8:29.

75. Acts 17:27, etc.

76. Malachi 3:2.

77. Bacon, *de interpretatione Naturae et regno Hominis,* Aphorism. CXXIV: "But I say that those foolish and apish images of worlds the fancies of men have created in philosophical systems must be utterly scattered to the winds. Be it known then how vast a difference there is between the Idols of the human mind and the Ideas of the divine. The former are nothing more than arbitrary abstractions; the latter are the creator's own stamp upon creation, impressed and defined in matter by true and exquisite lines. Truth therefore and utility are here the very same things: and the works of nature themselves are of greater value as pledges of truth than as contributing to the comforts of life" [Bacon, *Novum organum*, I, Aphorism 124, in *Works*, 4:110]. Elsewhere Bacon repeats this reminder that we should use the works of nature not only as amenities of living but also as pledges of truth.

78. [Homer, *Iliad* 1.1; Hamann omits the alphas and omegas in quoting the Greek, producing an effect similar to that of deleting the *a*'s and *o*'s from the English translation "Sing, O Goddess, the wrath of Peleus's son Achilles."]

79. "for the gods also have a sense of humor." Socrates in *Cratylus* [Plato, *Cratylus* 406c].

80. Socrates to Phaedrus: "They used to say, my friend, that the words of the oak in the holy place of Zeus at Dodona were the first prophetic utterances. The people of that time, not being so wise as you young folks, were content in their simplicity to

hear an oak or a rock, provided only it spoke the truth; but to you, perhaps, it makes a difference who the speaker is and where he comes from, for you do not consider only whether his words are true or not." [Plato, *Phaedrus* 275b-c; translated by H. N. Fowler, Loeb Classical Library (London, 1914).]

81. [A reference to such secular philosophers and freethinkers of the Enlightenment as Gassendi, La Mettrie, and Frederick the Great (who much admired the Epicurean philosophy of Lucretius).]

82. [A reference to modern scientific determinism, as a counterpart to the determinism of the ancient Stoics.]

83. [An allusion to Matthew 19:12 and to the church father Origen (c. 185-c. 254), who castrated himself for the sake of religion.]

84. [The "prince of this aeon" is Frederick the Great; the "court fools," "Gauls," and *esprits forts* are the French freethinkers (La Mettrie, Voltaire, etc.) with whom Frederick associated.]

85. 1 Samuel 14:24.

86. Brief is the lightning in the collied night,
    That (in a spleen) unfolds heav'n and earth
    And ere man has the power to say: Behold!
    The jaws of darkness do devour it up.

    Shakespeare, *A Midsummer Night's Dream*

87. "C'est l'effet ordinaire de notre ignorance de nous peindre tout semblable à nous et de repandre nos portraits dans toute la nature" [It is the usual effect of our ignorance to imagine everything resembles ourselves, and to spread our portraits throughout nature], says Fontenelle in his *Histoire du Théâtre Franç.* "Une grande passion est une espèce d'Ame, immortelle à sa manière et presque indépendant des Organes" [A great passion is a kind of soul, immortal in its fashion, and almost independent of physical organs], Fontenelle in *Eloge de M. du Verney.*

88. "For Plato alone is worth all of them to me." Cicero, *Brutus.* [Antimachus, in the anecdote alluded to, was reading a long poem, and all of his audience except Plato left the lecture room. He then made the remark quoted by Hamann (Cicero, *Brutus* 51.191).]

89. [Horace, *Ars poetica*, line 476 (the final line of the poem).]

90. [An allusion to Winckelmann, and an example of Hamann's hostility toward neoclassicism.]

91. Psalms 59:12.

92. See part 2 of the *Briefe, die neueste Literatur betreffend* (Letters concerning recent literature) passim, a little here, a little there, but mainly p. 131. [The reference is to an (anonymous) attack by Nicolai, in the *Letters* referred to, on a volume of poems that had impressed Hamann favorably. Hamann throws back at the anonymous critic some of the abuse the latter had directed at the poems. For further details, see Hans-Martin Lumpp, *Philologia crucis. Zu Johann Georg Hamanns Auffassung von der Dichtkunst* (Tübingen, 1970), pp. 87–89.]

93. Ovid, *Metamorph.*, lib. III. [Hamann, in this footnote, goes on to quote Ovid's version of the myth of Narcissus at length, from *Metamorphoses* 3.415–510.]

94. [See John 4:22.]

95. James 2:7.

96. [See Bacon, *Works*, 4:319–20: Pan (Nature) is the son of Penelope (formless matter) and her suitors (the Platonic Ideas or Forms), according to one myth discussed by Bacon, who himself suggests that Nature is rather the son of matter and Mercury (the Logos or Word of God). Hamann's following sentence presents Odysseus, the true master, as a typological forerunner of Christ, appearing in lowly form (as a beggar).]

97. [Allusion to a Danish scientific expedition (1761–67) to "Arabia felix" (Southern Arabia) under Carsten Niebuhr (1733–1815), which was mounted at the suggestion of Michaelis, who remains the chief target of Hamann's satire.]

98. "But indeed the chief business of magic was to note the correspondences between the architectures and fabrics of things natural and things civil. Neither are these only similitudes (as men of narrow observation may perhaps conceive them to be), but plainly the same footsteps of nature treading or printing upon different subjects and matters." So Bacon in the third book of *De augmentis scientiarum,* in which he claims to explain the magic art also by means of a "science of the universal consents of things," and in the light of this, the appearance of the Wise Men at Bethlehem. [Bacon, *Works,* 4:339 and 366.]

99. 1 Corinthians 12:31: "And yet I show unto you a more excellent way."

100. [Another allusion to Frederick the Great and his circle of *philosophes.*]

101. [See 2 Kings 4:38–42.]

102. [See Isaiah 63:10.]

103. [Psalms 50:13.]

104. [See John 1:18 and 13:23–25.]

105. Revelation 19:10.

106. [See John 2:8–10.]

107. See pp. 66 and 67 of the *Answer to the Question as to the Influence of Opinions on Language and of Language on Opinions* which received the prize awarded by the Royal Academy of Sciences in 1759. [The prize essay referred to is by Michaelis, and the reference is to remarks by him on Augustine's Punic (Carthaginian) origin and native language. Hamann goes on to pun on the word *Punic* in his footnote, and makes fun, at considerable length, of Michaelis's learned deliberations.] Also to be consulted in this connection: *Ars Punica sive Flos Linguarum: The Art of Punning; or, the Flower of Language in Seventy-nine Rules for the Farther Improvement of Conversation and Help of Memory.* By the Labor and Industry of TUM PUN-SIBI. [Hamann, as his subsequent comments make clear, shares the belief of his contemporaries that the work was by Jonathan Swift. It is now ascribed to Thomas Sheridan (see Jørgensen, p. 132).]

"Bons mots prompted by an equivocation are deemed the very wittiest, though not always concerned with jesting, but often even with what is important . . . for the power to divert the force of a word into a sense quite different from that in which other folk understand it seems to indicate a man of talent" (Cicero, *De Orat.,* lib. II) [Cicero, *De Oratore* 2.250 and 254].

See the second edition [of *Ars Punica*], 1719, octavo. The author of this learned work (of which I have, unfortunately, only a defective copy) is Swift, the glory of the priesthood ("The Glory of the Priesthood and the Shame!" *Essay on Criticism*) [Pope, *Essay on Criticism,* line 694 (on Erasmus)]. It begins with definitions: logical, physical, and moral. In the logical sense, "Punning is essentially something of which it is said that it applies to something else or is in any manner applied to something else." According to the natural science of the extravagant and whimsical Cardanus, "Punning is an Art of Harmonious Jingling upon Words, which passing in at the Ears and falling upon the Diaphragma, excites a titillary Motion in those Parts, and this being convey'd by the Animal Spirits into the Muscles of the Face raises the Cockles of the Heart." But according to casuistry, it is "a Virtue, that most effectually promotes the End of good Fellowship." An example of this artful virtue can be found among others of the same ilk in the answer quoted above to the Punic comparison between Mahomet the Prophet and Augustine the Church Father, which resembles a hybrid lover of poetry, with an imagination half-inspirational, half-scholastic, who is not nearly learned enough to appreciate the use of figurative language properly, let alone be able to scrutinize religious experience. [All of this is oblique criticism of Michaelis and his attempts to rationalize biblical references to miracles, etc., as merely figurative expressions.] The good bishop spoke Hebrew without knowing it, just as M. Jourdain spoke prose without knowing it, and just as even today this raising and answering of learned questions without knowing it, can reveal the barbarism of the age and the treachery of the heart, at the cost of this profound truth:

that we are all sinners, and devoid of the glory that is ascribed to us, the lying prophet of Arabia as much as the good African shepherd, as well as that clever wit (whom I should have named first of all) who thought up that farfetched comparison between the two believers in providence by putting together such ridiculous parallel passages according to the Punic theory of reason of our modern cabalists, for whom every fig leaf yields a sufficient reason, and every insinuation a fulfillment. [Satirical references to the philosophical doctrines of the Enlightenment such as the Leibnizian principle of sufficient reason.]

108. [The quotation is from St. Augustine's commentary (9.3) on St. John: see J. P. Migne, *Patrologia Latina* 35.1379f.]

109. Our Luther's words (reading Augustine, it is said, spoiled his taste somewhat), taken from his famous preface to the Epistle to the Romans [see Martin Luther, *Vorreden zur Heiligen Schrift* (Munich, 1934), pp. 78–93; Luther warns, in the passage referred to, against philosophical speculation on the mysteries of predestination and divine grace], which I never weary of reading, just as I never tire of his preface to the Psalms. I have introduced this passage by means of an accommodation, as they say, because in it Luther speaks of the abyss of Divine Providence, and, after his admirable custom, rests upon his dictum: "that one cannot without suffering the cross and the pains of death trade Providence against God without harm and secret rage."

110. The devout reader will be able to complete the hymnic cadence of this section for himself. [The quotation is from Luther's translation of the *Te Deum*.] My memory abandons me out of sheer willfulness; "Ever hastening to the end . . . and what he cannot hope to accomplish . . . he omits." [Fragmentary quotation from Horace, *Ars poetica* 148ff.]

111. [See 2 Kings 6:25.]

112. [The reference is to Cleopatra, who dissolved a pearl to drink Antony's health.]

113. 2 Peter 2:8.

114. [That is, in the Catholic mass (Rome) or the austere Calvinist church (Geneva).]

115. [Persius, *Satires* 1.113; snakes, sacred to the house, were used as a sign to warn against desecration. Here, the satirist responds ironically to protests by influential persons against his attacks.]

116. See note 76 of the editor, Lowth's *Praelect.*, XV; Algarotti, vol. III. [Michaelis, in his edition of Lowth, discusses wordplay at length, and considers it of little aesthetic merit; the second reference is to Francesco Algarotti's (1712–64) *Oeuvres*, 3:76 (*Essai sur la rime*).]

117. Gently rhyme creepeth into the heart, if 'tis not under compulsion; Harmony's staff and adornment, speech in our mem'ry it fixes. *Elegien und Briefe*, Strasburg, 1760. [The collection of poems quoted is by Ludwig Heinrich von Nicolay (1737–1820).]

118. [Plato, *Symposium* 185c–e; Paul Scarron (1610–60), French poet.]

119. See the editor's fourth note to Lowth's third lecture, p. 149, and the fifty-first letter in the third part of the *Letters concerning Recent Literature*.

120. [The "thorough critics" are Michaelis (as editor of Lowth's lecture) and Lessing, whose comments (in the *Letters concerning Recent Literature*) Hamann here quotes. The praise of the "thorough critics" is, of course, ironic. Hamann valued Klopstock for his piety and biblical language as well as for his verse.]

121. Wouldn't it be funny if Herr Klopstock were to specify to his printer or to some Margot la Ravaudeuse [according to Jørgensen, p. 142, the title of a novel by Fougeret de Monbron], as the philologist's muse, the reasons why he had his poetic feelings printed in separate lines, when the vulgar think they are concerned with *qualitatibus occultis* and the language of dalliance calls them feelings par excellence.

Despite the gibberish of my dialect, I would willingly acknowledge Herr Klopstock's prosaic manner to be a model of classical perfection. From having read a few small specimens, I would credit this writer with a profound knowledge of his mother tongue, particularly of its prosody. Indeed, his musical meter would seem highly appropriate as a lyrical garb for a poet who seeks to shun the commonplace. I distinguish the original compositions of our Asaph [psalmist (see Psalms 50 and 73–83); circumlocution for Klopstock as a singer of sacred songs] from his transformations of old church hymns, indeed even from his epic [references to Klopstock's *Geistliche Lieder* (1758) and his epic poem *The Messiah*, of which only part had been published when Hamann wrote], whose story is well known, and resembles Milton's in profile at least, if not entirely.

122. [Note Hamann's interest in folk poetry, which Herder was soon to echo more fully in his essay on Ossian.]

123. [Cicero, *Brutus* 75.262; that is, "who will merely use my writings as wastepaper."]

124. [Horace, *Odes* 1.2, lines 1–8 (translation by John Marshall); the reference in the poem to Deucalion's flood and the return of ancient chaos is for Hamann a figure for the coming Day of Judgment.]

125. "the rhapsodists—interpreters of the interpreters" (Socrates in Plato's *Ion*). [Plato, *Ion* 535a.]

126. Procopius, *De bello persico* 1.18.

127. "An asterisk [= little star] makes a light shine out, an obelisk [little dagger] stabs and pierces" (Jerome's preface to the Pentateuch, cf. Diogenes Laertius on Plato). In skillful hands, these Masoretic signs could equally well be used to rejuvenate the writings of Solomon, as one of the most recent commentators has interpreted two Epistles of St. Paul by the method of paragraphs and tables.

128. [Revelation 14:7.]

Notes by H. B. Nisbet

Johann Gottfried Herder

Johann Gottfried Herder (1744–1803) was born in East Prussia and studied theology at Königsberg, where he attended lectures by Kant and became friendly with Hamann. A tireless reader and prolific writer from an early age, his "fragments" *On Recent German Literature* (1766–67) and *Critical Forests* (1769) respond mainly to Lessing and Winckelmann, but already display a vast range of learning, and show the influence of Hamann. Leaving Riga, where he held a position as a teacher and preacher, in 1769, Herder traveled to France, Holland, and Hamburg, and in 1770 met Goethe in Strasbourg. His volume *On German Character and Art* (1773), which includes his essays on Shakespeare and on Ossian and folk poetry, also contains Goethe's essay "On German Architecture" (The German Library, volume 79). Herder's specific contribution to the study of literature, art, and culture was the historical relativism that made him able to show the value and function of the art of different nations and periods. He was also largely responsible for the interest in folk poetry that seized his younger contemporaries, including Goethe and Bürger. In 1776, Herder moved to Weimar as general superintendent of the church, and remained there for the rest of his life, in spite of many frustrations, including the obstacles to reforms of the church and the schools, and his eventual estrangement from Goethe. His enormous and diverse output includes works on the plastic arts, theology, linguistics, psychology, and history. His most important later works are the *Ideas for the Philosophy of the History of Mankind* (1784–91), and the *Letters for the Advancement of Humanity* (1793–97), which revise his earlier relativism in an attempt to reconcile it with a belief in progress. In his *Kalligone* (1800), he took issue with Kant's (and indirectly Schiller's) aesthetics.

The standard edition is *Sämtliche Werke,* ed. Bernhard Suphan et al., 33 vols. (Berlin: Weidmann, 1877–1913). For a useful introduction in English, see Wulf Koepke, *Johann Gottfried Herder* (Boston: Twayne, 1987).

On Recent German Literature: First Collection of Fragments

2. On the Ages of a Language

Just as the human being appears in various stages of life, so time changes everything. The whole human race, indeed, even the inanimate world, every nation, and every family are subject to the same law of change: from bad to good, from good to excellent, from excellent to worse and to bad: this is the cycle of all things. Thus it is with every art and science: they germinate, bear buds, blossom, and wilt. So it is too with language. That this has been perceived as little as possible until now, that the different ages have been constantly confused, is shown by the plans so often made for developing one stage from another: the child is brought on prematurely to grow an adolescent beard; the lively youth is fettered by gravity befitting a mature man; and the old man is supposed to return to his childhood, or even to possess the virtues of all ages. Perverse attempts, which would be harmful had not nature hindered many detrimental designs by combining them with sufficient weaknesses. A young graybeard, and a lad who is a man, are unbearable, and a monster who wants to be everything at the same time is nothing completely.

A language in its childhood bursts out with monosyllabic, rough, and high-pitched sounds. A nation in its first wild origins stares at everything like a child; alarm, fear, and then admiration are the only feelings of which both are capable, and the language of these feelings is sounds—and gestures. Their organs are still unused to making sounds, so these sounds are high-pitched and powerfully stressed; as sounds and gestures are signs of passions and feelings, they are vehement and strong; their language speaks for the eyes and ears, for the senses and passions, and they are capable of greater passions, because their way of life is full of danger and death and wildness: they therefore understand the language of emotion better than we, who only know this age from later accounts and inferences.

For just as memory cannot inform us about our earliest childhood, so it is equally impossible to hear news from this first age of language, when there was still no speech, but rather sounds; when there was still little thought, but all the more feeling; and when therefore there was writing least of all.

Just as the child or the nation changed, so did language with it. Horror, fear, and amazement gradually disappeared as familiarity with things increased; people became intimate with them and gave them names, names that were derived from nature and imitated it as much as possible in the sound. Where visible objects were concerned, gesture still had to help out a good deal, for the sake of comprehension, and their whole dictionary was still sensuous. Their linguistic organs became more flexible, and the stress less strident. They sang, therefore, as many peoples still do and as ancient historians consistently assert their ancestors did. They mimed, seeking the aid of body and gestures. At that time language was still very unordered in its connections and irregular in its forms.

The child grew up into a youth: wildness died down to civic calm, the way of living and thinking laid aside its roaring fire, and the song of language flowed sweetly from the tongue as from the tongue of Homer's Nestor,[1] and murmured in the ear. Concepts that were not sensuous were adopted into the language, but as is to be expected of course, they were called by familiar sensuous names. Hence the first languages must have been full of images and rich in metaphors.

And this youthful age of language was simply the poetic. People sang in everyday life, and the poet only raised his stresses in a rhythm chosen for the ear; language was sensuous and rich in bold images; it was still an expression of passion; it was still unfettered in its connections, the period fragmented as it pleased!—Behold! that is the language of poetry, the poetic period. The finest youthful blossom of language was the age of the poets, when the singers and rhapsodists sang. Since as yet there were no writers, they immortalized the most remarkable deeds in songs. They taught by means of hymns, in which were contained the battles and victories, fables and maxims, laws and mythology, known to that age of the world. That this was so among the Greeks the book titles of the most ancient lost writers prove, and the oldest reports attest that it was so in every people.

The older the youth becomes, and the more grave wisdom and judicious sobriety his character develops, the more he becomes a man and ceases to be a youth. A language in its manly age is not really poetry any more, but rather beautiful prose. Every peak of development tends to a new decline, and if we assume one point in time in language as the most poetic, then poetry must sink again after that point. The more it becomes art, the more it distances itself from nature. The more reserved and judicious manners become, and the less effect passions have in the world, the more subjects poetry loses. The more artifice is devoted to the period, the more inversions are done away with, the more civil and abstract words are introduced, and the more rules a language receives, the more perfect it may become, but the more it loses true poetry.

Now the period was born, and rounded: by dint of practice and observation this epoch, at its best, became the age of beautiful prose, which employed the wealth of its youth moderately, limited the willfulness of idioms without completely abolishing it, moderated the freedom of inversions without yet taking on itself the fetters of a philosophical construction, tuned down the poetic rhythm to the melodiousness of prose, and hemmed in the previously free arrangement of the words more into the roundedness of a period. This is the manly age of language.

Old age knows only rectitude instead of beauty. This rectitude detracts from its wealth, as Spartan discipline bans Attic sensuality. The more grammarians lay inversions in fetters, the more the philosopher seeks to distinguish between synonyms or throw them out, the more he is able to introduce direct instead of figurative words— the more language loses its charms, but also the less it will transgress. A foreigner in Sparta sees no disorder and no delights. This is the Philosophical Age of language.

Translated by Timothy J. Chamberlain

Notes

Original title: "Von den Lebensaltern einer Sprache," in *Über die neuere Deutsche Literatur. Erste Sammlung von Fragmenten* (1767).

1. [*Iliad* 1.249.]

Critical Forests: First Grove

Chapter 6

The great Winckelmann has shown us the beauty of Greek nature so masterfully that surely no one but a man devoid of knowledge and feeling will deny "their supreme law in the visual arts was beauty."[1] Nonetheless, it seems to me the first source and some of its veins still remain to be discovered. *Why* did the Greeks reach such heights in the cultivation of beauty that in this they take the prize in competition with all peoples of the earth? Lessing adds to this claim[2] when he shows us the Greek, in contrast to artistic taste in our time, as an artist who imposed narrow limitations on art: "his artist represented only the beautiful."

Only the beautiful? To be sure, my reader, I have read the wise animadversions and qualifications raised in a very scholarly way against this statement by Lessing; but he must first be understood before he is refuted. Does he intend to say that the Greeks depicted nothing ugly? I don't think so, and wish he hadn't written at another point,[3] "they never depicted a Fury." For if his thesis went that far, Klotz[4] would have the opportunity to adduce an example in every one of his future writings to show that the ancients also depicted Furies, Medusas, and so on—something surely everyone knows who has as much as passed through a museum.

Or does Lessing mean that the ancients had a law that even ugly figures were to be depicted as beautiful, because whatever is depicted must be beautiful? I know he has also been understood in this way, with the beautiful Medusa then cited as a sufficient example; but this is not how the meaning is to be taken.

This is how I understand him. The prevailing or supreme taste of the Greeks did not lie in representing and depicting some arbitrary object so as to prove one's worth simply by means of *imitation,* nor in showing oneself an artist simply by creating a likeness to the original. Rather, in these things their taste made the beautiful the supreme object, so that they didn't simply show off mere technique. And when understood in this way, the following qualifications ensue of necessity.

In order to gauge the *prevailing* taste, one mustn't cite every single example: for the Pausons, Pyreicuses, and other rhyparographers are irrelevant as long as they don't found schools and are not yet able to vie with the depicters of beauty for preeminence.

In order to gauge the prevailing taste, one doesn't have to take the words of a lawgiver,[5] a political philosopher, as proof of common practice: for they say what should be, not what is.

The best witnesses to the prevailing taste are the public works of art, the regulations of the authorities. Since Lessing concentrates on these, one teaches him nothing new by stating the opinion: " 'The Greek artist depicted only the beautiful'—Statements by writers and examples of artists bearing witness to the contrary *compel* me to impose narrower limitations on this observation, and to *confine* it merely to public monuments."[6] I think these were Lessing's prime sources, and he himself perhaps seeks regulations where there are none.[7]

In order to gauge a prevailing taste, one should further not take works from temples, where religion was the main motivation, or religious taste could not be changed. Lessing makes this qualification himself,[8] and this tones down his thesis so much that, I confess, he can surely mean as much or as little by it as he wants.

Finally, in order to gauge the prevailing taste one surely mustn't treat all periods alike, but rather focus on those in which taste is already formed, and does not appear corrupted by any imitation of bad examples. In the first case no law has yet been given, in the second it has for a while been swept aside, but nonetheless still remains the law of the land.—And these qualifications having been made, Lessing certainly can lay down as a law "that among the ancients beauty was the supreme law of the visual arts."

But among which ancients? Since when? For how long? With what subordinate and coordinate laws? And why did it become the supreme law preeminently among the Greeks, above all other nations? More weighty questions, and in the case of the last even Winckelmann seems to me barely adequate.

Lessing mentions two circumstances that bear on this issue: that "among the ancients the arts, too, were subject to the civil code," and that "the visual arts can have a particular influence on the character of a nation."[9] But he was only able to explain what he meant by these two points in passing. It must be possible to deduce from its causes how it was that among the Greeks laws governing art were not just *permitted*—which is as far as Lessing goes—but *necessary;* that among them art and poetry and music belonged much more to the essential nature of the state than now; that therefore the state could not exist without them, as its mainspring at that time, nor they without the state; that therefore the influence of the nation on art, and of art on the nation was not merely physical and psychological, but to a large extent political; that therefore among the Greeks for so many reasons, and not merely because of their national character, but also because of their education and way of life, and on account of the stage of development of their culture, their religion, and their state, the depiction of beauty was able to exercise greater influence, and had to absorb more influences. . . .

Chapter 9

Lessing seeks to grasp the first distinction between poetry and the visual arts in the *moment* to which art must confine itself by virtue of its material limitations.[10] This moment, therefore, cannot be chosen with too great a regard for its effect, and is only effective if it gives free rein to the imagination. Thus far all critics who have reflected on the limitations of the arts have come; but the use to which Lessing puts the observation belongs to him alone. For if art is bound to a moment, and if this moment persists, then, he says, let it not choose the climax of an emotion, otherwise the imagination can find nothing beyond it; let it express nothing transitory, for it immortalizes this transitory state.

There is nothing, on the other hand, "to compel the poet to compress his picture into one moment. He may, if he so chooses, take up each action at its origin and pursue it through all possible variations to its end. Each variation that would cost the artist a separate work costs the poet but a single pen stroke," and so forth.[11] This distinguishing mark, as I say, has long since been noted; but Lessing puts it to practical use.

Let art therefore select nothing transitory for its momentary object.[12] But what is actually, in nature, not transitory, what in nature is completely permanent? We live in a world of phenomena that follow on one another, in which one moment destroys the other. Everything in the world is bound to the wings of time, and movement, change, effect is the soul of nature. Metaphysically, therefore—but let's not talk metaphysically, let's talk of the senses. And as the senses understand it, according to the phenomena perceived by our eyes, are there not unceasing, lasting objects enough, which art should therefore imitate? Certainly, there are such objects, and these are so to speak all bodies in their quality as bodies. However much their successive moments and conditions may change, however quickly each moment of their existence may be altering them, this moment nonetheless doesn't pass away *before our eyes.* Therefore the artist can deliver phenomena for our eyes: let him depict bodies, let him imitate *lasting nature.*

But what if this lasting nature is also at the same time dead nature? What if the intransitoriness of a body attests precisely to its inanimateness? Then, if this lasting intransitoriness of the object is made the mark of art without qualification—what would that mean but that art would be deprived of *its best expression* by this principle? Imagine, reader, whatever expression of the soul you want in a body, and it's transitory. The more it characterizes a human passion, the more it denotes a changeable condition of human nature, and the more its "prolongation in art gives it an unnatural appearance, which makes a weaker impression the more often we look at it, until the whole object finally causes us disgust or horror."[13] However much room the imagination is left, however high it flies, in the end it has to reach a limit from which it must reluctantly return; indeed, the faster it goes, the more pregnant the chosen moment, the sooner it reaches this goal. As much as I can say to a laughing La Mettrie, when I see him still laughing the third or fourth time: "You're a fop!"—in the end I will equally well be able to say to Myron's cow:[14] "Be on your way then, why are you just standing there?" And however much cause I have to find a screaming, incessantly screaming Laocoön intolerable in the end, I will have just as much cause, just a little later, to become weary of the sighing Laocoön because he's still sighing. In the end I will react the same way to the standing Laocoön, because he's still standing and hasn't sat down yet; and finally to a rose by Huysum because it's still blooming, and hasn't wilted yet; ultimately I will grow weary of every imitation of nature by art. In nature, everything is transitory: the soul's passion and the body's feeling, the action of the soul and the movement of the body, every state of mutable finite nature. If art has only a moment into which everything is to be confined, then every changeable state of nature is unnaturally immortalized by art. Thus with this principle all imitation of nature by art ceases.

Nothing is more dangerous than to make a general principle of a delicate nuance of our taste, and then to make this principle into a law. If one good aspect results, so do ten unfortunate for sure.

Lessing wanted to exclude the highest degree of emotion from the forming of a statue: good! But the cause he gave for this was that this passion is transitory: not so good! Finally he made of this cause a principle: let art express nothing that cannot be imagined except as a transitory phenomenon—and this leads furthest astray. With this principle art is made inert and inanimate, it is sunk into that lazy repose that could only please medieval monastic saints: it loses the whole soul of its expression.

And what would the alleged reason for such cruel critical medicine be? Because a transitory phenomenon, whether agreeable or otherwise, receives by prolongation in art such an unnatural appearance that *each time we look at it again*[15]—I can't go on! When we look at it again! Each time we look at it again! Who will take this into account? Who, in his youth, will deny himself a pleasure because *in the end, each* time it is enjoyed the pleasure must be diminished? Who will nag at himself, quarrel with his feelings, instead of abandoning himself undisturbed to the agreeable present without a thought of the future? Without calling forth for himself shades from the future to shoo away his joys? All joys of the senses are only meant *for the first time they are viewed,* and the phenomena of the fine arts are also meant for that first view alone. "La Mettrie, who had himself portrayed in painting as a second Democritus, seems to you to be laughing only the first few times you look at him. You look at him more often and the philosopher turns into a fop. His laugh becomes a grin." Maybe! But what if this laughing Democritus only wanted to be portrayed for that first view? What then? If already at first sight his laughter was nothing but contemptible and disagreeable, and if this was enough to turn the philosopher in retrospect into a fop, and his face of Democritus into a grin: then to be sure it looks bad for him and the artist. He should have skipped his laughter—but on account of its contemptible, disagreeable aspect, not on account of its permanence. But if this wasn't the case, if the laughing philosopher only seems like a fop to you after repeated visits—then, my delicate friend! imagine you haven't seen him before, or else avoid him. But don't for this reason forbid us our first view of him, and still less form a law that in future no philosopher should be painted laughing. Why? Because laughter is something transitory. Every condition in the world is more or less transitory. Sulzer[16] had himself engraved with head inclined, chin supported on his finger, and a deep philosophical expression. According to Lessing's principle one would have to address his picture:

"Philosopher, will you have thought out your aesthetics soon? Aren't you getting cramps in your inclined head and your sublime finger? Sighing Laocoön, how long will you sigh? As often as I see you your chest is still constricted, your abdomen drawn in? A transitory moment, a sigh, is prolonged in you contrary to nature." Jupiter casting thunderbolts, Diana striding, Hercules carrying Atlas, and every figure with the least action and movement, indeed merely in any physical condition is by the same token prolonged contrary to nature, for none of these lasts forever. Thus, if the preceding opinion becomes a principle, the essence of art is destroyed.

This therefore cannot be a valid reason why art mustn't express any heightened emotion; the taste that decrees this isn't delicate so much as fastidious.

If we accept Aristotle's categories, every work of the visual arts is a *work* and not an energy.[17] It is there all at once in all its parts, its essence consists not in change, in succession, but in contiguous coexistence. If therefore the artist has perfectly satisfied the first but whole and most exact view, which must deliver a complete idea, then he has attained his purpose, the effect remains forever: it is a *work*. It stands there all at once, and so let it be contemplated: let the first view be permanent, exhaustive, eternal. Only human weakness, the slackness of our senses, and the unpleasantness of prolonged concentration makes perhaps a second, perhaps a hundredth repetition of this view necessary in the case of works that require profound investigation; but for all this, all these repetitions nonetheless only compose one view. What I have seen, I do not need to see again, and if something becomes disagreeable to me only by *repetition* and not by the whole *unity of its appearance,* the fault lies not in art, but in the jadedness of my taste. Now can this jadedness be made a principle of art? Can it even serve as a valid cause for another thesis?

Therefore I eliminate this cause of Lessing's as a cause and as a law, and think it suffices that extreme emotion is disagreeable to the first view, and as it were constricts the imagination too much. It must consequently be avoided in art, at least as the main object viewed. If the effect of art is a *work,* formed for a single but as it were eternal gaze, then this single view must contain as much beauty for the eye and as much that is fruitful to the imagination as it can. This is the source of the infinite and immeasurable quality of this visual art, which gives it an advantage over all other fine arts:

namely, a supreme ideal beauty for the eye, and for the imagination the quiet repose of Greek expression. For both are the means to maintain us in the arms of an eternal ecstasy, and in the profundity of a long, blissful view.

"How does it come about," asks an aesthetician,[18] "that an ideal beauty exists only in painting and sculpture, an *aliquid immensum infinitumque*[19] which artists take as an imaginary model, and poets do not?" I don't believe he has answered this question regarding art by his observation "that the ideal beauty is most difficult to attain in the fine arts," for the question remains the same: "Why must so difficult a goal be reached?" For no other reason, I believe, than because art delivers only *works* that represent a single moment and are formed for one great view, and that therefore must make their moment so pleasing, so beautiful, that nothing surpasses it, so that the soul sunk in its contemplation may repose, so to speak, and lose track of passing time. Those fine arts and letters, on the other hand, whose effect lies in time and in the alternation of individual moments, whose essence is energy, don't need to deliver something supreme at any one moment, and don't intend to absorb our soul into this momentary climax. For if they did, it would destroy the pleasure that lies in the succession, the connection, and alternation of these moments and actions, where each moment therefore is useful only as a link in the chain, and no further. If one of these moments, conditions, and actions becomes an island, a climax cut off from the rest, the essence of energetic art is lost. If on the other hand the one eternal moment of visual art is not such that it could afford an eternal view, then its essence is likewise not attained. In bodies, this single eternal view is perfect beauty, and insofar as the soul is supposed to have an effect through the body, it is the lofty repose of the Greeks. This is midway between inert inaction and agitated exaggerated effect; the imagination can drift further in both directions, and so is entertained longest by this view of the soul. Inert inaction cuts off the thread of the thoughts with one snip; the figure is dead, who will awaken it? The exaggerated expression again shortens the flight of fantasy on the other side; for who can think of something still higher beyond the highest? But the blissful repose of Greek expression sways our soul to both sides: and in its view we imagine at one and the same time the quiet sea from which this gentle wave of movement has risen, and the question: "What if the wave rose higher? What if this Zephyr's breath turned into a tearing storm of passion? How the floods would tower then, and the expression swell up!" So what a breadth of thoughts lies in the view of the quiet repose of Greek expression!

I believe I have found in the essence of art the explanation of two problems. *Why* is beauty the supreme law of the visual arts? Because their effect lies in *contiguity,* is therefore confined to *a single moment,* and its work creates *an eternal view.* Let this single view therefore deliver the highest thing that holds one fast in its arms for eternity—*beauty.*—Physical beauty, however, does not suffice: a soul looks through our eyes, so let a soul also look through the beauty represented to us. In what condition should this soul be? Doubtless in that which can maintain my view eternally, and create for me the longest contemplation. And which is that? No condition of lazy repose, which gives me no food for thought; nothing exaggerated in the expression, which clips the wings of my imagination; but rather movement as it were announcing itself, the beginning dawn, which allows us to look to both sides, and therefore is alone in affording an eternal view.

In this way the concepts of the distinction between the arts are generalized of themselves, and we no longer talk of sculpture and poetry, but in general of arts that deliver *works,* and those whose effect derives from uninterrupted energy. In this respect, what is true of poetry will be true of music and dance as well, for their effect also lies not in *a single view* but rather in a succession of moments, the connection of which makes up precisely the effect of the art: they therefore have quite different laws from those of the visual arts. I therefore can't explain the Roman Laocoön poet[20] by alleging that his *clamores horrendos ad sidera tollit*[21] doesn't show us a crooked screaming mouth and an ugly sight, for of course he wasn't working for the eye, and still less did this feature of his picture become an *eternal view* in the painterly understanding. But what if his whole description, which I regard as a painting *for my soul,* showed me no other inner condition of Laocoön than lies in this scream: doesn't this feature then remain the main image in the poet's picture? When I recall Virgil's Laocoön, do I not every time recall a screaming man? For in *his* pain he has not shown his soul in any other way. Now the viewpoint changes. The essence of poetry, the energetic purpose of the poet, must provide the explanation as to whether this feature of Laocoön, this *single* utterance of his feeling was supposed to become the main image, a lasting impression in my memory. It is not enough that *clamores horrendos ad sidera tollit* is a sublime feature for the ear (if I understand what a feature for the ear is); it must also have been the poet's concern to make it the main image of Laocoön in my imagination. If this is not the case, the poet, even if I don't demand a beautiful image, has still completely failed to make the impression he wanted on me.

It isn't my intention to investigate this in Virgil. I have justified Winckelmann, who (perhaps even only historically speaking) can say: "The artist's Laocoön doesn't scream like Virgil's." I have tested the reason Lessing gives for the distinction between the two arts, and followed it back to the *oneness of the view* in which only the visual arts and no others show themselves. I wish Lessing had made Aristotle's distinction between *work* and *energy* the basis of his entire work, for all the subdistinctions he mentions ultimately come down to this chief distinction.

Chapter 16

As a general point, it must not be thought that a philosopher who undertakes to elaborate the distinction between poetry and one of the fine arts thereby intends a complete explanation of the essence of poetry. Lessing shows what poetry isn't by comparing it to painting, but in order to see what it is in itself in the completeness of its essence, it would have to be compared with *all* its sister arts and sciences, e.g., music, dance, and rhetoric, and distinguished philosophically from them.

"Painting works in space; poetry in time. The former through figures and colors; the latter through articulated sounds. The true subjects of the former are therefore bodies, those of the latter actions." Thus far Lessing has come in his elaboration. Now let a philosophical composer take up his work: how far do poetry and music have common rules, since the effect of both is achieved by succession in time? How does poetry diverge, since it sings about *action*? Let the rhetorician continue: every kind of discourse can depict *action:* so how does poetry do so? How does it do it in its various genres and species?—Finally, put these theories together, and you have the essence of poetry.

Even given the one side of comparison under discussion, however, it seems to me that something is lacking in calculating the essence of poetry.—I take up Lessing's words at the point where he promises "to derive the matter from its first principles."[22]

He reasons thus: "If it is true that in its imitations painting uses completely different means or signs than does poetry, namely figures and colors in space rather than articulated sounds in time, and if these signs must indisputably bear a suitable relation to the thing signified, then signs existing in space can express only objects whose wholes or parts coexist, while signs that follow one another can express only objects whose wholes or parts are consecutive.

"Objects or parts of objects that exist in space are called bodies. Accordingly, bodies with their visible properties are the true subjects of painting.

"Objects or parts of objects that follow one another are called actions. Accordingly, actions are the true subjects of poetry."

Perhaps this whole chain of reasoning would be infallible if it started out from a stable point. But now let us at it. "If it is true that in its imitations painting uses completely different means or signs than does poetry"—true indeed!

"Namely figures and colors in space rather than articulated sounds in time." Already less precise! For articulated sounds are not to poetry what colors and figures are to painting!

"If these signs must indisputably bear a suitable relation to the thing signified"—with precisely this point all comparison falls away. Articulated sounds in poetry do not bear the same relation to the thing they signify as do figures and colors in painting to what they signify. Can therefore two so disparate things provide a third, a first principle of the distinction between and essence of the two arts?

The signs of painting are *natural:* the connection between the sign and the thing it signifies is based in the qualities of the thing signified itself. The signs of poetry are *arbitrary:* the articulated sounds have nothing in common with the thing they are supposed to express, but are only *accepted* as signs by a general convention. The natures of the two kinds of sign are therefore completely unalike, and the *tertium comparationis* disappears.

Painting works completely in space, by contiguity, by signs that show the thing *naturally.* But poetry does not work *in the same way by means of successivity* as painting by means of space. What rests *on the sequence* of its articulated sounds is not the same as what rested on the coexistence of the parts in painting. The successivity of its signs is nothing but the *conditio sine qua non,* and therefore simply a limitation, whereas the coexistence of signs in painting is the nature of the art, and the basis of the beauty of painting. Even if poetry, to be sure, works by means of consecutive sounds, that is, words, the consecutiveness of the sounds, the successivity of the words is not the central point of their effect.

In order to clarify this distinction, a comparison must be made between two arts that work by natural means, between painting and music. Here one can say: painting works completely *by means of space,* just as music does *by means of time.* What the coexistence of colors and figures is in painting, namely the basis of beauty, the consecutiveness of sounds is in music, the basis of euphony. As in painting the pleasure, the effect of the art rests on the sight of coexistent things, so in music the successivity, the connection and modulation of sounds is the means to musical effect. So as painting, I can continue, can only awaken the concept of time in us by illusion, let it never make this secondary work its main business, that is, to work as painting must by means of color and yet in time, for if it does, the essence and all the effect of the art is lost. The color piano bears witness to this.[23] Equally, music, on the other hand, which works completely by means of time, should never make its main business the musical description of objects in space, as inexperienced bunglers do. Let painting never stray from the coexistent, music never from succession: for both these are the *natural* means of their respective effects.

With poetry, however, it's different. Here what is natural in the signs, such as the letters, sound, sequence of tones, makes little or no contribution to the effect of poetry; the meaning that by arbitrary agreement lies in the words is everything. The successivity of sounds can't be reckoned as essential to poetry in the way that the coexistence of colors is to painting. For the signs do *not* have the same relation to the thing signified *at all.*

The foundation is shaky: how will the building be? Before we see this, let us first secure the foundation in a different manner. Painting works *in space,* and by means of an artful representation of space. Music, and all the energetic arts, do not work simply *in* but also by means of time, by means of an artful temporal variation of sounds. Couldn't the essence of poetry also be reduced to a similar main concept, since it works on the soul by means of arbitrary signs, through the meaning of words? Let us call the means to this effect *force,* and just as in metaphysics *space, time,* and *force* are three fundamental concepts, just as the mathematical sciences can all be derived from one of these concepts, so too in the theory of the fine arts and letters let us say: the arts that deliver *works* work in space; the arts that work by means of *energy,* in time; the various species of fine letters, or rather the only one, poetry, works by means of *force.* By *force,* which happens to be present in words, by force, which may pass through the ear, but works directly on the soul. This *force* is the essence of poetry, not coexistence or succession.

Now comes the question: which objects can this poetic force bring to the soul better, objects coexisting in space or objects succeeding one another in time? And to speak in terms of the senses again: in which medium does poetic force work more freely, in space or in time?

It works *in space* by making its whole discourse *sensuous.* With no sign must the sign itself, but rather the meaning of the sign, be felt; the soul mustn't feel the medium of the force, the words, but rather the force itself, *the meaning.* That is the first species of intuitive cognition. But poetry also brings so to speak each object visibly before the soul, that is, it assembles enough characteristics that in a single moment it makes the impression of bringing the object before the eyes of the imagination, creating the illusion of sight. This is the second species of intuitive cognition and the essence of poetry. The first can be a property of any lively discourse that isn't quibbling or philosophy, the second only of poetry, and makes up its essence, *the sensuously perfect in discourse.*[24] One can say, therefore, that the first essential quality of poetry really is a *species of painting, sensuous representation.*

It works *in time,* for it is *discourse.* Not simply inasmuch as discourse is the *natural* expression of passions, movement, etc., for this is only peripheral to poetry, but above all in that it affects the soul by means of the rapidity of its representations, their coming and going, and has the effect of energy partly in its alternation, partly in the whole that it builds up through succession in time. The first quality poetry shares with other varieties of discourse; but it is the second—that it is capable of alternation, of a melody of representations, as it were, and of a whole, whose parts are uttered gradually, whose perfection is therefore energized—it is this that makes it a music of the soul, as the Greeks called it; and this second form of successivity Lessing never touched on.

The whole essence of poetry is neither in isolation. Not the energy, the musical, for this can't exist without presupposing the sensuous nature of the representations it *paints* before the soul. But not the painterly either, for it works energetically: precisely by succession it builds into the soul the concept of the sensuously perfect *whole*. Only when both are taken together can I say that the essence of poetry is force whose effect derives *from space* (from objects it makes sensuous) in time (by means of a succession of many parts making up one poetic whole): in short, then, it is *sensuously perfect discourse*.

Having laid down these preconditions let us return to Lessing. For him the most excellent subject of poetry is *actions*—but only he can discover this concept in his concept of succession. I confess I can't.

"Objects or parts of objects that follow one another are actions."[25] How so? However many things I let follow one another, each is a body, an inert sight; succession doesn't suffice to make any of them action. I see time flee away, each moment chase the previous—does that mean I see action? Various natural scenes come before my eyes—isolated, inert, following one another: do I see action? Castel's color piano will never deliver actions by successively playing forth colors, even in waving and serpentine lines;[26] a melodic chain of sounds will never be called a chain of actions. I therefore deny that objects or parts of objects that follow one another are called *actions* at all simply on this account: and I deny equally that the subject of poetry is actions just because it delivers successions.

The concept of the successive is only half the idea of action: action arises when *successivity comes from force*. I imagine a being working in time, I imagine changes that follow one another by the force of a substance—thus arises *action*. And if actions are the subject of poetry, then I wager this subject can never be defined on the basis of the dry concept of succession: *force* is the focal point of its sphere.

And this is the force inherent in the inner nature of words, the magic force that affects my soul by means of the imagination and memory: it is the essence of poetry.—The reader sees that we are where we were, namely that poetry works by means of arbitrary signs; that the force of poetry lies entirely in this arbitrariness, in the meaning of the words; but not in *the sequence of sounds and words*, in the sounds as natural sounds.

Lessing, however, draws all his conclusions from this sequence of sounds and words; only very late does it occur to him that the signs of poetry are *arbitrary*,[27] but even then he doesn't weigh the implications of the objection that poetry works by means of arbitrary signs.

For how does he resolve this objection? By claiming "that the description of physical objects leads to the loss of illusion, the chief accomplishment of poetry, and that therefore discourse in itself, but not the sensuously most perfect discourse, poetry, can depict bodies."[28] The matter now seems better placed. Precisely because poetry can't be sufficiently painterly in its depiction of physical objects, it must not depict them. Not in order to avoid being painting, not because it depicts in successive sounds, not because space is the painter's field, and only time that of the poet—I see no cause in all this. As I say, the successivity of the sounds means little to the poet; he doesn't work by means of them as natural signs. But if his *force* leaves him, if he can't create an *illusion* for the soul with his representations independently of his sounds: then indeed the poet is lost, then nothing remains but a painter with words, a symbolic explainer of names. But Lessing's own example is the best witness that the matter is not yet best placed here.[29] If it is Haller's purpose in his poem "The Alps" to acquaint us by means of poetry with the gentian and its blue brother, and the herbs like and unalike it; then to be sure, for this reason alone and none other, he loses the poet's purpose of creating an illusion for me, and I as reader lose my purpose to let myself be deceived. But if I pass from Haller's poems to a botanical textbook, how will I be acquainted with the gentian and its brothers there? How else but again by means of successive sounds, discourse? The botanist will lead me from one part to another, he will elucidate the connection between these parts; he will seek to enumerate to my imagination in parts and as a whole something that, to be sure, the eye takes in at one glance; he will do everything that Lessing's poet is not supposed to do. Will he make himself comprehensible to me? There's no question about it, as long as I understand his words he must make himself clear to me, must create a certain illusion for me. If he can't do this, if I see the thing clearly merely in its details, but not as a whole, intuitively, then I will be able to prescribe to the author of a textbook of botany all the rules Lessing prescribes to the poet. I will say to him very earnestly:[30] "How do we arrive at a clear conception of an object in space, of an herb? We first look at its parts singly, then the combination of parts, and finally the totality. Our senses perform these various operations with such astonishing rapidity that they seem to us to be but one single operation, and this rapidity is absolutely necessary. . . . Now let us assume that the botanical writer takes us from one part of the object to the other in the best possible order; let us assume that he knows how to make the combination of these parts ever so clear to us; how much time would he use in doing this? That which the eye takes in at a single glance he counts out to us with perceptible slowness, and it often happens that when we arrive at the end of his description we have already forgotten the first features. And yet we are supposed to form a notion of the whole from these features. To the eye, parts once seen remain continually present; it can run over them again and again. For the ear, however, the parts once heard are lost unless they remain in the memory. And even if they do remain there, what trouble and effort it costs to renew all their impressions in the same order and with the same vividness; to review them in the mind all at once with only moderate rapidity, to arrive at an approximate idea of the whole! . . . It may be very nice to recite such descriptions, holding the flower in one's hand; but by themselves they say little or nothing."

That's how Lessing speaks to the poet, and why should I not speak in just the same way to the botanist who merely wants to teach me by means of words? I see no distinction between the two cases: the same object, a body, the same means of depicting it, discourse, the same obstacle in this means, the successivity of discourse, words. Consequently the lecture must apply to him just as well as to anyone who uses words to depict something.

Consequently the reason adduced, "successivity hinders the depiction of bodies," must actually lie outside the range of poetry, since it applies to all discourse, since every form of discourse in such a case intends not to make what is defined comprehensible, as a word, but intuitively known, as a thing.

Consequently within the range of poetry it can provide no true, at least no supreme law, but can only remain a secondary concept from which little or nothing can be deduced.—My whole chain of reasoning begins from a double basis. Firstly, the successive quality in the sounds of poetry is not the *chief,* not the *natural* means of its effect; rather, this means is the power that attaches to these sounds for arbitrary reasons, and affects the soul according to other laws than that of the succession of sounds. Secondly, the successivity of the sounds is not a property of *poetry alone,* but of *every form of discourse,* and can therefore determine or distinguish little of its inner essence. Now if Lessing makes succession the chief basis of the distinction between poetry and painting in his book, can the most correct drawing of their limits be expected?

Chapter 17

In order to get onto a more fruitful path than this dry secondary concept allows, Lessing makes a leap in which I do not follow him. "Poetry depicts by means of successive sounds; consequently it also depicts successions, consequently its subject is successions and actually nothing but successions. Successions are actions; consequently"[31]—consequently Lessing has what he wants, but where can he get it from? He found the concept of action in succession; and he concluded that poetry only depicts progressive objects because it depicts in successive sounds—now where is the chain of reasoning in this? Assuming the succession of sounds in poetry were what the contiguity of colors is in painting: in what relation does the successivity of the sounds stand to the successivity of the objects they depict? To what extent do the two successions keep step? How can it even occur to one to make the comparison? And how much less can one deduce the one from the other?—And even if it did depict successions, why must these successions be actions? And so forth. The drawing of the limits according to such a sketch can hardly be correct.

Hardly correct on the side of painting. "Its essence is to depict bodies"—I'm aware at least of more progressive actions in painting than the example Lessing gives, namely a drapery whose folds fall in such a way as to unite two moments.[32]

Still less however on the side of poetry, where little or nothing follows from the successivity of the sounds. It doesn't follow that poetry should depict no bodies: for if successive sounds cannot awaken the concept of coexisting things, then I don't see how any discourse, as merely audible speech, could produce the effect of *intuitive* cognition, for I would say, *images* are not audible. Then I don't see how discourse can awaken the concepts of *connected* images, for the successive sounds are not connected. Finally, I also don't see how a whole such as the ode, the proof, the tragedy, could arise in the soul *out of many partial concepts*. For the whole succession of sounds makes no such whole, for "the parts once heard are always lost."[33] So all or nothing can be deduced from this premise.

Still less does it follow *from these arguments* that all descriptive poetry is inviable, unpoetic.[34]

Still less from *this,* that the essence of poetry is progression, that poetry must only use one single characteristic of bodies, that unity of the painterly epithets is its rule.[35]

It doesn't even follow that "only on these principles can the grand style of Homer be defined and explained." I'm denying Lessing much—when it comes down to it, everything—but that doesn't mean I deny all the things that he alone builds on this foundation.— May I begin with Homer?

"Homer represents nothing but progressive actions. He depicts bodies and single objects only when they contribute toward these actions, and then only by a single trait. Even when Homer is forced by peculiar circumstances to fix our attention longer on a single object, by means of countless artistic devices he places this single object in a series of stages, in each of which it has a different appearance."[36] Beautiful! Splendid! Homer's true manner!—Only, that Homer chose this manner because he wanted *to depict using successive sounds,* because he despaired of depicting physical objects any other way, because he had to worry that even if he led us from one part of an object to another in the finest order, and managed to make the connection between these parts ever so clear, though the same parts observed in nature would constantly remain clear to the eye, yet for the ear, once heard, they would be lost, and with them the efforts of the poet—that Homer set his objects in a series of stages on *this* account has never occurred to me when reading Homer. . . .

However excellent Homer's language may be, though each word provides an image, progressing as rapidly as Diana in stride, without any of its relations being interrupted, if this rapid progression is supposed to be there in order so to speak to lessen the spatial hindrance, destroy it, in order to awaken thereby the illusion of seeing a *spatial* object, a body in space—no discourse can do this. Homer will surely hardly have remained so faithful to his progressive manner *to this end;* he will not have used a single trait for each thing *to this end,* least of all have chosen *to this end* the technique of consecutive development, "in order that the parts of the object keep pace with the flow of the discourse." No discourse can do this; still less does the discourse of the poet want to, least of all did the first among poets want to. His whole manner shows that he does not progress in order to give us by means of succession a *picture of the whole,* whatever that may be, but rather he progresses through the parts because he was completely unconcerned about the picture of the whole.

I wouldn't want for the world to have attributed the wrong

meaning to Lessing; I agree with him about the observation, but am perplexed by his conclusions and associations in explaining it. If anyone finds this distinction inconsiderable—it doesn't matter to me; it will seem considerable to others.

Homer always progresses in his actions because he *has to progress in them,* because all these partial actions are pieces of his whole actions, because he is an epic poet. I therefore don't need to get to know Juno's chariot, and Agamemnon's scepter, and Pandarus's bow[37] except insofar as they are supposed to contribute to the effect on my soul, when tied in to the action. That's why I hear the story of the bow—not as a *substitute* for a painting, but to plant in me in advance a notion of his strength, of the might of his arm, and with that the power of his sinew, of his arrow, of his shot. Then when Pandarus takes out his bow, strings it, sets the arrow to the string—shoots!—woe to Menelaus whom the arrow from such a bow strikes, we know its power. Lessing can therefore not say Homer was concerned about the picture, and only the picture of the bow when he told its story. This was the least of his concerns. The strength, the power of the bow was his business, that, and not the form of the bow belongs to the poem; that, and no other quality was supposed to contribute energetically to the effect, so that later, when Pandarus shoots, when the string whirs, the arrow strikes—we feel the arrow all the more. It is because of this energy that is the main object of a poem, that Homer allows himself to stroll from the battle to the hunt, and tell the story of the bow—for I see no other way to present this notion in all its strength except by the story. From an image we can really only learn form, and have to then deduce size from form and strength from size; from a story we learn this strength directly—and if the sole concern of the energetic artist, of the poet, is this strength, why should he burden himself with other labors? Let the painter paint image, form; the poet shall produce the effect of strength, of energy.—Homer does this, too, from the beginning to the end of the description; though not if I read him in the disguise in which Lessing clothes Pandarus's shot. In that disguise only a successive but not an energetic image can be discerned, but this energy is the main purpose of the poet, so that the successive sounds don't create the illusion of a painting, but each sound creates that of *energy,* so that we are supposed to *jump* when such a bow finally strikes.

The same is true of Agamemnon's scepter: I don't see its story at all "as an artistic device, by means of which the poet causes us to linger over a single object without entering into a tiring description of its parts."[38] His scepter is an ancient, regal, divine scepter! The notion is supposed to have an effect; I am unconcerned about all other artistic devices and allegories.

Juno's chariot is described.[39] Why? Because of course without the poet I haven't seen this chariot, because I have to get to know it in order to know a heavenly chariot. Why is it put together? Because of course we never get to know a heavenly chariot as well as when it first lies there in its parts and is then assembled. It is assembled, therefore, in order to depict the excellence of this divine chariot, the inner worth of all its parts, the artifice of its construction—but not in order to collect these parts successively, since one can't see them in coexistence. The assembling is no artistic device here, no quid pro quo, used as a means to give us the whole; it is no purpose of the poet to put together the sight as a whole; in the *assembling* itself lies the energy of the speech; nothing more. With each part we're supposed to exclaim: splendid! divine! regal!—if this is so, then the whole notion is sensuously perfect in our soul; the whole with its parts was no image for me—let a coachman learn that.—The chariot is together, the energy thus consummated: I exclaim again: splendid! divine! regal! and let Juno and Minerva drive off.

Achilles' shield[40] *develops* beneath Vulcan's hand. Why? Because it's supposed to, of course! Achilles needs weapons; Thetis implores Vulcan for them; he promises, stands up, works—why should he not work? In the whole of Homer's poem the gods are active: their scenes alternate with those of the humans. Now it is night, the action pauses, we haven't seen Vulcan for some time, since he appeared as the limping cupbearer of the gods. Achilles has lost his weapons with Patroclus, now let Thetis go to Vulcan, now Vulcan can forge; the shield is in development.—The whole scene belongs to the action of the poem, to the motion of the epic, and is not a figure that sticks out in the poem, nor a peculiarity of Homer's manner. In the development, in the creation of the shield lies indeed all the power of the energy, the whole purpose of the poet. With each figure Vulcan sculpts I admire the creative god, with each description of the measurements and the breadth I perceive the might of the shield being made for Achilles, for which the reader caught up in the interest of the action waits as eagerly as Thetis.

In short, I know of no successions in Homer that are there as artistic devices for making the best of a bad job, on account of an image, a depiction: they are the essence of his poem, they are the body of the epic action. In every trait of its development must lie energy, Homer's purpose; with every other hypothesis about artistic devices, disguises designed to avoid coexistent depiction, I lose Homer's tone. I know this is a major reproach, that no greater hindrance can be placed in the path of the force of a poet than not reading in his tone; but I don't retract my reproach on that account. Anyone who wants to see in the assembling of Juno's chariot and in the stories of the bow and the scepter and in the development of the shield nothing but an artistic device to escape a physical image, doesn't know what the action of a poem is; on him Homer has wasted his energy. When Homer needs a physical image, he depicts it, even if it were a Thersites; he knows of no artistic devices, of no poetic tricks and perils: progression is the soul of his epic.

Chapter 18

But now Homer isn't the only poet. Soon after him there came Tyrtaeus, Anacreon, Pindar, Aeschylus, etc. His επος, his progressive narrative, was transformed more and more into a μελος, into something lyrical, and then into an ειδος, a painting—genres that, however, still remained poetry. A lyrical singer (μελοποιος) and a lyric painter (ειδοποιος), Anacreon and Pindar, may therefore be set against the narrative poet (εποποιος) Homer.

Homer writes narrative poetry: "It happened! it came to pass!" So with him everything can be action, and must hasten to action. The energy of his muse strives in this direction: marvelous, moving *events* are his world. His is the creative word, "It came to pass!" Anacreon hovers between song and narrative: his narrative becomes a little song, his little song an επος of the god of love. His can therefore be the phrase, "There was!" or "I want!" or "Thou shalt!" as long as his μελος rings with pleasure and joy. The energy, the muse of each of his songs is a happy feeling.

Pindar has in mind a great lyric painting, the labyrinthine structure of an ode, which is supposed to become an energetic whole precisely by its apparent digressions, by secondary figures variously illumined. Here no part is supposed to appear for its own sake, but each is ordered with a view to the whole: an ειδος, a poetic painting in which the artist, not the art, is already visible everywhere. "I sing!"

Now how may they be compared? How different the ideal whole

of Homer, Anacreon, Pindar! How unalike the work on which they labor! The one wants to do nothing but compose: he narrates, he conjures, the whole event is his work, he is a poet whose subject is former times. The second does not want to speak; out of him sings joy; the expression of a pleasant feeling is his whole. The third speaks in person so that he will be heard: the whole of his ode is a building with symmetry and lofty art.—If each can arrive at his purpose in his own way, represent to me his whole perfectly, create for me an illusion in *this particular vision*—what more do I want?

The hypothesis has long been accepted, and in itself is innocent, that the whole of each kind of poem can be regarded as a kind of painting, building, or artwork, in which all parts should contribute to the effect of its main purpose, the whole. In all, the main purpose is poetic illusion, but in each in a different way. The lofty, marvelous illusion conjured up for me by the epic isn't the small sweet feeling with which the Anacreontic song wants to animate me; nor the tragic emotion in which I am put by a tragedy—yet each works to create its own illusion, in its own way, with its own means, to represent something intuitively in the most perfect degree; whether this something is epic action, or tragic action, or a single Anacreontic feeling, or a completed whole of Pindaric images, or whatever. But everything must be judged within its own limits, by its own means and its own purpose.

No Pindaric ode therefore should be seen as an epic lacking progression; no song as a picture lacking firm contours; no didactic poem as a fable, and no fable as descriptive poetry. As long as we don't want to argue about the one word, *poetry, poem,* every genre of poetry introduced has its own ideal—one a higher, more difficult, greater ideal than the other; but each its own. I must not transfer laws from one genre to another, let alone to poetry as a whole.

If therefore "Homer represents nothing but progressive actions, and only gives a single trait for each body, for each single thing, insofar as it participates in the action,"[41] then that may be adequate to *his* epic ideal. But perhaps an Ossian, a Milton, a Klopstock might have another ideal, where they do not progress with each trait, where their muse chose a different path? Perhaps, then, this progressive quality is simply *Homer's* epic *manner,* not even the manner of *his form of poetry* in general?—The critic should speak a timid "perhaps" here; the genius decides with the strong voice of example.

Still less, when Homer's practice leads me to the observation: "*Homer* depicts nothing but progressive actions," may I immediately top it with the major thesis: "*Poetry* depicts nothing but progressive actions—consequently actions are the true subject of poetry." If I observe in the case of Homer that "he depicts all single objects only when they contribute toward these actions, and then only by a single trait,"[42] then the seal may not immediately be set on it: "Consequently *poetry* also depicts bodies only by suggestion through actions; consequently *poetry* also can use only one single quality of bodies in its progressive imitations," and whatever else is supposed to follow from this in the way of rules about the unity of painterly epithets, restraint in the depiction of physical objects, etc. That these principles do not flow from a principal quality of poetry, e.g., from the successivity of its sounds, from which Lessing derives them, is proven. That they also, even if they all occurred in Homer's practice in the way that Lessing believes, still do not flow from the successivity of poetry in general, but rather from his narrower *epic* purpose, is also demonstrated. Now why should this epic tone of Homer's give tone and principle and law with no restriction to all poetry, as it claims to do in Lessing?

I tremble before the bloodbath that the following theses must cause among ancient and modern poets: "Actions are the true subjects of poetry; poetry depicts bodies, but only by suggestion through actions; each thing only by a single trait," etc.[43] Lessing didn't need to confess that Homer's practice brought him to these theses, one can almost see it in each of them, and yet barely even Homer remains a poet by these standards. From Tyrtaeus to Gleim, and from Gleim back to Anacreon; from Ossian to Milton, and from Klopstock to Virgil—the board is swept clear—terrible gaps. Not to mention the didactic, the painting, the idyllic poets.

Lessing has declared his opposition to a number of them, and on the basis of his principles must oppose more. "The detailed depictions of physical objects, without the above-mentioned Homeric device for transforming what is coexistent in them into what is really consecutive"—it is mentioned above that Homer knew nothing of such a device, and what could a device as a device do to such a great purpose?—"have always been recognized by the best critics as pieces of pedantic trifling, to which little or no genius can be attributed."[44] Of these best critics he adduces Horace, Pope, Kleist, Marmontel; but it seems to me that they don't prove Lessing's point without qualification. The citation from Horace[45] doesn't scold as poetasters those who paint a grove, an altar, a brook, a river, etc., but those who *paint in the wrong place:*

> Inceptis gravibus plerumque & magna professis
> Purpureus, late qui splendeat, unus & alter
> Assuitur pannus, cum lucus & ara Dianae &c.
> Aut flumen Rhenum, aut pluvius describitur arcus.
> Sed nunc non erat his locus.[46]

Pope declared a *purely descriptive* poem a banquet of nothing but sauces;[47] but didn't thereby declare "every detailed description of physical objects," appearing without the Homeric device, as a piece of pedantic trifling without genius. Von Kleist, it seems to me, wanted to place a kind of fable in his "Spring"—a plan is already in it insofar as his poem doesn't depict a crowd of images torn from the infinite space of rejuvenated creation at random, now here, now there, but rather, according to a critical essay,[48] it is a promenade depicting objects in the natural order in which they presented themselves to his eyes—he wanted, I say, to place a fable in it; but certainly not to throw out every detailed description of physical objects as pedantic trifling. And Marmontel, finally, to be sure wants more in the way of a moral and less physical images from the idyll, but whether that makes the idyll a sequence of feelings only sparingly interlaced with images, and thus also "a progressive sequence of actions, where bodies are only to be depicted with a single trait"—this I do not know, and according to Lessing it is otherwise not poetry.

Action, passion, feeling! I too love them in poems above all else; I too hate nothing so much as an inert, motionless craze for description, in particular when it takes up pages, sheets, poems; but not with such deadly hatred as to allow each body to participate in the action only by means of an epithet, and then not for the same reason, either, namely that poetry depicts in successive sounds, or because Homer does this or that, and avoids this or that— —not for that reason.

If I learn one thing from Homer, it's that poetry works its effect energetically: never with the purpose of delivering with its final trait (though successively) a work, image, painting, but rather so that already while the energy lasts the whole force must be experienced. I learn from Homer that the effect of poetry never works on the ear by sounds, nor on the memory, according to how long I retain a trait from the succession of details, but rather on my imagination. Therefore from this point, and from no other, must its effect be calculated. Thus I oppose it to painting and regret that Lessing didn't make his focus this central point of the essence of poetry, "effect on our soul, energy."

Translated by Timothy J. Chamberlain

Notes

Original title: *Kritische Wälder. Erstes Wäldchen* (1769). Herder explains the title with reference to Quintilian 10.3.17 to suggest the fragmentary and spontaneous character of his work.

1. [*Laocoön*, chapter 2.]
2. *Laocoön*, pp. 9–22 [chapter 2; Herder's references are to the first edition of *Laocoön* (Berlin, 1766)].
3. *Laocoön*, p. 16 [chapter 2].
4. [Christian Adolf Klotz (1738–71), philologist and professor of Rhetoric at Halle, was an outspoken critic of Lessing's *Laocoön*.]
5. *Laocoön*, p. 11, note b. [chapter 2, note 18], where Lessing cites the words of Aristotle.
6. Klotz, *Geschichte der Münzen* [*History of Coins*], pp. 41–42.
7. *Laocoön*, p. 12 [chapter 2]. I am still unconvinced about the Theban law εις το χειρον.
8. *Laocoön*, p. 103 [chapter 9].
9. *Laocoön*, pp. 12–15 [chapter 2; inexact quote].
10. *Laocoön*, p. 24 [chapter 3].
11. [*Laocoön*, chapter 4.]
12. *Laocoön*, p. 25 [chapter 3].
13. [*Laocoön*, chapter 3; quoted freely.]
14. [Myron of Eleutherae (fifth century B.C.) was famous for his lifelike sculptures of athletes and animals. His cow became proverbial.]
15. *Laocoön*, p. 25 [chapter 3].
16. *Sammlung vermischter Schriften* [Collected miscellaneous writings], part 5.
17. [Aristotle, *Nichomachean Ethics* 1.1.2.]
18. *Litteraturbriefe* [Letters concerning the newest literature], part 4, p. 285 [the author in question is Mendelssohn].
19. ["something immense and infinite."]
20. *Laocoön*, p. 30 [chapter 4; the poet is Virgil].
21. ["He lifted up his voice in horrible cries to the heavens."]
22. *Laocoön*, p. 153 [chapter 16].
23. [Eighteenth-century attempts to coordinate the effects of music and color led to the invention of L. B. Castel's "ocular harpsichord" or color piano.]
24. [This discussion rests on Baumgarten's definition of a poem in his *Meditationes* (1735) as "oratio sensitiva animi perfecta."]
25. *Laocoön*, p. 154 [chapter 16].
26. [A reference to William Hogarth's *Analysis of Beauty* (1753); the waving

line is termed the "line of beauty" (chapter 9), and the serpentine line the "line of grace" (chapter 10).]

27. *Laocoön*, p. 165 [chapter 17].
28. [*Laocoön*, chapter 17; quoted freely.]
29. *Laocoön*, p. 168 [chapter 17].
30. *Laocoön*, pp. 166–67 [chapter 17; with minor changes].
31. *Laocoön*, pp. 153–54 [chapter 16; quoted freely].
32. *Laocoön*, pp. 178–79 [chapter 18].
33. [*Laocoön*, chapter 17.]
34. *Laocoön*, pp. 174–75 [chapter 17].
35. *Laocoön*, pp. 154–55 [chapter 16].
36. *Laocoön*, p. 155 [chapter 16].
37. [*Laocoön*, chapter 16.]
38. *Laocoön*, pp. 159–63 [chapter 16].
39. *Iliad* 5.722–31.
40. *Iliad* 18.478ff.
41. *Laocoön*, p. 155 [chapter 16; quoted freely].
42. All bodies that are supposed to contribute to the effect of Homer's poems are depicted using as many traits as are supposed to contribute to the effect. Homer seldom limits himself to one, even in the case of a stone, a tool, a bow, etc. He always takes the time to adduce as many characteristics of the body as are supposed to be a vehicle of epic energy in this situation. If he describes a thing only with one trait, then this is usually general, and insignificant in this situation. These are the usual epithets he has for each frequently recurring thing.
43. *Laocoön*, pp. 154–55 [chapter 16; quoted freely].
44. *Laocoön*, pp. 173–74 [chapter 17].
45. *Ars poetica* 14ff.
46. [Poems beginning quite grandly and promising much, may have one
     or
     Two purple patches sewn on them as eye-catchers seen at a
     distance,—
     Striking effects, like "the altar and grove of Diana," for instance.
     . . .
     Maybe a view of the Rhine, or a rainbow,—but there was no cause
     for
     Mentioning any of these in the first place.
Translated by Charles E. Passage, in *The Complete Works of Horace* (Quintus Horatius Flaccus) (New York: Ungar, 1983), p. 360.]
47. [*Laocoön*, chapter 17.]
48. [Presumably Nicolai's anonymous *Ehrengedächtnis Herrn E. Chr. v. Kleist* (Berlin, 1760).]

Extract from a Correspondence on Ossian and the Songs of Ancient Peoples

My friend,[1] I share your delight at the translation of Ossian[2] for our language and our nation; it has pleased me as much as an original epic. A poet so full of the grandeur, innocence, simplicity, activity, and bliss of human life must assuredly make an impact—if we do not *in faece Romuli*[3] entirely despair of the effectiveness of good books—and move all those hearts that likewise would dwell in a poor Highland cottage and consecrate their houses to a cottage celebration. And Denis's translation shows such taste, such industry, partly a happy liveliness in the images, partly the vigor of the German language, that I too promptly ranged it among the favorite books in my library, and congratulated Germany on a bard of its own who has but been awakened by the Scottish bard. You used to be so obstinately skeptical of the Scottish Ossian's authenticity,[4] but listen to me now, who once defended him, not obstinately doubting, but nevertheless maintaining that despite all the taste and industry and liveliness and vigor of the German translation, our Ossian is assuredly not the true Ossian any more. I have not enough space to prove it here, so I can only offer my assertion as the Turkish Mufti utters his dictum, and here the name of the Mufti . . .[5]

My arguments against the German Ossian are not, as you kindly imagine, merely a general animus against the German hexameter; for what kind of feeling, of tone or harmony of soul do you credit me with, if I were to have no feeling for Ewald von Kleist's use of the hexameter, for example, or Klopstock's?[6] But—since you have yourself brought it up—what is Klopstock's hexameter doing in Ossian's poetry? *Hinc illae lacrimae*[7] indeed! If only Herr Denis had listened to Ossian's true style with his inner ear as well—Ossian so short and sharp, so strong, so virile, so abrupt in images and feelings; Klopstock's manner so leisurely, so admirable in the way it pours out feelings at length, making them advance in waves, break and die and advance again, letting the words and expressive combinations flow out. What a difference! And what is Ossian, when presented to us in Klopstock's hexameter? In Klopstock's style? I cannot think of two more different poets, even if Ossian were regarded as being a true writer of epics.

But he is not.—But I wanted to do no more than mention that, for I think some critical journal has already discussed this topic, and that has nothing to do with me.[8] What I wanted to do was to remind you that Ossian's poems are songs, songs of the people, folk songs, the songs of an unsophisticated people living close to the senses, songs that have been long handed down by oral tradition. And is that what they are when clad in our fine epic form? How could they possibly be? My friend, my first argument against your obstinate skepticism towards Ossian's originality relied above all upon an inner witness, the spirit of the work itself, which told us with prophetic voice that Macpherson could not possibly have invented something of this kind. Poetry of this kind could not possibly be composed in this century. And now, with that selfsame inner witness I cry just as loudly: "It is really impossible to sing that, impossible for a barbarous mountain people to sing it, hand it on, preserve it in a form such as this! Consequently it is not Ossian, the singer, whose songs were handed down." What do you say to my inner proof? Next time I shall perhaps send you pages on this!

. . . I did not believe you would cling so willfully to your German Ossian, nor try with your detailed comparisons and analyses to force me to admit "that he is certainly as good as the English Ossian." As far as sheer immediate feeling is concerned, what cannot be analyzed out of it! What cannot be proved by a brooding dissection—which at the very least is not the aforementioned immediate feeling. Have you considered in this case what you are usually very sensible of: what a different tone the discourse acquires from the omission of a word, the addition of another, the paraphrase or repetition of a third, from a different accent, glance, or voice? The sense may remain the same, but what of the tone, the color, the immediate feeling of the individuality of place and purpose? And does not all the beauty of the poem, all the spirit and strength of the discourse depend upon these factors? I grant you that our Ossian, as a work of poetry, is as good as the English, indeed better—but just because it is such a beautiful poetic work, it is no longer Ossian the ancient bard. That is what I wanted to say.[9]

Know then, that the more barbarous a people is—that is, the more alive, the more freely acting (for that is what the word means)—the more barbarous, that is, the more alive, the more free, the closer to the senses, the more lyrically dynamic its songs will be, if songs it has. The more remote a people is from an artificial, scientific manner of thinking, speaking, and writing, the less its songs are made for paper and print, the less its verses are written for the dead letter. The purpose, the nature, the miraculous power of these songs as the delight, the driving force, the traditional chant, and everlasting joy of the people—all this depends on the lyrical, living, dancelike quality of the song, on the living presence of the images, and the coherence and, as it were, compulsion of the content, the feelings; on the symmetry of the words and syllables, and sometimes even of the letters, on the flow of the melody, and on a hundred other things that belong to the living world, to the gnomic song of the nation, and vanish with it. These are the arrows of this barbarous Apollo with which he pierces our hearts and transfixes soul and memory. The longer the song is to last, the stronger and more attached to the senses these arousers of the soul must be to defy the power of time and the changes of the centuries—so which way does my argument turn now?

The Scandinavians, as we find them throughout Ossian too, were certainly a wilder, ruder people than the mild idealized Scots. I do not know of any Scandinavian song where a gentle feeling flows. They tread on rock and ice and frozen earth, and with regard to such treatment and culture, I do not know any Scandinavian poem that can be compared with Ossian's. But if once you look at their poems in the editions of Worm, Bartholin, Peringskiöld, or Verel[10]—how many kinds of meter! how exactly each one is determined by the ear's immediate susceptibility to rhythm! alliterative syllables symmetrically arranged within the lines like signals for the metrical beat, marching orders to the warrior band. Alliterative sounds as a call to arms, for the bardic song to resound against the shields. Distichs and lines corresponding! Vowels alike! Syllables harmonizing—truly a rhythmical pulse to the line so skilful, rapid, and exact that we study-bound readers have difficulty apprehending it with our eyes alone. But those peoples in all their vitality who did not read it from the page but heard it, heard it from childhood on and joined in singing it and adapted their ear to it—do not imagine that they had any difficulty with the rhythm! Nothing becomes habituated more strongly and enduringly, more rapidly and delicately than the ear. Once it has grasped a thing, how durably it retains it! Once apprehended in our youth with stumbling speech, how vividly it returns to us, and in swift association with every aspect of the living world, how richly and powerfully it returns! If I were minded to psychologize, I could relate you many a strange phenomenon from the realms of music, song, and speech![11]

And another thing. Read through Ossian's poems. In all the characteristics of bardic song they resemble another nation that still lives and sings and acts on earth today, and in whose history I have more than once recognized without illusion or prejudice the living story of Ossian and his forebears. They are the five Indian nations of North America: war cry and lament, battle song and funeral dirge, historical paeans on their forefathers and to their forefathers—all this is common to Ossian's bards and the North American savages alike. I make an exception of the Indians' songs promising torture and revenge; instead the gentle Caledonians colored their songs with the tender blood of love. Now look at how all the travelers, Charlevoix and Lafitau, Roger and Cadwallader Colden have described the tone, the rhythm, the power of these songs even for strangers' ears.[12] Examine how all the reports agree on how much these songs depend for their effect upon living movement, melody, gesture, and mime. And when travelers acquainted with the Scots who have also lived for long periods among the American Indians—Captain Timberlake,[13] for example—acknowledge the obvious similarities between the lays of both nations—you can draw your own conclusions. With Denis's translation our feet are firmly planted on dull earth: we can hear something of the content and meaning conveyed in our own decently poetic idiom; but not a sound, not a tone resembling all the barbarous tribes, not a single living breath from the Caledonian hills to raise our hearts and set our pulses racing and bring us the living sound of their songs. We sit and read with our feet firmly on dull earth.

I once hoped deep in my heart that I might someday travel to England. Dear friend, you cannot imagine how I counted on visiting those Scots too! First an insight, I thought, into the spirit of this nation, into its public institutions, into the English stage and the vast living drama of the English people to clarify my ideas about the history, philosophy, politics, and peculiarities of this marvelous nation that are so often obscure and confused in the mind of the foreigner. And then the great change of scenery—to the Scots, to Macpherson! There I wanted to hear a living performance of a living people's songs, see them in all their effectiveness, see the places that are so alive in all their poems, study in their customs the remains of that ancient world, become for a while an ancient Caledonian myself—and then back to England to increase my acquaintance with the living monuments of her literature, art collections, and the finer points of her national character—how much I looked forward to fulfilling this plan! And as a translator I would certainly have set about my task in a completely different way from Denis. For him, even the example of the original Gaelic offered by Macpherson was printed in vain.

. . . You mock my enthusiasm for these savages almost as Voltaire scoffed at Rousseau for wanting to go on all fours:[14] but do not think that this makes me despise the advantages of our own morals and manners, whatever they may be. The human race is destined to develop through a series of scenes in culture and customs; alas for the man who mislikes the scene on which he has to make his entrance, do his deeds, and live his life! But alas too for the philosopher of mankind and culture who thinks that his scene is the only one, and misjudges the primal scene to be the worst and the most primitive! If they all belong together as part of the great drama of history, then each one displays a new and remarkable aspect of humanity—and take care that I do not shortly afflict you with a psychology based on Ossian's poems! The ideas for one, at least, are stirring alive and deep in my heart, and would make very strange reading![15]

You know from travelers' accounts how vigorously and clearly savages always express themselves. Always with a sharp, vivid eye on the thing they want to say, using their senses, feeling the purpose of their utterance immediately and exactly, not distracted by shadowy concepts, half-ideas, and symbolic letter understanding (the words of their language are innocent of this, for they have virtually no abstract terms); still less corrupted by artifices, slavish expectations, timid creeping politics, and confusing premeditation—blissfully ignorant of all these debilitations of the mind, they comprehend the thought as a whole with the whole word, and the word with the thought. Either they are silent, or they speak at the moment of involvement with an unpremeditated soundness, sureness, and beauty, which learned Europeans of all times could not but admire—and were bound to leave untouched. Our pedants who have to cobble everything together in advance and learn it by rote before they can stammer it out with might and method; our schoolmasters, sextons, apothecaries, and all the tribe of the little-learned who raid the scholar's house and come out empty-handed until finally, like Shakespeare's gravediggers, his Lancelot or his Dogberry, they speak in the uncertain unauthentic tones of decline and death—compare these learned fellows with the savages! If you are seeking traces of their firm clarity in our own time, do not go looking for it among the pedants. Unspoiled children, women, folk of a sound natural sense, minds formed less by speculation than by activity—these, if what I have been describing is true eloquence, are the finest, nay the only orators of our time.

But in ancient times, it was the poets, the skalds, the scholars who best knew how to wed this sureness and clarity of expression to dignity, sonority, and beauty. And as they had thus united soul and voice and a firm bond, not to confound each other but to be a support and a helpmeet, thus it was that those (to us) half-miraculous works were composed by the ἀοίδοις,[16] singers, bards, minstrels—for that is what the greatest poets of ancient times were. Homer's rhapsodies and Ossian's songs were as it were impromptus, for at that time oratory was known only in impromptu delivery. Ossian was followed, though faintly and at a distance, by the minstrels, but still they did follow him, until finally Art arrived and extinguished Nature. From our youth we have tormented ourselves learning foreign languages and spelling out the syllabic quantity of their verses, to which our ear and nature can no longer respond; working according to rules virtually none of which a genius would acknowledge as rules of Nature; composing poetry about subject matter that gives us nothing to think about, still less to *sense,* and even less to imagine; feigning passions we do not feel; imitating faculties of the soul we do not possess—until finally it all turned false, insipid, and artificial. Even the best minds were confounded, and lost their sureness of eye and hand, their certainty of thought and expression and with them their true vitality and truth and urgency—everything was lost. Poetry, which should have been the most passionate, confident daughter of the human soul, became the most insecure, weak, and hesitant, and poems turned into schoolboys' exercises for correction. And if that is the way our time thinks, then of course we will admire Art rather than Nature in these ancient poems; we will find too much or too little Art in them, according to our predisposition, and we will rarely have ears to hear the voice that sings in them: the voice of Nature. I am sure that if Homer and Ossian were to come back to earth and hear their works read and praised, they would all too often be astonished at what we add to them and take away from them, at the artifices we apply to them, and at our lack of any immediate feeling for them.

Of course our hearts and minds have been formed differently from theirs by our education from youth and by the long-intervening generations. We scarcely see and feel any longer: we only think and brood. Our poetry does not emerge from a living world, nor exist in the storm and confluence of such objects and feelings. Instead we force either our theme or our treatment or both, and we have done so for so long and so often and from our tenderest years that if we attempted any free development, it would scarcely prosper; for how can a cripple get up and walk? That is why so many of our recent poems lack that certainty, that exactness, that full contour that comes only from the first spontaneous draft, not from any elaborate later revisions. Our ridiculous versifying would have appeared to Homer and Ossian as the weak scribbles of an apprentice would have appeared to Raphael, or to Apelles, whose barest sketch revealed his mastery.

. . . What I said recently about the first spontaneous draft of a poem in no way justifies the careless and bungling efforts of our young would-be poets. For what deficiency is more obvious in their work than the very indefiniteness of their thoughts and words? They themselves never know what they want or ought to say. But if someone lacks even that knowledge, how can any corrections ever teach him it? Can anyone make a marble statue of Apollo out of a kitchen skewer?

It seems to me, given the state of our poetry at present, that two main possibilities are open to us. If a poet recognizes that the mental faculties that are required partly by his subject and by the poetic genre he has chosen, and that also happen to be predominant within him, are the representational and cognitive faculties—he must reflect thoroughly on the content of his poem, comprehend it, turn it over, and order it clearly and distinctly until every letter is, as it were, engraved upon his soul, and his poem need only reproduce this in a complete and honest manner. But if his poem requires an outpouring of passion and feeling, or if this class of faculties supplies the most active and habitual kind of motivation he needs for his work—then he will abandon himself to the inspiration of the happy hour, and will write and enchant us.[17]

. . . You think that we Germans too probably had poems like the Scottish ballad I quoted.[18] I do not merely think so; I know it for certain. I know of folk songs, dialect songs, peasant songs from more than one province that certainly yield nothing in the way of rhythm and liveliness, simplicity and vigor of language, to many such ballads. But who is there to collect them? to care about them? to care about the songs of the people, from the streets and alleys and fishmarkets? about the unsophisticated roundelays of country folk? about songs that often do not scan, whose rhymes are often false? who would take the trouble to collect them—who would bother to print them for our critics who are so clever at scansion and syllable counting? We would rather read our prettily printed modern poets—just to pass the time, of course. Let the French collect their old chansons! Let the English publish their ancient songs and ballads and romances in splendid volumes! Let Lessing be the only one in Germany to bother about Logau and Scultetus and the old bardic lays![19] Our recent poets, of course, are better printed and more agreeable to read; at most we print extracts from Opitz, Fleming, and Gryphius.[20] Let the remnants of the old, true folk poetry vanish entirely with the daily advance of our so-called culture, just as many such treasures have already vanished—after all, we have metaphysics and dogmatics and bureaucratics—and we dream peacefully on—

And yet, believe me, if we were to go in search of our local songs, each one of us, in our own province, we might well gather poems together, perhaps half as many as in Percy's *Reliques,* but almost their equal in value! How often have I been reminded as I read poems from his collection, particularly the best Scottish pieces, of German customs and German poems, some of which I have heard myself. If you have friends in Alsace, in Switzerland, in the Tyrol, in Franconia or Swabia, then beg of them—first that they should not be ashamed of these poems—for the sturdy Englishmen were not ashamed of theirs, nor did they need to be.[21]

All the songs of these savage peoples move around objects, actions, events, around a living world! How rich and various are the details, incidents, immediate features! And the eye has seen it all, the mind has imagined it all. This implies leaps and gaps and sudden transitions. There is the same connection between the sections of these songs as there is between the trees and bushes of the forest; the same between the cliffs and grottoes of the wilderness as there is between the scenes of the event itself. When the Greenlander tells of the seal hunt, he does not speak; he paints all the details with words and gestures, for they are all part of the picture in his mind. When he holds a graveside eulogy and sings a funeral dirge for his departed, he does not praise or lament, but paints, and the dead man's life, vividly portrayed with all the sudden leaps of the imagination, cannot but speak and cry.[22]

Look at the overloaded artificial Gothick style of the recent so-called philosophical and pindaric odes by the English poets Gray, Akenside, Mason,[23] etc., which they regard as masterpieces! Does the content or the meter or the wording produce the least effect of an ode? Look at the artificial Horatian style we Germans have fallen into at times—Ossian, the songs of the savage tribes and the old Norse skalds, romances, dialect poems could show us a better path, but only if we are ready to learn more than the form, the wording, or the language. But unfortunately this is only our starting point, and if we stay there, we will get nowhere. Am I wrong, or is it not true that the most beautiful lyric poems we have now—and long have had—are consonant with this virile, firm, vigorous German tone, or at least approach it—so what can we not hope from the awakening of more of that kind![24]

Translated by Joyce P. Crick,
with modifications by H. B. Nisbet

Notes

Original title: *Auszug aus einem Briefwechsel über Ossian und die Lieder alter Völker.* This work was first published in an anonymous collection of five essays, edited by Herder, entitled *Von deutscher Art und Kunst. Einige fliegende Blätter* (On German character and art. A collection of broadsheets) (Hamburg, 1773). Herder's epistolary essay on Ossian was the first item in the collection. His essay on Shakespeare, also included here, was the second. The remaining contributions were Goethe's "Von deutscher Baukunst" (On German architecture; German Library, vol. 79), a eulogy of Gothic architecture, and of Strasbourg Cathedral in particular; Paolo Frisi's "Versuch über die Gothische Baukunst" (Essay on Gothic architecture), translated from the Italian original of 1766; and Justus Möser's "Deutsche Geschichte" (German history), an extract from the preface to Möser's *History of Osnabrück* (1768). The present translation of Herder's essay on Ossian omits the numerous folk songs and ballads from various countries that Herder cites as examples of folk poetry, as well as sections in which he discusses Klopstock and various lesser poets of the time.

1. [The correspondent is fictitious. His supposed contempt for folk poetry is a rhetorical device that enables Herder to defend such literature in a direct and vigorous manner.]
2. [James Macpherson's *The Works of Ossian, the Son of Fingal,* 2 vols. (London, 1765) appeared in the German translation of Michael Denis as *Die Gedichte Ossians, eines alten celtischen Dichters,* 3 vols. (Vienna, 1768–69).]
3. ["among the dregs of Rome" (Cicero, *Letters to Atticus* 2.1).]
4. [Herder dismissed all (justified) suggestions that the poems were largely the work of Macpherson himself, and accepted the latter's claim that he had merely translated authentic poems by the ancient Celtic bard.]
5. [The break in the text is Herder's. It is designed to preserve the fiction that this is a series of extracts from an actual correspondence.]
6. [Denis's translation is in German hexameters, a form popularized in Germany by the poets Klopstock and Kleist.]
7. ["hence the tears" (Terence, *Andria* 1.126).]

8. [Herder here ironically alludes to his own earlier review of Denis's translation in the periodical *Allgemeine deutsche Bibliothek* (1768).]

9. [The following passage, in which Herder cites other popular poems that would resist translation into the formal hexameter, is omitted.]

10. [The references are to Olaus Wormius (1588–1654), author of *Danica litteratura antiquissima vulga gothica dicta* (Copenhagen, 1636) and other works on ancient Norse poetry; Thomas Bartholinus (died 1690), author of *Antiquitatum de causis contemptae a Danis adhuc gentilibus mortis libri tres* (Copenhagen, 1689); Johann Peringer de Peringskiöld (1654–1720), author of *Monumenta Sueo-Gothica* (Stockholm, 1710–19); and Olaus Verelius (1618–82), editor of the *Hervarar-Saga* (Upsala, 1672) and other Norse sagas.]

11. [The following short discussion of alliterative verse-forms in Old Norse poetry is omitted here.]

12. [Pierre François Xavier de Charlevoix (1682–1761), *Histoire et description générale de la Nouvelle-France* (Paris, 1744); Joseph-François Lafitau, *Moeurs des Sauvages Amériquains, comparées aux moeurs des premiers temps* (Paris, 1723); Woodes Rogers (died 1732), *A Cruising Voyage round the World* (London, 1712); Cadwallader Colden (1688–1776), *The History of the Five Indian Nations* (New York, 1727).]

13. [Henry Timberlake, *Memoirs of Lt. Henry Timberlake . . .* (London, 1765).]

14. [In his letter to Rousseau of 30 August 1755, Voltaire ironically distanced himself in such terms from Rousseau's praise of primitive society in his *Discours sur les origines et les fondements de l'inégalité parmi les hommes.*]

15. [A long section follows, in which Herder describes how his appreciation for primitive poetry was first awakened by reading it in an appropriately "natural" environment (on board ship, in stormy weather, on his voyage from the Baltic to France in 1769). He then describes hearing Latvian folk songs at first hand, and, after further criticisms of Denis's hexameter translation of Ossian, quotes a selection of folk poems from various countries, including the ballad "Edward" from Thomas Percy's *Reliques of Ancient English Poetry.*]

16. ["poets" or "singers."]

17. [There follows a discussion (omitted here) of various contemporary German poets, who are classified under the two headings which Herder has just specified. More examples of genuine folk song, including "Sweet William's Ghost" from *Percy's Reliques*, are then quoted.]

18. ["Sweet William's Ghost," which Herder has just quoted in full in his own German translation.]

19. [Lessing edited and published a collection of epigrams by the German baroque poet Friedrich von Logau (1604–55) in 1759, and a collection of poems by Andreas Scultetus (c. 1622–47) in 1771.]

20. [Justus Friedrich Wilhelm Zachariae (1726–77), a friend of Lessing's and himself a poet, published a two-volume anthology (Brunswick, 1766–71) of German poetry that included works by the baroque poets Martin Opitz (1597–1639), Paul Fleming (1609–40), and Andreas Gryphius (1616–64).]

21. [Herder proceeds, in the following (omitted) passage, to quote German poems, including Goethe's famous "Heidenröslein," which is presented as an anonymous folk song like the rest. He praises its popular language and elisions as the antithesis of overpolished modern verse.]

22. [Herder goes on to quote further examples of the free use of language in popular poetry, and praises Luther's hymns in particular. He again attacks slavish adherents of (neoclassical) poetic rules, and defends Klopstock's odes for their bold inversions and innovative language.]

23. [Thomas Gray (1716–71), *Odes* ("The Progress of Poesy," "The Bard") (Strawberry Hill, 1757); Mark Akenside (1721–70), author of *The Pleasures of the*

Imagination (1744) and of various odes that appeared in his collected poems in 1772; William Mason (1725–97), a friend of Gray and author of *Poems* (London, 1764).]

24. [The essay concludes with a "Postscript," in which Herder ecstatically praises Klopstock's newly published *Odes* (1771), and laments the inadequacy of recent musical settings of German poetry.]

Notes by H. B. Nisbet

Shakespeare

If there is any man to conjure up in our minds that tremendous image of one "seated high on the craggy hilltop, storm, tempest, and the roaring sea at his feet, but with the radiance of the heavens about his head,"[1] that man is Shakespeare. Only with the addition that below him, at the foot of his rocky throne, there murmur the masses who explain him, apologize for him, condemn him, excuse him, worship, calumniate, translate, and traduce him—and to all of whom he is deaf!

What a library of books has already been written about him, for him, against him! And I have no wish to add to it. I would rather that no one in the small circle of my readers would ever again dream of writing about him, for him, against him, excusing him or slandering him; but would rather explain him, feel him as he is, use him, and—if possible—make him alive for us in Germany. May this essay help in the task.

Shakespeare's boldest enemies have, in so many guises, mocked at him and declared that though he may be a great poet, he is not a good dramatist; and even if he is a good dramatist, he is incapable of the great classical tragedies of Sophocles, Euripides, Corneille, and Voltaire, who have taken this art to its furthest limits. And Shakespeare's boldest friends have mostly been satisfied with finding excuses and making apologies for him, always treating his beauties as compensations for his transgressions against the rules, uttering an *Absolvo te* over the accused and then idolizing his greatness the more extravagantly, the more they are obliged to shrug their shoulders at his flaws. This is still the case with his most recent editors and commentators.[2] I hope these pages will change the perspective and throw a fuller light upon his image.

But is this not too bold, too presumptuous a hope, when so many of the great have written about him? I think not. If I can demonstrate that both sides have been building on prejudice, on illusion, on nothing; if I have only to draw a cloud from their eyes or at most adjust the image without in the least altering anything in either eye or image, then perhaps I can ascribe it to my time or even to chance that I should have found the place on which to position my reader: here is the place to stand, else you will see nothing but caricature. But if we go on winding and unwinding at the great tangle of pedantry without ever getting any further, what a grievous destiny we shall weave!

It is from Greece that we have inherited the words drama, tragedy, comedy. And as the lettered culture of the human race has, in a narrow region of the world, made its way solely through tradition, a certain store of rules that seemed inseparable from its teaching has naturally been carried everywhere with it as in its womb and in its language. Since of course it is impossible to educate a child by way of reason, but only by way of authority, impression, and the divinity of example and of habit, so also entire nations are to an even greater extent children in all that they learn. The kernel will not grow without the husk, and they will never harvest the kernel without the husk, even if they have no use for it. That is the case with Greek and northern drama.

In Greece drama developed in a way in which it could not develop in the north. In Greece it was what it could not be in the north. Therefore in the north it is not and cannot be what it was in Greece. Thus Sophocles' drama and Shakespeare's drama are two things that in a certain respect have scarcely the name in common. I believe I can demonstrate these propositions from Greece itself and thereby decipher in no small measure the nature of northern drama and of the greatest northern dramatist, Shakespeare. We will perceive the origins of the one by means of the other, but at the same time see it transformed, so that it does not remain the same thing.

Greek tragedy developed as it were out of *one* scene, out of the impromptu dithyramb, the mimed dance, the chorus. This underwent accretions, adaptations: instead of one acting figure, Aeschylus introduced two onto the stage, invented the concept of the protagonist, and reduced the choric element. Sophocles added the third figure, invented the stage—out of such origins, but relatively late, Greek tragedy rose to its great heights, became a masterpiece of the human spirit, the summit of poetry that Aristotle honors so highly, and we, looking at Sophocles and Euripides, cannot admire deeply enough.

But at the same time we see that certain things can be explained in terms of these origins that, if we were to look upon them as dead rules, we would be bound to misjudge dreadfully. That simplicity of the Greek plot, that austerity of Greek manners, that sustained, buskined quality of expression, the music, the stage, the unity of place and time—all this lay so fundamentally and naturally, without any art or magic, in the origins of Greek tragedy—that it could come into being only in the sublimation of all these characteristics. They were the husk in which the fruit grew.

Go back to the childhood of that time: simplicity of plot really was so deeply embedded in what was called the deeds of ancient times, republican, patriotic, religious, heroic action, that the poet's difficulty lay in discerning parts in this simple whole, in introducing a dramatic beginning, middle, and end, rather than in forcing them apart, lopping them off, or in shaping a whole out of disparate events. Any reader of Aeschylus or Sophocles would see nothing incomprehensible in that. In Aeschylus's drama, what is tragedy often but an allegorical, mythological, semiepic tableau, almost without sequence of scenes, story, feelings? It was, as the Ancients said, nothing but chorus, with a certain amount of story in between. Could there be the least labor or art expended on simplicity of plot in such a case? And was it any different in most of Sophocles' plays? His *Philoctetes, Ajax, Oedipus Coloneus,* etc., are all still very close to the uniform nature of their origin: the dramatic tableau surrounded by the chorus. No doubt about it! This is the genesis of the Greek stage!

Now see how much follows from this simple observation. Nothing less than: "The artificiality of their rules was—not artifice at all! it was Nature!" Unity of plot was unity of the action before them that, according to the circumstances of their time, country, religion, manners, could not be other than single and simple. Unity of place—was unity of place; for the one brief solemn act took place only in one location, in the temple, the palace, as it were in the nation's marketplace. There it first admitted only mimed enactments and narrated interpolations; then at last the entrances and exits and the separate scenes were added—but of course it was still but one scene, where everything was held together by the chorus, where in the nature of things the stage could never remain empty, and so on. And now what child needs to have it spelled out that the natural accompaniment and consequence of all this is unity of time? All these elements lay in the very nature of things, so for all his skill, without them the poet could do nothing!

So it is also obvious that the art of the Greek poets took a path completely opposite to the one that we have had ascribed to them nowadays. They did not simplify, I think, but they complicated.[3] Aeschylus made the chorus more complex. Sophocles elaborated on Aeschylus. And if we compare Sophocles' most cunning dramas and his masterpiece *Oedipus Rex* with Aeschylus's *Prometheus Bound* or with what information we have of the ancient dithyrambs, we shall perceive the astonishing art that he succeeded in bringing to them. But it was never the art of making many into one, but really the art of turning simplicity into a multiplicity, into a beautiful labyrinth of scenes. And his greatest care was still, when he had reached the most complicated point of the labyrinth, to transform his spectators' perception back into the illusion of that earlier simplicity, and to unwind the tangled knot of their feelings so gently and gradually as to make them feel that they had never lost it, that previous dithyrambic feeling of oneness. That is why he separated out the scenes for them, at the same time retaining the choruses and making them the points of rest for the action. That is why, with every individual word, he did not let them lose sight of the whole, in the expectation, in the illusion of development and of completion (all these things the ingenious Euripides, when the stage had scarcely been established, promptly failed to do!). In short, Sophocles gave the action *grandeur* (which is something that has been terribly misunderstood).[4]

And anyone who reads him with clear eyes and from the point of view of Sophocles' own time will appreciate how highly Aristotle valued the genius of his art, and will realize that everything he says was virtually the opposite of what modern times have been pleased to make of it. The very fact that Aristotle moved away from Thespis and Aeschylus and based himself on the complexity of Sophocles' poetry; that he took this innovation as his starting point and located the essence of the new poetic genre there; that it became his dearest wish to develop a new Homer of the drama and compare him to his advantage with the first; that he omitted not the slightest detail that might in performance support his conception of the action of scale and grandeur—all this shows that the great philosopher too was theorizing according to the great tendency of his time, and that he is in no way to blame for the restrictive and childish follies that have turned him into the paper scaffolding of our modern stage![5] In his excellent chapter on the nature of the plot,[6] he clearly knew and recognized no other rule than the eye of the spectator, soul, illusion, and expressly stated that limitations of length, still less of kind or time or place of the structure, do not admit of being determined by any other rules. Oh, if Aristotle were alive today and saw the false, perverted use of his rules in dramas of a wholly different kind! But we had better stick to calm and dispassionate inquiry!

As everything in the world changes, so the Nature that was the true creator of Greek drama was bound to change also. Their view of the world, their customs, the state of the republics, the tradition of the heroic age, religion, even music, expression, and the degrees of illusion changed. And in the natural course of things the material for plots vanished, the opportunity for their use, the incentive for using them. True, poets could work on old material and even take over their material from other nations and dress it in the accustomed manner. But that did not achieve the effect. In consequence it lacked the soul. In consequence it was no longer (why should we mince our words) the thing itself. Puppet, imitation, ape, image, in which only the most blinkered devotee could find the moving spirit that once filled the statue with life. Let us turn straightaway (for the Romans were too stupid, or too clever, or too savage and immoderate to create a totally hellenizing theater) to the new Athenians[7] of Europe, and the matter will, I think, become obvious.

There is no doubt: everything that makes for this stuffed likeness of the Greek theater has scarcely been more perfectly conceived and produced than in France. I do not only mean the rules of the theater, so-called, which are laid at the good Aristotle's door: unity of time, place, action, connection between scenes, verisimilitude of setting, and so on. What I really want to ask is whether there is anything in the world possible beyond that glib classical thing that Corneille, Racine, and Voltaire have produced, beyond that sequence of beautiful scenes, of dialogue, of lines and rhymes with their measure, their decorum, their polish? The writer of this essay not only doubts it, but all the admirers of Voltaire and the French, especially those noble Athenians themselves, will deny it outright—they have done so often enough in the past, they are still at it, and they will go on doing so: "There is nothing above it; it cannot be bettered!" And in the light of this general agreement, with that stuffed and stilted image there on the stage, they are right, and are bound to become more so, the more all the countries of Europe lose their heads to this glib smoothness and continue to ape it.

But all the time there is that oppressive, incontrovertible feeling: "This is not Greek tragedy, not in purpose, effect, kind, or nature," and the most partial admirer of the French cannot deny this, once he has experienced the Greeks. I will not even attempt to inquire whether they observe their Aristotle's rules as much as they claim, for Lessing has recently raised the most terrible doubts about the loudest pretensions.[8] But granted all that, the drama is not the same, because it has nothing in common with Greek drama at its very heart: neither action, nor customs, nor language, nor purpose—nothing. So what is the point of all these externals, this scrupulously preserved uniformity? Does anyone believe that a single one of the great Corneille's heroes is a Roman or a French hero? Spanish heroes! Heroes out of Seneca! Gallant heroes; adventurous, brave, magnanimous, amorous heroes, cruel heroes—dramatic fictions who outside the theater would be called fools and who even then, at least in France, were almost as alien as they are now—that is what they are. Racine speaks the language of sensibility—and it is widely agreed that, in this respect, he is unrivaled. But even so, I would not know where sensibility ever spoke such a language as this. These are pictures of sensibility at third hand; they are never, or but rarely, the first, immediate, naked emotions, groping for words and then finding them at last. Is not Voltaire's beautiful poetic line—its mold, content, treatment of imagery, brilliance, wit, philosophy—a beautiful line indeed? Of course! The most beautiful you could imagine; and if I were a Frenchman, I would despair of writing a single line after Voltaire—but beautiful or not, it is not *theatrical* verse, appropriate to the action, language, morals, passions, purpose of a *drama* (other than French drama); it is false; pedantic balderdash! And the ultimate aim and end of it all? Certainly not a Greek end, certainly not a tragic aim and purpose. To stage a beautiful play—as long as it is a beautiful action as well—to have a number of ladies and gentlemen of elegant dress and deportment utter fine speeches and recite philosophy both sweet and useful in beautiful verse, to put them all into a story that gives an illusion of reality and holds our attention, finally to have it all performed by a cast of well-rehearsed ladies and gentlemen who go to great lengths to win our applause and approval with their declamation, the stilted gait of the sentiments, and the externalities of feeling—all this might serve most excellently as a living textbook, as an exercise in expression, deportment, and decorum, as a pattern of good, even heroic, behavior, and even as a complete academy of national wisdom and propriety in matters of living and dying (quite apart from all secondary purposes). Beautiful, instructive, educative, most excellent it may be—but it contains not a hint of the aim and purpose of the Greek theater.

And what was this aim? According to Aristotle (and there has been enough dispute about it ever since), it is no more nor less than a certain convulsion of the heart, an agitation of the soul to a certain degree and in certain aspects—in short, a specific kind of illusion that, believe me, no French play has yet achieved, or will achieve. And consequently, whatever splendid or useful name it may bear, it is not Greek drama! it is not Sophoclean tragedy! It resembles Greek drama as an effigy might! The effigy lacks spirit, life, nature, truth—that is, all the elements that move us; that is, the tragic purpose and the achievement of that purpose—so how can it be the same thing?

This in itself proves nothing as to its merit or lack of merit, but only raises the question of difference, which I think my previous remarks have established beyond doubt. And now I leave it to the reader to decide for himself whether a copy of foreign ages, customs, and actions that is only half-true, with the entertaining purpose of adapting them to a two-hour performance on a wooden stage, could compare with, let alone be regarded as greater than, an imitation that in a certain sense was the epitome of a country's national identity? I leave it to the reader to judge (and a Frenchman will have to do his best to get round this one) whether a poetic drama that really has no purpose at all as a whole—for according to the best thinkers its greatest virtue lies only in the selection of detail—whether this can be compared with a national institution in which each minute particular has its effect and is the bearer of the richest, deepest culture. Whether finally a time was not bound to come when, with most of Corneille's most artificial plays already forgotten, we will regard Crébillon and Voltaire with the same admiration with which we now look on d'Urfé's *Astrea*[9] and all the *Clelias*[10] and *Aspasias*[11] from the times of chivalry: "So clever, so wise, so inventive and well made, there might be so much to learn from them, but what a pity it is in *Astrea* and *Clelia*." Their entire art is unnatural, extravagant, tedious! We would be fortunate if our taste for truth had already reached that stage! The entire French repertory would have been transformed into a collection of pretty lines, maxims, and sentiments—but the great Sophocles would still stand where he is now!

So let us now assume a nation that, on account of circumstances that we will not pursue, had no desire to ape ancient drama and run off with the walnut shell, but rather wanted to create its own drama. Then, I think, our first question would still be: when, where, under what conditions, out of what materials should it do so? And it needs no proof that its creation can and will be the result of these questions. If it does not develop its drama out of the chorus and the dithyramb, then it will not have any trace of a choric, dithyrambic character. If its world did not offer such simplicity in its history, traditions, domestic, political, and religious conditions, then of course it will not display it either. If possible, it will create its drama out of its own history, the spirit of its age, customs, views, language, national attitudes, traditions, and pastimes, even if they are carnival farces or puppet plays (just as the Greeks did from the chorus)—and what they create will be drama, as long as it achieves the true purpose of drama among this nation. Clearly, I am referring to the

toto divisis ab orbe Britannis[12]

and their great Shakespeare.

That this was not Greece, neither then nor earlier, will not be denied by any *pullulus Aristotelis*,[13] and so to demand that Greek drama should develop naturally then and there (I am not speaking of mere imitation) is worse than expecting a sheep to give birth to lion cubs. Our first and last question is solely: what is the soil like? what harvest has it been prepared for? what has been sown in it? what is its most suitable produce? And great heavens, how far we are from Greece! History, tradition, customs, religion, the spirit of the time, of the nation, of emotion, of language—how far from Greece! Whether the reader knows both periods well or but a little, he will not for a moment confuse things that have nothing in common. And if in this different time—changed for good or ill, but changed— there happened to be an age, a genius who might create a dramatic oeuvre out of this raw material as naturally, impressively, and originally as the Greeks did from theirs; and if this creation were to attain the same end, though taking very different paths; and if it were essentially a far more complexly simple and simply complex entity, that is (according to all the metaphysical definitions) a perfect whole—then what fool would compare and condemn because this latter was not the former? For its very nature, virtue, and perfection consist in the fact that it is not the same as the first; that out of the soil of the age there grew a different plant.

Shakespeare's age offered him anything but the simplicity of national customs, deeds, inclinations, and historical traditions that shaped Greek drama. And since, according to the first maxim in metaphysics, nothing will come of nothing, not only, if it were left to the philosophers, would there be no Greek drama, but, if nothing else existed besides, there would and could no longer be any drama at all. But since it is well known that genius is more than philosophy, and creation a very different thing from analysis, there came a mortal man, endowed with divine powers, who conjured out of utterly different material and with a wholly different approach the selfsame effect: *fear* and *pity!* and both to a degree that the earlier treatment and material could scarcely produce. How the gods favored his venture! It was the very freshness, innovation, and difference that demonstrated the primal power of his vocation.

Shakespeare did not have a chorus to start from, but he did have puppet plays and popular historical dramas; so out of the inferior clay of these dramas and puppet plays he shaped the splendid creation that lives and moves before us! He found nothing like the simplicity of the Greek national character, but a multiplicity of estates, ways of life, attitudes, nations, and styles of speech. To grieve for the former would be labor lost; so he concentrated the estates and the individuals, the different peoples and styles of speech, the kings and fools, fools and kings, into a splendid poetic whole! He found no such simple spirit of history, story, action: he took history as he found it, and his creative spirit combined the most various stuff into a marvelous whole; and though we cannot call it plot in the Greek sense, we could refer to it by the middle-period term *action* or by the modern term *event (événement),* "great occurrence"—O Aristotle, if you were to appear now, what Homeric odes you would sing to the new Sophocles! You would invent a theory to fit him, such as his fellow countrymen Home[14] and Hurd,[15] Pope, and Johnson have not yet created! You would rejoice to draw lines for each of your plays on plot, character, sentiments, expression, stage, as it were from the two points at the base of a triangle to meet above at the point of destination—perfection! You would say to Sophocles: "Paint the sacred panel of this altar; and thou, northern bard, paint all the sides and walls of this temple with thy immortal fresco!"

Let me continue expounding and rhapsodizing, for I am closer to Shakespeare than to the Greek. Whereas in Sophocles' drama the unity of a single action is dominant, Shakespeare aims at the entirety of an event, an occurrence. Whereas Sophocles makes a single tone predominate in his characters, Shakespeare uses all the characters, estates, walks of life he requires to produce the concerted sound of his drama. Whereas in Sophocles a single ethereal diction sings as it were in the Empyrean, Shakespeare speaks the language of all ages, of all sorts and conditions of men; he is the interpreter of Nature in all her tongues—and in such different ways can they both be the familiars of the same Divinity? And if Sophocles represented and taught and moved and educated Greeks, Shakespeare taught and moved and educated northern men! When I read him, it seems to me as if theater, actors, scenery all vanish! Single leaves from the book of events, providence, the world, blowing in the storm of history. Individual impressions of nations, classes, souls, all the most various and disparate machines, all the ignorant blind instruments—which is what we ourselves are in the hand of the creator of the world— which combine to form a whole theatrical image, a grand event whose totality only the poet can survey. Who can imagine a greater poet of mankind in the northern world, and a greater poet of his age?

Step then before his stage, as before an ocean of events, where wave thunders upon wave. Scenes from nature come and go before our eyes; however disparate they seem, they are dynamically related; they create and destroy one another so that the intention of their creator, who seems to have put them together according to a crazy and disorderly plan, may be fulfilled—dark little symbols that form the silhouette of a divine theodicy. Lear, the rash, hotheaded old man, noble in his weakness as he stands before his map giving away crowns and tearing countries apart—the very first scene already bears within its seed the harvest of his fate in the dark future. Behold, soon we shall see the generous spendthrift, the hasty tyrant, the childish father even in his daughters' antechambers, pleading, praying, begging, cursing, raving, blessing—o Heavens, and presaging madness! Then he will soon go bareheaded in the thunder and lightning, cast down to the lowest of the low, in the company of a fool, in a crazy beggar's cave, almost calling down madness from above. And now see him as he is, in all the light-yoked majesty of the poor abandoned wretch; and now restored to himself, illumined by the last rays of hope only for them to be extinguished forever! Imprisoned, dead in his arms the child and daughter who had comforted and forgiven him; dying over her body; and his faithful servant dying after the old king! O God, what vicissitudes of times, circumstances, tempests, climes, and ages! And all of it not merely a single story, a heroic political action, if you will, moving from a single beginning to a single end according to Aristotle's strictest rule;[16] but draw nearer and feel too the human spirit that integrated every person and age and character, down to the smallest secondary thing, into the picture. Two old fathers and all their very different children. The son of the one, grateful in his misfortune toward his deceived father; the other hideously ungrateful toward his affectionate father, even in his abominable good fortune. One father against his daughters, his daughters against him, their husbands, suitors, and all their accomplices in fortune and misfortune! Blind Gloucester supported by his unrecognized son, and mad Lear at the feet of his rejected daughter! And now the moment at the crossroads of fortune, when Gloucester dies beneath his tree, and the trumpet calls, all the incidental circumstances, motives, characters, and situations concentrated into the poetic work, all in a world of fiction, all developing into a whole, a whole made up of fathers, children, kings and fools, beggars and misery, but throughout which the soul of the great event breathes even in the most disparate scenes, in which places, times, circumstances, even, I would say, the pagan philosophy of fate and the stars that reigns throughout, all belong so essentially to the whole that I could change nothing, move nothing, nor transfer parts from other plays, or to other plays. And that is not a drama? Shakespeare is not a dramatic poet? The poet who embraces a hundred scenes of a world event in his arms, composes them with his glance, breathes into them an all-animating soul, and enraptures us, our attention, our heart, all our passions, our entire soul from beginning to end—if not more, then let father Aristotle be witness: "The scale of the living creature must allow it to be comprehended with *one* glance"[17]—and here—great Heavens! How Shakespeare feels the whole course of events in the depths of his soul and draws them to a close! A world of dramatic history, as great and as profound as Nature; but it is the creator who gives us the eye and perspective to see its greatness and profundity.

In *Othello*, the Moor, what a world! what a whole! the living history of how the passion of this noble, unhappy man emerges, develops, erupts, and comes to its sad end. And what richness and complexity in the mechanism that goes to make *one* drama! How this Iago, this devil in human form, has to view the world in a certain way and treat everyone around him as his playthings; and how the other figures, Cassio and Roderigo, Othello and Desdemona, with their susceptibilities as tinder to his diabolical flame, have to be grouped around him; how all are caught in his net and exploited by him, and everything hastens to its sorrowful end. If an angel of providence were to weigh human passions against one another, and compose groups of souls and characters, and endow them with occasions for each to act in the illusion of free will, while he led them by this illusion, as if by the chain of fate, towards his controlling idea—this is how the human mind that conceived this work devised, pondered, planned, and guided its course.

It should not be necessary to point out that time and place are as essential to the action as husk is to kernel, and yet these are what provoke the loudest outcry. If Shakespeare discovered the godlike art of conceiving an entire world of the most disparate scenes as one great event, then of course it was part of the truth of his events also to idealize time and place for each scene in such a way that they too contributed to the illusion. Is there anyone in the world who is indifferent to the time and place of even trivial events in his life? And are they not particularly important in matters where the entire soul is moved, formed, and transformed? In our youth, in scenes of passion, in all the decisive actions of our lives! Is it not place and time and the fullness of external circumstances that endow the whole story with its direction, duration, and existence? And can one remove from a child, a youth, a lover, a man in the field of action, a single localizing circumstance, a single how? where? or when? without prejudicing our whole grasp of his personality? In this respect, Shakespeare is the greatest master, simply because he is only and always the servant of Nature. When he created the events in his dramas and pondered them in his mind, he pondered times and places too. From out of all the scenes and conjunctures in the world, Shakespeare chose, as though by some law of fatality, just those that are the most powerful, the most appropriate to the feeling of the action; in which the strangest, boldest circumstances best support the illusion of truth; in which the changes of time and place over which the poet rules, proclaim most loudly: "This is not a poet, but a creator! Here is the history of the world!"

For example, when the poet was turning over in his mind as a fact of creation the terrible regicide, the tragedy called *Macbeth*—if then, dear reader, you were too timid to enter into the feeling of place and setting in any scene, then alas for Shakespeare, and for the withered page in your hand! For you will have felt nothing of its opening, with the witches on the blasted heath, nothing of the scene with the bloody man bringing the news of Macbeth's deeds, nothing of the king's tidings to him; you will have felt nothing of the change of scene when Macbeth is ready to listen to the witches' prophetic spirit and identifies their greeting with Duncan's previous message. You will not have seen his wife walking the castle with that fateful letter, nor how she will walk there later so terribly transformed. Nor finally will you have enjoyed with the gentle king the sweet evening air where fearlessly the martlet breeds and haunts, while you, King Duncan—this lies in the workings of the invisible—are drawing near your murderous grave. The house in a bustle, making ready for guests, and Macbeth making ready for murder! Banquo's preparatory scene at night with torches and sword! The dagger, the terrible dagger in the vision! The bell—the deed has scarcely been done when there comes that knocking on the door! The discovery— the assembled guests—you may travel all ages and places and you will find that the intention behind this creation could not have been realized other than there and in this way. The scene of Banquo's murder in the forest, the nocturnal banquet and Banquo's ghost— then again on the witches' heath (for his terrible and fateful deed is done!). Then the witches' cavern, spells, prophecies, rage, despair! The death of Macduff's children, with only their mother to shelter them beneath her wing! and the two outlaws beneath the tree, and then the frightful queen sleepwalking in the castle, and the marvelous fulfillment of the prophecy—Birnam Wood drawing near— Macbeth's death at the sword of one not of woman born—I would have to enumerate all the scenes, all of them, to give a local habitation to the ineffable whole, a world of magic and regicide and destiny that is the soul of the play and breathes life into it right down to the smallest detail of time, place, and apparently wayward interlude. I would have to enumerate them so that I could summon it all before the soul as a terrible, indissoluble whole—and yet withal I would say nothing.

The individual quality of each drama, of each separate universe, pulses through place and time and composition in all the plays. Lessing compared certain aspects of *Hamlet* with that theatrical queen Semiramis.[18] How the spirit of the place fills the entire drama from beginning to end! The castle platform and the bitter cold—the watch relieved, tales told in the night, disbelief and credulity, the star, and then it appears! Is there anyone who does not sense art and nature in every word and detail! And so it proceeds. All ghostly and human guises exhausted! The cock crows and the drum rolls, the silent beckoning and the nearby hill, speech and silence—what a setting! what a profound revelation of the truth! See how the frightened king kneels, and Hamlet strays past his father's picture in his mother's chamber! And now the other scene! Hamlet at Ophelia's grave! The touching good fellow in all his dealings with Horatio, Ophelia, Laertes, Fortinbras! the young man's playing with action, which runs through the play and almost until the end never becomes action—if for one moment you feel and look for the boards of a stage and a series of decorous versified speeches upon them, neither Shakespeare nor Sophocles nor any true poet in the world has written for you.

Oh, if only I had words for the one main feeling prevailing in each drama, pulsing through it like a world soul. As it does in *Othello,* belonging as an essential part to the drama, as in his searching for Desdemona at night, as in their fabulous love, the sea crossing, the tempest, as in Othello's raging passion, in Desdemona's manner of death, which has been so much derided, singing her willow song as she undresses, while the wind knocks; as in the nature of the sin and passion itself, his entrance, his address to the candle—if only it were possible to comprehend all this in words, to express how it all belongs deeply and organically to *one* world, one great tragic event—but it is not possible. Words cannot describe or reproduce the merest most miserable painting, so how can they render the feeling of a living world in all the scenes, circumstances, and enchantments of Nature? Peruse what you will, gentle reader, *Lear* or the *Henries, Caesar* or the two *Richards,* even the magical plays and the interludes; *Romeo* in particular, the sweet drama of love, a romance indeed in every detail of time and place and dream and poetry—attempt to remove something of its quality, to change it, even to simplify it for the French stage—a living world in all the authenticity of its truth transformed into this wooden nullity—a fine metamorphosis! Deprive this plant of its soil, juices, and vigor, and plant it in the air, deprive this human being of place, time, individuality—you have robbed them of breath and soul, and you have a mere image of the living creature.

For Shakespeare is Sophocles' brother, precisely where he seems to be so dissimilar, and inwardly he is wholly like him. His whole dramatic illusion is attained by means of this authenticity, truth, and historical creativity. Without it, not merely would illusion be left unachieved, but nothing of Shakespeare's drama and dramatic spirit would remain—or else I have written in vain. Hence the entire world is but the body to this great spirit. All the scenes of Nature are the limbs of this body, even as all the characters and styles of thought are the features of this spirit—and the whole might well bear the name of Spinoza's giant god: Pan! Universum![19] Sophocles was true to Nature when he treated of *one* action in *one* place and at *one* time. Shakespeare could only be true to Nature when he rolled his great world events and human destinies through all the places and times—where they took place. And woe betide the frivolous Frenchman who arrives in time for Shakespeare's fifth act, expecting it will provide him with the quintessence of the play's touching sentiment. This may be true of many French plays, where everything is versified and paraded in scenes only for immediate theatrical effect. But here, he would go home empty-handed. For the great world event would already be over. He would witness but its last and least-important consequences, men falling like flies. He would leave the theater and scoff: Shakespeare is an affront to him, and his drama the merest foolishness.

The whole tangled question of time and place would long ago have been unraveled if some philosophical mind had only taken the trouble to ask what time and place really mean in drama.[20] If the place is the stage and the length of time that of a *divertissement au théâtre*, then the only people in the world to have observed the unity of place and the measure of time and scenes are—the French. The Greeks, with a degree of illusion higher than we can conceive, whose stage was a public institution and whose theater was a temple of worship, never gave the unities a thought. What kind of illusion is experienced by a spectator who looks at his watch at the end of every scene to check whether such an action could take place in such a span of time, and whose chief delight it is that the poet has not cheated him out of a second, but has showed him on the stage only what would take the same length of time in the snail's pace of his own life? What kind of creature could find this his greatest pleasure? And what kind of poet would regard this as his chiefest end, and pride himself on this nonsense of rules? "How much pretty perform-ance I have crammed so neatly into the narrow space of this pit made of boards, called *le théâtre français;* how elegantly I have fitted it all into the prescribed length of time of a polite visit! How I have sewed and stitched, polished and patched!"—miserable master of cere-monies, a theatrical posturer, not a creator, poet, god of the drama! The clock does not strike on tower or temple for you if you are a true dramatic poet, for you create your own space and time; and if you are capable of creating a world that can only exist in the categories of time and space, behold, your measure of space and duration is there within you, and you must conjure all your spectators to accept it, and urge it upon them—or else you are, as I have said, anything but a true dramatic poet.

Is there anyone in the world who needs to have it demonstrated that space and time are in themselves nothing, that in respect of being, action, passion, sequence of thought, and degree of attention within and without the soul, they are utterly relative? Has there never been any occasion in your life, good timekeeper of the drama, when hours seemed to you moments, and days seemed hours; and conversely times when hours turned into days and the watches of the night into years? Have you never known situations in your life when your soul dwelt sometimes outside you? Here, in your beloved's romantic chamber? there, gazing upon that frozen corpse? again, in the oppression of external shame and distress—or occasions when your soul fled far beyond world and time, overleaping the places and regions of the earth, unmindful of itself, to inhabit heaven, or the soul, the heart of the one whose being you feel so deeply? And if something of this kind is possible in your slow and sluggish, vermiculate and vegetable life, where there are roots enough to hold you fast to the dead ground, and each slow length you drag along is measure enough for your snail's pace, then imagine yourself for just one moment into another, poetic world, transpose yourself into a dream. Have you never perceived how in dreams space and time vanish? What insignificant things they are, what *shadows* they must be in comparison with action, with the working of the soul? Have you never observed how the soul creates its own space, world, and tempo as and where it will? And if you had experienced that only once in your life, and wakened after a mere quarter of an hour, the dark remnants of your actions in the dream would cause you to swear that you had slept and dreamed and acted whole nights away, and Mahomet's dream would not for one moment seem absurd to you.[21] And is it not the first and sole duty of every genius, of every poet, above all of the dramatic poet, to carry you off into such a dream? And now think what worlds you would be throwing into disarray if you were to show the poet your pocket watch or your drawing room, and ask him to teach you to dream according to their prescriptions!

The poet's space and time lie in the movement of his great event, in the *ordine successivorum et simultaneorum*[22] of *his* world. How

and where does he transport you? As long as he sees to it that you
are transported, you are in his world. However slowly or quickly he
causes the course of time to pass, it is he who makes it pass; it is he
who impresses its sequence upon you: that is his measure of time.
And what a master Shakespeare is in this respect too! His grand
events begin slowly and ponderously in his nature, as they do in
Nature itself, for it is this he renders, but on a smaller scale. How
laborious his presentation, before the springs of action are set in
motion! But once they are, how the scenes race by, how fleeting the
speeches, how winged the souls, the passion, the action, and how
powerful then the hastening movement, the pell-mell interjection of
single words when time has run out for everyone. And finally, when
the reader is entirely caught up in the illusion he has created, and is
lost in the dark abyss of his world and his passion, how bold he
becomes, what trains of events he commands! Lear dies after Cor-
delia! And Kent after Lear! It is virtually the end of his world; the
Last Judgment is upon us, when everything, the Heavens included,
lurches and collapses, and the mountains fall! The measure of time
is no more. Not for our merry clockwatcher, of course, who turns up
unscathed for the fifth act to measure by his timepiece how many
died and how long it took. But Great Heavens, if that is supposed to
be criticism, theater, illusion—so much the worse for criticism,
theater, illusion! What do all these empty words mean?

At this point the heart of my inquiry might begin: what art, what
creator's skills did Shakespeare employ to turn some base romance
or tale or fabulous history into such a living poetic whole? What
laws of historical, philosophical, or dramatic art are revealed in all
his doings, in all the secrets of his craft? What an inquiry! How
much it could contribute to our reading of history, our philosophy
of the human soul, our drama! But I am not a member of all our
academies of history and philosophy and the fine arts, where in any
case they turn their minds to anything but such a question. Even
Shakespeare's own countrymen do not consider it. What historical
errors his commentators have so often castigated him for, what
beautiful historical passages have been faulted—for example in that
bulky edition by Warburton![23] And has it occurred to the author of
the most recent essay on him[24] to raise my fundamental question:
"How did Shakespeare turn tales and romances into poetic
drama?"? Hardly. Just as it scarcely occurred to the Aristotle of this
British Sophocles, Lord Home.

So just a nod in the direction of the usual classifications of his plays. Not long ago a writer who certainly had a deep feeling for his Shakespeare had the bright idea of making that fishmonger of a courtier with his gray beard and wrinkled face, his eyes purging thick amber and his plentiful lack of wit together with weak hams, of making the childish Polonius, I say, into his Aristotle, and suggesting that the string of—als and—cals he splutters out should be taken seriously as the basis of classification for all of Shakespeare's plays.[25] I doubt it. True, it is Shakespeare's mischievous habit to put into the mouths of children and fools all those empty commonplaces, moral sentiments, and classifications that, when applied to a hundred instances, are appropriate to all and to none. And a new Stobaeus or *Florilegium* or cornucopia of Shakespeare's wisdom, such as the English already possess and we Germans, praise be, are supposed to have had of late,[26] would give the greatest pleasure precisely to figures like Polonius and Lancelot, the fools and harlequins, poor Dickon or bombastic king of knights,[27] because all the sane and sensible human beings in Shakespeare do not have any more to say than the moment requires. But even here I still have my doubts. It is probable that in this passage Polonius is intended to be just a great baby who takes clouds to be camels and camels to be bass viols and in his youth once enacted Julius Caesar and was accounted a good actor and was killed by Brutus and knows very well

Why day is day, night night and time is time[28]

—spinning a top of theatrical words here too. But who would want to build a theory upon that? And what virtue lies in the distinctions tragedy, comedy, history, pastoral, tragical-historical or historical-pastoral, pastoral-comical or comical-historical-pastoral? And were we to shuffle those—cals a hundred times, what insight would we have in the end? Not one single play would be a Greek tragedy, comedy or pastoral, nor should it be. Every play is history in the widest sense, which of course from time to time shades off in varying degrees into tragedy, comedy, etc., but the colors are so infinitely nuanced that in the last resort each play remains and cannot but remain—what it is: history! the heroic drama of the nation's destiny conjuring the illusion of the Middle Ages or (with the exception of a few plays that are really entertainments and interludes) a great and entire enactment of a world event, of a human destiny.

Sadder and more important is the thought that even this great creator of history and the world soul grows older himself, that the words and customs and categories of the age fall into the sere and yellow leaf, and that we ourselves are already so remote from these great ruins of the days of chivalry that even Garrick,[29] who has revived Shakespeare and been the guardian angel of his grave, has had to change, cut, and mutilate his works so much. And soon, perhaps, as everything gets blurred and tends in different directions, even his drama will become incapable of living performance, and will become the fragment of a Colossus, an Egyptian pyramid everyone gazes at in amazement and no one understands. Happy am I that, though time is running out, I still live at a time when it is possible for me to understand him; and when you, my friend,[30] who feel and recognize yourself in reading his dramas, and whom I have embraced more than once before his sacred image, can still dream the sweet dream worthy of your powers, that one day you will raise a monument to him here in our degenerate country, drawn from our age of chivalry and written in our language.[31] I envy you that dream. May your noble German powers not flag until the garland hangs aloft. And should you too in later times perceive how the ground shakes beneath your feet, and the rabble round about stand still and gape or jeer, and the everlasting pyramids cannot reawaken the spirit of ancient Egypt—your work will still stand. And a faithful successor will seek out your grave and write with pious hand the words that have summed up the lives of almost all the worthies in the world:

Voluit! quiescit![32]

Translated by Joyce P. Crick,
with modifications by H. B. Nisbet

Notes

On the original edition of this essay, see the note to the preceding essay by Herder.

1. [The image is taken from Mark Akenside's didactic poem *The Pleasures of the Imagination* (1744), III, 550–59, which Herder paraphrases; cf. also note 23 to Herder's essay on Ossian.]

2. [The editors whom Herder has in mind probably include Alexander Pope, Samuel Johnson, and Christoph Martin Wieland, whose eight-volume translation of *Shakespears theatralische Werke* was published at Zurich in 1762–66.]

3. [Herder, without naming him, is here contradicting Lessing who, in section 46 of his *Hamburg Dramaturgy* (German Library, vol. 83), had declared that the Greek tragedies simplified originally complex plots in the interests of those unities of place and time that were necessitated by the constant presence of one and the same chorus on stage: see Lessing, *Werke*, edited by Herbert G. Göpfert, 8 vols. (Munich, 1970–79), 4:443.]

4. [Herder's account of Greek tragedy in this paragraph closely follows that of Aristotle in chapters 4 and 6 of his *Poetics*.]

5. [Herder's criticism is directed at the poetics of Corneille and French classical tragedy, and at its German imitators such as Gottsched.]

6. [Aristotle's *Poetics*, chapter 7.]

7. [That is, the French. Herder's contemptuous remarks on French neoclassicism echo Lessing's strictures on it in his *Hamburg Dramaturgy* of 1767–69.]

8. [The reference is again to Lessing's *Hamburg Dramaturgy*, particularly sections 46–48 (German Library, vol. 83): see Lessing's *Werke*, ed. Göpfert, 4:443–56.]

9. [*Astrée*, a pastoral romance in five volumes (Paris, 1607–28) by Honoré d'Urfé (1567–1625).]

10. [*Clélie*, a romance in ten volumes (Paris, 1654–60) by Madeleine de Scudéry.]

11. [*Aspasia:* the name of more than one French novel of the eighteenth century. It is uncertain whether Herder is referring to one of them in particular, or to them all as a class. Aspasia is also, however, a character in Madeleine de Scudéry's romance of chivalry *Artamène ou le Grand Cyrus* (1648).]

12. ["The Britons, divided from the rest of the world"; after Virgil, *Eclogues* 1.66.]

13. ["pupil (literally 'chicken') of Aristotle."]

14. [Henry Home (Lord Kames) (1696–1782); author of *Elements of Criticism* (Edinburgh, 1762).]

15. [Richard Hurd (1720–1808), editor of *Q. Horatii Flacci Ars Poetica. Epistola ad Pisones* (London, 1749), the commentary to which contained an analysis of the different kinds of drama.]

16. [Aristotle, *Poetics*, chapter 7: "A whole is that which has a beginning, a middle, and an end. . . . Well-constructed plots must neither begin nor end in a haphazard way, but must conform to the pattern I have been describing."]

17. [Aristotle, *Poetics*, chapter 7: "In just the same way as living creatures and organisms compounded of many parts must be of a reasonable size, so that they can be easily taken in by the eye, so too plots must be of a reasonable length, so that they may be easily held in the memory."]

18. [In his comparison, in the *Hamburg Dramaturgy* (sections 11–12), of the unconvincing ghost in Voltaire's *Sémiramis* with the far more effective ghost in Shakespeare's *Hamlet* (Lessing's *Werke*, ed. Göpfert, 4:281–86).]

19. [The young Herder was already studying the much-decried heretic Spinoza. Along with Lessing and Goethe, he was shortly to initiate a wave of enthusiasm in Germany for Spinoza's nature pantheism, an enthusiasm that was shared by Schelling, Novalis, and other German Romantics: see David Bell, *Spinoza in Germany from 1670 to the Age of Goethe* (London, 1984), especially pp. 38–70 and 97–146.]

20. [Herder's criticisms here are directed in particular at Pierre Corneille's *Discours des trois unités* (*Théâtre de Pierre Corneille*, vol. 3 (Amsterdam, 1664)).]

21. [Mohammed's dream of his assumption into heaven.]

22. [Order of succession and simultaneity (order in time and space); cf. Lessing's use of these categories in chapter 16 of his *Laocoön*.]

23. [The reference is to William Warburton's (1698–1779) eight-volume edition of Shakespeare (London, 1747).]

24. [Elizabeth Montagu (1720–1800), *An Essay on the Writings and Genius*

of *Shakespeare, Compared with the Greek and French Dramatic Poets, with Some Remarks upon the Misrepresentations of Mons. de Voltaire* (London, 1769); Herder reviewed the German translation (by J. J. Eschenburg) of the work in 1771 (*Sämtliche Werke*, 5:312–17).]

25. [Heinrich Wilhelm von Gerstenberg (1737–1823), "Versuch über Shake-spears Werke und Genie," in Gerstenberg's periodical *Briefe über Merkwürdigkeiten der Literatur* 2, Letters 14–18 (1766); the classification after Polonius occurs in Letter 17 (reprinted in *Sturm und Drang. Kritische Schriften,* edited by Erich Loewenthal, third edition (Heidelberg, 1972), pp. 27–30).]

26. [Johannes Stobaeus, Greek anthologist of the sixth century A.D., whose *Florilegium* contained numerous extracts from a wide range of Greek authors. The English anthology of Shakespeare to which Herder refers is William Dodd's *The Beauties of Shakespeare*, 2 vols. (London, 1752). J. J. Eschenburg (1743–1820), German translator of Shakespeare, planned a similar anthology in German.]

27. [Richard II and Falstaff.]

28. [*Hamlet* 2.2.88.]

29. [The actor David Garrick (1717–79).]

30. [These words are addressed to the young Goethe, who had already been infected by Herder's enthusiasm for Shakespeare, and whose essay "Von deutscher Baukunst" (On German architecture), in praise of Gothic architecture, was printed immediately after Herder's essay on Shakespeare in the collection *On German Character and Art* (1773) in which these works first appeared.]

31. [The reference is to the original version (1771) of Goethe's drama of chivalry, *Götz von Berlichingen,* which was entitled *History of Gottfried von Berlichingen with the Iron Hand.* Although Herder was privately much impressed by the drama, the sharp criticisms he sent in a (now-lost) letter to Goethe led Goethe to revise the play before it was published in 1773.]

32. ["He has striven! now he rests!"]

Notes by H. B. Nisbet

Letters for the Advancement of Humanity.
Eighth Collection (1796)

Ninth Fragment. Letter 107.

*Comparison of the Poetry of Various Ancient
and Modern Peoples: Conclusions*

Poetry is a Proteus among the peoples. It changes its form according to language, manners, customs, temperament, and climate, even the accent of the peoples.

Nations migrate, languages mingle and change, human beings encounter new objects, their inclinations tend in another direction, their exercises toward another goal, new models affect the way they put together images and concepts, even the tongue, this small member, moves differently and the ear accustoms itself to different sounds. With all these changes, poetry changes not only from nation to nation, but even in the same people. Among the Greeks, poetry, and even the concept of poetry, was a different thing in the age of Homer than in that of Longinus. Completely different notions of poetry were held by the Roman and the monk, the Arab and the Crusader, or after the rediscovery of the ancients by the scholar, and at varying ages of various nations by the poet and the people. The name itself is an abstract concept embracing so much that if not clearly grounded in individual cases it disappears like an illusion into the clouds. The quarrel about whether the *ancients or the moderns were better* was therefore very empty, and the thoughts it occasioned were poorly defined.[1]

The quarrel became still emptier by the fact that either a false standard of comparison was assumed, or none at all: for what was supposed to decide about rank here? The *objective* art of the poetry? How many fine definitions would be required to find out the height of perfection in each kind and genre according to time and place, purpose and means, and to apply this without bias to each thing compared! Or was the *subjective* art of the poet supposed to be regarded—how far this one excelled that in fortunate natural gifts, more favorable circumstances, greater diligence in using what had been there before him and lay around him, a more noble goal, a wiser application of his powers to reach this goal and make it his own—another ocean of comparison! As many standards as have been set up for poets of a single nation or of various peoples, so much futile labor has been taken on. Each critic values and ranks them according to his pet notions, according to the way he became acquainted with them, according to the effect this one or that had on him. The cultivated man bears in himself both his own ideal of perfection and his standard of how this is to be reached, and is reluctant to exchange them for anyone else's.

We therefore must not hold it against any nation if it loves its own poets above all others and wouldn't like to exchange them for foreign poets; for these are *their* poets. They have thought in *their* language, their imagination has worked in the circle of *their* objects; they felt the needs of the nation in which they were brought up, and endeavored to relieve them. So why shouldn't their nation feel *with them* too, since a single bond of language, thoughts, needs, and feelings ties them firmly to each other.

The Italians, French, and English place a prejudicially high value on their own poets, and often despise other peoples unjustly; only the Germans have let themselves be led astray into exaggerating beyond all measure the merits of foreign peoples, especially the English and French, and neglecting themselves as a result. To be sure, I don't at all begrudge a Young (for the talk here is not of Shakespeare, Milton, Thomson, Fielding, Goldsmith, Sterne) the perhaps somewhat excessive admiration we give him, since he was introduced by Ebert's translation,[2] a translation that not only has all the merit of an original, but even as it were corrects and tones down the exaggerations of its English original by the construction of a harmonious prose and by the rich moral annotations drawn from other nations. But otherwise the Germans will always bring upon themselves the reproach of indecisive lukewarmness by so forgetting the purest poets of their language, and placing them at such a disadvantage in their schools and in the education of youth in general, in a way that no neighbor nation does. By what means shall our taste, our style be developed? By what means shall our language be defined and regulated if not by the best writers of our nation? Indeed, by what means shall we attain patriotism and love of our fatherland, other than by its language, by the most excellent thoughts and feelings expressed in it, and laid in it like a treasure. We would surely not now, after our language has been written for a millennium, still wander around indecisively among many turns of phrase, if from our youth on we knew our best writers and chose them as our guides.

However, no love for our own nation should hinder us from

recognizing *everywhere* that good that can only be effected *progressively in the great course of ages and peoples*. A certain sultan rejoiced in the many religions that each honored God in their own way in his empire; it appeared to him as a beautiful, colorful meadow, where flowers of many kinds blossomed. Thus it is with the poetry of different peoples and ages on our globe; in each age and language it was the quintessence of the flaws and perfections of a nation, a mirror of its attitudes, the expression of the highest toward which *it* strove (*oratio sensitiva animi perfecta*).[3] To set these pictures (more and less perfect, true and false ideals) against one another is an amusement from which much can be learned. In this gallery of various ways of thinking, endeavors, and wishes we surely get to know ages and nations more deeply than on the deceptive disconsolate path of their political and military history. In this latter we rarely see more of a people than how it let itself be ruled and killed; in the former we learn how it thought, what it wished and wanted, how it found joy, and was guided by its teachers or its inclinations. To be sure we still lack many aids to this overview into the souls of the peoples. Greeks and Romans set aside, dark clouds still hang over the Middle Ages, which are nonetheless the source of everything for us Europeans. Meinhard's feeble *Essay on the Italian Poets* has not even been continued as far as Tasso,[4] still less has anything similar been carried out for other nations. An *Essay on the Spanish Poets* died with the learned expert in this literature, Diez, the editor of Velasquez.[5]

There are three ways to provide oneself with an overview of this field of human thought rich in flowers and fruit, and each has been trodden.

Eschenburg's popular collection of examples[6] chooses in agreement with his theory[7] the path of *genres and species;* a path on which youths can learn much from a skillful leader, for often a single name designating very different things can lead far astray. The works of Homer, Virgil, Ariosto, Milton, and Klopstock bear the single name "epic," and yet are quite different artistic products even down to the concept of art that lies in the work, let alone judging by the spirit that animates them. Sophocles, Corneille and Shakespeare only have the name of tragic playwright in common; the genius of their representations is quite different. So it is with all poetic genres, all the way down to the epigram.

Others have ordered poets according to *feelings,* among whom Schiller in particular has said many fine and excellent things.[8] But how much feelings overlap! What poet remains so faithful to a single way of feeling that it could designate his character, even in different works? Often he touches the strings of many, indeed all notes, which cancel one another out precisely by their disharmonies. The world of feelings is a realm of spirits, often of atoms; only the hand of the creator is able to order figures from it.

The third, and if I may say so, natural method, is to leave each flower in its place, and to contemplate it there exactly as it is, according to its age and species, from root to crown. The most humble genius hates hierarchy and comparison. He prefers to be the first in the village rather than second to Caesar.[9] Lichen, moss, fern, and the richest scented flower: each blossoms in its place in *God's* order.

Poetry has been ordered *subjectively* and *objectively* according to the objects it depicts, and the feelings with which it represents objects; a true and useful perspective, which also seems the right one for the characterization of individual poets, e.g., Homer and Ossian, Thomson and Kleist. For Homer tells the stories of the world of his ancestors without noticeable particular personal involvement; Ossian sings them from his wounded heart, from his sad-happy memory. Thomson depicts the seasons as nature gives them; Kleist sings his spring with feeling, as a rhapsody of sights, often interrupted by thoughts of himself and his friends. However, this distinction also barely describes different poets and ages of poetry: for Homer is also involved with his subjects, as a Greek, and as a narrator, and so were the balladeers and fablers in the Middle Ages, and in more recent times Ariosto and Spenser, Cervantes and Wieland. To be otherwise would have been outside his calling and would have disturbed his narrative. But in the arrangement and characterization of his figures Homer too sings in a supremely human manner; where it doesn't seem that way to us, the difference is easily explicable by the difference between the way of thinking of his times and of ours. I am confident I can discover in the Greeks every pure human sentiment, perhaps even in the most beautiful measure and most beautifully expressed; only everything in its appropriate place. Aristotle's *Poetics* has ordered *fables, characters, passions, sentiments* in a way that cannot be improved on.

Man has been the same in all ages; but he expressed himself in each case according to the circumstances in which he lived. The poetry of the Greeks and Romans is very varied, in its wishes and laments, in its descriptions full of pleasure and joy. So is the poetry of the monks, the Arabs, the more recent peoples. The great distinction that arose between East and West, the Greeks and us, was effected by no new category, but rather by the mixing of peoples, religions, and languages, finally by the development of manners, inventions, knowledge, and experience; a distinction that could hardly be expressed by a single word. If I employed the words *reflective poet* for some modern writers, this was also inadequate, for a "purely reflective" poet is actually no poet at all.

The basis and ground of poetry is *imagination* and *mind,* the *land of the soul.* By words and characters it awakens an ideal of happiness, beauty, and dignity that slumbers in your heart; it is the most perfect expression of language, of the senses and of the mind. No poet can escape the law that inheres in it; he reveals what he has and what he lacks.

Nor can one separate *ear* and *eye* in poetry. Poetry is not mere painting or sculpture, capable like them of representing pictures without intention; it is *speech* and has *intention.* It affects the inner sense, not the outer eye of the artist; and to that inner sense belongs in every cultivated human being or one capable of cultivation *the mind, moral nature,* and therefore in the poet a *rational and humane intention.* Speech has something *infinite* in it; it makes deep impressions, which indeed precisely poetry strengthens by means of its harmonious art. Therefore the poet can never want to be simply a painter. He is an artist by the power of his penetrating speech, which paints the object it paints or represents on a *spiritual, moral,* as it were *infinite* ground into the *mind,* into the *soul.*

Should therefore with poetry, too, *progress* be inevitable, as with all sequences of sustained natural effects? I have no doubt about it, as long as progress is properly understood. In language and manners we will never be Greeks and Romans; we don't want to be, either. But that the spirit of poetry in the course of all the periodic oscillations and eccentricities through which its endeavors until now have led, from nation to nation, and age to age, strives to throw off both all coarseness of feeling and all false adornment and seeks the focal point of all human endeavors, namely the *genuine, whole, moral nature of man, philosophy of life*—this the comparison of the ages makes very credible to me. Even in those ages where taste is most corrupt we can say in accordance with the great rule of nature: *tendimus in Arcadium, tendimus!*[10] Our path leads to the land of simplicity, truth, and ethics.

Translated by Timothy J. Chamberlain

Notes

Original title: *Briefe zu Beförderung der Humanität* (1793–97).

1. [Herder is referring to the "querelle des anciens et des modernes" in the late seventeenth and early eighteenth century in France and England.]

2. [Johann Arnold Ebert (1723–95), a major translator and advocate of English literature and aesthetics, published his translation *Youngs Klagen oder Nachtgedanken deutsch* in 1751.]

3. ["A sensuous and perfect discourse of the soul"; the definition of a poem given by Baumgarten in his *Meditationes* (1735). Cf. Herder's use and discussion of this definition in *Critical Forests,* chapter 16.]

4. [The reference is to Johann Nikolaus Meinhard's (1727–67) *Versuche über den Charakter und die Werke der besten italienischen Dichter* (Essays on the character and works of the best Italian poets). Vols. 1 and 2 appeared in 1763 and 1764; a third volume was added after Meinhard's death (1774) by Christian Joseph Jagemann (1735–1804).]

5. [Johann Andreas Dieze (1729–85) translated *Origines de la Poesie Castellana* (Origins of Castilian poetry) by Luis Jose Velasquez de Velasco (1722–72).]

6. [*Beispielsammlung zur Theorie und Literatur der schönen Wissenschaften* (Anthology for the theory and literature of the arts) (1788–94) by Johann Joachim Eschenburg (1743–1820).]

7. [*Entwurf einer Theorie und Literatur der schönen Wissenschaften* (Sketch of a theory and literature of the arts) (1783).]

8. See *Die Horen,* November and December 1795, January 1796 [*Über Naive und Sentimentalische Dichtung* (On naive and sentimental poetry); German Library, vol. 17.]

9. [According to Plutarch's *Lives,* Caesar declared he would rather be first in a village than second in Rome.]

10. ["We are making our way to Arcadia"; cf. Virgil, *Aeneid* 1.204: "tendimus in Latium."]

Johann Wolfgang von Goethe

Johann Wolfgang von Goethe (1749–1832) studied law at Leipzig and Strasbourg, where in 1770 he met Herder. Under Herder's influence, he adopted folk poetry as a model for his own lyrics, and Shakespeare as his inspiration in the theater. His historical drama *Götz von Berlichingen* (1773) made him famous throughout Germany, his first novel, *The Sorrows of Young Werther* (1774; The German Library, volume 19), in all Europe. Hailed as the great genius German literature had been awaiting, he accepted Duke Karl August's invitation to Weimar in 1775, and remained there for the rest of his life as a state official. His only prolonged absence was his stay in Italy from 1786 to 1788, where his studies of the visual arts confirmed his turn to classical models, reflected in the plays *Iphigenia in Tauris* (1787) and *Torquato Tasso* (1790). His friendship and alliance with Schiller from 1794 until Schiller's death in 1805 enabled the two writers to produce the aesthetic ideology and canonical works of Weimar Classicism. Goethe's later years saw a new broadening of his interests, to include, for example, Persian poetry, taken as an inspiration for his poems in the *West-Eastern Divan* (1819). His greatest work, *Faust* (The German Library, volume 18), occupied him from the mid-1770s until his death, and in its diversity and range reflects every stage of his development. Other major works include the novels *Wilhelm Meister's Apprenticeship* (1795–96), *Elective Affinities* (1809; The German Library, volume 19), and *Wilhelm Meister's Journeyman Years* (1829), and the epic poem *Hermann and Dorothea* (1796–97). Goethe himself also attached considerable importance to his scientific writings, particularly his *Theory of Colors* (1810). The most commonly cited edition is the Hamburg edition, *Goethes Werke,* ed. Erich Trunz, 14 vols. (Hamburg: Wegner, 1948–64).

On Shakespeare's Day

It seems to me this is the noblest of our feelings, the hope to abide, even when fate appears to have brought us back to the general condition of nonexistence. This life, gentlemen, is much too short for our soul—witness the fact that every human being, the lowest and the highest, the least fit and the most worthy, tires of everything sooner than of living; and that nobody reaches the goal he set out for with such longing—for however long someone may enjoy success on his way, yet in the end he falls, often within sight of the goal he hoped for, into a pit dug for him by God knows whom, and is reckoned as nought.

Reckoned as nought! I! Who am my all, since I know everything only through myself! This is the cry of everyone who feels his existence and takes great steps through this life, a preparation for the endless road beyond. To be sure, each according to his measure. Though one may start out at the most vigorous hiking pace, the other wears seven-league boots, steps over him, and two steps for the latter mark out a day's journey for the former. Be that as it may, this busy hiker remains our friend and our companion, even if we stare in amazement and respect at the other's gigantic steps, follow his footprints, measure his steps against ours.

Off on the journey, gentlemen! Contemplating a single such footprint makes our soul more ardent and greater than gaping at a royal entrance with its thousand feet.

Today we honor the memory of the greatest wanderer, and bring honor on ourselves by doing so. We have in ourselves the seed of merits we know how to value.

Don't expect me to write a lot, or anything organized, a tranquil soul is no festive dress; and until now I have still thought little about Shakespeare; sensed, felt, at most, is all I've been able to do. The first page I read in him made me his for life, and when I had finished the first play I stood there like a man born blind who in the blink of an eye had been given his sight by a miracle-working hand. I recognized, I felt in the most vivid way that my existence was infinitely expanded, everything seemed new to me, unknown, and the unaccustomed light made my eyes hurt. By and by I learned to see, and thanks be to my grateful genius, I still feel vividly what I have gained.

I didn't hesitate for a moment to renounce the conventional theater. The unity of place seemed to me as anxiety ridden as a prison, the unities of action and time burdensome fetters on the imagination. I leaped into the open air and felt for the first time that I had hands and feet. And now that I saw how much injustice the masters of the rules had done me in their dungeon, and how many free souls still writhe in there, my heart would have burst had I not declared a feud against them, striving day by day to cast down their towers.

In its inward qualities and its externals, the Greek theater the French took as their model was such that a marquis could sooner imitate Alcibiades[1] than it was possible for Corneille to follow Sophocles.

First an intermezzo in the religious service, then solemnly political, the tragedy showed the people individual great actions of their fathers with the pure simplicity of perfection, aroused whole, great feelings in their souls, for it was whole and great itself.

And in what kind of souls!

Greek! I cannot explain what that means, but I feel it, and for the sake of brevity cite Homer and Sophocles, and Theocritus, as my authorities—they taught me to feel it.

Now I add swiftly, "Little Frenchman, what do you want with Greek armor? It's too big and heavy for you."

That's why all French tragedies are self-parodies.

How they proceed so according to the rules, and are as alike as peas in a pod and occasionally boring, too, especially in general in the fourth act, you, gentlemen, unfortunately know from experience, and I say nothing about it.

Who actually first hit on the idea of bringing grandiose affairs of state onto the stage, I don't know; there's an opportunity here for the amateur to write a critical treatise. I doubt if the honor of invention belongs to Shakespeare; suffice it to say, he brought this kind of play to a level that has always appeared the highest, and still does, since so few eyes reach up to it, and it can therefore hardly be hoped that anyone could see, let alone climb beyond it.

Shakespeare, my friend, if you were still among us, I could live nowhere but with you, how gladly I would play the supporting role of Pylades if you were Orestes,[2] rather than the most venerated character of a chief priest in the temple at Delphi.

Let me break off, gentlemen, and continue writing tomorrow, for I am writing in a tone that, though it comes right from my heart, you may not find so edifying.

Shakespeare's theater is a beautiful peep show in which the history of the world flows by before our eyes on the invisible thread of time. His plots are not plots at all according to conventional definitions, but his plays all revolve around the secret point, which no philosopher has yet perceived or defined, in which our own individuality, the free will we lay claim to, collides with the necessary course of the world as a whole. But our corrupted taste beclouds our eyes so much that we almost need a new creation to disentangle ourselves from this darkness.

All the French, and the Germans infected by them, even Wieland, have done themselves little honor in this matter as in various others. Voltaire, who always made it his profession to disparage all majesty, has shown himself here too to be a genuine Thersites. If I were Ulysses, he should bend his back beneath my scepter.[3]

Most of these gentlemen object particularly to his characters.

And I cry out: Nature! Nature! Nowhere is nature so itself as in Shakespeare's people.

Now I've really stirred them all up.

Give me air so I can speak!

He competed with Prometheus, re-created his human beings feature by feature, but *on a colossal scale.* That's the reason we don't recognize them as our brothers. And then he animated them all with the breath of *his* spirit, *he* speaks from them all, and one recognizes their kinship.

And how should our century presume to pass judgment on what is nature? Whence should we draw our knowledge of it, when from our youth on we feel everything about ourselves tightly laced and affected, and see that's the way others are too. I'm often ashamed, facing Shakespeare, for it sometimes happens that at first glance I think, "I would have done that differently." Afterwards I recognize I'm merely a poor sinner, and Nature herself prophesies through Shakespeare, while my people are bubbles blown by whims derived from romances.

And now to conclude, although I haven't yet begun.

What noble philosophers have said of the world holds true of Shakespeare, too: what we call evil is only the other side of the good, and belongs as necessarily to its existence and as part of the whole as the tropics must burn and Lapland freeze in order for there to be a moderate clime. He guides us through the whole world, but we coddled, inexperienced people scream at the sight of every unknown grasshopper we encounter, "Lord, he wants to eat us!"

Arise, gentlemen! Trumpet me all noble souls out of the Elysium of so-called good taste, where, drunk with sleep in tedious twilight they half are, and half are not, have passions in their heart and no marrow in their bones, and, because they are not tired enough to rest, and yet are too lazy to be active, waste their shadowy lives sauntering and yawning amongst myrtles and laurel bushes.

Translated by Timothy J. Chamberlain

Notes

Original title: *Zum Shakespeares-Tag*. Written 1771, first published 1854.

1. [An Athenian of great wealth, power, and abilities, friend of Socrates and character in Plato's *Symposium*.]
2. [Pylades is the faithful friend of Orestes in Greek legend and literature.]
3. [See *Iliad* 2.212–77, where Odysseus beats Thersites for disparaging Agamemnon.]

Review of *The Fine Arts in Their Origin, Their True Nature and Best Application,* by J. G. Sulzer.

Very easy to translate into French, could also very well be translated from French. Sulzer, according to the testimony of one of our *famous* men just as great a philosopher as any from antiquity, seems in his theory, in the manner of the ancients, to fob the poor public off with an esoteric doctrine, and these sheets are, if possible, less significant than everything else he has written.

The *fine arts,* an article in his general theory,[1] take central stage here, in order to put both amateurs and connoisseurs in a position to judge of the whole so much the sooner. Reading the great work until now we have already had many a doubt; but now that we investigate the very principles on which it is built, the lime that is supposed to stick together the scattered limbs of the lexicon, we find our opinion confirmed only too much: nothing is done for anyone here except the student seeking a basic primer, and the quite superficial fashionable dilettante.

We have already previously voiced our thoughts that a theory of the arts might not yet be ready for our times in Germany.[2] We do not presume to expect such an opinion to be able to prevent the publishing of such a book; we can only, indeed we must, warn our good young friends against works of this kind. Anyone who lacks sensuous experience of the arts should rather leave them alone. Why should he occupy himself with them? Because it's fashionable? Let him consider that all theory bars his way to true enjoyment, for a more harmful nullity than theory has not been invented.

The *fine arts,* the fundamental article of Sulzer's theory. So there they are, of course, all together again, whether they're related or not. What doesn't stand listed in the lexicon? What cannot be connected by means of such a philosophy? Painting and dance, oratory and architecture, poetry and sculpture, all conjured by the magic light of a little philosophical lantern through a single hole onto the white wall, they dance up and down in the marvelous light, many-colored, and the delighted spectators pant for breath in their joy.

That some man who reasoned rather badly hit on the idea that certain human occupations and joys that became a labor and an effort for unspontaneous imitators without genius, could be classified under the rubric of arts, fine arts, for the benefit of theoretical sleight of hand—on account of its convenience this idea then remained the main theme for philosophy about the arts, even though they bear no closer relation to one another than the seven liberal arts of the old priestly schools.

We are astonished that Sulzer, even without reflecting on it, didn't become aware during the execution of his work of the great inconvenience that as long as one keeps to generalities one says nothing, and at most can conceal the lack of material from the inexperienced by means of declamation.

He wants to oust the indefinite principle of *imitation of nature*, and gives us in its place an equally meaningless one: *the embellishment of things*. He wants, in the traditional manner, to make inferences from nature to art: "Everything in all creation is in harmony, to touch the eye and the other senses from all sides with pleasant impressions." So does that which makes unpleasant impressions on us not belong just as much to nature's plan as her most lovely aspects? Are the raging storms, floods, rains of fire, subterranean glow, and death in all the elements not just as much true witnesses of her eternal life as the sun rising in splendor over full vineyards, and fragrant orange groves? What would Sulzer say to the loving mother nature if it were to swallow into its belly a metropolis he had built up and populated with all the fine arts and their handmaidens?

This inference stands up just as little: "In general, nature wanted to educate our hearts to gentleness and sensitivity by means of the pleasant impressions streaming in on us from all sides." *In general* it never does that, rather, it hardens its genuine children, thank God, against the pains and evils it continually causes them, so that we can call that man the happiest who was able to encounter evils with the greatest strength, turn them away from him, and in defiance of them proceed according to his own will. Now that is too arduous, indeed impossible, for a great part of humankind; hence most of them, particularly the philosophers, beat a hasty retreat and retrench; which is why they then *in general* argue with such adequacy.

How selective and limited is the following observation, and how much it is supposed to prove! "Above all, this tender mother has placed all the charms of attractiveness in those objects that are most necessary to our happiness, in particular in the blissful union in which the man finds a spouse." We honor beauty with all our heart, have never been insensitive to its attractions; but to make it the prime mover in this sphere is only possible for one who has no inkling of the mysterious powers by which each is drawn to *its like,* and everything under the sun mates and is happy.

So even if it were true that the effect of the arts is the embellishment of things around us, it is nonetheless false to say that they do so following the example of nature.

What we see of nature is power, this power devours; nothing is present, everything passing, a thousand seeds are crushed, a thousand born each moment, it is great and significant, infinitely diverse; beautiful and ugly, good and evil, all exists side by side with equal right. And *art* is precisely the opposite; it arises from the endeavors of the individual to preserve itself from the destroying power of the whole. Even the animal by its artful instincts *sets itself apart, preserves itself;* the human being in all conditions fortifies himself against nature in order to avoid its thousandfold evils and enjoy only the measure of goodness it accords; until he finally succeeds as far as possible in encasing the circle of all his genuine and acquired needs within a palace, in holding all the scattered beauty and happiness spellbound within its glass walls, where he then becomes softer and softer, substitutes joys of the soul for joys of the body, and his powers, with nothing disagreeable to tauten them to natural uses, melt away into virtue, beneficence, sensibility.

Sulzer continues on his way, which we would rather not follow; he cannot lack a great troop of disciples, for he feeds them with milk, not strong foods;[3] talks a lot about the essence of the arts, their purpose; and praises their great usefulness as a means to the furtherance of human happiness. Anyone who knows human nature just a little, and the arts, and happiness, will have little hope of this; the many kings will occur to him who were eaten to death by ennui in the midst of the glory of their splendor. For if only connoisseurship is envisaged, if one does not enjoy with active participation, hunger and disgust, the two most inimical drives, must soon combine to torment the wretched *Pococurante*.[4]

Following this he embarks on a portrayal of the history of the fine arts and their present condition, projected imaginatively with the finest colors, just as good and no better than the histories of mankind to which we are so accustomed these days, in which the fairy tale of the four ages of the world always suffices,[5] and told in the tone of history rewritten for practical application—as a novel.

Now Sulzer comes to our times and, as befits a prophet, scolds his own century roundly; admittedly doesn't deny that the fine arts have found more than enough promoters and friends, but because they have still not been used to the great end, the *moral improvement* of the people, our rulers have done nothing. He dreams, with others, that a wise legislature would both animate geniuses and be able to indicate the true goal to work towards, and more along those lines.

Finally he raises the question whose answer is supposed to open the way to the true theory: "What initiatives can be taken so that man's innate sensual tendencies can be used to elevate his way of thinking and can be employed in specific cases as a means to attract him irresistibly to his duty?" As half- and misunderstood and vain as Cicero's wish to lead virtue to his son in the form of physical beauty.[6] And Sulzer doesn't answer the question, but rather merely suggests what is important here—and we close his little book. His audience of disciples and petty connoisseurs may remain faithful to him, we know that all true artists and lovers of art are on our side, and will laugh at the philosopher just as until now they have complained about the academics. And to these listeners a few words more, confined to a few arts, which may apply to as many as it can.

If any speculative endeavor is to benefit the arts, it must address the artist directly, provide a draft to his natural fire, so that it can spread and prove active. For it's all a matter of the artist, that he feels no bliss in life but in his art, that he lives sunk in the instrument of his art, with all his feelings and powers. What does the gaping audience matter, what does it matter whether or not it can account for why it gaped, when it has done with gaping?

So anyone who in writing, speech, or by means of example—in ascending order—could raise the so-called amateur, the artist's only true audience, nearer and nearer to the spirit of the artist, so that his soul might also flow into the instrument of his art, would have done more than all psychological theorists. These gentlemen are so high up there in the empyrean of transcendental virtuous beauty that they don't care about petty details down here, which are all that matter. Which of us sons of the earth, on the other hand, doesn't see with deep regret how many good souls remain stuck with meticulous mechanical execution, e.g., in music, and perish beneath it?

May God preserve our senses, and preserve us from the theory of sensuousness, and give every beginner a good master! And since these are not to be had everywhere and always, and yet one has to write, let the artist and amateur give us a περὶ ἑαυτοῦ[7] of his endeavors, of the difficulties that delayed him most, the powers with which he overcame them, the chance events that helped him, the spirit that in certain moments came over him and gave him light for his life, until in the end, always growing, he swung himself up to mighty possession and as king and conqueror compelled the neighboring arts, indeed the whole of nature, to pay tribute.

In this way we would gradually assemble a living theory, passing from the mechanical to the intellectual, from the mixing of paints and the tuning of strings to the true *influence of the arts on heart and mind,* would give the amateur joy and courage, and perhaps help the genius a little.

Translated by Timothy J. Chamberlain

Notes

Goethe's review of Sulzer's *Die schönen Künste in ihrem Ursprung, ihrer wahren Natur und besten Anwendung* appeared on December 18, 1772, in the *Frankfurter Gelehrte Anzeigen,* a literary newspaper to which at this time Herder, Goethe, and Johann Heinrich Merck (1741–91) were major contributors.

1. [Sulzer's *Allgemeine Theorie der schönen Künste und Wissenschaften* (General theory of the fine arts and letters), which appeared between 1771 and 1774, was a major work of academic classicism in Germany. Much criticized by the Storm and Stress, its influence on Weimar Classicism has later been recognized.]
2. [A reference to Merck's review of Sulzer's *General Theory,* also in the *Frankfurter Gelehrte Anzeigen,* which had reproached Sulzer for failing to follow the lead of Lessing's *Laocoön* and Herder's *Critical Forests.*]
3. [1 Corinthians 3:2.]
4. [In Voltaire's *Candide* (chapter 27), the rich Venetian senator Pococurante remains dissatisfied despite enjoying all the pleasures of life.]
5. [Probably a reference to the division of world history into the four empires of the Assyrians, Medes, Macedonians, and Romans, made popular by St. Jerome in his commentary on Daniel. In some interpretations, the Holy Roman Empire still sustained the fourth empire until its dissolution in 1806.]
6. [Cicero, *De officiis* 1.5.15.]
7. [(Here) "report."]

From Goethe's Pocketbook

It's high time people stopped talking about the form of dramatic plays, their length and brevity, their unities, their beginning, middle, and end, and whatever all that stuff is called. And our author[1] sets out fairly directly for the content, which it used to seem could be taken so much for granted.

All the same, there does exist a form that differs from the one mentioned as the inner sense differs from the outer, which is not obvious, but has to be felt. Our mind must have a clear view of what another mind can conceive; our heart must feel what can fill another. Confounding the rules doesn't mean there are no constraints, and even if the example were to be dangerous, it's nonetheless fundamentally better to write a confused play than a cold one.

To be sure, if more people had the feeling for this inward form,[2] which embraces all forms, there would be fewer monsters of the spirit to disgust us. It wouldn't occur to people to stretch out every tragic event into a drama, nor to cut up every novel into plays! I wish some clever person would parody this twofold nuisance and rework for example Aesop's fable of the wolf and the lamb as a tragedy in five acts.

Every form, even the most intensely felt, has an element of untruth; but form is once and for all the glass through which we focus the holy rays of diffused nature into a fiery gaze directed at the human heart. But the glass! Anyone not given it won't hunt it down, like the mysterious stone of the alchemists it is both vessel and substance, fire and cooling bath. So simple that it lies before every door, and so wondrous a thing that precisely the people who possess it for the most part can make no use of it.

Anyone, by the way, who really wants to work for the stage should study the stage, the effect of painted backgrounds, of the lights, makeup, glazed linen, and glitter, should leave nature in its place and be sure to give assiduous thought to avoiding setting up anything but what can be performed before children on planks fixed between slats, cardboard, and canvas—as a puppet play.

Translated by Timothy J. Chamberlain

Notes

An excerpt from *Aus Goethes Brieftasche,* a contribution by Goethe to Heinrich Leopold Wagner's (1747–79) translation of Louis Sébastien Mercier's *Du théâtre ou nouvel essai sur l'art dramatique* (1773). The translation appeared as *Neuer Versuch über die Schauspielkunst* in 1776.

1. [I.e., Mercier.]
2. [Goethe adopts this concept from Shaftesbury (*Characteristics of Men, Manners, Opinions, Times* (1714), treatise 7, chapter 3.7).]

Simple Imitation of Nature, Manner, Style

It does not seem to be superfluous to define clearly the meaning we attach to these words, of which we shall often have occasion to make use. For, however long we may have been in the habit of using them, and however they may seem to have been defined in theoretical works, still everyone continues to use them in a way of his own, and means more or less by them, according to the degree of clearness or uncertainty with which he has seized the ideas they express.

Simple Imitation of Nature

If an artist, in whom we must of course suppose a natural talent, is in the first stage of progress, and after having in some measure practiced eye and hand, turns to natural objects, uses all care and fidelity in the most perfect imitation of their forms and colors, never knowingly departs from nature, begins and ends in her presence every picture that he undertakes—such an artist must possess high merit, for he cannot fail of attaining the greatest accuracy, and his work must be full of certainty, variety, and strength.

If these conditions are clearly considered, it will easily be seen that a capable but limited talent can in this way treat agreeable but limited subjects.

Such subjects must always be easy to find. Leisurely observation and quiet imitation must be allowed for; the disposition that occupies itself in such works must be a quiet one, self-contained, and satisfied with moderate gratification.

This sort of imitation will thus be practiced by men of quiet, true, limited nature, in the representation of dead or still-life subjects. It does not by its nature exclude a high degree of perfection.

Manner

But man finds, usually, such a mode of proceeding too timid and inadequate. He perceives a harmony among many objects, which can only be brought into a picture by sacrificing the individual. He gets tired of using nature's letters each time to spell after her. He invents a way, devises a language for himself, so as to express in his own fashion the idea his soul has attained, and give to the object he has so many times repeated a distinctive form, without having recourse to nature herself each time he repeats it, or even without recalling exactly the individual form.

Thus a language is created, in which the mind of the speaker expresses and utters itself immediately; and as in each individual who thinks, the conceptions of spiritual objects are formed and arranged differently, so will every artist of this class see, understand, and imitate the outward world in a different manner, will seize its phenomena with a more or less observant eye, and reproduce them more accurately or loosely.

We see that this species of imitation is applied with the best effect in cases where a great whole comprehends many subordinate objects. These last must be sacrificed in order to attain the general expression of the whole, as is the case in landscapes, for instance, where the aim would be missed if we attended too closely to the details, instead of keeping in view the idea of the whole.

Style

When at last art, by means of imitation of nature, of efforts to create a common language, and of clear and profound study of objects themselves, has acquired a clearer and clearer knowledge of the peculiarities of objects and their mode of being, oversees the classes of forms, and knows how to connect and imitate those that are distinct and characteristic—then will *style* reach the highest point it is capable of, the point where it may be placed on a par with the highest efforts of the human mind.

Simple imitation springs from quiet existence and an agreeable subject; manner seizes with facile capacity upon an appearance; style rests upon the deepest foundations of knowledge, upon the essence of things, so far as we are able to recognize it in visible and comprehensible forms.

The elaboration of what we have advanced above would fill whole volumes; and much is said upon the subject in books, but a true conception of it can only be arrived at by the study of nature and works of art. We subjoin some additional considerations, and shall have occasion to refer to these remarks whenever plastic art is in question.

It is easy to see that these three several ways of producing works of art are closely related, and that one may imperceptibly run into the others.

The simple imitation of subjects of easy comprehension (we shall take fruits and flowers as an example) may be carried to a high point of perfection. It is natural that he who paints roses should soon learn to distinguish and select the most beautiful, and seek for such only among the thousand that summer affords. Thus we have arrived at selection, although the artist may have formed no general idea of the beauty of roses. He has to do with comprehensible forms; everything depends upon the manifold purpose and the color of the surface. The downy peach, the finely dusted plum, the smooth apple, the burnished cherry, the dazzling rose, the manifold pink, the variegated tulip, all these he can have at will in his quiet studio in the perfection of their bloom and ripeness. He can put them in a favorable light; his eye will become accustomed to the harmonious play of glittering colors; each year would give him a fresh opportunity of renewing the same models, and he would be enabled, without laborious abstraction, by means of quiet imitative observation, to know and seize the peculiarities of the simple existence of these subjects. In this way were produced the masterpieces of a Huysum and Rachel Ruysch, artists who seem almost to have accomplished the impossible. It is evident that an artist of this sort must become greater and more characteristic, if in addition to his talent, he is also acquainted with botany; if he knows, from the root up, the influences of the several parts upon the expansion and growth of the plant, their office, and reciprocal action; if he understands and reflects upon the successive development of leaves, fruit, flowers, and the new germ. By this means he will not only exhibit his taste in the selection of superficial appearance, but will at once win admiration and give instruction through a correct representation of properties. In this wise it might be said that he had formed a style; while, on the other hand, it is easy to see how such a master, if he proceeded with less thoroughness, if he endeavored to give only the striking and dazzling, would soon pass into mannerism.

Simple imitation therefore labors in the antechamber that leads to style. In proportion to the truth, care, and purity with which it goes to work, the composure with which it examines and feels, the calmness with which it proceeds to imitate, the degree of reflection it uses, that is to say, with which it learns to compare the like and separate the unlike, and to arrange separate objects under one general idea—will be its title to step upon the threshold of the sanctuary itself.

If now we consider manner more carefully, we shall see that it may be, in the highest sense and purest signification of the word, the middle ground between simple imitation of nature and style.

The nearer it approaches, with its more facile treatment, to faithful imitation and on the other side, the more earnestly it endeavors to seize and comprehensibly express the character of objects, the more it strives, by means of a pure, lively, and active individuality, to combine the two, the higher, greater, and more worthy of respect it will become. But if such an artist ceases to hold fast by and reflect upon nature, he will soon lose sight of the true principles of art, and his manner will become more and more empty and insignificant in proportion as he leaves behind simple imitation and style.

We need not here repeat that we use the word *manner* in a high and honorable sense, so that artists who, according to our definition, would be termed mannerists, have nothing to complain of. It is only incumbent upon us to preserve the word *style* in the highest honor, in order to have an expression for the highest point art has attained or ever can attain. To be aware of this point is in itself a great good fortune, and to enter upon its consideration in company with sensible people, a noble pleasure, for which we hope to have many opportunities in the sequel.

Translated by S. G. Ward

Notes

Original title: *Einfache Nachahmung der Natur, Manier, Stil.* First published 1789.

On Epic and Dramatic Poetry

The epic and the dramatic writer are both subject to the universal poetic laws, especially the law of unity and the law of progressive development. Furthermore they both deal with similar subjects and both can use a great variety of motives. The essential difference consists in this, that an epic poet narrates an event as completely past, while the dramatist presents it as completely present. If one wished to develop in detail from the nature of man these laws both have to follow, one would continually have to keep before his mind a rhapsodist and an actor, each in the character of a poet, the former surrounded by a circle of listeners quietly following with rapt attention, the latter by an impatient throng that has come simply to see and to hear. It would then not be difficult to deduce what is most advantageous to either of these two forms of poetry, what subjects either will choose preeminently, nor what motives either will make use of most frequently; as I remarked in the beginning, neither can lay claim to any one thing exclusively.

The subject of the epic as well as of tragedy should be based on the purely human, it should be vital, and it should make an appeal to one's feelings. The best effect is produced when the characters stand upon a certain plane of cultural advancement, so that their actions are purely the expression of their personality and are not influenced by moral, political, or mechanical considerations. The myths of the heroic times were especially useful to the poets on these grounds.

The epic poem represents more especially action restricted to individuals; tragedy, suffering restricted to individuals. The epic poem represents man as an external agent, engaged in battles, journeys, in fact in every possible kind of undertaking, and so demands a certain elaborateness of treatment. Tragedy, on the other hand, represents man as an internal agent, and the action, therefore, requires but little space in a genuine tragedy.

There are five kinds of motives:

(1) Progressive motives, which advance the action. These the drama uses preeminently.

(2) Retrogressive, which draw the action away from its goal. These the epic poem uses almost exclusively.

(3) Retarding, which delay the progress of the action or lengthen its course. Both epic and tragic poetry use these to very great advantage.

(4) Retrospective, which introduce into the poem events that happened before the time of the poem.

(5) Prospective, which anticipate what will happen after the time of the poem. The epic as well as the dramatic poet uses the last two kinds of motives to make his poem complete.

The worlds that are to be represented are common to both, namely:

(1) The physical world, which consists first of all of the immediate world to which the persons represented belong and which surrounds them. In it the dramatist limits himself mostly to one locality, while the epic poet moves about with greater freedom and in a larger sphere. Secondly, the physical world, containing the more remote world in which all of nature is included. This world the epic poet, who appeals exclusively to the imagination, makes more intelligible through the use of similes and metaphors, which figures of speech are employed more sparingly by the dramatist.

(2) The moral world, which is absolutely common to both, and, whether normal or pathological, is best represented in its simplicity.

(3) The world of fancies, forebodings, apparitions, chance, and fate. This is available to both, only it must of course be approximated to the world of the senses. In this world there arises a special difficulty for us moderns, because we cannot easily find substitutes for the fabulous creatures, gods, soothsayers, and oracles of the ancients, however much we may desire to.

If we consider the manner of treatment as a whole, we shall find the rhapsodist, who recites what is completely past, appearing as a wise man, with calm deliberation surveying the events. It will be the purpose of his recital to get his hearers into an even frame of mind, so that they will listen to him long and willingly. He will divide the interest evenly, because it is impossible for him to counteract quickly a too-vivid impression. He will, according to his pleasure, go back in point of time or anticipate what is to come. We may follow him everywhere, for he makes his appeal only to the imagination, which originates its own images and which is to a certain extent indifferent as to what images are called up. The rhapsodist as a higher being ought not to appear himself in his poem; he would read best of all behind a curtain, so that we may separate everything personal from his work, and may believe we are hearing only the voice of the muses.

The actor represents the very reverse of this. He presents himself as a definite individuality. It is his desire to have us take interest exclusively in him and in his immediate surroundings, so that we may feel with him the sufferings of his soul and of his body, may share his embarrassments, and forget ourselves in him. To be sure he, too, will proceed by degrees, but he can risk far more vivid effects, because by his actual presence before the eyes of the audience he can neutralize a stronger impression even by a weaker one. The senses of spectators and listeners must be constantly stimulated. They must not rise to a contemplative frame of mind, but must follow eagerly; their imagination must be completely suppressed; no demands must be made upon it; and even what is narrated must be vividly brought before their vision, as it were, in terms of action.

Translated by F. W. J. Heuser

Notes

Original title: *Über epische und dramatische Dichtung.* The result of discussions between Goethe and Schiller, it was written down by Goethe in 1797, but first published in 1827.

Literary Sansculottism

Those who consider it an absolute duty to connect definite concepts with the words they employ in speaking and writing will very rarely use the expressions, *classical author* and *classical work*.

What are the conditions that produce a classical national author? He must, in the first place, be born in a great commonwealth, which after a series of great and historic events has become a happy and unified nation. He must find in his countrymen loftiness of disposition, depth of feeling, and vigor and consistency of action. He must be thoroughly pervaded with the national spirit, and through his innate genius feel capable of sympathizing with the past as well as the present. He must find his nation in a high state of civilization, so that he will have no difficulty in obtaining for himself a high degree of culture. He must find much material already collected and ready for his use, and a large number of more or less perfect attempts made by his predecessors. And finally, there must be such a happy conjuncture of outer and inner circumstances that he will not have to pay dearly for his mistakes, but that in the prime of his life he may be able to see the possibilities of a great theme and to develop it according to some uniform plan into a well-arranged and well-constructed literary work.

If anyone, who is endowed with clearness of vision and fairness of mind, contrasts these conditions under which alone a classic writer, especially a classic prose writer, is possible, with the conditions under which the best Germans of this century have worked, he will respect and admire what they have succeeded in doing, and notice with tactful regret in what they have failed.

An important piece of writing, like an important speech, can only be the outgrowth of actual life. The author no more than the man of action can fashion the conditions under which he is born and under which he acts. Each one, even the greatest genius, suffers in some respects from the social and political conditions of his age, just as in other respects he benefits by them. And only from a real nation can a national writer of the highest order be expected. It is unfair, however, to reproach the German nation because, though closely held together by its geographical position, it is divided politically. We do not wish for Germany those political revolutions that might prepare the way for classical works.

And so any criticism that approaches the question from such a false point of view is most unfair. The critic must look at our conditions, as they were and as they now are; he must consider the individual circumstances under which German writers obtained their training, and he will easily find the correct point of view. There is nowhere in Germany a common center of social culture, where men of letters might gather together and perfect themselves, each one in his particular field, in conformity with the same standard. Born in the most widely scattered portions of the land, educated in the most diverse ways, left almost entirely to themselves or to impressions derived from the most varied environments, carried away by a special liking for this or that example of German or foreign literature, the German men of letters are forced, without any guidance, to indulge in all sorts of experiments, even in botched work, in order to try their powers. Only gradually and after considerable reflection do they realize what they ought to do. Practice alone teaches them what they can do. Again and again the bad taste of a large public, which devours the bad and the good with equal pleasure, leads them into doubt. Then again an acquaintance with the educated though widely scattered population of the great empire encourages them, and the common labors and endeavors of their contemporaries fortify them. Such are the conditions under which German writers finally reach man's estate. Then concern for their own support, concern for a family, force them to look about in the world at large, and often with the most depressing feeling, to do work for which they have no respect themselves, in order to earn a livelihood, so that they can devote themselves to that kind of work with which alone their cultured minds would occupy themselves. What German author of note will not recognize himself in this picture, and will not confess with modest regret that he often enough sighed for an opportunity to subordinate sooner the peculiarities of his original genius to a general national culture, which unfortunately did not exist?

For foreign customs and literatures, irrespective of the many advantages they have contributed to the advancement of the higher classes, have prevented the Germans from developing sooner as Germans.

And now let us look at the work of German poets and prose writers of recognized ability. With what care and what devotion did they not follow in their labors an enlightened conviction! It is, for example, not saying too much, when we maintain that a capable and industrious literary critic, through a comparison of all the editions of our Wieland—a man of whom we may proudly boast in spite of the snarling of all our literary parasites—could develop the whole theory of good taste simply from the successive corrections of this author, who has so indefatigably worked toward his own improvement. We hope that every librarian will take pains to have such a collection made, while it is still possible, and then the next century will know how to make grateful use of it.

In the future we may perhaps be bold enough to lay before the public a history of the development of our foremost writers, as it is shown in their works. We do not expect any confessions, but if they would only themselves impart to us, as far as they see fit, those facts that contributed most to their development, and those that stood most in the way of it, the influence of the good they have done would become still more far-reaching.

For if we consider what superficial critics take least notice of—the good fortune young men of talent enjoy nowadays in being able to develop earlier, and to attain sooner a pure style appropriate to the subject at hand—to whom do they owe it but to their predecessors in the last half of this century, each of whom in his own way has trained himself with unceasing endeavor amidst all sorts of hindrances? Through this circumstance a sort of invisible school has sprung up, and the young man who now enters it gets into a much larger and brighter circle than the earliest author, who had to roam through it first himself in the faint light of dawn, in order to help widen it gradually and as it were only by chance. The pseudocritic, who would light the way for us with his little lamp, comes much too late; the day has dawned, and we shall not close our shutters again.

Men do not give vent to their ill humor in good society; and he must be in a very bad humor, who at this present moment, when almost everybody writes well, denies that Germany has writers of the first order. One does not need to go far to find an agreeable novel, a clever sketch, a clearly written essay on this or that subject. What proof do not our critical papers, journals, and compendiums furnish of a uniformly good style? The Germans show a more and more thorough mastery of facts, and the arrangement of the material steadily gains in clearness. A dignified philosophy, in spite of all the opposition of wavering opinions, makes them more and more acquainted with their intellectual powers, and facilitates the use of them. The numerous examples of style, the preliminary labors and endeavors of so many men, enable a young man now sooner to present with clearness and grace and in an appropriate manner what he has received from without and developed within himself. Thus a healthy and fair-minded German sees the writers of his nation at a fair stage of development, and is convinced that the public, too, will not let itself be misled by an ill-humored criticaster. Such a one ought to be barred from society, from which everyone should be excluded whose destructive work might only make productive writers disheartened, the sympathetic public listless, and the onlookers distrustful and indifferent.

Translated by F. W. J. Heuser,
Revised by Timothy J. Chamberlain

Notes

First published 1795. The title (*Literarischer Sansculottismus*) draws a parallel between the unjustified dismissal of writers of value by inferior critics, and the campaign of the Sansculottes in the French Revolution against those better than themselves. Goethe's specific target is an essay by Daniel Jenisch (1762–1804). This translation omits the first four paragraphs of Goethe's essay.

Jakob Michael Reinhold Lenz

Jakob Michael Reinhold Lenz (1751–92) studied theology in Königsberg, where he attended lectures by Kant, who remains an important influence in Lenz's philosophical essays. In Strasbourg in 1771, he met Goethe, who rapidly came to dominate his imagination. Lenz's first play, *The Tutor* (1774), appeared anonymously and was generally attributed to Goethe. This play, like *The Soldiers* (1776; The German Library, volume 14), breaks new ground in the realistic portrayal of middle- and lower-class Germany, and in the development of a drama beyond the traditional genres. Lenz's other plays include *The New Menoza* (1776), and the literary satire *Pandemonium Germanicum* (1775). He also wrote stories, notably "Zerbin" (1776) and "The Country Vicar" (1777), philosophical and religious essays, including the "Opinions of a Layman" (1775), and essays on literature, in particular his "Notes on the Theater" (1774; excerpts appear in The German Library, volume 83). In 1778, Lenz suffered a complete mental collapse; fetched back to his family in Riga, he wandered on to St. Petersburg and Moscow, where he supported himself by translation and the charity of friends, until his death in 1792. Goethe's later unfavorable judgment long decided his reputation, though Georg Büchner made him the subject of his powerful story "Lenz" (1835–36; The German Library, volume 28). In the twentieth century, Lenz has come into his own as a living force in the German theater, and an important influence on naturalism, expressionism, and the epic theater. A good selection of his works is provided in *Werke und Schriften,* ed. Britta Titel and Hellmut Haug, 2 vols. (Stuttgart: Govert, 1966–67). For a study in English, see John Osborne, *J. M. R. Lenz: The Renunciation of Heroism* (Göttingen: Vandenhoeck & Ruprecht, 1975).

On *Götz von Berlichingen*

We are born—our parents give us bread and clothing—our teachers thrust into our minds words, languages, sciences—some charming girl or another thrusts into our heart the desire to make her our own, to fold her in our arms as our property, if indeed some more bestial need isn't involved—there arises some opening in the state where we fit in—our friends, relatives, patrons set to and manage to shove us into it—we turn in this spot for a while like the other wheels and push and drive—until, if all continues as it should, we are dulled with use and in the end in turn have to make way for a new wheel—that, gentlemen! speaking with due modesty, is our biography—and now what does that leave man other than a small machine of outstanding artifice, fitting better or worse into the big machine we call the world, world events, world history.

No wonder philosophers philosophize this way if that's the way people live.[1] But can one call that living? can one call that feeling one's existence, one's independent existence, the divine spark? Ha, the appeal of life must consist of something better: for to be a ball others play with is a sad, depressing thought, eternal slavery, animal nature that is merely more artful, rational, but precisely for that reason more wretched. What do we learn from this? This isn't intended as a declamation, gentlemen—if your own feelings don't tell you that I'm right, then I'd damn all oratorical arts that might incline you to take my part without convincing you. What do we learn from this? This is what we learn, that action, action is the soul of the world, not enjoyment, not emotional sensitivity, not intellectual hairsplitting, that only by action do we come to resemble God who acts without ceasing and without ceasing delights in his works. This is what we learn, that the power of action in us is our spirit, our highest faculty, that it alone gives to our body with all its sensuality and sensitivity true life, true consistency, true worth, that without this spirit all our pleasure, all our feelings, all our knowledge are only passivity, only death delayed. This is what we learn, that this our power of action should not rest, should not desist from effectiveness, from motion, from tumult until it has created freedom around us, room for action: good God, room for action, even if it were chaos you had created, wild and void, but freedom dwelled only there and we could brood over it in imitation of you until something emerged from it[2]—bliss! bliss! A feeling fit for gods!

Forgive my enthusiasm! One cannot talk about these things too enthusiastically; for when our opponents waste so much heat presenting passivity to us as sweet and pleasant, shall we not rake together fires from heaven and hell to recommend activity? There our modern-day theatrical heroes stand, sighing away their last vital power in order to please a mask painted up to the ears—rascals and not heroes! What have you *done* to earn the name heroes?

Let me explain myself more precisely. Our stages today teem with nothing but masterpieces, which however, to be sure, are masterpieces only in the minds of their masters. But that aside, let them be what they may, what does it matter to me? For let us adopt another way of judging plays, my brothers, let us for a change look at their consequences, at the overall effect they have. It seems to me that must after all be the surest way. If you throw a stone into the water, you judge the size, mass, and weight of the stone by the circles it makes in the water. Therefore, let our question of every newly appearing play be the great, the divine Cui bono?[3] Cui bono did God create light? In order that it give light and warmth. Cui bono did He create the planets? So that they order the seasons and years for us. And so it goes on without ceasing in nature, nothing lacks purpose, everything has its great, manifold purpose, which can never be measured adequately by human nor by angelic standards. And where would the genius find another, higher, deeper, greater, more beautiful model than God and His nature?

Therefore, cui bono? What sort of effect do the products of all the thousand French geniuses have on our spirit, on our heart, on our whole existence? Heaven forbid I should be unjust. We take home with us a beautiful, delightful sweet feeling, as if we had downed a bottle of champagne—but that's all. Sleep on it for a night and the whole thing's wiped out again. Where is the *living* impression, which afterwards mixes itself into attitudes, deeds, and *actions,* the Promethean spark that has stolen into our innermost soul so unnoticed that it fills our whole life with bliss, if we do not let it die away again by lying completely still? Let that therefore be the judicial scale according to which, even with our eyes blindfolded, we determine the true worth of a play. Which is heavier, which has more weight, power, makes the greater impression on our opinions and actions? And now decide about Götz. And I would like to call out to the audience of all Germany, if my voice were that loud: one and all, first imitate Götz, first learn to think, feel, act again, and if you find that pleases you, then decide about Götz.

So, my worthy brothers! I now admonish and beg you, let us not lay this book from our hand unused right after the first reading, let us first weigh the character of this German man of old with heated soul, and if we find it good, make it our own, so that we may again become Germans, from which we've deviated so far, so far. I shall jot down here a few traits of his character. A man who pretends to neither fame nor name, who wants to be nothing but what he is: a man.—Who has a wife worthy of him, earned not by begging and flattery but by his own merit—a family, a circle of friends all of whom he loves much more strongly than he could tell them, but for whom he *acts*—applies his all to provide for them peace, safety from the unjust attacks of outsiders, joy, and pleasure—see, there he is, the whole man, always busy, active, warming, and beneficent like the sun, but also just as much a devouring fire, when people get too close to him—and at the end of his life he goes down like the sun, satisfied that he will see better places, where there is more liberty than he could provide for himself and his own here, and leaves light and radiance behind him still. One who has lived thus, verily, he has fulfilled his destiny, God, *you* know how fully, how *well*, he knows only as much of it as suffices to make him happy. For what in the world can surpass the awareness that one has given much joy?

We are all, gentlemen! in a certain sense still silent players in the great theater of the world, until it shall please the directors to give us a role. Whatever it may be, we must all hold ourselves ready to act in it, and according as we act better rather than worse, more strongly rather than more weakly, so we have played better rather than worse, and improved the happiness of our souls and our circumstances.

What could be a finer preparatory exercise for this great drama of life than if we now, when our hands and feet are still bound, attempt to perform in some room or another our *Götz von Berlichingen,* written by one of our own—what a grand idea! Let me take responsibility for carrying out this project, it shall not be as difficult as you imagine at first. No theater, no curtain, no scenery—it's all a matter of action. Choose the roles of your favorite characters, or permit me to give them out. It really will be very useful entertainment for us. Through imitation, through acting, a character makes a deeper impression. And entertainment will also be involved, I guarantee it, far more than you could ever imagine now. I demand from you nothing but seriousness and vigor in this undertaking, for gentlemen, you are men now—and I hope I don't need to call out to you the words of the apostle Paul: "When I was a child I acted like a child, but when I became a man I laid aside childish ways."[4] If everyone gets to the very bottom of his role and makes everything of it that can be made of it—think, gentlemen! what an idea! what a divine play! No need for curtain or benches! We're beyond the externals. Two swing doors opened and closed between scenes—if really necessary, we can mark off the acts by a little piece of music we can play ourselves—And no mortal may come to our Eleusinian mysteries[5] before we have rehearsed three or four times—and then everyone's invited who still feels a living breath in them—i.e., strength, spirit, and life to act with vigor.

Translated by Timothy J. Chamberlain

Notes

Original title: *Über Götz von Berlichingen*. Goethe's first major drama, a historical play written in emulation of Shakespeare with demonstrative disregard of the classical rules, took Germany by storm in 1773. Lenz's speech was probably delivered at a literary club in Strasbourg in 1774.

1. [Lenz has in mind the French mechanistic philosophers La Mettrie and Helvétius.]
2. [See Genesis 1.]
3. ["For whose advantage?"]
4. [1 Corinthians 13:11.]
5. [The cult of Demeter at Eleusis near Athens reached its annual climax in the "mysteries" celebrated by initiates from all of Greece, which probably involved a dramatic representation of Demeter's quest for her daughter, abducted by Pluto.]

Letters on the Morality of *The Sorrows* of *Young Werther*

First Letter

Dear Friend!

You write, you wish in all seriousness Goethe had never had *The Sorrows of Young Werther* printed. Forgive me, but this wish is so strange that I have the right to demand of a friend whose understanding and heart I have to esteem, that he should be obliged, indeed compelled to justify it.

Shall I prove to you I have this right? I know that the fine arts constitute the highest delight of your life—at least my heart has only become the sister of yours on this condition and can only be united with any heart on this condition. A man who is dead to the true feeling of all that is beautiful, great, noble in nature or in the arts always remains in my eyes a dangerous man, however pious and tame he may appear. Even if he has too little understanding to do me actual harm, too little resolution to be a villain, he will make himself more fearful to me than the most cunning and boldest enemy by his lack of understanding in interpreting my intentions and actions, by inactivity in the matters most urgent to my heart, indeed perhaps even by working against my most innocent and noblest endeavors at the urging of a morality he has abstracted from his own character and of the itch to achieve something irrespective of his laziness. After all that's the way it is even in nature—the noblest and strongest animals always shy away most from the most inconsiderable and wretched of all. The crowing of a cock can destroy the composure of a lion, the grunting of a pig that of an elephant. In general the greatest and most astonishing effects of nature are always subordinate to the sad rule that they can be destroyed by the most insignificant chance events, often by a simple suspension of the active powers, which can be caused by the very least counteraction. Thus the bear that uproots trees is felled by the blow of a rod on the nose, and the victory of an eager army is thwarted by a contrary wind.

This digression doesn't apply to you, since you are agreed with me that all happiness in human life consists in the feeling of beauty. Beauty can be called simply the quintessence of goodness, so how could a human heart do without it, without becoming a wretched heart? Now just look at *Werther's Sorrows* as a product of beauty, as which you must recognize it—and dare to sign so unjust a judgment with your name a second time.

Second Letter

You consider it a subtle defense of suicide. That seems to me like describing Homer's *Iliad* as a subtle encouragement of anger, quarreling, and enmity. Why on earth do people always impute to the poet moral purposes he never thought of? There has been enough laughter at that French geometrician who asked of every poem: "What does that prove?"—and yet every day people make the same mistake. As if the poet sat himself on his Delphic tripod[1] in order to prove a philosophical thesis. That may be the case with the author who bites his nails, but why measure a giant by a dwarf? Goethe wanted to represent nothing more and nothing less than the sorrows of young Werther, to follow them to their final goal as Homer pursues the wrath of Achilles. And the whole great work has made so little impression on you that at the end you can still ask about its moral?

With some of my comedies people have imputed to me all kinds of moral purposes and philosophical theses. They've racked their brains about whether I really consider private tutors as a class so dangerous to society, and haven't borne in mind that I only wanted to give a specific picture of things as they are and that the philosophy of the privy councilor is motivated only by his individuality.[2] In the same way they look for an attack on religious reforms in *The New Menoza,* when the new Menoza simply couldn't speak and act any other way under these circumstances if he wanted to retain a bit of personality. But this just by the way—the best I could do was to remain silent when I saw myself wrongly saddled with these virtues, since they were a sad proof to me of how little I must have succeeded so far in capturing the heart and imagination of my readers.

But that people sit down just as calmly and ask about the moral of *The Sorrows of Young Werther,* when my senses passed away when I read it, when I was transported magically into his world and loved with Werther, suffered with Werther, died with Werther—that I couldn't tolerate, even if I knew the author of this book not even by his name.

Third Letter

You say the representation of such violent passions is dangerous to the public?—Now I have you where I wanted you. I shall talk earnestly with you, my friendship gives me the right to do so and you can conclude what you want after reading this letter. If you want to suspend relations with a heart whose feelings diverge so far from your own, then you have the authority to act or not as you please.

When I had read the book for the first time, I ran around, full of the sweet tumult it had aroused in my breast and praised it to all my friends. The first copy I had (a present from the author) I gave to that woman whom among all my acquaintances I esteemed most highly and who found herself in a position that in its externals resembled that of Lotte quite closely. Far from it even occurring to me that the book could be dangerous to her, I gave it with the most unconcerned, firmest trust that it would cultivate in her heart those feelings that alone can constitute and secure the future happiness of her husband. How nervous I was when afterwards I saw almost everyone convinced of the opposite! And how doubt and pusillanimity struggled later in my heart, even though in the case of the fair lady reader mentioned, to whom I here pay the public tribute of my high esteem, I had not found myself deceived in my expectation. "There's a great deal of morality in it," were the first words I heard from her mouth about this book, and I am determined these words should put the whole philosophizing public to shame.

So let us just investigate the morality of the novel, not the moral purpose the poet has set himself (for there he ceases to be a poet), but rather the moral effect the reading of this novel can and must have on the hearts of the public. It must be the concern of every writer not to have caused damage, and woe betide the poet who can look calmly upon the ill consequences of his writings. The greatest virtue of a poet in all eternity is a noble heart, and since nobody can be found among the great heap of admirers and heralds who will tender my friend this service of love, to defend his heart, since even his enemies must do justice to his understanding and his talents: so I take this sweet occupation upon myself, unhired and uncalled, and want at least to make myself immortal by being capable of feeling the full worth of this my contemporary.

This testimony will do him no harm. To be proud of one's heart is a higher virtue than all shabby humility and feigned modesty.

Sixth Letter

Werther will not always find such readers as me, you write, who know how to interpret everything so correctly. Thank you for the compliment, I think heaven has apportioned to each a modicum of reason, to lead him through this life. But I shall concede to you that the greatest part of that readership that swallows Werther most avidly is a mass of young people lacking reflection and experience, ready to fling themselves into the first abyss of passion they come to wherever that may lead. *The Sorrows of Young Werther is written precisely for these and their kind.* . . . And what other sort of book should be written for them, should make them aware and sensible of that which is beautiful and noble? The Bible—which they have never read? Sermons—which they listen to but never hear? Philosophical miscellanies in pocketbook format which they can use for nothing on earth? Novels and comedies from the monstrous land of ideas that have never descended to our world, and whose dissimilarity to what we experience stamps as a fool a man who forms himself according to their model as soon as he steps into any good society? They'll read such stuff when they've taken a laxative and don't know how else to fill out the condition between sleep and waking. They'll burst with laughter at a human being who took it into his head to play the role of Grandison[3] or Medon[4] in reality, characters they found quite tolerable in theory. But to see a human being with their own feelings and their own way of acting, let me say, shaped like them, fall passionately for the finest creature in nature; to be moved, shaken, devastated by his fate, as with all that we love; to take on his emotions, imperceptibly make his outlook their own, distinguish a girl full of soul, full of the most delicate feeling of her position with regard to others from a glittering doll, to prefer her, to attempt to please her, to honor her, to adore her, to die for her—would to God we had a world full of Werthers, we'd find ourselves better off for it.

Oh, how wise Nicolai is to have discovered the weighty secret of preventing the damage that reading this novel would cause in so skillful a way. As if it were so unknown, so unheard-of a truth, that nobody reads a novel just because he wants to be converted but rather because and as long as it pleases him. But none of these gentlemen has a good enough heart to confess about *Werther* this truth: that every novel that is able to grasp and move the heart in its most hidden recesses also of necessity *improves* the heart, whatever this novel might look like.

Werther's merit consists precisely in this: that he acquaints us with passions and emotions everyone feels obscurely in himself, but to which he is unable to give a name. Therein consists the merit of *every poet.*

Eighth Letter

. . . There stands Laocoön[5] before his goddess with every expression of his pain . . . , there he stands, nailed to the rock of his duty, and weeps out his pain to heaven, until he dies the slow death decided for him in the council of the gods. What hothead capable of feeling this pain *in its entirety* will still desire to imitate him, will not of his own accord turn around when he's wandered just a few steps on these thorns? Why all the raised voices, I beg you, the thing speaks and warns of its own accord, only people incapable of daring the attempt, or of feeling it even remotely, can fear any danger. Young people who can chatter away whole nights with an old graybeard about it[6] are the very furthest from ever becoming Werther. A young, quiet, speechless feeling heart would soonest arouse my concern, but precisely for these the book is a remedy. If such a one has no Mentor behind him to thrust him directly from the cliff into the sea[7]—let him err for a while, he'll find his way. He will feel moments in his soul where the violence of passion subsides and makes room for a peaceful stillness, leaving him time enough for the decision to make a friend of the lover, and not to end so gruesomely as Werther, whose reasons for suicide would all be rendered powerless by one happy moment. A moment in which such a reader warms himself in the presence, even in the mere thought of his beloved, is more powerful than ten convincing arguments. And hope never leaves him, can never leave him. Go after the unfortunate man shipwrecked on a barren island, sitting there lonely and abandoned—you'll find hope with him. What are all these warnings supposed to achieve? Do you think we're hawking our life for pennies? Do you think suicide is as quickly committed as the word is spoken? Leave the young men alone—they'll do themselves no harm, even without the help of chronology and heraldry.[8] For perhaps they will be helped still sooner by a novel—our imagination at least wants to be entertained if it is to turn away from a charming object. And I can thank the poet for no secret of his art more than for placing in his goodness the antidote for this consuming fire precisely where these gentlemen fear to find the poison—I mean occupation for the well-disposed heart and the happily tuned imagination. These occupations will soon lead him to more serious ones, and thus a happy harmony will be restored in his soul, a harmony that must always without fail arise out of strong and manly labors and choice enjoyments of the imagination and the senses, and that will not allow the love of life to be extinguished. All that Werther would also have—but Werther is an image, gentlemen, a Prometheus crucified, in whose example you can mirror yourselves; and it is left up to your own genius to apply this example as usefully as you can.

Doesn't it occur to you that the poet can only paint the one side of the soul that serves his purpose, and must leave the others to reflection? That in order to satisfy your foolish demands he would have to write a chronicle of twenty-four folios that would demand just as much time to read as Werther could have lived and suffered?

That Werther is an image it is physically and metaphysically impossible to imitate fully?

That until you make of yourselves what he was before he began to suffer and what he had to be in order to suffer *in this way,* half your life could pass?

That you therefore needn't immediately chatter about imitation, before you feel in yourselves the possibility that you could imitate him?

And that in that case there would be no danger of imitation?

Translated by Timothy J. Chamberlain

Notes

Original title: *Briefe über die Moralität der Leiden des jungen Werthers* (1775). Goethe's best-selling novel (German Library, vol. 19), published in 1774, aroused bitter controversy on account of the hero's suicide, which incurred the disapproval of many civil and ecclesiastical authorities, and of older writers including Lessing and Nicolai. It is against Nicolai's parody *Die Freuden des jungen Werthers* (The joys of young Werther), 1775, that Lenz is writing in particular.

1. [The priestess of Apollo delivered oracles from a tripod at Delphi.]
2. [Lenz is referring to his play *Der Hofmeister* (The tutor).]
3. [The virtuous hero of Richardson's novel *Sir Charles Grandison.*]
4. [Herald of the wooers in the *Odyssey,* who warns Penelope of a plot against her son Telemachus.]

5. [I.e., Werther.]

6. [As in J. C. Riebe's *Über die Leiden des jungen Werthers. Gespräche.* (Conversations on *The Sorrows of Young Werther*) (1775).]

7. [A service Mentor performs Télémaque to preserve him from the seductions of Calypso's island in Fénelon's *Aventures de Télémaque,* book 7.]

8. [Riebe recommended studies of this kind to cool the blood.]

Review of *The New Menoza,* Composed by the Author Himself

... What I consistently call a comedy is not a performance that simply arouses laughter, but rather one that is for everybody. Tragedy is only for the more serious part of the audience, which is capable of regarding heroes of an earlier age in their own light and of measuring their worth accordingly. Thus the Greek tragedies immortalized remarkable persons of their fatherland in the actions or fates that distinguished them; thus also Shakespeare's tragedies were true representations of characters taken from the histories of ancient and modern nations. But the comedies of the Greeks were for the people, and the distinction between laughter and tears was only an invention of later critics who did not perceive why the coarser part of the audience had to be more inclined to laughter than to tears, and that the more it approached a savage condition rather than leaving it behind, the more its comedies had to approach the comic. Hence the distinction between ancient and modern comedy, hence the necessity of the French tearful dramas[1] that cannot be reasoned away by any amount of mockery, and will only fall completely when the morals of the nation are totally corrupted. Comedy is a painting of human society, and when this becomes serious, the painting cannot laugh. Hence Plautus wrote in a more comic way than Terence, and Molière more comically than Destouches and Beaumarchais. Hence our German writers of comedies have to write comically and tragically simultaneously, because the people for which they are writing, or at least should be writing, is such a mishmash of culture and coarseness, manneredness and wildness. Thus the comic poet creates an audience for the tragic. I have spoken enough for those able and willing to understand me. I am not denying a single artist anything, but simply want to present to the public the principles of my art, which I have derived from the most famous ancient artists, and have thought through for a long time with a soul full of heated concern. Anyone who considers the influence the theater can have on a nation will join me in my interest in a subject that will certainly not be settled in theater newspapers and yearbooks.

Translated by Timothy J. Chamberlain

Notes

Original title: *Rezension des Neuen Menoza, von dem Verfasser selbst aufgesetzt.* Lenz wrote the review, published in the *Frankfurter Gelehrte Anzeigen* (1775), because he was disappointed at the reception of his comedy *Der Neue Menoza.*

1. [The *comédie larmoyante,* a form of serious or sentimental comedy, was fashionable in the eighteenth century in France.]

Friedrich von Blanckenburg

Friedrich von Blanckenburg (1744–96) served as an officer in the Prussian army until his retirement for reasons of health in 1776. A dedicated and perceptive amateur of literature and bibliophile, he published his major work, *Essay on the Novel*, in 1774. From 1778 until his death he lived in Leipzig, where he was active as an editor and translator.

Essay on the Novel

Preface

I'm not sure from what point of view this work might be seen if I didn't indicate the appropriate viewpoint myself, and that is the purpose this preface is intended to serve.

It may appear to many people a very audacious and unfortunate idea to want to write a kind of theory for *novels*. If there were not so many difficulties in this undertaking, so many centuries might perhaps not have passed, and so many novels have been written without some speculator conceiving the idea of thinking about this genre of writings, comparing the existing works with their purpose and intention, and pointing out the means whereby this purpose can best be reached, taking into account the disposition of human nature.

But perhaps it has not been considered worth the trouble of giving much thought to a genre of writings that is only written for the entertainment of the *masses?*—This seems in fact to be the case; but precisely *this* consideration makes such neglect reprehensible.

Shouldn't one think *first and foremost* about how to provide the greatest part of the human race with healthy fare?

It is not my intention to write a complete theory for a genre of writings that can assume such manifold forms, nor am I capable of doing so; but for the reasons given, I consider observations about this form of literature very necessary.

That these writings, being after all the entertainment of the masses, have naturally had an influence on their *taste*—and also on their *manners*—is surely undeniable.

Not that we just want to hear what the epigrammatist who wrote in Zigler's *Asiatische Banise*[1] has to say about it:

> With daring faithful pious knights
> Our good mothers' *taste* was *spoiled;*
> With finer wit, sentimental jests,
> They *spoil* our daughters' *hearts.*
> Kästner's *Lectures. Second Collection,* p. 114.[2]

What is to be expected of a text "in which the heroine is usually a virtuous woman whom the author leads through all manner of perils on land and at sea, exposing her to a thousand temptations, occasionally even violent enterprises, and in the end crowning her through some peripeteia or another? The girl has to be shipwrecked, in order to be made a slave; her virtue is put to the test, either by a Bassa or a Thersander, or a young knight of love in Paris, London, or wherever.—The novels of all nations seem to have this in common: *That men sacrifice their time, their peace of mind, their higher calling, occasionally their health or even their life to the other sex.*" What, I say, is to be expected for the cultivation of *good* taste, for the propagation of *good* manners, from such a piece of writing, characterized thus by a novelist himself, or at least by a translator of novels?[3]

Now in order that this taste may be less spoiled, in order that the bad influence of novels on manners may be less bemoaned by our good mothers—to this end I have written down these observations. They are intended, if possible, to lead the novel back to truth and nature.

I confess in all honesty that I believe a novel can be made a very pleasant and very instructive pastime; and not, as might be supposed, for an idle woman, but also for the thinking mind.

We have perhaps no more than two or three novels of *this* kind—

perhaps even just *one*. I have studied *these* existing works with all the diligence necessary to discover by what means they have become what they are.

Even before I thought of writing this essay, I read the novels of Fielding and Wieland, *Tom Jones* and *Agathon,* for my instruction and my amusement, and at each step taken in them compared them with human nature and found in them what Pope says of Homer:

Nature and [they] were . . . the same.[4]

And of the other works that have appeared in this genre, I have surely read the most important, and in general as many as have been necessary for me to recognize how excellent those two are.—Not that it is my intention when I name the two together to put them on the same level and declare them two of a kind; Wieland is indisputably *one* degree more perfect; but Fielding deserves to be placed second only to him. The demonstration of this belongs elsewhere.—

But will readers be willing to accept and find valid what I have learned and abstracted from these two writers, and therefore from human nature?—If the *poets* care about receiving justified applause, then I think they can quarrel with no one who takes the trouble to tell them at least something of what they must do to win the applause of the best readers. And if the spreading of good taste and the improvement of manners are those final purposes they must duly set themselves, if they don't want to be counted among the *useless diversions:* then the *means* whereby these *final purposes* can be attained should be sought out with the greatest care.—And who will not find it at least worth the trouble of testing what is said, when he sees that Fielding and Wieland have become what they are by the qualities he will here find noted? Who will not want to become a Fielding or a Wieland—if he can?

The *readers* themselves, or the *masses,* if you will, could easily be annoyed the most if all the suggestions that can be deduced from the patterns given were followed. For they have claimed for themselves the office of judgment over these writings; perhaps they believe they will lose out if a critic so much as dismisses one novel in his criticism. Who will willingly allow his accustomed fare to be taken from him?—I can only assure them that however strange and heavy the new fare may seem to them at first sight, they will lose nothing by it, but will only become all the more healthy from it.—And also, the novelists will surely take care that they will not be short of the *accustomed* fare so soon.

From everything I have so far said, it can be deduced that it is not my intention to present *arbitrary* principles and prescriptions. Nor have I begun, as might be expected, with an investigation of the word *novel*, and deduced from this the necessary qualities of this genre. I haven't even read Huet's book *On the Origin of Novels;*[5] though I would have wished I could have laid my hands on it.

As far as I'm concerned, the word *Roman* ["novel"] may derive from 'Ρωμη (strength), or from the city of Rheims, or from the name of the language in which the bards wrote their poetry! Readers who look for an explanation of that in me could easily find themselves disappointed.

And so could those who expect a lot of observations on the merely *external* organization of the novel. The *internals* still look too desolate and wild for one to start out by bothering oneself with the dress. By rights, this dress should always be the last thing, and unfortunately it is almost always the first; it has almost always been regarded as the most essential thing. Shall we never cease to be like the lad in Gellert's fables who was determined to make a nightingale of the siskin?[6]

So nothing will be found here about the dimensions of the whole, nor the chance form, nor the setting (except that I recommend *German* manners), nor about the number and selection of characters, except what has to be said of them in connection with more important matters.

I regard the novel, the *good novel,* as that which, in the first ages of Greece, the epic was for the Greeks; at least I believe that is what the *good novel* could become for us.—But by this I don't mean that these two genres of works are precisely the same in all respects, and resemble one another exactly.

The novel did not arise from the genius of the authors alone; the *manners* of the age gave it its being. *Places* where *citizens* were not needed; and *times* in which *citizens* no longer existed transformed the heroic poems of the ancients, an *Iliad* or *Odyssey,* into a novel. If he had been born and educated in times when human beings were full-fledged citizens, the first novelist would certainly have written an epic instead of a novel.—It is not that the heroic poems of the ancients were so supplanted by these novels that they could not exist together with them, and in fact they did live on; rather, novels were written for the entertainment of their times, just as epics were for the entertainment of theirs. The impression that, at that time, only epics could make, novels now make; insofar, that is, as they are now the entertainment of the public, as epics were previously.

Naturally, differences in the organization of these different works arose from this. The novel is of more manifold scope than the epic, because there are more objects to entertain the *human being* than the *citizen*. And there are further differences of this kind. But all may be derived from the distinction that exists between the manners and organization of the world at that time and at present.

If the novel is actually for us what the epic was, correspondingly, for the Greeks; if we are now primarily only capable of taking an interest in that which is of concern to the *human being* as such (without thinking of him as a member of a specific state): then the demands I believe I may justly make of the novelist can easily be foreseen.—This change in our interests can bring the human race closer to perfection. The novelist should help to lead it there.

He should show us the *human being* as he is able to do, according to the organization peculiar to his work. All the rest is ornament and peripheral. The various forms a novel can have must all be forms given to a single substance. What I am talking about here is this substance alone, as what is most essential; not the form, the design of the thing.

And I have such esteem for *naked humanity, stripped* of all that it can be given by manners and status and chance; I would like so much to see it reinstated in its true privileges; I would like so much to convince the whole world that a clear head and a pure heart are the *most important* elements of our station:—and I still find these opinions spread about so little that naturally I have come back to them more than once, and have even given myself over to a few short digressions in order to make them the more capable of application. For if we must see and seek humanity above all in the *human being:* then we must be educated in such a way, and the human being must be shown us in such a manner that *the first thing we see in him is this, and then we can also observe* how he came into the possession of these qualities.

For the philosopher, the prospect that arises from the change in the objects of our interest cannot be unpleasant. If we are and should be human above all, if we can only achieve our destiny by being human, then he must welcome the fact that the interest of human beings is directed primarily to what concerns the human being alone, and not the human being as a citizen.—Perhaps he concludes from this that a part of this universe, of this earth, is nearer to its perfection than ever another part was—that a few more windings and detours on the path to the goal and general final purpose of nature have been passed through—that all the perfections and advantages possessed by the Greeks and Orientals are not what they are actually believed to be—that the alteration and recasting of our taste in this respect are not a decline, and the perfections of Greek literature are not the *highest* perfections.

Happy the poet who can contribute something to enlarge these prospects for the philosopher; who, while showing us the human being, teaching us to know him, and to become him ourselves, still never forgets his own people with its peculiarities in the process, but rather in his way is as national as the Greek poets were for their people.

By this means, I believe, the novelist can become classical, and his work worth reading. I have insisted above all on this, because the novelist occupies himself above all with the *human being;* and that concern is the source of this essay. It is obvious that those other trivial and peripheral matters had no place in it.

That my notions accord very well with the notions of critics in other genres I am fully convinced. But I do not insist on having presented things completely new and until now unheard-of. For the most part, I have applied to the novel principles and observations that have long been known and accepted.

Nor am I writing for the *masters of this art,* and don't claim to have written for them. I feel myself too weak for that. But precisely because I don't write for them, but for young, aspiring novelists, I have in a few places gone more into basics than may perhaps seem necessary to the masters. But I ask them to consider the state of affairs among our usual novelists.

A few more details!—I have very often cited examples from the epic or the drama, rather than the novel, where they proved what they were supposed to prove. There are a variety of causes; one of them is that on the whole, the epic and the drama are better known than the novel.—Further, I have more often brought foreigners to mind than my countrymen; but I hate and despise wars among critics and authors. I have almost always cited right away translations of the passages from foreign and classical authors used. This precaution also will surely not be completely useless given our reading public—at least for the *usual writers* of novels.

Further, I have often censured works with a great reputation. Among these belong above all Richardson's novels. But it wasn't my intention to belittle them. Let no one who thinks he hears me speaking too absolutely or too judgmentally attribute this to pride and vanity. I value Richardson; but I value truth higher than him. I have always written without secondary motives, out of inner conviction, and *after testing what I had to say.*

Finally, my work falls naturally into two parts. In the *first,* there are remarks on the *attractiveness* some subjects have; in the second the talk is of the art of the poet as far as the ordering and development of the parts and the whole of the novel are concerned.

Part 1. Chapter 1

. . . If the contents of the novel must diverge from that of the epic, because they arose from a difference in the way of thinking people had, then this must naturally have had an influence on other aspects of the novel's organization. Let us therefore seek out the distinction there must be between the epic and the novel, in order to define the idea of a novel more clearly, and to distinguish it all the more surely from the genres that border on it and are so closely related to it.— But I have no intention of exhausting this material, and listing all the details that can be counted as distinctions. I will only touch on the *most essential* things.

Firstly, therefore, the heroic poet is only allowed an action of *a certain magnitude,* a certain scope. Aristotle gave this prescription[7] not just in accordance with the final purpose all poets have, to *amuse* and to *instruct;* in determining this magnitude more closely he also consulted the way of thinking peculiar to his people, and the subjects the epic poets treated. One cannot suppose otherwise of the philosopher surveying his material from all points of view; and I think this supposition cannot disgrace him.

The closer determination of this magnitude is of no further concern to us than that the scope appropriate to the novel comprehends more, or at least can comprehend more, than that magnitude. The most important human events can be united within a single perspective, and bound together into a whole of cause and effect, neither minute nor vast, even though Aristotle would never have recognized it as the whole appropriate to a heroic poem. Since we really see this is the case in at least two examples, of which furthermore the most beautiful is of *German* birth and origin, my opinion needs no further proof than that I name—*Agathon*. Let anyone who is surprised that I account this excellent work without further ado among the novels, please also consider that it does not, as he might suppose, happen because I value as its equal everything that is and is called a novel, but rather because I wish all novels would resemble it, because it alone has all the qualities such a work, in accordance with its nature, can have. It is not, as you might suppose, its particular content that causes me to acknowledge it has these advantages; it is the manner in which its author has treated the material, events and characters that raises this work so far above all others of its kind. Given this treatment, the hero could be a Tristram,[8] and the work would still be excellent; still excellent, even if we didn't see developing in it *a pattern for life.*

If we investigate *Agathon,* we immediately find that the point in which all its events are united is none other than the whole current moral being of Agathon, his current way of thinking and manners, which, formed by all these events, are as it were the result, the effect of them all, so that this piece of writing makes up a perfectly poetic whole, a chain of cause and effect. Neither in the prescriptions of Aristotle, nor in the existing heroic poems do we find a plan for a work of such scope. We see in it a prime example of the distinction observed with regard to the magnitude of the action, which exists between the epic and the novel. To be sure, we have many novels that appear broader in scope than *Agathon*. Without mentioning here novels like *Clelia* and *Artamène,*[9] the works of Richardson appear to have a much greater scope as far as their action is concerned, and yet in fact they don't have this scope. When Agathon comes to Tarent, he is at least some thirty years old, and all the events of his previous life insofar, that is, as they have not remained without effect on him, are united in a single point. This cannot be said of *Grandison,* nor of *Clarissa,* nor of those larger works, even if in other regards they had the other perfections a work of this kind can have.

A natural consequence of this distinction observed between the epic poem and the novel is the question: why does the novel rather than the epic poem receive this greater scope? The investigation of this question is not so very indifferent, if we want to acquaint ourselves with the nature of the novel. If, in the twenty-third chapter of the *Poetics,* Aristotle also seems to criticize those epic poets who sing of an entire war, or of all the adventures of a single person, it can certainly be the case that these poets brought on themselves the philosopher's criticisms by failing to unite these events in a single perspective; nor will I ever believe that if Aristotle were to judge *Agathon* as a whole, he would not concede that it affords as much pleasure as any complete work of nature ever can afford; but in spite of that I am just as firmly convinced that even if Wieland were to give his work the stylistic qualities of an epic, it would never become an epic poem for Aristotle. Aristotle demanded for the heroic poem a *great* action,[10] and although the word with which he expresses the subject of epic poems can have more than one meaning, and has also been a stumbling block to the translators, who have explained it now this way, now that, have applied it now to the characters, now to the action; it nonetheless seems very probable to me that the actual meaning of the philosopher can very easily be found, if one here, as one by rights always should with him, abstracts the meaning of the word, in accordance with the intention he had when he used it, from the way of thinking and the notions the Greeks had to have of the thing by virtue of their political organization, religion, manners, and whole condition. If Aristotle's commentators wanted to become practical, they should always attempt to discover the causes that may have led him to one rule or another. It is certain that the philosopher can mean nothing here other than an action and characters who should have much to make them attractive to the Greeks, taking into account the way of thinking of that age. Now according to these notions, I make bold to say that a poem in which all the actions only had the purpose of forming the mind and character of a single man, even if this single man were Ulysses or Achilles, would not have had the characteristic magnitude Aristotle demands for a heroic poem.[11] And nor would Aristotle have recommended this kind of magnitude to the poet when selecting his action, if he had not been sure it would win him the greatest applause, unless, that is, such an action had the greatest influence on the public of that time, and was considered important by it.

With respect to the scope and content of the action, the epic poets of more recent times (if I perhaps except my faithful friend Ariosto and a few others, whom strict critics usually hardly place among heroic poets), have, on the whole, modeled themselves so much after the Homeric heroic poem, they have subjected themselves so faithfully to the rules of Aristotle,[12] and our critics have followed the philosopher so exactly in their prescriptions concerning this genre of poems, that I surely need not fear censure when I assume that Aristotle's concept of the epic (which perhaps gave rise to the

German title *heroic poem*) is generally accepted, and then conclude that the distinction between heroic poem and novel with respect to the scope of the action therefore appears to spring from the selection of the different events. Thus at the same time a second distinction would also be observed that exists between the two genres, and both distinctions are contained in this: that as the heroic poem sings of *public deeds* and *events,* that is, *actions of the citizen* (in a certain sense of this word), so the novel occupies itself with the *actions and feelings of the human being.*

These two distinctions have their basis in the difference in the manners and organization of the world. But just as in the epic it is above all the *deeds* of the citizen that come into consideration, in the novel the main thing seems to be the *being* of the human, his *inner condition.* In the case of those *deeds,* an attractive entertainment for the citizen can be imagined, because they can either comprise the fame of the forefathers, or the good fortunes of their country. If the epic is to make the appropriate impression, then its content must be taken from the people for which it is written. How could the Christian epic please the Muslim? And if the novelist wanted to limit himself solely to *human* deeds and enterprises, what could come out of it that would be as interesting as the deeds mentioned above? But the *inner being* of a human can certainly occupy us very pleasantly. In the case of a won battle, it's not the inner nature of the general we're concerned with, its appeal for us lies in the thing itself; but in the case of events that befall our fellow humans, it's the state of their feelings that leads us to be more or less interested when these happenings are narrated. Experience will teach everyone this is so. Is it *deeds* and *events* that entertain us so pleasantly in *Tom Jones,* or is it not rather this Jones himself, this human with his being and his feelings? He does nothing, at least very little, that we can even approve of, and yet we love him dearly, and are therefore very interested in his adventures.

I have already previously indicated some of the *advantages* that arise for humankind from this, if novelists use these hints of nature, these consequences of the organization of our current times, and I will draw attention to the *characteristic qualities* that result from this for the novel in the appropriate place.

That the emotions and actions of *humankind* are the proper content of novels is not refuted by the fact that in some works of this kind kings and heroes, Clelias and Artamènes appear.[13] The authors of these works treat their characters as *human beings,* and not as citizens; at least the basis of the actions is the feeling of the mere human and not of the citizen, even though these actions *seem to have the appearance of civil action.*

It goes without saying that the scope previously accorded the novel is the broadest possible; but not that absolutely every novel must have this scope in order to be a novel. More details about this can only come later.

Further, most of the following observations are calculated with regard to the highest effect a novel is able to produce, without my wanting to deny this name to every piece of writing that doesn't produce all these effects (if the public wants to call it a novel, or the author has been pleased to name it so). Anyway, it's not the name that matters. And that criterion might also really exclude so many works that only a very few might remain that, as *Lessing* says of *Agathon,* deserved to be read by a man of classical taste.[14] Let it suffice that I intend to elaborate in the most careful way all that can become of a work that *occupies itself with the human actions and feelings.*

There are all kinds of other distinctions between the epic poem and the novel, which seem to derive from the first, and for which I can only account most adequately when I regard them as its natural consequences. One of these distinctions is the *style.*

All kinds of public actions are performed with a *solemnity* and *dignity* that would be more than affectation in the case of private events. Who speaks among friends in the same way that he speaks in a public speech, before a public assembly? Even if the style of the heroic poem has more beauties than that all its effect and appeal should have arisen solely from this congruence, on account of which it was introduced, it still seems certain to me that the public nature of the epic actions must have been one of the causes of the poetic style. And so too it would sound very precious and very improbable if a novelist were to adopt the epic tone. But surely it goes without saying that this doesn't mean everything that can create for us the *ideal* presence of the objects treated and presented is rejected.

A *third* distinction may be observed between the heroic poem and the novel that, like the previous one, seems to be a consequence of the first. The epic allows certain supernatural effects that are called machines;[15] and the novel might perhaps not tolerate them.

More recent commentators seem to believe that the dignity and importance of epic action allows, indeed can even demand the support and intervention of the gods and of higher beings, according to the very unphilosophical principle that these beings must be more concerned about the whole than about the individual. They also believe that the appearance of the marvelous given to the epic poem by this means makes it much more attractive; and by this argument they seem to want to justify submitting themselves here too so absolutely to the prescriptions of Aristotle and the example of Homer. But the actual causes of these prescriptions and of this use of superior beings surely lie elsewhere. Firstly, they were supplied more by the religion of the ancients than by ours. When Jupiter and Juno, Mars and Venus declared themselves for or against the Greeks, it was *family quarrels* in which they were intervening. And that made these interventions extremely attractive, because among Homer's readers there could still be very many to whom naturally the reminders of such close relations between them and their gods had to seem very flattering and pleasant. The machines therefore certainly won Homer more than one reader, because the particular interest of so many Greeks was tied to them; whether they win our epic poets more readers I don't know. But since the novelist can have none of these reasons for using machines in his work, because they don't accord and can't be combined so well with the objects he treats as with the subject of the epic poem; further, since he has to accommodate himself to the prejudices and opinions of people as a whole—however unphilosophically they may think—if he wants to please them all; for all these reasons, he probably restrains himself from machines in his work, especially since the *appeal of the marvelous* (the only reason he could still use them) would rob him of greater advantages than it can grant him, as we shall see in the appropriate place. From these comparisons of the epic poem and the novel, a few observations seem to have resulted that make it comprehensible to us why some aspects of the organization of the two kinds of works are the way they are. And this seems to us to be perhaps not so completely unimportant if we want to acquaint ourselves more closely with the nature of one of the two.

Part 1. Chapter 18

I have very often heard it said that in the peculiar quality of our nation there lies nothing particularly attractive for the poet, and the writer in general, to use. I certainly don't belong among the flatterers of my fatherland—I think I have already given the reader proofs of this—but how people have been able to say this so absolutely, without qualification, has always been beyond my comprehension. Firstly, we are still *human;* and if the author of the book on moral beauty is right, we are more human than all other nations. And in their works, good poets have always drawn those traits that are most attractive principally from the human heart. And should these traits not be capable of combination with the outward characteristics of our people as a nation? Or have we by our outward forms become so incapable of all feelings that the poet would offend all probability by giving us a feeling, human heart? Such an opinion could hardly be asserted consistently in all seriousness; at least to the extent to which it is true of us, it would also have to be true of other nations, and perhaps of some still more. Yet here it is not a matter of our greater or lesser sensibility, of the qualities of our heart and the state of our *inner* being: the question is whether the *peculiarities in the manners of our people* are of such a kind that the poet cannot use them at all?

Let us suppose for a moment that as little about us as one will is striking, attractive, and as much, on the other hand, commonplace, banal, bare. Let us just first come to an agreement on what I understand by the peculiarity of manners, and by the advantage the poet can derive from it, and by the necessity he stands in to use it.

With each character in his work, the poet *must* presuppose a certain *context* in which he has become what he is, in the real world. And once he has had him born and brought up in his little world, he has become what he is in the context that exists in his work, and whose basis is always taken from the real world. Now through this context, in other words, through the education he has received, the social position he holds, the people he has lived with, the affairs he has presided over, he will receive certain peculiarities; and these peculiarities in his manners, in his whole behavior, will have an influence on his way of thinking, and his way of acting, on the *expression* of his passions, etc.; so that all these small traits from his life and his whole being stand in the closest connection with the whole of this character as *cause* and *effect.* Consequently, we must also see a lot of these smaller traits—as many, that is, as is consistent with the main business of the characters—if we are not to have a skeleton of a character before us, but rather are to recognize his full, rounded figure and account for all he does and does not do. For the bare expression of the passions of a character, his simply doing something, roughly as may follow from the character's temperament and present situation, is so far from enough for a good poet—though for most so much the rule—that he will prefer to show nothing of the character than only this shallow surface. It is impossible for the picture to stand out against its background, and receive the roundedness by the power of which alone we recognize it as living, as real, without these small traits. Without them, as I said, every character is a gaunt skeleton. He can no more be imagined *sensuously* than the mathematician's square number. Now these traits in manners are to be found not just in the nation, but, to put it more properly, in the various classes and institutions of a people; and therefore they must exist among us as well. Of course they can also be found in foreign manners; but I just believe that since the poet always has his own nation before his eyes, he can sooner be alert to these peculiarities, these details, when drawing the characters of his figures, if he takes them from his own people, and when he has his characters act can sooner have them express their actions and passions in accordance with these traits, than if he fetches his characters from abroad.—Even conceding, then, that German manners, customs, etc., as a *whole* have nothing attractive and striking—conceding that they are as cold, as monotonous, as conceited or as derivative as they really are: the poet can nonetheless find in them with less effort and more certainty all the thousand details whereby all the events and characters in his work receive that peculiarity that individualizes them and gives them life and truth. . . .

Part 2. Chapter 1

. . . All poets have the general final purpose of instructing by means of pleasure. This final purpose is so noble, the business so important, that, at the risk of being laughed at a bit, I say with confidence and conviction that I concede precedence over the poet only to the *civil lawgiver,* and can only set alongside him the clergyman who is what Hagedorn's Theophilus is[16]—and only this clergyman, not any whatever—and, additionally, only the man "whose nocturnal lamp illumines the whole globe" (Kleist).[17] And shouldn't this hierarchy take first place among the others, since its members contribute to the true well-being of the human race?

But if the poets concede that they all have the intention of instructing by giving pleasure, isn't it surprising that only so few know how to order the means they have in their hands in accordance with this final purpose, and with the nature of these means? It seems as if many do not take the trouble to become what they nonetheless would like so dearly to be.

It is perhaps not so very easy to discover the right ordering according to which a work should be constructed. There are great poets who consider the ordering of a work a minor matter. Voltaire says somewhere (I think in the preface to *Mariamne*), that nothing is easier than to order a plot; but his works do not convince me that this art is necessarily so very common. There are other critics who declare the ordering of a work of any scope the most important thing. Among these is Aristotle,[18] and a few other honest people.

The prescription to instruct by pleasing is indisputably too generally formulated not to need a more precise definition. I think I can justly paraphrase it thus. The poet should create in his readers, in the principal way allowed by his means, ideas and feelings that can further the perfection of the human being and his vocation. Visions that occupy us pleasantly, while they teach us to think, and feelings that are instructive at the same time as they please us, that is, of the kind we must have according to the disposition of our nature and by virtue of our calling. The poet will order his work just as the works of nature are ordered, which, while they afford us pleasure, at the same time contain seeds for thought. The gentle color green, so formed because according to our eye it must be so formed if it is to please us, clothes the greatest part of creation, which occupies our power of thought in the most pleasant way.

I don't believe that the poet can properly be a teacher in any way other than by occupying our powers of thought and feeling through his art in ordering and developing his work. He must not set himself up explicitly as a teacher; still less must his characters do this. We ourselves, without him lecturing us, must be able to learn from him; and we will learn all the more surely and better if we have the opportunity to become our own instructors through his work. Human beings with their virtues and weaknesses, events that can and must follow from these, cannot possibly step forward and give explicit lectures on the moral of the case. They would become untrue to their nature. Genuine virtue doesn't like to prattle much, unless hired to do so by the community; and the moralizing of vice and folly is unlikely to do much good. One would very quickly forget their words, seeing their deeds; or if the poet lets these deeds happen simply for the sake of a lesson, one would forget the lesson itself very quickly. And if moralizing becomes a duty and a compulsion, the other condition under which alone we want to see the poet's work can easily fail to be fulfilled: it can bore us instead of pleasing us as it should.

So *how* must the novelist order his events and characters in order to arouse in the readers such ideas and feelings as we as rational human beings should principally have? As we have seen, he has everything that a *human being* can be and do at his disposal. Every novel is a mass of events and characters. In such a work, either a character or an event can be the main object. The end, that is, the conclusion of a work can be the *completion* of an event, so that we can be satisfied with regard to it, or the *completion* of a character, so that this character who has arisen and developed in the course of the work has now come as far as the poet intended he should, and we now need know nothing more to be satisfied. Who fails to see that in the first instance the event is the most important thing, insofar, that is, as without its completion we would lack something for which the mere existence of the characters cannot compensate? In this case, the characters are as it were brought together by the poet so that the event can result. It is still too soon to say how far this is right or wrong; I only want to characterize the genre. Here, the selection and ordering of the events is the main purpose of the poet. Without this ordering, the result, that is, that event that is the purpose of the novel cannot be realized. From this of course it follows that the character can then only come into consideration insofar as the purpose the poet has set himself can best be reconciled with him. It wouldn't necessarily have to be a Clarissa (to cite an example from a novel), it could also be another adorable girl who is seduced and made unhappy by Lovelace, and who would allow the attaining of the unhappy event, the end of the work, the poet's purpose, just as well as Clarissa does.—In the second instance, the final event is of so little importance to us that we can also imagine Agathon at some other place than Tarent without hesitation. Only if the whole being of this Agathon, his way of thinking and acting were other than it now is would we be unsatisfied. In this case the events are merely there for the sake of the characters. . . .

Part 2. Chapter 2

In his work, the novelist shows us *people* who are at least *possible* in the *real* world. What do we see of these people, or rather, what must we see of them if we want to observe their being, their action in a way that accords with the truth?

If mere *seeing* is enough, then we first run into figure, beauty, deportment, dignity in behavior.—But all these things show us so little of the true nature of the human being that a writer can only then perhaps still use them to arouse attention if, as a pretext and excuse for his very honorable intentions, he unfortunately knows from Dacier's translation of Plato only that Socrates believed a beautiful soul must necessarily keep company with a beautiful body.[19] The most beautiful, most seemly figure that gives rise to Phaedrus's "O quanta species—cerebrum non habet!"[20] is only gaped at by the *rabble*. And surely that must not hold true of people with whom we're supposed to make the effort to seek acquaintance.

The second thing we see in people is honors, dignities, wealth. If this were what we had to regard, in order to see the true nature of a human being, then the clever man would more often remove his hat before the prince and his farmer-general in order to get into their company.

I do not say that in all these excellent things there is absolutely nothing to see if we want to observe the human being as he truly is. But then all that we have observed appears merely as the cause of an effect, simply in *relation* to the *real* human being; it is shown us merely as a means, not as an intention or an end purpose. We see beauty merely insofar as it affects Conti or the prince; dignity only because it makes the abominable *Marchese* a refined chamberlain;[21] wealth merely because it wins the good Timon (in Shakespeare) many friends—who are no friends.[22]

The poet who apparently wants to show merely these things in his characters, or to claim they are the most important, will certainly drive some of his readers—perhaps the ones who should be most dear to him—to their ugly and impoverished Aesop or to the hunchback Scarron with his worn-out black doublet, rather than enduring any longer in such company.

And what will they seek in the company of Aesop and Scarron? They will want to see the people there feel and act. Mere *hearsay* will naturally be able to amuse them less than personally witnessing every idea, every mockery, every satire themselves. And they will never learn from others' reports what they can from what they *see*.

So if we are to *see* something of the human being, the poet must bring us into the company of his characters so absolutely that we have his characters with their *whole* being before us.

If we want to see all we must observe in order to see human beings as they truly are, then it is natural that we have to rely on their utterances and their enterprises. But merely narrating, "It came to pass! it happened!" gives us nothing to see but the surface, the exterior of the things that have happened. And can that be called seeing the human being as he truly is, seeing *what* and *how* he is?

In real life the mere narration of things that have happened is so rare that we constantly hear, and ourselves pose the question: "*How* is that possible? *How* could that happen?" This question is on our tongue even when we are witnesses of an occurrence in which a well-known man acts in a way that just doesn't match the way we imagined he would act.

It is never the mere *outward* circumstances of a human being that bring him to do something. If this were possible, then Agathon and Danae hewn in marble would have to be able to love one another just as cordially as the characters themselves do. Who fails to see that there is a medium, as it were, through which a character or an event must pass in order to have an effect on another? This medium is the heart, the whole mental and emotional constitution of the character affected. The expression that we occasionally use of some people in real life, that they act like a machine, that is, that no effect on their mental and emotional constitution is required in order to move them to do something, is so unflattering that we would prefer to be able to declare these people *are* machines. And the *human being* should never be a machine; not even the machine of the poet.

Every event that is realized has a dual relation; firstly, it is the *effect* of previous, and secondly, the *cause* of subsequent events. When it is said that we have been moved by someone else, or by this thing or that, to do one thing or another, in other words, when some outward effect is visible, who doesn't see that that actually means we have been put into the emotional state required to do this or that?

When causes affect us that are followed in a particular way by a particular emotional state, it is not just a matter of the cause affecting us, but also of the state of our emotional constitution at the time, and of a thousand other details that must all come together if a certain effect is to follow. The whole united, merged sum of our ideas and feelings, our physical condition, sickness or health, the company and the weather, and many nameless, apparently very insignificant things can have attuned this emotional state more or less favorably, so that the tone follows or does not. The influence of our body on the state of our intellectual feelings is only too strong.

In one of Shakespeare's tragedies, which our compatriots still do not possess in German, Menenius is confident his mission to Coriolanus will enjoy greater success if he undertakes it in the afternoon.[23] Only at the *table,* at the table at which *Musarion* presided, and *Chloe* waited, only by virtue of the assistance of that *basket* Chloe brought along, and of many minor circumstances, all of which we find in the poet, could the effect result whereby Phanias became a happy and truly wise man.[24]

When this same event becomes the *cause* of subsequent events, the same relations occur. It then affects the emotional state of the person, so that the event can ensue, which is actually an effect of it.

That is how it is in real life. The *inner* and the *outer* sides of the human being are so precisely interdependent that we simply have to know the former if we want to explain and make comprehensible to ourselves the outward phenomena, and all the outward manifestations of the human being. If in the real world we *cannot* every time comprehend and observe all the *causes* that bring forth an event in one way, rather than in another, then this happens because the sum of efficient causes is too great and diverse, and the whole is too interwoven for us to be able to discover them in it. Also, we often don't *want* the explanation of the event, because normal events rarely need this elaboration of the whole emotional state of a person, in order to be simply *believed;* because we usually don't seek instruction in the events of the real world; and because narrators and listeners often do not know how to observe, state, and comprehend the mental operations involved—or are accustomed to thinking in too machinelike a way to be able even to think of their very existence. So when the question "How is that possible?" follows on some improbable event, it is usually satisfied by assurances, the citing of witnesses, etc.

I have often been very inclined to ask many novelists for such an eyewitness interview. For what we read in many of them would certainly need still more credentials than the *most uncommon* events of the real world. And yet when relating such events, the conscientious historian often has the documents printed, in order not to bring his readers to shake their heads.

If the principal intention of the poet is and should be to show us of his people, of his characters, what we can in *truth* see of a human being, then he cannot neglect this *outer* and *inner* connection of the efficient cause of any event he has carried out by a character, if only for the reason that if he does neglect it we would never see what we should see in his work.

If he doesn't want to dishonor himself, the *poet* cannot have the pretext that he does not know the *inner being* of his characters. He is their creator, they have received all their qualities, their whole being from him; they live in a world he has ordered.

Given this presupposition, when some event is realized we shall now have to see the whole *inner* being of the characters, with all the *causes* that set them in motion, in the work of the *poet*, if the *poet* is not to transform himself into the mere *narrator*. . . .

Translated by Timothy J. Chamberlain

Notes

Original title: *Versuch über den Roman* (1774); the reprint (Stuttgart: Metzler, 1974) has a useful afterword by Eberhard Lämmert.

1. [*Die Asiatische Banise* (1689), a popular novel by Heinrich Anshelm von Zigler und Kliphausen (1663–97).]

2. [*Vorlesungen in der Königlichen deutschen Gesellschaft zu Göttingen gehalten. Zweite Sammlung* (1773), by Abraham Gotthelf Kästner (1719–1800).]

3. [Early in his academic career, Kästner, later a famous mathematician, supported himself in part by translations. He produced German versions of Richardson's *Sir Charles Grandison* and *Pamela*.]

4. [Pope, *Essay on Criticism* 135: "Nature and Homer were, he found, the same."]

5. [*Traité de l'origine des romans* (1670), by Pierre Daniel Huet (1630–1721).]

6. [In Gellert's fable "Der Zeisig," a boy shown a siskin and a nightingale wrongly believes the bird with the more attractive plumage must also have the more attractive voice.]

7. [See Aristotle, *Poetics,* chapters 23–24.]

8. [A reference to Laurence Sterne's novel *The Life and Opinions of Tristram Shandy.*]

9. [Novels by Madeleine de Scudéry, each of which ran to ten volumes.]

10. It goes without saying that inner greatness is meant here.

11. If only our critics (as a few of them have very laudably done) would always pay a little attention to the origin, cause, actual purpose, and true content of the laws of Aristotle, when they present them to us as so utterly absolute! Or if only a new Aristotle would arise and write a *German* poetics, as Aristotle actually wrote a *Greek* poetics. Though of course it would have to be someone other than a Gottsched who had this idea, as Gottsched once did. But perhaps at present there is nothing in our whole political condition, way of thinking, and manners a critic could refer to when composing his rules, as Aristotle was able to do, once he had taken human nature into account, of course.—This question would be worth investigating. But I don't

want for example a *Celtic* poetics to be written, or whatever Ossian and the bards sang to be declared the property of our fatherland.

12. With what justice or injustice I do not want to determine so very precisely; but since we have neither such a fatherland, nor such laws, nor such a way of thinking as the Greeks had (a matter I think I have to repeat here), it seems impossible that *such* actions as Homer treated can have the same influence on a *German* as they had on a Greek audience. What's more, I doubt outright that any action could be discovered for the epic that would have such an effect on us Germans as the *Iliad,* for example, had on the Greeks at a certain time. Even the *Aeneid* never made the same impression on the Romans as the works of Homer made on the Greeks. And nor could it. The heroic poem contains above all *deeds, enterprises,* and in these, no interest can lie for the merely *subject* population. It is so often and so much lamented that Homer is read so little now, compared with the times when there was still a Greece; that our heroic poets have so very few readers, and moreover such very cold readers, compared with the readers Homer had in those days; that we neglect the model of the ancients more and more every day, and our taste is getting worse and worse. There are people who claim that however excellent Homer's style may be, there are nonetheless a few of our poets who—*if one takes into account the differences arising from language and a few other circumstances* in the matter (and if one does, if poetry loses, the nation does not feel the loss, because it cannot know *what* it has lost)—these admittedly very few poets are, in their way, and as far as the whole situation of their times makes it possible, *almost* as excellent *for us,* as only Homer could be for the Greeks—without them ever having been read, or it being possible for them to be read, as he was. The conclusion is very rightly drawn from this that the reason lies in the selection of the subject the different poets treat—and yet the attempt is not made to determine the principal quality the subject matter must have, in accordance with all the circumstances in which we find ourselves, if it is to attract us as the content of the *Iliad* attracted the Greeks. The more remote we are from the Greeks, the more all that related only to that people must seem indifferent to us, and so nothing but that which concerns humankind as such can interest us in these works. Therefore, anyone who wants to become *our Homer* in the true sense must first discover a subject matter that is just as attractive as the subject Homer treated was for the Greeks; and then, to be sure, he must treat it as Homer did. Those more recent epic poets who have taken the content for their heroic poems from religion seem to have judged rightly the attractive nature such a subject matter must always have, and despite the god of Ferney (as an epigrammatist calls old Voltaire somewhere) will always retain; but I do not know if this alone suffices. It does not help to shift the blame for our indifference and negligence always and only onto the people, which often devours an insignificant French novel, or a tasteless novella; and it is perhaps unfair to do so. For if a people can have an appetite for such a dish, how delighted would it be with another, in which human nature, and all the peculiarities it has received through religion, legislation, etc., had been consulted?—"But perhaps . . ." I understand! But then first pity the people that can have no taste for anything but French farces. The fault is not *its alone!* And in the end, one thing at least remains to it, which cannot be taken away by any means. We must always remain *human,* and the peculiarities of taste in our own and in neighboring nations confirm that we are increasingly reverting to this. And humankind, ultimately, loses nothing by this process, as will already have been seen. Let us therefore cultivate this field in the most careful way! Until now it has still been in part very neglected. It still does not seem from a few of our genres of poetry that we are limited to that field alone, they have rather grown in a place where *for us* flowers no longer grow. How I pity our German Pindars and Horaces! I would not pity them so much if I did not respect them so highly.

13. [Clelia is a heroic young Roman woman, and Artamène is a Persian prince.]

14. [Lessing, *Hamburg Dramaturgy,* no. 69.]

15. [See Aristotle, *Poetics,* chapter 24. Aristotle accords the marvelous greater scope in the epic than in tragedy, though he only explicitly mentions "machines" in connection with tragedy in chapter 15.]

16. [Theophilus is the model clergyman in Hagedorn's poem "Charakter eines würdigen Predigers."]

17. ["Der Frühling" 134–35.]

18. [*Poetics,* chapter 7.]

19. [The harmony of body and soul is a topic in a number of Plato's dialogues; as Blanckenburg implies, only a superficial reading will allow such a simplistic interpretation as the one cited.]

20. ["Oh that such a splendid face—should lack a brain." See Phaedrus, *Fables* 1.7. These are the words of the fox on seeing the empty mask of a tragic actor; Phaedrus applies the fable to those who have rank and renown, but lack common sense.]

21. [Characters in Lessing's tragedy *Emilia Galotti.*]

22. [In *Timon of Athens.*]

23. [Shakespeare, *Coriolanus* 5.1.]

24. [Wieland, *Musarion.*]

Christoph Martin Wieland

Christoph Martin Wieland (1733–1813) was educated according to pietistic principles, but in the early 1760s came under the influence of rationalism and sensualism. This development stands behind his playful erotic verse narratives of the 1760s, but also more seriously behind the novels *Don Sylvio* (1764) and *The History of Agathon* (1766–67), which is generally regarded as the first Bildungsroman. The narrative poem *Musarion; or, the Philosophy of the Graces* (1768) presents moderation as the key to wisdom. Wieland's political novel, *The Golden Mirror* (1772), led Duchess Anna Amalia of Sachsen-Weimar to appoint him tutor to her two sons. Wieland spent the remainder of his life in or near Weimar. His later works include the satirical *History of the Abderites* (1774; book 4 appears in The German Library, volume 10) and the verse romance *Oberon* (1780). Witty, urbane, and tolerant, Wieland became the great spokesman of his generation for a cosmopolitan vision of literature. He translated twenty-two plays of Shakespeare in the 1760s, yet always retained the greatest respect for French literature. Attacked by the young Goethe and Lenz, he responded with a quiet tolerance that eventually compelled respect. In later life, Wieland showed an ability to appreciate younger writers, including Jean Paul and Heinrich von Kleist, which Goethe and Schiller lacked. Apart from his novels, poems, and translations, Wieland's major contribution to German intellectual life was the periodical *Der Deutsche Merkur* (1773–1810). For a useful edition, see *Werke,* ed. Fritz Martini and Hans Werner Seiffert, 5 vols. (Munich: Hanser, 1964–68). For an introduction in English, see John A. McCarthy, *Christoph Martin Wieland* (Boston: Twayne, 1979).

The Eagerness to Give
Our Poetry a National Character

The reasons why the German nation cannot have so pronounced a national character as the French and the English are familiar enough. They lie in our constitution, and can therefore also only cease with our constitution. The German nation is properly speaking not a single nation, but rather a conglomerate of many nations, just as the ancient Greeks, among whom Corinthians, Spartans, Thebans, Athenians, Megarians, Thessalians, etc., were much too distinct from one another to resemble one another other than through very general characteristics, which consequently were not very distinctive. If, at the time when they flourished most, the Greeks as a whole excelled in comparison to all other known peoples, the reason was merely that the other peoples were all more or less slaves or barbarians. If at that time the greatest part of Europe had already enjoyed a high degree of civilization, they would not have appeared anything like as exceptional. Yet for all this the Greeks as a whole did have a national character, and we Germans have ours. If we ourselves should be too biased to judge of it, let a Swede or a Russian with as much taste and knowledge as is required for such a judgment, make a comparison of the best German poets and prose writers with the best writers in Italy, France, and England, and then declare whether he does not perceive in our writers some taste of our native soil, if I may so put it—whether there are not traits in each one that distinguish the German writer from the Italian, French, English, and that must not be attributed to national character.—And this, it seems to me, is all one can reasonably demand in this matter. But this apparently doesn't satisfy certain individuals blustering with self-styled patriotism. By the national character they would like to give our poetry or our works of genius in general they understand something more: though one almost has to doubt if they understand their own demands properly. If they mean that we Germans should have a national literature just as distinctive and just as peculiar to us as in times past Greek and Celtic literature were peculiar to the Greeks and Celts, and contrasting with others by means of strong national characteristics—then they have presumably not considered that they are demanding something that is neither possible given the present-day constitution of the world, nor desirable in any respect at all. Would the Romans in Trajan's times[1] not have been ridiculous if they had bemoaned the loss of their ancient, peculiar poetry, of their fescennine and saturnine verses,[2] and had spoken contemptuously of their Virgil, Horace, Ovid, Catullus, etc., as imitators of the Greeks? Would we be less so if we refused to recognize our poets as native because they have formed themselves not according to the model of the bards of the ancient Celts—but according to Greek models, or the more recent models of those European nations that have become enlightened and refined earlier than us? Every nation has its original poetry, brought forth by nature alone, and it is undeniable that for all its wildness it has beauties art cannot attain: a strength that is only possible in a state of freedom where humanity still has all its powers gathered together unbridled and unspent; a fire as violent and wild as the passions of childish souls in Herculean bodies. But of course we won't want to revive the times in which the great Ossian wrote in order to refurnish our poetry with these wild beauties, this sinewy strength. Yet surely we can transport ourselves into those times by the effort of our imagination? Oh, why not? This we can do as well as we can tickle ourselves in order to laugh. But to what end should we do that? Our constitution, our way of living, our manners, our whole condition are—thank heaven!—so very different from those of our ancestors in the time of the bards that there would hardly be a surer means to make our poetry useless and ridiculous than to want to disguise it as a Veleda.[3] I would think that in this case too we would still remain only imitators, wanting to acquire by the force of art that unrefined forest song nature taught its sons. And so if we really want to or have to imitate, why should we not rather take our models from a nation among whom every noble and beautiful art that puts man in possession of his privileges over the animals was pursued to perfection? Weren't the Greeks really the teachers of all other civilized peoples in the ancient world? Have we more recent Europeans less to thank them for than the ancient Romans? To what do we owe our transformation into man-nered human beings, our superior constitutions, our superior civil order, our arts, our taste, our refinement, if not to the spirit they have kindled in us, the light they have passed on to us, the patterns they have left us? Is it not the poets, the artists, the philosophers, the doctors, the orators, the statesmen, the generals of the Greeks and Romans, who have formed our greatest men in all these categories for more than two hundred years? And now, having enjoyed their instruction, their examples, their models for so long, we should take it into our heads to leave the trails blazed in poetry—and in poetry alone (for in which other art would we really want to follow the example of the ancient Celts, Teutons, Goths, and Vandals?)—in order to wander around in the forests of the ancient Germans, and to affect in our songs a national character that has so long since ceased to be ours?

The more I reflect on the prime duty of human beings to draw closer together, to form connections, and to labor with united forces to their communal perfecting as members of a single great society instituted by nature, the more reasons I think I find to consider it a firm step forward on the path that leads to the goal of the public happiness of the human race, that the nations of Europe at least are losing more and more of what formerly constituted their respective particular characters, which was what distanced them to a greater or lesser degree from the character of enlightened and mannered peoples. The less sociable a people is, the more it lives, like the ancient Egyptians, and even the modern Chinese and Japanese, for itself, cut off from all others, the better to be sure it sustains itself in its national character, but the more imperfect its national condition also remains. Here the same seems to be true of whole peoples as the author of the reflections "On the Contradictions in Human Nature" (*Der Deutsche Merkur* [vol. 1] no. 2, p. 162) asserts of individual people. By this separation and the care they take not to mingle foreign concepts and manners with their own, they attain a kind of individuality that often borders on caricature; and just as (according to this same author) association with people of all classes, from all countries, adhering to all ways of thinking, lends the concepts of the individual person greater range, and his manners greater elegance, the same can also be claimed of the peoples of which human society as a whole is composed, as if of so many moral persons. Nature has already seen to it that each nation has its own culture, its own temperament, its own assets and deficiencies. All the outward physical and ethical causes that have an effect on the human being affect different peoples in such different ways, in such unequal degrees, in so varied directions, that one need not worry at all that they could acquire a uniformity detrimental to perfection from the effects of sociability, and from reciprocal communication of what each possesses as its own in the way of products of nature and art. But this *will* lead to the loss of the unyielding, the excessively divergent quality that causes a displeasing dissonance in the whole; and the intermediate tints and gentle gradations that arise from the refraction of the color peculiar to each nation will give the great living painting of the civilized world a beauty and harmony at the sight of which (if we may employ a Homeric expression) a god in flight might stay to take delight in the sight of a spectacle so fair.

The true calling of literature is to impart beauty and nobility to human nature; and who can define the limits of the beneficial influence it could have on human society if it were to work toward this great purpose in union with philosophy and with its other sister arts, both visual and musical? But in order that it attain this purpose, it must rise above the mere imitation of individual instances in nature, above the narrow concepts of single societies, above the imperfect models of single works of art, must create for itself ideal forms out of the assembled features of beauty poured out over all of nature, and compose of these forms the archetypes according to which it works. This, I at least am utterly convinced, is the best way to proceed, and the general basic law of art, which connects with equal force the Italian, French, English, German, and every other writer. The whole realm of nature and art stands at his disposal in this process, and as each in his way seeks to enrich himself from these treasures, he will ultimately approach a perfection that constitutes the common character of poetic virtuosos, at whatever time and among whatever people they may have lived, and in whatever language they may have worked. Schoolboyish, slavish imitators, apes of the great masters, limited minds who hold fast to the individual and characteristic qualities of a famous artist they find pleasing, and believe they are like him if they meticulously copy his manner (as they imagine it, for actually the great master has no manner)—such people there will always be in the fine arts. These people will, according to which circumstances happen to control them, hold onto individual patterns now native, now foreign, and then critics of equally limited conceptions will come and in inconsistent expressions that alternately say too much and too little, scream about the lack of a national literature, national music, etc., will confuse as is their custom the emulation of the genius with the imitation of the mechanical worker, and even perhaps in the end award the prize of excellence only to the writer who, in his desire to be an original, says things which no one has said before him, and no one will say after him.

Many are of the opinion that our literature could gain infinitely from the treatment of indigenous subjects, the depiction of indigenous manners, and particularly from a direct connection to our national interest and to great events important for the whole of

Germany, and that it could only become a true national literature if employed in this way. This matter is important; but the problems it presents for solution are too complicated to be investigated in this note, which is in any case already too extensive. But I am thinking of perhaps making it the content of a separate examination in the next forthcoming part of the *Merkur,* and of presenting my thoughts on it to the reader for him to judge himself.[4]

Translated by Timothy J. Chamberlain

Notes

Original title: *Der Eifer, unsrer Dichtkunst einen National-Charakter zu geben etc.* Published in *Der Deutsche Merkur,* vol. 2, no. 2 (May 1773).

1. [Trajan ruled 98–117.]
2. [Ancient drinking and dancing songs, characterized by Wieland elsewhere as indecent and inartistic.]
3. [According to Tacitus, a Germanic maiden from the tribe of the Bructeri honored as a prophetess (*Histories* 4.61, 65).]
4. [This plan was not realized.]

Letters to a Young Poet: Letter Three

. . . I am as convinced as anybody can be that Sophocles' *Oedipus* is the most perfect example of tragedy; and that therefore the rules that have been derived from this highest model of tragic art are rules by the observation of which a man who had inherited the spirit of Sophocles and had had the advantage of discovering an equally fortunate subject as is Oedipus would produce just as excellent a tragedy. But that does not mean the mere observation of these rules, in particular of the so-called three unities, is enough to make an excellent work. Surely no one will deny that the most irregular play written with Shakespeare's genius, knowledge of human nature, deep gaze into the innermost folds of the heart, liveliness and energy of imagination, warmth of feeling, and inexhaustible wealth of thoughts and images, would be worth infinitely more than Gottsched's *Cato*, for all its observation of the rules of the divine Aristotle. Who will not rather read or hear an excellent performance of the former than of the latter? Who wouldn't rather spend time with a most irregularly built Aesop than with a second Antinous, who is only a mindless doll?[1]

Shakespeare's plays are for the most part grandiose dramas of state affairs, or dramatized novellas and fairy tales, and when he composed them he thought as little of the plot of *Oedipus* as of the Tribunal of Ceremonies at Peking. So much the worse! says Herr von A.,[2] and I might almost say it too, if I were convinced that Shakespeare wouldn't have lost more than he would have gained by observing the rules. But be that as it may! He is and remains nonetheless (begging the pardon of my noble friend) the foremost dramatic poet of all ages and peoples—not because he disregarded the rules of Greek tragedy; not on account of the way he jumbled the most sublime tragedy with the lowest comedy; not on account of certain flaws he had in common with the greatest writers of his nation and his age, nor on account of the sacrifices he knowingly made to the bad taste of his audience, from which he had to derive his support—this, I would think, should surely be understood of itself once and for all! Rather, it is because in everything that constitutes the most essential quality of a great poet in general, and of a dramatic poet in particular, in the strength of all his mental powers, in his intense feeling for nature, in the ardor of his imagination, and his gift of transforming himself into every character, and putting himself into every situation and passion, neither Corneille nor Racine, neither Crébillon nor Voltaire, has surpassed him, and indeed (if we want to judge without prejudice and after adequate investigation and comparison of the matter) they have been far from equaling him. Anyone who speaks of traces of a great genius that are often to be found in his works[3] awakens the suspicion he has never read them. It is not traces but the continuous radiance and ample outpourings of the mightiest, richest, most sublime genius that ever inspired a poet that overwhelm me as I read his works, make me insensitive to his flaws and irregularities, and allow me beneath the magic of his omnipotent imagination to think as little of French rules and French models, as it could occur to me in a majestic forest, illumined by the warmest sun, to lament that Lenôtre hadn't come to the aid of nature here with his measuring tape and pruning shears.[4] Shakespeare's works are only monsters (as Herr von A. calls them) compared with rule-governed tragedies, insofar as the cathedral in Milan or Westminster Abbey are monsters compared with Greek temples, or the facade of Strasbourg Minster compared with the facade of the Louvre. A mediocre little temple built according to the Ionic order would to be sure be more elegant than the majestic cathedral church in York, which is one of the most splendid monuments in the so-called Gothic style: but what sort of a mind would it take to want to have the latter torn down to be replaced by the former, if it were up to him?

Shakespeare's irregularity will never in itself be beauty, though in his work it often gives rise to great beauties; and his flaws remain flaws, even though they are the flaws of a great man. It is not a good thing to imitate his irregularity without having been fitted out by nature with mental powers like his; and it is ridiculous to ape his flaws. But what could the *servum pecus* of spiritless imitators[5] imitate in a Shakespeare other than his flaws? His genius certainly can't be duplicated. Yet it is, however, merely Shakespeare's apes whose shoddy work he is now supposed to pay for, because they have taken his faulty side as their model. Certainly, let those who follow him without calling, understanding, or taste be censured! But what has Shakespeare to do with them? He stands on his own merits. His works, in which nature has so great and art so small a part, will eternally remain the pleasure of all readers of unspoiled taste, and the study of all true artists—they are made, read, felt, studied, but not to be imitated except insofar as the faithful impressions of nature they represent to us in such great abundance can be regarded as just so many models. In spite of the fact that the cultivated person becomes all that he is to some extent through imitation, it is nonetheless certain that only those born with the spirit of the fine arts, only those of true decided talent, are capable of imitating the great masters whose teacher was nature herself, with wisdom and discretion. The model may be a Shakespeare or a Corneille, a Raphael or a Rembrandt, if the one who wants to form himself in his image is a *servum pecus* or an ape, nothing decent can come of it. Even if Shakespeare had never become known among us, or had never even existed, we would in all probability have not a single excellent work more and not a single bad work less. Those of the latter kind would only be bad in other forms and in another manner: instead of miscreate imitations of the Englishman we would have received a greater number of shallow, spiritless, rhymed or unrhymed imitations of the French; instead of savage cannibals, lunatics, bandits, and heroes who belong on the wheel or at least in galley chains, we would see on our stages novelistic heroes à la Scudéry and Calprenède, or Greeks, Romans, and Orientals metamorphosed into sophisticated Parisian gentlemen and ladies: and then what would art or our literature have gained from this?—So once more, it is not in our taking bad models, but in going about their imitation in the wrong manner, for the most part, that the evil lies that must be remedied, and probably will be remedied as soon as a German city large and prosperous enough to maintain a good standing theater has a large enough number of people with taste to set the tone for the rest of the public—and as soon therefore as it will be worth the effort, i.e., sufficiently honorable and rewarding, for men of genius, knowledge, and talent to devote themselves wholly to the stage.

Since Herr von A. in giving vent to his displeasure at the imitators of Shakespeare and of the English in general also mentions the play *Götz von Berlichingen,* let me in this context say a few words about this work that occasioned such a great and general sensation when it first appeared.—"I am wholly of the opinion," says Herr von A., "that in every respect *Götz von Berlichingen* is the equal of every masterpiece of the divine Shakespeare." And since he thinks this means he has said the worst that can be said of the work of our compatriot, he believes he owes the author a kind of compensation, and so adds: "Please don't consider this as mockery of the author of *Götz.* His *Werther's Sorrows* raises him to the rank of our best writers: but I cannot possibly approve of his theatrical taste, his plays,[6] however many beautiful details may be found in them."—I don't insist on denying what Herr von A. seems to believe, and frequently gives us to understand, namely, that *Götz von Berlichingen* has given at least as much innocent occasion as Shakespeare himself for the mischief people of very varied kind have brought about on our stages in the past ten years by more or less immature, or nonsensical freaks of genius or pseudogenius, of daydreaming, of imitation mania, of the vain belief that they too can fly above the mundane, etc. But I deny outright that the author of *Götz* intended in his work to produce a workable play for our mostly traveling troupes of actors, or to supplant from our stages those rule-governed plays whose least virtue was their regularity. His purpose was surely in the main to test his powers on a great dramatic painting of an age and its manners, for which he took the subject matter from the history of our own fatherland in part so that he himself could think his way into it more vividly, in part to make it more interesting for the nation. I suppose he felt himself strongly tempted at the time to yield to the call of his genius, which drew him to a dramatic career; he perhaps wanted merely to legitimize his sending in the eyes of the nation by this first effort; and he showed us what a man who started thus could achieve subsequently. The public was amazed at the marvel, was at first dazzled by the mass and diversity of such completely unaccustomed beauties, but soon enraptured and overwhelmed by the natural truth and the living spirit that breathes in so many, so varied persons of all classes, from the Emperor Maximilian to the groom, and from the groom right down to the gypsy lad. The initial rapture was unanimous. The small number of connoisseurs with sound feeling and unprejudiced mind, who were not so accustomed to artificial and conventional forms that their absence could have made them insensitive to the least beauty of a work nature had marked so visibly with the stamp of genius: these few saw with heartfelt joy, perhaps also with envy, Shakespeare's genius return to life in a young German; and promised our literature and stage the most splendid fruits from the full maturity of a mind whose first product already revealed so much virile strength, so much thoughtful understanding, an imagination so powerful and yet already so controlled, so correct a feeling for what is natural and what is conventional in mankind, a so finely discerning sense for what characterizes centuries, epochs in time, classes, sexes, and individual persons. Fate seems not to have favored these hopes with respect to the stage. But anyone who has read or heard *Iphigenia in Tauris,* a tragedy in iambic verse that has yet to be printed, by this same author, written just as wholly in the spirit of Sophocles as his *Götz* is in the spirit of Shakespeare, and (if indeed so great a value lies in the rules) more regular than any French tragedy—such a reader, I say, will not hold it against any enthusiastic friend of our literature if, with respect to this case too, a few humble doubts arise against Master Pangloss's favorite saying.[7] Who else but a poet who, according as his genius impelled him, could contend with equal success with Shakespeare or Sophocles, would have been more suited to remedy the ailments of our stage, to put a stop to the excesses of the imitators, and by combining nature, which is the soul of Shakespeare's works, with the beautiful simplicity of the Greeks, and with the art and taste the French are so proud of, to create for our dramatic muse a character of its own and a superiority that no other nation could so easily have rivaled?

In the meantime I am assured that already *Götz von Berlichingen* alone—irrespective of the fact that it was neither suited nor written for performance, and that (like all other good things in this world) it has occasioned abuses of many kinds by its mere existence—has performed a very important service for us; and that an advocate of the public against the insulting reproaches of certain amateurs who seem to go to just as great excess in their respect for French literature as others in their contempt for it, could produce quite considerable evidence in its defense. Let me explain myself more clearly.

When Gottsched began to pursue the reform of the stage with his well-known zeal, they made do, since nature makes no leaps,[8] with bad or mediocre translations and imitations of the French. A play in tolerably fluent rhymes, in which the three unities were precisely observed, was a good play as defined by him and his school. Schlegel's *Canute* was as far as I know the first that rose above mediocrity. A few others followed by and by. But whether it was that the circumstances were not sufficiently favorable, or that the choice of the subject, or the manner of treatment had insufficient interest, or whatever else may have been the reason: suffice it to say that our dramatic muses dragged along in a feeble condition and were still unable to gain any national character. Almost everything seen on our stages was foreign property; and after everyone had wearied of seeing plays by Racine, Molière, Destouches, Voltaire, La Chaussée, etc., in German disguise, it came to the point that they had to call in the assistance even of a Goldoni. The German who went to the theater had suddenly to become a Parisian or a Venetian in order to be able to take any interest in what was put on for him. Admittedly, from time to time the new fashions that came from Paris gave us again the pleasure of a change; unable to laugh any more in comedies, people began to find it very pleasant to cry in them; when bored with expending pity on the Mithridateses,[9] the Bajazets,[10] the Orosmanes,[11] and the whole family of the Atrides,[12] who were of so little relevance to us, they gave a warm welcome to the domestic tragedy and the so-called drama, which approximates the comedy of Terence: but a single *Père de famille*,[13] a single *Eugénie*[14] or *Cénie*[15] engendered so many misbegotten German-French half-breeds, and our stage was flooded with such a deluge of dramatized novels and everyday occurrences in dialogue form, that in the end people began to be heartily weary of these wares too. During the course of all these changes in the theater a man of great talents, genuine erudition, and profound knowledge of human nature, though more a philosopher than a poet, in a word, Lessing, had arisen, and had attempted to improve taste and bring our dramatic poets onto the right path, partly by criticism, partly by his own plays, which contrasted strongly with the accustomed fare on our stages. His *Sara Sampson, Minna von Barnhelm,* and *Emilia Galotti,* three plays written with much spirit, though in a variety of manners, had caused a great sensation; but the intervals between their appearance had been too great for them to do the stage any fundamental and permanent service; and, truth be told, they also had in them too much of the author's individual way of thinking for them, when taken as models, not to frequently lead astray the poor imitators, who limped along behind a man of far too superior powers. So although we thereby gained the advantage of approaching the English taste more nearly, and bringing more nature, more action, and therefore also more interest into our dramas, yet all the same our theater taken as a whole still remained a true junk shop. The small number of good original plays was lost in the endless mass of copies and imitations devoid of genius and taste, which drew contributions from all nations of the earth; and we were cast back into the old condition of confusion again and again, in part by the unfortunate good naturedness of our public, which was ready to make do with whatever it was served, and in part by the inactivity of our best minds, who either did nothing at all, or much too little, to win supremacy for superior taste. In this condition, irrespective of the fact that we could exhibit an enormous mass of plays of all genres, forms, manners, and tones, and a large number of traveling companies of actors, it would all the same have been almost ridiculous to boast to foreigners of a German stage.

Thus matters lay when in a moment in which everyone yearned for change, and in more ways than one was prepared and in the mood to welcome any innovation, no matter how daring, *Götz von Berlichingen* appeared in print, and by the extraordinary effect it had particularly on the younger half of the reading public, made the seventh decade of this century, which is so singularly striking in our literature, remarkable for the stage too. It could easily be anticipated that it would effect the revolution Herr von A. laments so bitterly, and by which we (as cannot be denied) have seen all kinds of strange, in part misbegotten products, unworthy of an enlightened age, crowned with the liveliest applause on German stages. At first sight, the fact is peculiar enough; but nothing like as unnatural or as shameful for our public as it might appear to a one-sided spectator. Among the plays that probably have jealousy at the success of *Götz von Berlichingen* to thank for their existence, and that offend Herr von Ayrenhoff no more than all other persons of sound and educated taste, I could name not a few (if they were not in any case well-known enough) that have received the warmest, most decided applause on our most distinguished stages, in the noblest cities of Germany, in Vienna, Berlin, Munich, Mannheim, indeed even in Herr Adelung's German Athens,[16] and in Hamburg, where one would have expected Lessing's *Dramaturgy* to have created a particularly enlightened audience. It can be said with good reason that from that time on these have been the audience's favorite plays; and just as one cannot hold it against any dramatic author if he congratulates himself on general applause, and considers the way in which he received it the best: so also, on the other hand, it is impossible that an entire nation[17] find the most vivid pleasure in a play without it having some merits that justify this pleasure. In short, the audience can never be completely wrong in matters where its own advantage or pleasure is at issue; and if we investigate properly why the plays under discussion here received such great applause, it will be found that they are basically the same reasons for which plays have caused a particular sensation among every people in the world, ever since there have been peoples and plays. In the case of by far the most tragedies, comedies, dramas, etc., with which we were entertained from Gottsched's times on, we had to allow ourselves to be transposed now to Greece, now Italy, now France or England, now to Constantinople, Babylon, Memphis, or Peking. These foreign countries were, so to speak, the native land peculiar to our tragedy. German history, German heroes, a German scene, German characters, manners, and customs were something completely new on German stages. Now what can be more natural than that German audiences had to feel the liveliest pleasure when they finally saw themselves moved as if by a magic wand into their own fatherland, into well-known cities and localities, into the midst of their own countrymen and ancestors, into their own history and conditions—in short, into the company of people with whom they were at home, and in whom they recognized more or less the traits that characterize our own nation? This single circumstance would already suffice to explain the phenomenon; but it is not yet all. The plays mentioned—however wild and irregular their plot, exaggerated their characters and passions, turgid, bombastic, uneven, incorrect, even, it's true, indecent and dirty their speech and expression may in part be—have the merit of riveting the audience to the scene by strongly drawn and unusual characters, violent explosions of powerful, strongly contrasting passions, extraordinary situations, a great diversity of dramatic pictures, much pomp and action, a lot of stage transformations and operatic settings, in short, by everything that strongly engages the eyes and the heart—and of always arousing in the audience expectation, disquiet, and alternating convulsions of love and hate, admiration and pity, fear and hope, terror and horror, joy and sadness, in short, all the emotions that all or at least most people like so much to have aroused in themselves, as long as the matter doesn't concern them directly. What a difference from the tedium, or at most weak interest produced by the monotony, the little action toiling along, the dialogues or monologues that were uninteresting or even incomprehensible for the greater part of the audience, the passions, always set more into rhetorical declamation than true action, and the mostly frosty fifth acts of most of the French plays or their imitations! Is it any wonder if everyone abandoned the latter and flocked to the former? And does the audience deserve to be scolded because it prefers to be entertained as much as possible, and moved in a lively way, rather than be bored? Why in all the world should we always make do with plays that make us neither hot nor cold, and fit neither our national temperament nor our manners and our conditions? Why should the stage never be a true, living representation of nature; and why should we always hear, instead of true copies, only abstract ideals, instead of the living accents of emotion and the energetic language of the passions, only morals drawn from compendiums, aphorisms, and the language of compliments and courtesy of the refined world? If *Götz von Berlichingen* and its well- and ill-formed imitations had no other merit than that the experience of their effect had shown us the way in which we can gain a true national stage: then that would already be merit enough. Men of genius, but men, not rough, untamed youths, equally lacking in knowledge of nature, art, and the world, who without noticing it are constantly torn beyond the bounds of what is natural and seemly by a half-crazy imagination—men of true genius and talent, I say, will in the end (as the example of the author of *Götz* and of *Iphigenia* has already shown us) unfailingly encounter on their way an Aeschylus and a Sophocles, of their own accord, and then it will be found that the forms of the Greeks do not exclude all other forms; that among the rules that can be derived from their works various were merely conventional and local;[18] and that poetry knows no other indispensable laws than those without which it would not be in a position to exercise its omnipotence over the imagination and heart of human beings in that way that is simultaneously the most pleasant and the most beneficial to the purposes of human society. For this last point, to be sure, neither should nor may be lost from sight in any art that is pursued in civil society.

So, my dear M.,[19] if I said I wished to see a versified and rhymed German tragedy capable of standing alongside one by Racine or Voltaire,[20] what I meant by that was neither more nor less than that, as far as I knew, we still had no such play; and that it ill befits us to want to belittle the French before we have shown that we can outdo them in their own manner. But I was far from considering this manner, this form, the only one, or even just the best; far from elevating a Racine or Voltaire, on account of their agreement with the rules, on account of a more or less artful plot, on account of the greater purity of speech, beauty of versification, and in general on account of the more sophisticated and more noble taste of their age, above Shakespeare, to whom they are as inferior in genius and imagination, in depth of feeling and faithful representation of nature as the aphoristic, philosophical *Henriade*[21] is inferior to the *Iliad*. I was just as far from considering our *Götz von Berlichingen* a monster, as *Lear, Hamlet,* or *Othello,* or from considering the more recent imitations of these plays fit to be thrown out because the unities of time and place and other rules are not observed in them. If I fault them, it is on account of flaws, excesses, and absurdities that would also be such in the most rule-abiding play. I don't wish for us to form ourselves slavishly after the model of the Greeks or the French: but rather that we had a stage as well suited to us as the stage of Sophocles and Aristophanes was to the age of Pericles, or that of Racine and Molière to the court and capital of Louis XIV; but which, purified of all the flaws that offend common sense and are contrary to the true purpose of dramas,[22] would in its manner be excellent enough also to please people of sense and taste, of whatever country and people they might be, by beauties that are independent of national and local circumstances and all kinds of conventional form. I believe one can do the French justice without for that reason taking sides against the English. In my opinion, a man of talent can produce estimable works in all genres, and (if I may here borrow an expression of Voltaire's) the only genre I would wish to see banished from our literature is—the boring genre.[23] . . .

Translated by Timothy J. Chamberlain

Notes

Original title: *Briefe an einen jungen Dichter. Dritter Brief.* First published in *Der Teutsche Merkur,* March 1784. In the second of these (fictional) letters (1782), Wieland had expressed the view that German literature still lacked works comparable with the achievements of French neoclassicism. In response, the Austrian neoclassical dramatist Cornelius Hermann von Ayrenhoff had dedicated to Wieland his tragedy *Kleopatra und Antonius* (1783). The dedication, which expressed opinions far narrower than Wieland's, provoked this third letter.

1. [Aesop is said to have been very ugly. Antinous was a beautiful Roman youth favored by the emperor Hadrian (ruled 117–38).]
2. [Ayrenhoff, in his dedication to Wieland.]
3. [As Ayrenhoff had.]
4. [André Lenôtre (1613–1700) designed strictly geometrical French gardens for Louis XIV.]
5. [Horace, *Epistles* 1.19.19: "O imitatores, servum pecus" ("O imitators, servile herd").]
6. But surely with the exception of *Clavigo,* which abides very closely by the rules?
7. ["All is for the best in this world!" (Voltaire, *Candide*).]
8. ["Natura non facit saltus," a celebrated phrase from the *Philosophia botanica* by Carolus Linnaeus (1707–78).]
9. [Protagonist in Racine's play by the same name.]
10. [Protagonist in Racine's tragedy by the same name.]
11. [Protagonist in Voltaire's *Zaïre.*]
12. [Agamemnon, Iphigenia, and Orestes were the subjects of many dramas.]
13. [By Diderot (1761), translated by Lessing.]

14. [By Beaumarchais (1767).]

15. [By Françoise de Graffigny (1753).]

16. [Dresden.]

17. As the number of dissidents against the majority is hardly in the proportion of one to a hundred, it can surely be seen that they can't come into consideration here at all.

18. Thus the rule of the unity of place, for example, which Aristotle never even mentioned, is based merely on the fact that in ancient tragedy the chorus, which always remained on the stage, was an essential and indispensable part of the play: now that this is not the case, there is also no adequate basis for making this unity a law.

19. [Wieland's fictitious correspondent.]

20. [In the second letter, to which von Ayrenhoff responded.]

21. [By Voltaire.]

22. Such as the arousal of such convulsions as without any admixture of pleasure merely cause nausea, horror, and an uncomfortable feeling of constriction—or the representation of fools the like of which one at most only finds in madhouses, and of such villains as one can only imagine possible as devils incarnate—the overburdening with episodes beneath which the main characters are crushed, etc.

23. ["Encore une fois, tous les genres sont bons, hors le genre ennuyeux"; preface to *L'enfant prodigue* (1736).]

Karl Philipp Moritz

Karl Philipp Moritz (1756–93) came from a bitterly poor, rigidly quietist background, described in his autobiographical "psychological novel" *Anton Reiser* (1785–90; book 1 is included in The German Library, volume 10). Escaping this intellectual and material deprivation, he attempted without success to become an actor, and studied briefly in Erfurt and Wittenberg before becoming a teacher in Berlin. There freemasonry brought him into contact with leading figures in the Berlin Enlightenment, and he soon made the acquaintance of Moses Mendelssohn, who supported his pioneering psychological periodical *Know Thyself; or, Magazine of Experiential Psychology* (1783–93). Always restless, he traveled in England and Italy, and wrote important accounts of these journeys. In Italy from 1786 to 1788, he spent much time with Goethe, developing the ideas reflected in his own writings on aesthetics, and in those of Goethe in the following years, and so helping to prepare the way for Weimar Classicism. Back in Berlin, he became professor of the Theory of the Fine Arts (1789), and a member of the Academy of Sciences (1791). Before his early death, he discovered and gave vital assistance to the novelist Jean Paul.

A good selection of Moritz's works was published as *Werke*, ed. Jürgen Jahn, 2 volumes (Berlin: Aufbau-Verlag, 1973). For a study in English, see Mark Boulby, *At the Fringe of Genius* (Toronto: University of Toronto Press, 1979).

On the Concept of That Which Is Perfect in Itself

It is probably true that *we have to draw sharper lines between things* than exist in nature, as soon as we want to make the distinction between two things the actual object of our thought.

However, the concepts of usefulness and pleasure fade into one another so much, and coincide so nearly that it is almost impossible to imagine an opposition between the pleasant and the useful. Like the beautiful, the useful is only a particular species of the pleasant.

The principle of imitation of nature as the chief purpose of the fine arts has been rejected and subordinated to the purpose of pleasure, which has been made in its place the first basic law of the fine arts. The intention of these arts, it is said, is actually merely pleasure, as that of the mechanical arts is usefulness.

However, we find pleasure both in the beautiful and in the useful: so how is the former distinguished from the latter?

In the case of the merely useful, I find pleasure not only in the object itself, but also and primarily in imagining the convenience or comfort that will accrue to me or to someone else from its employment.

I make myself the focal point, as it were, to which I relate all parts of the object, i.e., I regard it merely as a means of which I am the end, inasmuch as my perfection is furthered by it.

The merely useful object is therefore nothing whole or perfect in itself, but rather only becomes so by achieving its purpose or becoming perfected in me.

When I look at the beautiful, however, I shift the purpose back from myself into the object itself: I look at it as something that is perfected not in me, but in itself, something that therefore constitutes a whole in itself, and affords me pleasure for its own sake; in that I do not so much relate the beautiful object to myself, as myself to it. Now since the beautiful pleases me more for its own sake, but the useful merely for my sake, the beautiful therefore affords me a higher and more unselfish pleasure than the merely useful.

The pleasure in the merely useful is coarser and more common, pleasure in the beautiful finer and rarer.

Since the useful has its purpose not in itself, but outside itself in something else, whose perfection is to be increased by it, the one who wants to produce something useful must constantly keep this extrinsic end before his eyes when engaged in his work.

And as long as the work achieves its extrinsic purpose, in other respects it may be however it chooses, in itself; this, insofar as it is merely useful, doesn't come into consideration at all.

As long as a clock shows the hours correctly, and a knife cuts well, I do not care, with regard to the actual use, about the splendor of the clock's case, or about the handle of the knife; nor do I pay attention to whether the mechanism in the clock or the handle of the knife appeals to my eye or not. The clock and the knife have their end outside themselves, in the person employing them for his convenience; they are therefore nothing perfected in themselves, and have no peculiar value in and of themselves without the possible or actual achievement of their extrinsic end.

They only give me pleasure regarded as a whole in combination with their extrinsic purpose; cut off from this purpose, they are completely indifferent to me.

I only look at the clock and the knife with pleasure insofar as I can employ them, and do not employ them for the sake of looking at them.

In the case of the beautiful, the opposite holds.

The beautiful does not have its purpose outside itself, and does not exist for the perfection of something else, but rather for its own intrinsic perfection. One does not look at it because one wants to employ it, but only employs it because one wants to look at it.

We do not so much need the beautiful in order to be delighted by it, as the beautiful needs us in order to be recognized. We can very well exist without looking at beautiful artworks, but they cannot well exist as such without our gaze.

The more, therefore, we can do without them, the more we look at them for their own sake, in order as it were to endow them with their true existence by means of our gaze.

For by our growing recognition of the beautiful in a beautiful artwork we increase, as it were, its very beauty, and fill it with greater and greater value.

Hence the impatient desire that all should pay homage to the beautiful we have recognized as such: the more generally it is recognized and admired as beautiful, the more value it acquires in our eyes, too.

If we felt pleasure in the beautiful more for our sake than for its own, what would it matter to us whether it were recognized by anyone outside ourselves?

We use our influence and make strenuous efforts on behalf of the beautiful, in order to win it admirers, wherever we may encounter it: indeed, we even feel a kind of pity when we see a beautiful artwork that, trodden into the dust, is looked at by passersby with indifferent gaze.

The sweet astonishment, the pleasant oblivion with which we look at a beautiful artwork is another proof that our pleasure here is something subordinate, and that, of our own free will, we allow it to be determined by the beautiful, to which we concede for a time a kind of supreme authority over our feelings.

While the beautiful draws our gaze wholly to itself, it draws it for a while away from ourselves and makes us appear to lose ourselves in the beautiful object; and just this loss, this oblivion of ourselves is the highest degree of the pure and unselfish pleasure the beautiful affords us.

In that moment we sacrifice our individual, limited existence to a kind of higher existence. Pleasure in the beautiful must therefore approach nearer and nearer to unselfish love, if it is to be genuine.

Every specific relation to myself in a beautiful artwork gives the pleasure that I feel in it something extra, which is lost for someone else; for me, what is beautiful in the artwork is not pure and unalloyed until I completely rid myself of the thought of its particular relation to myself and look at it as something that is produced merely for its own sake, so that it may be something perfect in itself.

Now, however, just as love and benevolence can to some extent become a necessity to the noble philanthropist, without this making him selfish, so too pleasure in the beautiful can by custom become a necessity to the man of taste, without losing its original purity on this account.

We need the beautiful merely because we wish to have the opportunity to pay homage to it by recognizing its beauty.

So a thing cannot be beautiful because it gives us pleasure, otherwise everything useful would also have to be beautiful; rather, we call beautiful that which gives us pleasure without actually being useful.

However, it is impossible for that which lacks a use or a purpose to give pleasure to a rational being.

Where, therefore, an object lacks an extrinsic use or purpose, this must be sought in the object itself, if it is to arouse pleasure in me; or I must find in its individual parts so much purposefulness that I forget to ask what the whole thing is actually supposed to do. In other words, I must find pleasure in a beautiful object only for its own sake; to this end, the lacking extrinsic purposefulness must be replaced by its intrinsic purposefulness; the object must be something perfected in itself.

Now if the intrinsic purposefulness in a beautiful artwork is not sufficiently great to let me forget extrinsic purposefulness, I naturally ask, "What's the point of the whole thing?" If the artist replies,

"To give you pleasure," I ask him further, "What reason do you have to arouse in me pleasure rather than displeasure by your artwork? Does my pleasure matter so much to you that you would consciously make your work less perfect than it is, just so as to accord with my perhaps corrupted taste; or doesn't your work rather matter so much to you, that you will attempt to attune my pleasure to its pitch, so that its beauties are felt by me?

"If the latter is the case, I do not see how my chance pleasure could be the purpose of your work, since that pleasure first had to be woken and determined in me by your work itself.

"My pleasure is only agreeable to you insofar as you know that I have accustomed myself to feel pleasure in what really is perfect in itself; but you would not be so concerned about this if you were merely concerned with my pleasure and not rather that the perfection of your work should be confirmed by the interest I take in it.

"If pleasure were not so subordinate an end or rather only a natural consequence of works of the fine arts, then why would the genuine artist not attempt to spread it to as many people as possible, instead of often sacrificing to the perfection of his work the pleasant feelings of many thousands who have no sense for his beauty?"

But if the artist says, "If my work pleases or awakens pleasure, then I must have achieved my purpose," then I reply, "On the contrary! Because you have achieved your purpose, your work pleases, or that your work pleases can perhaps be a sign that you have achieved your purpose in the work itself.

"But if the actual purpose of your work was more the pleasure you wanted to effect through it, than the perfection of the work in itself, then that is already enough to make the applause your work has received from this person or that suspect to me."

"But I only endeavor to please the most noble!"—"Fine! But this is not your final purpose. For I may still ask: why is it precisely the most noble you endeavor to please? Surely because these have accustomed themselves to feeling the greatest pleasure in what is most perfect? You refer their pleasure back to your work, the perfection of which you want to see confirmed by it.

"Encourage yourself in your work as much as you want by the thought of the applause of the noble; but do not make it in itself your final and highest goal, otherwise that is the surest way to miss it.

"Even the fairest applause must not be pursued, but rather only accepted in passing.

"Let the perfection of your work fill your entire soul while you labor on it and put even the sweetest thought of fame in the shade, so that this only steps forth occasionally to enliven you anew when your spirit begins to flag; then you will receive unsought what thousands strive for in vain. But if imagining the applause is your chief thought, and if your work is only valuable to you insofar as it brings you fame, then you must go without the applause of the noble.

"Your labors tend in a selfish direction: the focus of the work will fall outside the work, you do not produce it for its own sake, and for that same reason do not produce anything whole, perfected in itself.

"You will seek false glitter, which perhaps dazzles the eye of the rabble for a while, but vanishes like mist before the gaze of the wise.

"The true artist will seek to bring the greatest intrinsic purposefulness or perfection into his work; and if it then finds applause, he will be happy, but he has already attained his actual purpose with the perfecting of his work. Just as the true sage seeks to bring the highest purposefulness, in harmony with the course of all things, into all his actions and regards the purest happiness or the enduring condition of pleasant feelings as a sure consequence of that endeavor, but not as its goal.

"For even the purest line of happiness only runs parallel to the line of perfection; as soon as the former is made the goal, the line of perfection of necessity goes all awry.

"Individual actions, insofar as they merely aim to realize a condition of pleasant feelings, may acquire an apparent purposefulness, but taken together they do not constitute a consistent, harmonious whole.

"It is just the same in the fine arts when the concept of perfection or that which is perfected in itself is subordinated to the concept of pleasure."

"So pleasure isn't the purpose at all?"—I reply: "What else is pleasure, or from what else does it arise than from the contemplation of purposefulness? Now if there were something of which pleasure itself were the sole purpose, then I could only judge the purposefulness of the thing from the pleasure that accrues to me from it.

"But of course my pleasure itself must first arise from this judgment; it would therefore have to exist before it were there. Also, the end of course must always be something simpler than the means that aim to produce it: but since the pleasure in a beautiful artwork is just as composite as the artwork itself, how can I regard it as something simpler the individual parts of the artwork should aim to produce? Just as little as the representation of a painting in a mirror can be the purpose of its composition; for this will always follow of itself, without my having to pay the least attention to it during my work.

"Now if the imperfection of the image of my artwork represented by a dull mirror increases in proportion to the perfection of the work, I will surely not make the work less perfect so that less beauties are lost in the dull mirror?"

Translated by Timothy J. Chamberlain

Notes

Original title: *Über den Begriff des in sich selbst Vollendeten.* First published in 1785.

Gottfried August Bürger

Gottfried August Bürger (1747–94) won fame with his powerful ballad "Lenore" (1773; The German Library, volume 39), and in the following decade was among the most popular German poets. In addition to his poetry, his adaptation of *Macbeth* (1782) enjoyed considerable success, and his version of the *Adventures of Baron Münchhausen* (1786) became a perennial favorite. Having resigned his position as a magistrate to concentrate on writing, he struggled to support himself and his family as editor of the Göttingen *Musen-Almanach* and unsalaried professor at Göttingen University, where he gave private lectures, mainly on stylistics. To professional frustrations and financial vicissitudes were added the personal trials of the early death of his second wife ("Molly" in his poems), and his disastrous third marriage. Schiller's devastating review of his poems (included in this volume) dealt a final blow to his prestige, and his reputation has never fully recovered.

A fair introduction to his life and works is provided by William A. Little, *Gottfried August Bürger* (New York: Twayne, 1974). The German texts of the present selections may be found in *Sturm und Drang: Dichtungen und theoretische Texte,* ed. Heinz Nicolai, 2 vols. (Munich: Winkler, 1971).

Outpourings from the Heart on Folk Poetry

Why are Apollo and his Muses merely in action on the pinnacle of Pindus?[1] Why does their song merely enrapture the ears of the gods, or the few with enough breath and strength to scale the steep battlements of Olympus? Should they not descend and walk on earth, as Apollo did long ago among the shepherds of Arcadia?[2]

Should they not leave their robes of light, the sight of which so often blinds the human eye, up there, and put on human nature? Come and go among the children of men, both in palaces and huts, and sing for the human race as a whole, in a way equally comprehensible and equally entertaining for all? To be sure they should do this! But how little the German muses have done so until now!

Our nation enjoys the unfortunate reputation of being—not exactly wise, but learned. This reputation might be quite estimable if only it were not so much a matter of trivial learning. It is largely the fault of this trivial learning that our poetry cannot boast of the general access to ears and hearts it has already found in many other nations. We are so deeply and highly learned that we can speak the languages of almost all peoples; we know their actions, manners, and customs, all their wisdom and folly inside out; we are thoroughly acquainted with their fields and forests, cities and villages, temples and palaces, houses and stables, their kitchens, cellars, attics and rooms, wardrobes, coffers, and heaven knows what else. And this is why we are so distant and foreign in our thoughts, speech, and action, that our unlearned countrymen can rarely make head or tail of us. The worst thing is that we learn all this merely in order to know it and thus join the clique. For the most part it remains dead capital; and how can coin that often has no intrinsic value at all, and whose impression has long since gone out of fashion, go into circulation?

As far as I'm concerned, this could go on as usual in all spheres—except in poetry. By rights, the German muse should not go off on learned journeys, but rather stay home and learn its natural catechism by heart. But where is it written in the natural catechism of the Germans that the German muse should procure foreign fantasies and feelings, or wrap its own in foreign costumes? Where is it written that she should stammer a divine language, as it were, rather than the human language of the Germans? Divine language? Dear God have mercy! This divine language, which many of our muse's infants claim to babble, is often nothing but the coarse roaring of lions and bulls, the neighing of stallions, howling of wolves, barking of dogs, and cackling of geese. Instead of letting the stream of song pour down a gradual slope, with distinct, audible, melodious sounds, they stand on a precipitous crag, throw their head back in ghastly ecstasy, roll their eyes, and cast their jugful down, hurly-burly, with indistinct, confused noises—and yet in the end there's probably not enough for a gnat to drink its fill.

They want to paint not human, but heavenly suns; in the manner not of their own sort but of peoples of other ages and climes; they often even want to feel as the good Lord and His holy angels feel. This is the reason, you German poets, and not the coldness and sloth of the audience, as you wrongly imagine, that your poems are not common knowledge throughout the whole people.

To be sure, there is no more powerful means to remedy this evil than the Book of Nature, so often described and cited, but so rarely read. One should get to know the people in its entirety, explore its imagination and sensibility, in order to fill the former with suitable images, and to hit on the right register for the latter. Then pull out the magic wand of the natural epos! Set it all in swarming tumult! Chase it before the eyes of the imagination! Let fly the golden arrows! Truly! Then things shall go differently from the way they have until now! I promise anyone who achieves this that his song will enrapture the refined sage just as much as the rude forest dweller, the lady at her dressing table as much as the daughter of nature at her spinning wheel and at the laundry. Let this be the real ultimate height of poetry!

Here I have a feeling I see many makers of poems and theories smiling at me in wise condescension. They mean to say that not all subjects can be treated in so generally comprehensible and agreeable a manner, particularly not the amusements of the understanding and wit. I have a feeling the most charming didactic poem, the epigram, and many other poems of their class, which also have their little place in theories of poetry, are about to jump up and cause an uproar.—My dear people, your theory doesn't disturb the theory of nature at all. Nature, if I am not much mistaken, assigns the domain of imagination and feeling to poetry, but the realm of the understanding and wit to another lady, the art of versifying. Each should disport itself primarily on the property it is assigned. Yet nature doesn't mean to separate the two completely at all, or provoke dissension between them. Let them dwell side by side as peaceable neighbors; let them even go hand in hand as friendly neighbors now and then; let them borrow dishes, pots, brooms and yardsticks from each other; let them, finally, also speak the same language, distinguished only by dialect, as it were! But nonetheless, at bottom they remain apart. This delimitation of boundaries isn't meant to wound the honor and dignity of the art of versifying in the least. She may be a nice woman, and her realm a fair realm. But the question as to which of the two has precedence, and deservedly so, should be decided without bias, since until now the members of both states have frequently been in the habit of strolling back and forth so very amicably. And let it always remain this way in future.

The concerns of the art of versifying are none of my business here. It is the weal and woe of poetry that are near to my heart. I would like to make all its products in harmony with the people. I am talking primarily of the lyric and epic-lyric genres.

But the magic wand of the epos, which should animate and stir up the machinery of the imagination and the feelings, is in few hands. Many sought it and didn't find it, because it really isn't easy to find, and they didn't seek it in the right place. Where it is still to be found first and most easily is in our old folk songs. Only recently have a few genuine sons of nature come upon its traces here.[3]

These ancient folk songs present to the maturing poet a very important opportunity for studying art that is naturally poetic, particularly lyric and epic-lyric art. They are mostly true outpourings of indigenous nature both in imagination and feeling. To be sure, the oral tradition has often added and taken away a lot, thereby introducing much ridiculous nonsense. But truly, anyone who knows how to separate the gold from the dross will capture a treasure that is far from contemptible. And wouldn't it be well worth the effort for a man with a critical, Hemsterhuis-like nose[4] to strive to remove the heterogeneous incrustations and restore the ancient reading that is obscured or even lost?

With this in mind, my ear has often listened at dusk to the magic sound of ballads and popular songs, beneath the linden trees in a village, at the laundry, and in spinning rooms. Rarely has a little ditty, as they call it, been too nonsensical and absurd not to have offered at least something, even if only a brush stroke of magically rusty coloration, which edified me poetically. How to recite ballads and romances, or the lyric and epic-lyric genre—for the two are one and the same; and everything lyrical and epic-lyrical should be a ballad or folk song!—how to recite them, I say, can be learned quite splendidly in this way, and almost solely in this way.

Here, to be sure, so-called higher lyric poetry, which doesn't want to be classified in this genre, and no doubt thinks a lot of itself, gets right in my way again. I know works that are very much in harmony with the people, in spite of belonging to this higher lyric genre. That which is not for the people may take itself off wherever it wants. May it have the most sublime value for gods and sons of gods! For the earthly race it has no more value than the most remote star, whose light glimmers over to us from a deep, dark distance. I would utter this verdict even if I were such a son of the gods myself, for I am more concerned with my beloved human race than with gods and sons of gods.

It is my opinion that by means of popularity poetry should again become what God created it to be, and for which purpose He laid it in the souls of the elect. A living breath, which wafts over the hearts and senses of all men! The breath of God, which wakens from sleep and death! Makes the blind see, the deaf hear, the lame walk, and the lepers clean! And all this for the benefit of the human race in this vale of tears!

From the muse of the romance and the ballad alone may our people hope for a revival of the general popular shorter epic for all classes, from pharaoh to the son of the maid behind the mill! For this reason I fail to understand why some people make this muse a pseudomuse, or the maid of one of the nine true Muses, and will put in her hand no instrument but the bagpipes; when on the contrary she rules the whole immeasurable domain of the imagination and the feelings; when after all it is she who has sung *Orlando Furioso,*[5] *The Fairy Queen,*[6] *Fingal* and *Temora,*[7] and—believe it or not—the *Iliad* and the *Odyssey.* It's true! For the peoples to whom they were sung, all these poems were nothing but ballads, romances, and folk songs. Precisely for that reason they received that general national applause so many petty people find incomprehensible. To be sure, they are no longer in harmony with the *German* people; but then we are not the Greeks, not the Italians, not the Britons. We are Germans! Germans, who should not make Greek, Roman, cosmopolitan poems in the German tongue, but German poems in the German tongue, digestible and nourishing for the whole people. You poets who have not done anything like this, and therefore are read little or not at all, don't blame the "cold and slothful" audience, blame yourselves! Give us a great national poem of the kind described, and we'll make it our vade mecum. Come down from the peaks of your cloudy learning, and don't demand that we, the many who live on earth, should climb up to you few.

That folk poetry has been neglected until now, that the ballad and the romance have become almost contemptible and a poetic toy, is largely the fault of those naive poetic youngsters who imagine they could also surely make ballads and romances, and consider this kind of poetry the poetic ABC. They take the first little tale they come across, without any purpose or interest, drone it out from head to tail in boring, miserable strophes, interlarded vapidly here and there with antiquated words and phrases, in a way that's supposed to be quaint, they include all the insignificant incidentals of the little story, and title it "ballad," "romance." There's no life in it! No breath! There's no happy conception! No bold sudden transitions in the images or the feelings! Nothing exciting anywhere, neither for the head nor for the heart!—My dear poetic youngsters, from now on don't forget it: folk poetry, just because it is the ultimate height of art, is the most difficult of all. Let us no longer be misled by the motto "ut sibi quivis speret idem,"[8] into wooing the most chaste of all muses!

I check the outpouring of my heart with the wish that a German Percy may finally arise, collect the remnants of our old folk songs, and in the process uncover the secrets of this magic art more than has happened until now.[9] To be sure, I have already frequently expressed this wish to my friends orally, and said it should be communicated further, and someone or other should be prompted to carry it out. But until now in vain! Among our peasants, shepherds, huntsmen, miners, journeymen, tinkers, flax workers, boatmen, carters, peddlers, Tirolean men and women, an astonishing multitude of songs really is current, of which there will hardly be one from which the poet couldn't learn at least something for the people. Some of those I have heard had true poetic merit as a whole, many in individual passages; I am sure the same is true of far more I have not seen. A collection of this kind, put together and annotated by a man who understands art!—What wouldn't I give for this!—It wouldn't be suitable for imitation as a whole, nor for the common reader, to be sure; but it would be a rich source for art, for insightful art. But those poetic youngsters especially would have to keep their paws, which grope at everything, out of it, or be struck on the knuckles by the golden plectrum.

Translated by Timothy J. Chamberlain

Notes

Original title: *Herzensausguß über Volkspoesie.* First published 1776.

1. [Mountain range in northern Greece.]
2. [In the Peloponnesus; in eighteenth-century poetry, a land of idyllic peace and simplicity.]

3. [Bürger is thinking above all of Herder.]
4. [A reference to the Dutch philosophers Tiberius Hemsterhuis (1685–1766) and his son Frans Hemsterhuis (1721–90).]
5. [By Ariosto.]
6. [By Spenser.]
7. [By Ossian.]
8. ["Let each hope to achieve the same." Horace, *Ars poetica* 240–41.]
9. [Nicolai responded to this plea with his anthology *Eyn feyner kleyner Almanach vol schönerr echterr liblicherr Volckslieder, lustigerr Reyen undt kleglicherr Mordgeschichten* (A fine little yearbook full of beautiful, genuine, charming folk songs, merry rounds, and lamentable tales of murder) (1777–78), which in spite of its satirical title was the first significant collection of German folk songs.]

On Popularity in Poetry

The German word *Dichtkunst* doesn't correspond at all to the Greek *poetry*. This word would be more correctly translated by *Bildnerei* [the forming of images]. For writers do not always *dichten*, or tell stories; on the other hand, they always form images.

If the claim were made that *dichten* doesn't always mean "to tell stories," but also means the activating of certain mental powers, in order that they produce something, then this definition would have been hunted out from one of the most remote corners, not from the common linguistic archive.

On the concept of forming images depends that of form, and on this in turn the concept of the sensuous and the physical. By short steps we have therefore come far enough to know that poetry is concerned with the forming of images of sensuous, physical objects.

But not every image of a physical, sensuous object is poetry. The particular quality required of a physical, sensuous object if the forming of its image is to belong to poetry is beauty.

But the word *Bildnerei* does not yet correspond to the matter completely, any more than the word *poetry* does.

Nature forms images in one way, the poet in another. Nature forms original images for the outward senses. The poet forms replicas for the inward sense, i.e., for that point where everything that the outward senses pick up is brought together.

Therefore, if it mattered to us to encompass the thing with a single word, we could call poetry *Nachbildnerei* [the forming of replicas].

Even though this expression isn't an exhaustive definition either, it nonetheless encompasses the essential and principal matter, which can be reduced to immutable rules which must be valid from East to West.

Replicas cannot be formed of all objects, nor should they be. For just as not all original images in nature are pleasing, so neither are all replicas in poetry pleasing. Here human taste enters the scene and asserts its rights. Nature and taste are the lawgivers in poetry. Nature is the monarch; it decrees without consultation. What it once decrees, it decrees in all ages, in all lands. Taste is an individual composed of a thousand voices. The majority decides.

It is easier to satisfy the law of nature than the law of taste. If the poet looks at the original image in nature as his law book, and at his replica, and compares the two, then if he does not entirely lack discretionary judgment, he must swiftly perceive whether he has done the best possible.

But he can't go around gathering the votes of taste. Great powers of judgment and extensive experience are required to judge whether a majority of votes will support his work. . . .

All forming of images is in its final roots nothing but the representation of the original object. The difference between the materials used in representation then divides the trunk into various branches. Thus painting arises from representation using colors, music from the use of sounds, and poetry from the use of words. My attention here is directed only to the last branch.

Now from that root thesis arise two questions: *what* is to be represented, and *how?* The answer to these questions encompasses the whole of poetics, and can only be brief. In truth, it was unnecessary to write so many thick books about it, from Aristotle on.

I don't know whether what I will say has already been said somewhere. For I wouldn't want to read through all those thick books to find out, not to atone for my sins. Yet I have the feeling I will disturb a wasp's nest. Ugh! How much buzzing, humming, and stinging there'll be!

Whether already said, or still unsaid, whether believed or doubted, let this be set down in the archive of my age. I have wanted for a long time to unburden myself of my creed in this matter, without caring about the applause or dissension of my contemporaries.

What is *representation?* The word itself says it more clearly than any explanation. But be it known to anyone who is so impoverished in language and concepts as not to understand the word: representation is the mirror and mirror image of the original object.—By the way, before I forget it, let me preface this once and for all by saying that I'm speaking to men, not to schoolboys, I can't engage in contortions, and always prefer a concise, brief, quick style.

It is already obvious that I set representation in the place previously occupied in poetics by the miserable word *imitation*. Imitation is an image reflected weakly from a dull surface; but representation returns in bodily, living form from a bright mirror.—Imitator, here, as everywhere, you are the impotent, marrowless slave! But you, representer, are the mighty ruler, whose staff extends over all of nature. . . .

Treatises are written for the understanding; representations are for the senses. The senses are inward or outward. They have access to the inner person by the well-known five instruments, as by means of tubes. Inside they converge in a single point, which is the inward sense corresponding to the outward senses, or the imagination. All forming of images that can be taken up by one or other of these senses, and is represented animated with passion, is pure, genuine poetry, valid from the beginning of the world to its end.

And this shouldn't be meant for the people, but only for a few pepper merchants? Ha! As if not all human beings were—human beings. As if nature had not endowed them everywhere with the instruments of sensuous receptiveness. Of course there are unfortunate people who are robbed of one or more senses. But that doesn't make it any less true that all human beings have five senses, have the power of imagination, and passions.

If a whole people existed whose noses were organized in such a way that they preferred the smell of asafetida[1] to that of roses, for this people one should sing about asafetida instead of the rose. I'd like to see the man who tries to overturn this principle from a poetics written for such a people.

The original object is changeable according to taste. Representation itself rests on laws unchanged until the end of days.

You can represent the horrors of a battle, of a military hospital, in such a way that your representation must always, eternally count as genuine poetry. But will it please? That depends on the nerves of the outward or inward senses, which no theorist can tune to a different pitch than that given them by nature. . . .

Imagination and *feeling* are the sources of all poetry. Objects the sensuous imaginative faculty cannot take up, and that strike no string in the sensuous faculty of feeling, are beyond the bounds of poetry. These objects include all kinds of abstract didactic theorems the imagination cannot embody and dress up.

By people I don't mean rabble. If someone is required to write legibly, what is meant is surely not that even one who can't read or write at all should be able to read him. With the muse it is not as with virtue. Virtue may pride itself on only pleasing the noble few. But in the case of the poet, it's inability or lack of judgment if he can't keep to the highway. The greatest, most immortal poets of all nations have been *popular* poets. Throughout the whole history of poetry, poetry has been loved most and has held the most universal appeal precisely among those nations that have not introduced poetry from foreign countries, but where it has rather sprouted from their own nature. That gives rise to genuine, true popularity, which harmonizes the most with the faculties of the imagination and feeling of the people as a whole.

Here and there I have been called *our folk poet,* indeed even the *greatest* folk poet. That would be the highest praise my complacency could wish for, if by folk poetry was understood what I want understood by it. For then I would be more than Homer, Ossian, and Shakespeare, who as far as I know were the greatest folk poets on earth.

But nobody, not even those who called me the greatest folk poet, will place me above Homer, Ossian and Shakespeare on that account. My earlier, brief, and casual remarks on folk poetry have been an annoyance to many, a folly to still more. I see that the theorists make folk poetry a *genre,* and concede it as such at most a chapter in their theories. All this convinces me that few people, indeed none at all, have understood what I mean. No matter, however I have pondered and still ponder this subject, this principle becomes ever more certain to my mind: all poetry should be in harmony with the people, for this is the seal of its perfection.

Translated by Timothy J. Chamberlain

Notes

Original title: *Von der Popularität der Poesie.* Probably written in 1784; first published 1835.

1. [A resin with a strong odor, used medicinally as an antispasmodic. Its German name, *Teufelsdreck* (literally, "devil's shit"), makes a much more direct impression.]

Friedrich Schiller

Friedrich Schiller (1759–1805) achieved celebrity with his first play, *The Robbers* (1781), which was followed by *Fiesco* (1783), and *Intrigue and Love* (1784). In the following years he completed *Don Carlos* (1787), but increasingly turned to history, and wrote studies on the history of the Netherlands and on the Thirty Years' War. He taught history at Jena University from 1789 until 1791, until enabled by a grant to devote himself to the study of Kant. These philosophical studies resulted in a series of significant works on aesthetics and literature, most notably *On the Aesthetic Education of Man* (1795), and *On Naive and Sentimental Literature* (1795–96). In 1794, Schiller came into close contact with Goethe, and in the ensuing years they collaborated closely in developing the ideas and producing the works of Weimar Classicism. Schiller returned to drama, writing his great historical trilogy *Wallenstein* (1799), *Mary Stuart* (1800), *The Maid of Orleans* (1801), *The Bride of Messina* (1803), and *William Tell* (1804). Schiller also wrote poetry, much of it with a strongly philosophical content.

A useful edition of Schiller's works is *Sämtliche Werke*, ed. G. Fricke, H. G. Göpfert and H. Stubenrauch, 4th. edition, 5 vols. (Munich: Hanser, 1965–67). In The German Library, Schiller's plays appear in volumes 14, 15, and 16, his major theoretical writings in volume 17.

On Bürger's Poems

The indifference with which our philosophizing age is beginning to look down on the games of the muses seems to affect no genre of poetry more seriously than the *lyric*. The institutions of social life at least still provide *dramatic* poetry with some protection, and *narrative* poetry is allowed by its freer form to accommodate itself more to the tone of the world, and absorb the spirit of the times. But the yearbooks, the songs for social occasions, the liking our ladies have for music, are only a weak check to the decline of lyric poetry. And yet it would be a very depressing thought for the lover of beauty if these youthful blooms of the spirit were to die out when the time of fruition comes, if the greater maturity of culture were to be bought at the cost of even a single opportunity for enjoying beauty. Rather, even in our so unpoetic days, a very worthy purpose might be discovered for poetry in general, and therefore also for lyric poetry; it might perhaps be demonstrated that even if from one perspective it has to take second place to higher intellectual occupations, from another it has only become all the more necessary. While the expanded sphere of knowledge, and the specialization of professional occupations, necessitate the isolation of our mental powers, and their separate functioning, it is poetry almost alone that reunites the separated powers of the soul, that occupies head and heart, acumen and wit, reason and imagination in a harmonious cooperation that, as it were, restores in us *human wholeness*. It alone can turn aside the saddest fate deliberative reason can encounter, namely to lose the prize of its endeavors by the diligence of its research, and to perish for the joys of the real world in an abstract rational world. Returning from the most divergent paths the spirit would find itself again in poetry, and in her rejuvenating light escape the rigidity of premature old age. Poetry would be Hebe, blooming in her youth, serving the immortal gods in Jove's hall.

But this would require poetry itself to progress with the age for which it is supposed to perform this important service, to adopt all the advantages and acquisitions of this age. What experience and reason have amassed in the way of treasures for mankind would have to win life and fruitfulness and clothe itself in grace in poetry's creative hand. It would have to gather in its mirror the manners, the character, the whole wisdom of its times, purified and ennobled, and with idealizing art create from the century itself a model for its century. But this would presuppose that poetry itself fell into none but *mature* and *cultivated* hands. As long as this is *not* the case, as long as there is any distinction between the morally cultivated, unprejudiced mind and the poet, other than that the latter possesses poetic talent as a further addition to the former's advantages, poetry may fail to exercise an ennobling influence on the age, and all the progress of scientific culture will only diminish the number of poetry's admirers. The cultivated man cannot possibly seek refreshment for spirit and heart from an immature youth, cannot possibly want to rediscover in poems the prejudices, vulgar manners, and spiritual emptiness, which repel him in real life. He rightly demands from the poet who is to be a faithful companion through life, as Horace is to the Roman, that he should stand on the same level as him intellectually and morally, because he does not want to sink beneath himself even in hours of pleasure. So it is not enough for the poet to depict feelings with exalted colors; he must also feel in an exalted manner. Enthusiasm *alone* is not enough; the enthusiasm of a cultivated mind is demanded. All the poet can give us is his *individuality*. This must therefore be worthy of being displayed before the world and posterity. To ennoble this—his individuality— as much as possible, to raise it to the purest, most splendid humanity, is his first and most important occupation, before he is permitted to undertake to move those who are excellent. The highest value of his poem can be none other than that it is the pure, perfect image of an interesting emotional state felt by an interesting, perfected mind. Only such a mind should be stamped in artworks for us; it will be recognizable to us in its least utterance, and the one who is *not* such a mind will seek in vain to conceal this essential failing by art. Just the same is true of the aesthetic as of the ethical; just as here it is only the morally excellent character of a person that can impress on any single action the stamp of ethical goodness, so in aesthetics it is only the mature, the perfect mind from whom the mature and perfect issues forth. No talent, however great, can lend the individual artwork what its creator lacks, and shortcomings that spring from this source even the file cannot remove.

We would be not a little embarrassed if we were charged with wandering through the contemporary German Parnassus with this measure in hand. But it seems to us that experience must surely teach us how great an effect the greater number of our lyric poets has on the better members of the public, for all the praise they receive; it also sometimes happens that one poet or another surprises us with his confessions, or provides us with evidence of his character, even if we hadn't perceived it in his poems. For now we will confine ourselves to applying what we have said to *Bürger*.

But may a poet who explicitly announces himself as a "folk poet," and makes *popularity* his highest law (see preface to part 1 of his *Poems*),[1] really be subjected to this standard, too? Far be it from us to bother Bürger with the varying meanings of *popular;* perhaps it requires only a few words to come to an agreement with him about the term. A popular poet in the sense in which Homer was for his age, or the troubadours for theirs, might be sought in vain in our time. Our world is no longer that of Homer, where all members of society shared more or less the same level in their feelings and opinions, and could therefore easily meet in the same description, in the same feelings. Now, a very great disparity is evident between the *elite* of a nation, and its *masses;* the cause of this lies already, in part, in that conceptual enlightenment and the ennobling of manners constitute a coherent whole, from the fragments of which nothing is to be gained. Apart from and in addition to this cultural difference, it is social conventions that make the members of the nation so extremely dissimilar to one another in their way of feeling and in the expression of their feelings. It would therefore be futile to cast together arbitrarily in a single concept what has long since ceased to be one. A popular poet for our times would therefore merely have the choice between the *easiest thing in the world,* and the *hardest:* either to accommodate himself exclusively to the powers of comprehension of the great mass, and to renounce the applause of the cultivated class, or to compensate for the enormous distance between the two by the greatness of his art, and to pursue both ends together. We have no lack of poets who have been fortunate in the first genre, and have earned the thanks of *their* audience; but a poet of Bürger's genius can never have devalued art and his talent so far as to strive for such a goal. For him, popularity, far from easing the poet's labors, or concealing mediocre talents, is one difficulty *more,* and indeed a task so difficult that its happy resolution can be called the highest triumph of the genius. What an undertaking, to satisfy the fastidious taste of the connoisseur, without thereby being unpalatable to the great mass—to adapt to the childish understanding of the people without compromising the dignity of art. This difficulty is great, yet not insuperable, the whole secret of resolving it—a fortunate choice of subject matter, and the utmost simplicity in its treatment. The poet would have to select the subject matter exclusively from situations and feelings peculiar to the human being as a human being. He would have to take care to abstain from all that requires experiences, information, skills attained only in specific social circumstances, and by this pure distillation of the merely *human* in the human being restore, as it were, the lost state of nature. In tacit accord with the most excellent people of his age he would seize the hearts of the people where they are softest and most educable, lend assistance to the ethical instincts by his practiced feeling of beauty, and employ the need for passion, which the every-day poet sates in so vapid, and often so harmful a manner, in order to purge the passions. As the enlightened, refined *spokesman for the feelings of the people,* he would provide the emotions of love, joy, devotion, sadness, hope, etc., which gush forth seeking a tongue, with a purer and more intelligent text; by lending them expression, he would make himself master of these emotions, and ennoble their rude, unformed, often brutal outbursts even on the lips of the people. Such a poet would suffuse the simple feelings of nature with even the most sublime philosophy of life, transmit the results of the most laborious research to the imagination, and allow the secrets of thought to be guessed by the childish mind in an easily decipherable language of images. A precursor of clear cognition, he would bring the boldest truths of reason to the people in charming and un-suspicious garb, long before the philosopher and lawgiver could dare to raise them up in their full glory. Before they had become the property of conviction, they would already have proved their quiet power in the heart, through the influence of the poet, and an impatient, unanimous desire would finally demand them from rea-son of its own accord.

Taken in this sense, the popular poet seems to us to deserve very high status, whether he is measured by the abilities presupposed in him, or by his sphere of influence. It is granted only to the great talent to play with the results of deep thought, to free the thought from the form to which it was originally bound, from which per-haps it arose, to transplant it into an unrelated context, to conceal so much art in so little display, so much wealth in such simple trappings. Bürger therefore does not exaggerate at all when he declares "the popularity of a poem is the seal of its perfection." But when he asserts this he tacitly assumes what many who read him might completely overlook in this assertion, namely, that the first indispensable condition of a poem's perfection is that it possess an absolute intrinsic worth, utterly independent of his readers' varied powers of comprehension. "If a poem," he seems to want to say, "survives the test of genuine taste and combines this merit addi-tionally with a clarity and comprehensibility that make it able to live in the mouth of the people, then the seal of perfection is stamped upon it." That sentence is absolutely identical with this: That which pleases the excellent is good; that which pleases everyone without distinction is still better.

So far from its being possible to relax the highest demands of art somewhat when it comes to poems intended for the people, it is rather essential and necessary to the determination of their value (which consists only in the happy combination of such divergent qualities), to begin with the question: has no element of superior beauty been sacrificed to popularity? Have these poems not lost for the connoisseur the interest they have gained for the mass of the people?

And here we must confess that Bürger's poems have still left a great deal to be desired, that in most of them we miss the mild, consistent, always clear, manly spirit that, initiated into the mysteries of the beautiful, noble, and true, descends to educate the people, but never denies its heavenly origins even in the most intimate communion with them. Bürger not infrequently *mingles* with the people, to whom he should only condescend, and instead of drawing them up to him in jest and play, it often pleases him to make himself their equal. The people for whom he writes are unfortunately not always those he wants imagined by this title. It cannot possibly be the same readers for whom he wrote down his "Nachtfeier der Venus," his "Lenore," his song "An die Hoffnung," "Die Elemente," the "Göttingische Jubelfeier," "Männerkeuschheit," "Vorgefühl der Gesundheit," etc., on the one hand, and "Frau Schnips," "Fortunens Pranger," "Menagerie der Götter," "An die Menschengesichter," etc., on the other.[2] But if we judge a popular poet at all correctly, his merit does not consist in providing each class with some song particularly enjoyable to it, but rather in satisfying every class in every single song.

However, let us not dwell on errors for which an occasional lapse is to blame, and that can be remedied by a more rigorous selection of his poems. But that this unevenness of taste is very often found in one and the same poem might be as difficult to improve as to excuse. The reviewer must confess that among all of Bürger's poems (speaking of those he endowed most richly) he can hardly name one that afforded him a wholly pure enjoyment, at the cost of no displeasure at all. Whatever it was that disturbed the harmonious effect of the whole—lack of congruence between the image and the thought, or the way the dignity of the content was offended, or a symbol too lacking in spirit, even just an ignoble image that distorted the beauty of the thoughts, an expression that fell flat, needlessly wordy ostentation, an impure rhyme, or unrhythmical line (though these are his most rarely encountered faults)—this disturbance in the midst of such ample enjoyment was all the more disagreeable to us because it compelled us to judge that the mind representing itself in these poems was not a mature, perfected mind, and that his products perhaps only lacked the final touch because—he himself lacked it. . . . [3]

One of the first requirements of the poet is idealization, ennoblement, without which he ceases to deserve his name. It is his role to free what is excellent in his subject (whether this is a figure, feeling, or action, residing *within* him or *outside* him), from coarser, at least alien admixtures, to gather in a single object the beams of perfection scattered among several objects, to subordinate individual traits that disturb the proportions to the harmony of the whole, to raise the individual and local to the level of the general. All ideals he forms individually in this way are, as it were, only emanations of an inward ideal of perfection that resides in the soul of the poet. The greater the purity and fullness to which he has cultivated this inward, general ideal, the nearer those individual ideals will also approach the highest perfection. It is *this* idealizing art we miss in Bürger. Apart from the fact that his muse seems to us in general to have a too sensual, often vulgarly sensual character—that for him love is seldom anything but sensual gratification or a feast for the eyes; beauty is often only youth, health; happiness is only living in high style—we might call the paintings he displays to us more a jumble of images, a compilation of traits, a kind of *mosaic,* than ideals. If, for example, he wants to paint womanly beauty for us, he seeks for each of his beloved's individual charms an image from nature that corresponds to it, and from these images he creates his goddess. . . . [4] But how little paintings of this kind say to the more refined artistic sense, which is satisfied never by abundance, but by wise economy, never by material, but only by the beauty of the form, never by the ingredients, only by the delicacy with which they are blended! We do not want to investigate how much or how little art is required by this manner of invention; but in this context, we realize from our own example how little such youthful bravado endures the test of manly taste. For the same reason it could not be a very pleasant surprise either to rediscover in this collection of poems, an enterprise of more mature years, both whole poems and individual passages and expressions that only the poetic childhood of their author could excuse and only the ambivalent applause of the great mass could allow to survive so long—not to forget the "Klinglingling," "Hopp Hopp Hopp," "Huhu," "Sasa," "Trallyrum larum," and so forth. If a poet like Bürger affords such trifles protection by the magical power of his pen, the weight of his example, how is the unmanly, childish tone introduced into our lyric poetry by a host of bunglers to be lost? . . . [5]

One misses the art of idealization in Bürger most when he describes feelings; this reproach is directed particularly at the more recent poems, addressed mainly to Molly, with which he has enriched this edition. Inimitably beautiful though most of them are in diction and versification, poetically as they are *sung,* they seem to us just as *unpoetically felt.* The law Lessing gives the writer of tragedies somewhere,[6] not to represent anything uncommon, any strictly individual characters and situations, is still more valid for the lyric poet. The latter has still less sanction to depart from a certain general quality in the emotions he describes, since he is granted correspondingly less space to enlarge upon the peculiarity of the circumstances that occasion them. Bürger's new poems are largely products of a quite singular situation of this kind, which admittedly is neither so strictly individual, nor so exceptional as, say, Terence's Heauton Timorumenos,[7] but is just individual enough as to be neither fully, nor sufficiently purely grasped by the reader for those unideal elements, which are inseparable from it, not to disturb his enjoyment. Now this circumstance would merely deprive the poems in which it is encountered of one perfection; but a second is added, which does them fundamental damage. For they are not merely *paintings* of this singular (and very unpoetic) state of mind, but also obviously *products* of the same. The poet's irritability, anger, depression are not merely the *subject* he sings of; unfortunately they are also often the *Apollo* who inspires him. But the goddesses of charm and beauty are very willful divinities. They only reward *that* passion they themselves aroused; they do not gladly tolerate on their altar any fire other than the fire of a pure, unselfish enthusiasm. An angry actor will hardly seem to us a noble representer of indignation; let a poet take good care not to sing of pain in the midst of pain. To the extent that the poet himself is merely a suffering party, his feeling must inevitably sink from its ideal generality to an imperfect individuality. He may write poems about it from a milder, distancing memory, and then the more he has personally experienced what he sings about, so much the better for him; but he must never write while dominated by the emotion to which he is to give sensuous *beauty*. Even in poems of which it is customarily said that love, friendship, etc., themselves guided the poet's pen, he had to begin by becoming a stranger to himself, disentangling the object of his enthusiasm from his individuality, contemplating his passion from a distance that made it milder. The beauty of the ideal is simply only made possible by freedom of the spirit, by an autonomy that suppresses the predominance of passion.

Bürger's more recent poems are characterized by a certain bitterness, an almost sickly melancholy. This costs in particular the most outstanding piece in this collection, "Das hohe Lied von der Einzigen,"[8] much of its otherwise inapproachable worth. Other critics have already expressed themselves in more detail on this beautiful product of Bürger's muse, and we concur with pleasure with *much* of the praise they have bestowed on it. We merely wonder how it was possible to forgive the poet's élan, the ardor of his feeling, his wealth of images, the power of his language, and the harmony of his versification so many transgressions of good taste; how it was possible to overlook the fact that the poet's enthusiasm not infrequently strays over the border into *madness*, that his ardor often becomes *fury*, that for that very reason the mood in which one puts this song aside is absolutely not the beneficial harmonious mood in which we want to see ourselves put by the poet. We understand how Bürger, carried away by the emotion that dictated this song to him, captivated by the close relation of this song to his own situation, which he placed in it as in a shrine, could exclaim to himself at the conclusion of this song that it bears the seal of perfection—but for this very reason, in spite of its brilliant merits, we might call it simply an outstanding *occasional poem*—a poem, that is, in which one may find that its origin and *intention* excuse any lack of that ideal purity and perfection that alone satisfy good taste.

Precisely the great and close participation of the poet's own *self* in this and a few other songs in this collection explains to us, incidentally, why we are reminded with such exaggerated frequency of *him*, the author, in these songs. The reviewer knows none among recent poets who abuses Horace's "sublimi feriam sidera vertice"[9] as much as Bürger. We do not want on this account to suspect that the little flower wondrous fair[10] has fallen from his breast on such occasions; it is obvious that one can only squander so much self-praise on oneself in jest. But assuming he only means a tenth of such jocular expressions seriously, a tenth recurring ten times still makes a whole, bitter seriousness. Even a Horace can only be *forgiven* self-praise, and the enraptured reader is reluctant to *forgive* the poet he would so like—*only* to admire.

These general hints concerning the poet's mind seem to us all that could be said in a newspaper about a collection of more than a hundred poems, of which many are worth a thorough analysis. The unanimous judgment of the public, decided long since, makes it superfluous for us to talk about his ballads, a form of poetry in which no German poet will easily surpass Bürger. In the case of his sonnets, models of their kind, which transform themselves into song on the lips of the reciter, we share his wish that they may find no imitator who cannot, like him and his excellent friend *Schlegel*,[11] play the lyre of the Pythian god.[12] We would gladly have done without all the merely *witty* pieces, above all the epigrams, in this collection, just as in general we would like to see Bürger abandon the light, jocular genre, which doesn't agree with his strong, sinewy manner. To be convinced of this, compare for example the drinking song (part 1, p. 142), with one of similar content by Anacreon or Horace. Finally, if we were asked on our conscience which of Bürger's poems we prefer, the serious or the satirical, the completely lyrical or the lyrical narrative poems, the earlier or the later, our verdict would favor the serious, the narrative, and the earlier poems. One cannot fail to recognize that Bürger has gained in poetic *power* and *abundance,* in the force of his language and the beauty of his versification; but his manner has not grown more noble, nor his taste more pure.

If we have only called attention to the flawed aspects of poems of which no end of beautiful things can be said, this is, one might say, an injustice of which we could only make ourselves guilty towards a poet of Bürger's talent and fame. It is only worth the effort of taking *the side of art* against a poet whom so many imitating pens lie in wait for; and only the greatest poetic genius is capable of reminding the lover of beauty of the *highest* demands of art, which in the case of a mediocre talent he either voluntarily suppresses, or is in danger of completely forgetting. We gladly admit that we see the whole host of our living poets, who wrestle with Bürger for the lyric laurel wreath, just as far beneath *him,* as he himself, in our opinion, has remained beneath the highest beauty. We are also well aware that much of what we found reproachable in his products is attributable to *external* circumstances, which hampered the power of his genius in exercising its most beautiful effectiveness, and of which his poems themselves give such moving hints. Only the serene, calm soul gives birth to the perfect. The struggle with external situations and hypochondria must burden least of all the heart of the poet, who is supposed to disentangle himself from the present and rise freely and boldly into the world of ideals. However stormy it is in his breast, the clarity of the sun must surround his brow.

But if any of our poets deserves to perfect himself in order to achieve something perfect, that poet is Bürger. The abundance in his poetic paintings, the glowing, energetic language of the heart, the stream of poetry, now surging splendidly, now lilting sweetly, which makes his products so outstandingly distinctive, lastly, the honest heart that, one is tempted to say, speaks from every line, deserves to wed itself to an always constant aesthetic and moral grace, to manly dignity, to substantial thought, to lofty and calm greatness, and thus to win the highest crown of classicality.

The reading public has a fine opportunity to do the art of our fatherland a service. Bürger, we hear, is preparing a new, *more beautiful* edition of his poems, and it will depend on the degree of support given him by the friends of his muse whether it is to be at the same time an *improved,* a *perfected* edition.

Translated by Timothy J. Chamberlain

Notes

Original title: *Über Bürgers Gedichte.* First published in 1791 as a review of the second edition of Bürger's *Gedichte* (1789).

1. [The preface referred to takes up substantially the same ideas as those in the texts by Bürger in this volume.]
2. ["Venus's Nocturnal Celebration," "Lenore," "To Hope," "The Elements," "The Anniversary Celebration in Göttingen," "Male Chastity," "Presentiment of Health;" and "Frau Schnips," "Fortuna's Pillory," "The Divine Menagerie," "To Human Visages."]
3. [Schiller provides some examples from Bürger's poem "Elegie, als Molly sich losreißen wollte" (Elegy: When Molly wanted to tear herself away), omitted here.]
4. [Schiller gives an example, omitted here, from "Die beiden Liebenden" (The two lovers).]
5. [Schiller cites as an example the poem "Blümchen Wunderhold" (The little flower wondrous fair), omitted here.]
6. [Lessing discusses this issue at length in his *Hamburg Dramaturgy*, nos. 87–95.]
7. [*The Self-Tormentor,* a comedy by Terence discussed by Lessing in *Hamburg Dramaturgy*, nos. 87–88.]

8. ["The Song of Songs on the Peerless Woman."]

9. [Ode to Maecenas, *Carminae* 1.1.36: "I shall touch with raised brow the stars."]

10. [A symbol of modesty in the poem referred to in note 5.]

11. [A. W. Schlegel, the Romantic critic, was also known for his sonnets; Bürger was his teacher.]

12. [Apollo.]

Biographical Notes
on Writers and Artists

JOSEPH ADDISON (1672–1719). English author, known for his classicistic tragedy *Cato* (1713), and editor of the moral weeklies *The Tatler* (1709–11) and *The Spectator* (1711–12).

JOHANN CHRISTOPH ADELUNG (1732–1806). Compiled the first important German dictionary (1774–86); also an authority on style.

ANACREON (C. 580–C. 495 B.C.). Greek lyric poet. His poems, of which few survive, celebrate love and wine.

APELLES (fourth century B.C.). Most celebrated Greek painter; said to have written a treatise on painting, now lost.

LUDOVICO ARIOSTO (1474–1533). Italian poet, best known for his epic *Orlando Furioso* (1532).

FRANCIS BACON, baron of Verulam, viscount of St. Albans (1561–1626). English philosopher and statesman. Major works: *Novum Organum* (1620); *De dignitate et augmentis scientiarum* (1623).

ALEXANDER GOTTLIEB BAUMGARTEN (1714–62). Established aesthetics as a philosophical discipline with his *Aesthetica* (1750).

PIERRE AUGUSTIN CARON DE BEAUMARCHAIS (1732–99). French dramatist, best known for *The Barber of Seville* (1775) and *The Marriage of Figaro* (1785).

BENJAMIN BODEN (1737–82). Author of *De umbra poetica dissertationes* (1764).

JOHANN JAKOB BREITINGER (1701–76). Swiss critic, opponent of Gottsched's strict rationalism, and advocate of descriptive poetry and the limited use of the marvelous; best known for his *Critische Dichtkunst* (1740).

PIERRE BRUMOY (1688–1722). French scholar, author of *Théâtre des Grecs* (1730).

GAIUS VALERIUS CATULLUS (c. 84–c. 54 B.C.). Roman lyric poet.

COUNT CAYLUS. Anne Claude Philippe de Tubières (1692–1765). French art critic and patron of painters, author of *Tableaux tirés de l'Iliade, de l'Odysée, d'Homère et de l'Énéide de Virgile, avec des observations générales sur le costume* (1757).

JEAN-BAPTISTE VIVIEN DE CHATEAUBRUN (1686–1775). French dramatist.

PIERRE CORNEILLE (1606–84). Creator of French classical tragedy. Major works include: *Medea* (1635), *Le Cid* (1637), *Cinna* (1641), *Polyeucte* (1643), *Rodogune* (1644).

PROSPER JOLYOT DE CRÉBILLON (1674–1762). French dramatist.

MICHAEL KONRAD CURTIUS (1724–1802). German philologist and historian; translated Aristotle's *Poetics* (1753).

ANDRÉ DACIER (1651–1722). French classical scholar; translated Horace, Aristotle's *Poetics*, Plutarch's *Lives* and dialogues by Plato.

ANNE LEFEBVRE DACIER (1654–1720). Editor and translator of classical literature, including the *Iliad,* the *Odyssey,* and works by Anacreon, Sappho, Aristophanes, Terence, Plautus, and Horace.

DEMOCRITUS (c. 460–c. 370 B.C.). Greek philosopher, developer of "atomism"; represented by later writers as always laughing at human follies.

PHILIPPE DESTOUCHES (1680–1754). French dramatist. Author of more than twenty comedies in the tradition of Molière, but with greater emphasis on character and moral seriousness.

DENIS DIDEROT (1713–84). French Enlightenment author and philosopher.

DIONYSIUS HALICARNASSUS (first century B.C.). Greek rhetor and historian. Main work: *Antiquitates Romanae.*

EPICURUS (341–270 B.C.). Greek philosopher who taught that the highest good is happiness, attainable only by the practical wisdom of the philosopher; later misrepresented as an advocate of sensual pleasure.

FRANÇOIS DE SALIGNAC DE LA MOTHE-FÉNELON (1651–1715). Archbishop of Cambrai, and educator of Louis XIV, for whom he wrote the pedagogical novel *Les Aventures de Télémaque* (1717).

HENRY FIELDING (1707–54). English novelist, author of *The History of Tom Jones* (1749). He opposed Richardson, and established the realistic humorous novel in England.

BERNARD LE BOVIER DE FONTENELLE (1657–1757). French writer of plays and poetry, and of works on science, politics, religion, and philosophy.

THOMAS GALE (c. 1636–1702). English classical scholar.

CHRISTIAN FÜRCHTEGOTT GELLERT (1715–69). Popular author of moralistic verse fables; also wrote comedies, poems, and a novel.

JOHANN MATTHIAS GESNER (1691–1761). Philologist and pedagogue, compiler of the *Novus linguae et eruditionis Romanae thesaurus* (1747).

JOHANN WILHELM LUDWIG GLEIM (1719–1803). Author of Anacreontic and patriotic poems.

CARLO GOLDONI (1707–93). Prolific Italian dramatist; reformer of Italian comedy.

OLIVER GOLDSMITH (1728–74). English writer popular in Germany for his novel *The Vicar of Wakefield* (1766).

FRANÇOISE D'ISSEMBOURG D'HAPPONCOURT DE GRAFFIGNY (1695–1758). French novelist.

FRIEDRICH VON HAGEDORN (1708–54). Author of didactic poems, odes, and fables, known in his day as "the German Horace."

ALBRECHT VON HALLER (1708–77). Swiss physician and poet, best known for his didactic descriptive poem "Die Alpen" (The Alps), 1732.

JEAN HARDOUIN (1646–1729). French scholar; edited Pliny (1685).

CLAUDE ADRIEN HELVÉTIUS (1715–71). French Enlightenment philosopher, for a time at the court of Frederick the Great.

HORACE (65–8 B.C.). Roman poet, known for his odes, satires, and epistles. His Epistle to the Pisos, conventionally known as the *Ars Poetica*, exercised a decisive influence on neoclassical poetics in France, England, and Germany.

JAN VAN HUYSUM (1682–1749). Dutch still-life painter.

HYPERIDES (390/89–322 B.C.). Athenian orator. In a famous speech, he defended the hetaera Phryne.

SAMUEL JOHNSON (1709–84). English neoclassical critic and author, compiler of the first major English dictionary (1755), and editor of moral weeklies, and of Shakespeare.

FRANCISCUS JUNIUS (FRANÇOIS DU JON, 1589–1678). German scholar known for his *De pictura veterum* (On the painting of the ancients), published in 1637.

EWALD CHRISTIAN VON KLEIST (1715–59). Prussian officer, friend of Nicolai and Lessing, author of patriotic poems and odes; died in the Seven Years' War. His most successful poem was "Der Frühling" (Spring), 1749.

JOACHIM KÜHN (1647–97). German scholar, editor of Aelian and Pausanias.

GAUTIER DE COSTES DE LA CALPRENÈDE (c. 1610–63). French dramatist and author of romantic historical novels, popular until the end of the eighteenth century.

PIERRE CLAUDE NIVELLE DE LA CHAUSSÉE (1692–1754). French dramatist, creator of the "comédie larmoyante."

JULIEN OFFROY DE LA METTRIE (1709–51). French materialist, among the philosophers at the court of Frederick the Great; author of *L'Homme Machine* (1748).

GOTTFRIED WILHELM VON LEIBNIZ (1646–1716). German mathematician, philosopher, and polymath. In his *Essays on Theodicy* (1710), he argued that this is the best of all possible worlds; his *Monadology* (1720) set forth the theory of monads and of pre-established harmony.

GEORGE LILLO (1693–1739). English dramatist; *The London Merchant* (1731) was the first domestic tragedy on the German stage.

KASSIOS LONGINUS (c. 213–273). Greek Neoplatonist. The treatise *On the Sublime* was long attributed to him.

LUCRETIUS (97–55 B.C.). Roman poet, author of the didactic poem *De Rerum Natura*, which expounds the doctrines of Epicurus.

JAMES MACPHERSON (1736–96). Scottish poet; his "translations" of poems by Ossian, based only loosely on ancient material, and largely his own creation, were widely regarded as authentic from their appearance in the 1760s until after his death.

SCIPIONE MAFFEI (1675–1755). Italian playwright, translator, and scholar. His best-known tragedy is *Merope* (1713).

JEAN FRANÇOIS MARMONTEL (1723–99). French author of tragedies, philosophical novels, and a *Poétique Française* (1763).

ANTON RAPHAEL MENGS (1728–79). German neoclassical painter and art critic, close friend of Winckelmann.

Louis Sébastien Mercier (1740–1814). French dramatist and critic.

Metrodorus (fl. 168 b.c.). Athenian artist and philosopher of the Atomistic school.

John Milton (1608–74). English poet, author of the epic *Paradise Lost* (1667).

Molière (Jean Baptiste Poquelin, 1622–73). Most important author of French classical comedies.

Bernard de Montfaucon (1655–1741). French antiquarian, author of *Antiquitée expliquée* (15 vols., 1719–24).

Ossian (third century a.d.). Legendary Celtic bard and hero (see Macpherson).

Pauson (fifth century b.c.). Athenian painter.

Thomas Percy (1729–1811). Editor of the first important collection of British folk poetry, *Reliques of Ancient English Poetry* (1765).

Persius (34–62). Roman satirical poet.

Petronius (first century a.d.). Roman writer, author of the satirical narrative the *Satyricon*.

Philostratus (170–c. 245). Greek sophist. Author of a life of Apollonius of Tyana, and a history of the heroes of the Trojan war.

Pindar (c. 522/518–after 446 b.c.). Greek lyric poet, famous for his sublime and obscure verse.

Plautus (c. 250–184 b.c.). The most celebrated Roman comic poet.

Alexander Pope (1688–1744). Chief representative of neo-classicism in England. Author of *An Essay on Criticism* (1711), satires, including *The Dunciad* (1728), epistles, and *An Essay on Man* (1733); translator of Homer.

PROCOPIUS (c. 500–after 562). Byzantine historian.

PROTOGENES (fourth century B.C.). Greek painter, said to have written works on painting and poetry.

PYREICUS (probably fourth century B.C.). Greek painter.

PYTHAGORAS LEONTINUS (480–20 B.C.). Greek sculptor.

JEAN RACINE (1639–99). Writer of French classical tragedies, including *Bajazet* (1672), *Mithridates* (1673), *Iphigenia in Aulis* (1674), and *Phaedra* (1677).

SAMUEL RICHARDSON (1689–1761). English author of epistolary novels celebrating virtue, notably *Pamela* (1740), *Clarissa* (1747–48), and *Sir Charles Grandison* (1753).

RACHEL RUYSCH (1664–1750). Dutch still-life painter.

JACOPO SADOLETO (1477–1547). Italian poet, author of a poem on the Laocoön group.

PAUL SCARRON (1610–60). French humorous poet.

JOHANN ELIAS SCHLEGEL (1719–49). German playwright and critic. His plays follow Gottsched's rules; most notable are *Canute* (1746) and the patriotic *Hermann* (1743). His critical works are more independent, e.g., in their advocacy of Shakespeare.

MADELEINE DE SCUDÉRY (1607–1701). French novelist, author of *Artaméne ou le Grand Cyrus* (1649–53), and *Clélie* (1654–60).

EDMUND SPENSER (c. 1552–99). English poet, author of *The Faerie Queene* (1590–96).

LAURENCE STERNE (1713–68). English novelist, famous in Germany for *The Life and Opinions of Tristram Shandy* (1760–67), and *A Sentimental Journey through France and Italy* (1768).

JOHANN GEORG SULZER (1720–79). Swiss philosopher and aesthetician; his major work is *Allgemeine Theorie der schönen Künste und Wissenschaften* (1771–74).

TORQUATO TASSO (1544–95). Italian poet, best known for his epic *Jerusalem Delivered* (1581).

TERENCE (c. 195–159 B.C.). Roman comic poet; six of his comedies survive, and from the Renaissance were much used in schools.

THEOCRITUS (c. 310–c. 250 B.C.). Greek bucolic poet.

THESPIS (sixth century B.C.). Celebrated as the father of Greek tragedy.

JAMES THOMSON (1700–1748). Scottish poet, author of *The Seasons* (1730).

THUCYDIDES (c. 460–c. 400 B.C.). Athenian historian.

TIBULLUS (c. 54–19 B.C.). Roman elegiac and bucolic poet.

TIMANTHES (fl. 400 B.C.). Greek painter.

TIMOMACHUS (late fourth century B.C.). Painter from Byzantium.

TYRTAEUS (seventh century B.C.). Greek lyric poet.

VALERIUS MAXIMUS (first century A.D.). Roman historian.

VOLTAIRE (François-Marie Arouet, 1694–1778). French enlightenment writer and philosopher, famed for his wit, controversial on account of his deism; a favorite of Frederick the Great of Prussia. He spent periods of his life in England and Berlin, and the last twenty years in Ferney, near Geneva. His tragedies include *Brutus* (1730), *Zaïre* (1732), *Alzire* (1736), *Mahomet* (1742), *Mérope* (1743), and *Sémiramis* (1748). He also wrote an epic poem, the *Henriade* (1723). His most durable work has proved his novel *Candide* (1758).

JOHANN JOACHIM WINCKELMANN (1717–68). German art historian. His conception of ancient art as embodying "noble simplicity and tranquil grandeur" decisively influenced German classicism. Major works: *Gedanken über die Nachahmung der griechischen Werke in der Malerei und Bildhauerkunst* (1755), and *Geschichte der Kunst des Altertums* (1764).

EDWARD YOUNG (1683–1765). English poet, celebrated for his *Night Thoughts on Life, Death, and Immortality* (1742–44).

ACKNOWLEDGMENTS

Every reasonable effort has been made to locate the owners of rights to previously published works and the translations printed here. We gratefully acknowledge permission to reprint the following material:

From *German Aesthetic and Literary Criticism,* edited and introduced by H. B. Nisbet, "Aesthetics in nuce" by Johann Georg Hamann (pp. 139–50, 275–86), and "Extract from a Correspondence on Ossian and the Songs of Ancient Peoples" by Johann Gottfried Herder (pp. 154–76, 286–89). Copyright © 1985 by Cambridge University Press. Reprinted with the permission of Cambridge University Press.

THE GERMAN LIBRARY
in 100 Volumes

All volumes available in hardcover and paperback editions at your bookstore or from the publisher. For more information on The German Library write to: The Continuum Publishing Company, 370 Lexington Avenue, New York, NY 10017.